GOING AROUND

GOING AROUND

selected journalism

MURRAY KEMPTON

EDITED BY **ANDREW HOLTER**

FOREWORD BY **DARRYL PINCKNEY**

SEVEN STORIES PRESS
New York ✧ Oakland ✧ London

Seven Stories Press
140 Watts Street
New York, NY 10013
www.sevenstories.com

Library of Congress Cataloging-in-Publication Data

Names: Kempton, Murray, 1917-1997, author. | Holter, Andrew, editor. | Pinckney, Darryl, 1953- writer of foreword.
Title: Going around : selected journalism / Murray Kempton ; edited by Andrew Holter ; with a foreword by Darryl Pinckney.
Description: New York : Seven Stories Press, [2025] | Includes bibliographical references.
Identifiers: LCCN 2024058600 (print) | LCCN 2024058601 (ebook) | ISBN 9781644214510 (trade paperback) | ISBN 9781644214527 (ebook)
Subjects: LCSH: Journalism--United States. | United States--Civilization--20th century.
Classification: LCC PN4725 .K46 2025 (print) | LCC PN4725 (ebook) | DDC 070.92--dc23/eng/20250131
LC record available at https://lccn.loc.gov/2024058600
LC ebook record available at https://lccn.loc.gov/2024058601

Printed in the United States of America

9 8 7 6 5 4 3 2 1

Contents

I: Losing-Side Consciousness

II: "From the gifted typewriter of Murray Kempton"

III: Disillusion, Revision, Comedy

IV: Watchman's Rounds

V: Late Style

Foreword

DARRYL PINCKNEY

Thirty years ago or more, when on my way home to Indiana or on my way back to England, I would stop off in New York City. Barbara Epstein would put me up at her home on West Sixty-Seventh Street. Sometimes I overlapped with Diane Johnson, in from Paris, or Barbara's daughter, Helen, on her way to Berkeley or London or Kampala. Elizabeth Hardwick said it sounded pretty crowded over there, but it worked, because Barbara and Murray were out all day, whereas she was home all day, and she had only one bathroom. Barbara, too, had only one bathroom, so Lizzie didn't see how she could stand having us there. She and Barbara's apartments were on the same block and were of the same design. Lizzie stressed that however imposing their living rooms were, the rest was tight. I stayed in what had been Barbara's son Jacob's room when he was growing up, right off the kitchen.

A small beige quilted pillow sat among plants and Murray's cassette player on Barbara's kitchen windowsill. I don't remember exactly the words sewn into it in red lettering, but the motto said something like "People who are interesting in the morning are boring." I could hear Barbara's front door slamming and then her feet as she entered the kitchen with the *New York Times* that had been delivered. She wore long white cotton nightdresses and spread the newspaper so that it took up most of her round kitchen table. I could hear her make coffee. I knew not to intrude.

Murray also left Barbara alone with the newspaper first thing in the mornings. Then I could hear the changing of the guard over the newspaper in the kitchen. Barbara would head back upstairs, leaving Murray barefoot in a dishrag version of a plaid terrycloth bathrobe and shaking out cereal into a bowl. It was Murray's turn to head upstairs to get ready as Barbara was coming back down to head out. They confirmed the evening's plans at the front door. She was generally amused by his itinerary for the day. While she sat behind her desk until after dark, he moved around the city on his bicycle, from office to courthouse to boxing gym, on the trail, following a story. He knew so much about New York City and its politics, a history he told through its ever-renewable cast of outrageous characters. The city was his beat, Barbara often said.

That tough little pillow was in the windowsill for a reason. There was an element of monologue escape in my polite guest's morning timing. But at last, I was looting Barbara's refrigerator. Murray would return to the kitchen in suit and tie, his pipe clamped at the side of his mouth, the better to reminisce about, say, H. L. Mencken. He was thinking of making a collection of columns and calling it *Bigotries*, an echo of Mencken's *Prejudices*. Murray spoke in complete sentences, whole paragraphs. He digressed from a point he would not forget to go back to in order to say that Mencken said that Stalin was from Georgia, which meant the same thing in the USSR as it did in the USA. He was ready to laugh in the mornings, humanity being what it was.

New York always got Murray Kempton at full sail. He had a deep, resonant voice that could not be ignored. It was made for philosophic utterance. More than one subject could be broached between our turning off the kitchen lights, slamming Barbara's heavy dark wooden door, and waiting for the elevator. A threatening morning could lead to a conversation with a doorman as we descended about how different Waterloo might have turned out for Napoleon had it not poured with rain the night before the battle. Murray had beautiful manners, and he believed in being courteous to secretaries, assistants, underlings, people whose jobs meant that they got kicked around by supposed higher ups. He addressed everyone as being on the same plane, regardless of their status.

I see Murray on the sidewalk in front of Barbara's building—he looked like he sounded, early American: a pale pink face behind heavy glasses and under hair that had been ginger but was now white and still impressively thick. He is remembered for his accessories: bicycle clips on his trousers, that pipe, headphones around his neck for the Walkman waiting in his pocket. He cannot get on the bike he is holding. One more story detains him. Murray said he was once talking to Gore Vidal, and because he was en route to some place, Gore, in the middle of an anecdote, got on the subway with him. There was a blind man beating his seeing eye dog with a cane. Murray said he was sorry to interrupt Gore, but he was in a bind. He didn't like to interfere with the pleasures of the disabled, but he felt for the dog. Gore said, "Didn't you know the blind were the meanest people on earth?" Murray said the sadness in Gore's voice made him wonder if he hadn't been talking about his grandfather, the blind senator.

Daily life tested one's principles. His principles troubled him. *The New York Review of Books* had a fantastic party for Václav Havel at Lincoln Center, and among the hundred or more guests was Henry Kissinger, conspicuous because he was alone, shunned. I heard someone say that he wanted to go over and slap the creep he considered a war criminal. Then I saw Murray enter the bright, empty space around Kissinger. His socialism had been high church, and his Christianity was an extension of the labor unionism of his youth. He said later that Kissinger should not have been invited, but once he had been, he became the *Review*'s guest, like everyone else there. He said when someone asked Kissinger's brother why he had no accent while Kissinger's accent was so heavy, his brother replied that that was because Kissinger never listened to anyone else. Murray had wit, a man of honor who was not a bore. His principles were private, an inner flame, the self alone with the self.

An ancestor of his was the author of the notorious Fugitive Slave Act of 1851, which, among other provisions, made a criminal of any white person in the North aiding a black person who had fled bondage in the South. It was not a history Murray saw himself as needing to atone for so much as to heed closely. Ancestry on the unjust side made this history very personal to him. From his decades of reporting, he knew more about twentieth-century Black history than I did. He was from that era when civil rights organizations were desperate to have the mainstream, i.e., white, press interested in their campaigns and on hand to witness, to describe, especially before the television cameras began to cover demonstrations. In the early days of civil disobedience and sit-ins and trials, Black leaders believed that the presence of white journalists acted as a restraint on local and state police forces.

Murray's sympathy for the Wobblies and the Popular Front expressed the hope for what used to be called a more pluralistic America. I told him about a book on the Communists in Harlem, who in 1934 decided to make their white guys take dance lessons so that Black women comrades would have partners at Party functions, because the Black men were always so busy with the white women. He liked to say that for guys like him, World War II had been their first chance to meet people different from themselves. But he'd already been doing that as a young white guy in Baltimore in the 1930s drawn to Black music and not afraid to venture into the Black part of town.

In the evenings, Murray's bicycle was parked between the elevator and Barbara's big brown door, and if it was not press week, then she'd organized dinner by telephone. She'd slam the front door not long after the chicken and vegetables had been delivered. Murray would be busy quoting Louis Armstrong as she placed a platter in his hands, or he'd follow her from the kitchen into the dining room while she carried a bowl, he on to something Duke Ellington or Billy Strayhorn had said. We'd hear the elevator and soon the most astonishing people would be walking through the door.

Edward Said and Barbara agreed that there was little difference between a Likud and a Labor government, and that realization was what made Rita Hauser so smart. Mariam Said remembered that the first time she was taken to Baghdad, they went to the movies, and the audience drank from the same cup when refreshments were handed around. Edward and Murray agreed on the Latinate awfulness of the King James Bible and the elegance of the Coverdale Psalter. Edward once had breakfast with Jimmy Carter. He had asked an aide if he was accessible, then Carter himself came down the stairs and said that he was, and he would give him his private number to prove it.

Murray did not need much of a prompt to tell Richard Nixon stories. Nixon always referred to Murray as an old friend and trusted adviser, which Murray said was the language of the friendless. Murray once said that Nixon said the country was vindictive. That was a favorite word of

Nixon's. Barbara Bush was the most vindictive woman in Washington, according to Nixon. Murray said Nixon hated successful Republican presidents and loathed Reagan most of all because he got away with everything.

It was a mystery to me, Murray's succor of Richard Nixon. After all, the subjects Murray was most passionate about were people who suffered and lost and lost yet again. I heard that when Murray's eldest son was killed on his honeymoon in an automobile accident, Nixon wrote him a long letter of condolence. Murray's son had objected to the Vietnam War draft, and I wondered if his eventual anger at Bill Clinton, the draft dodger who became commander-in-chief, did not contain rage toward a dead son that he could not express otherwise.

Family life was a shadow that never lifted. Barbara's version of West Sixty-Seventh Street had its complications. After more than a decade with Barbara, Murray was still technically married to his second wife. Every other weekend, he had custody of his adult son, Christopher, who suffered from severe autism, and for whom he kept his grimly functional apartment on West Eighty-Seventh Street. Estranged for a time, Murray's daughter Sally had changed her name and gone to head an ashram upstate, and her little brother, David, had followed her into the sect. His second son, Arthur, had the wavy hair Murray had when young and would go on to write a history of Motown. Their mother, Murray's first wife, still lived in the house down in Princeton.

When Jacob Epstein got married, his father told him he could not see a bride without seeing a plaintiff. But even after Jacob's father remarried, he telephoned Barbara every day for the rest of her life. Murray called Jason Epstein my husband-in-law. Lizzie sometimes let herself notice that Jason and Murray, both brilliant, eccentric, attractive, could not have been more unalike in their treatment of her friend. Murray was gallant and guilty, and Jason was, well, not those things. Either feminism was another doctrine to be skeptical toward or it wasn't. "There is a little bit of farce in every tragedy," I once heard Barbara say. Murray was a bold declaimer of his love as we cleared dishes. He defined a great beauty as the woman no man was not better for having known. Barbara pretended he was talking about Elizabeth Taylor.

Some mornings Murray did not hit the streets right away. His pipe waited for him to remember to relight it. In my memory, I associate his kitchen quiet with Samuel Johnson's *An Account of the Life of Mr. Richard Savage*, which Murray never seemed to cease from studying. Richard Savage, eighteenth-century failed dramatist, irregular poet, satirist, dead in a debtor's prison—Murray believed that Johnson had a clear sense of Savage's disastrous temperament, his follies, his self-inflicted misfortunes, even if he overvalued the work. It was the sheer mess Savage made of his life that seduced Johnson. Savage never found a stranger whom he didn't leave a friend nor had a friend he did not oblige to become a stranger, Johnson said. Samuel Johnson can sound like Murray Kempton writing about the moral challenges in the lives of losers. He would not reproach a criminal already in the executioner's hands. Savage appreciated virtue but was not himself virtuous, Johnson said. He was "the friend of goodness." Pure Murray.

Introduction

ANDREW HOLTER

"All I want to see journalism do is cover everything the way it covers the Mafia," Murray Kempton once told an interviewer. "That's all it needs to do. I don't mean the way it covers the Mafia when it says the Mafia runs the country as it takes over a little more of Union, New Jersey. I mean as they write about the Mafia with all the detail." The Genovese family has a crisis of succession, and the richness of motivation and morality, "the intimation of human selfishness and ambition and greed," is all there in the copy. Where are these resources of description, Kempton wondered, when the Republican Party finds its capo? And if it is a given that when someone like Joe Profaci, emperor of olive oil and boss of the Colombo crime family, gives thousands of dollars to a church in Brooklyn it is to burnish the veneer of his respectability, what is it when the executives at General Motors—or at Starbucks, we might ask—do more or less the same thing?

"If you talk to gangsters long enough," Kempton said, "you'll find they're just as bad as respectable people."

Murray Kempton wrote for newspapers between 1935 and 1997, with a break during the Second World War and for two excursions into magazines. Few American reporters left as many words in the twentieth century—perhaps eleven thousand columns—and none had quite the range of concern, the indelibility of style, the quality of mercy, and the force of reproach that make his work so compelling more than twenty-five years after he filed his last piece. In Joan Didion's estimation, he was "the best we have, and better than we deserve."

Kempton reported on subjects including organized labor, organized crime, radicals and reactionaries, political candidates and conventions, the Civil Rights Movement in the South and entrenched racism in the North, murder trials, baseball, jazz, Italy, Central America, New York City. Other people wrote about these things. The difference with Kempton comes down to his style, in the first place, and to the deeper questions of his journalism and criticism—the seven-decade-spanning inquiry into how the indignities of this country, this age, even this personal inheritance of sin, might be redeemed or at least resisted for a heroic moment, recorded for all time in a thousand words. His beat was hypocrisy, irony, hubris, courage. The characters and scenery changed; the dialog and blocking were liable to surprise; but the essential dramas remained pretty much the same.

"I usually call in at 8:30, find out what's on the Associated Press daybook, decide where to go," Kempton explained in 1994, at age seventy-six. He often took his bicycle, the trouser legs of a neatly tailored suit cinched with rubber bands while a Walkman around his neck spun Bach or Bessie Smith. "Sometimes the first place won't work out, so I'll move on to something else. Sometimes that won't work out, either." In this peripatetic, freestyle manner, he made literature from a genre, the newspaper column, that is here today, gone tomorrow. Writing books did not suit him. Criticism was not enough. His self-respect as a reporter—the only job title he would permit himself—demanded he keep the soles of his oxfords warm on the pavement. To H. L. Mencken it was "the life of kings"; Kempton called it "going around."

Finding the victim, Kempton thought, was the reporter's "one commanding duty." He was for the downtrodden, instinctively: His columns upheld the valor of the mother on welfare, the veteran in rags, "the good man in the bad job" whom he supposed was his favorite subject. "There's no use kicking somebody unless he's up," he said. Kempton's embrace of also-rans, losers, and guilty parties, though, became something of a trademark, the consequence of what William F. Buckley Jr. called "a compassion that is sometimes unruly." Kempton pleaded clemency for Julius and Ethel Rosenberg not because he thought the accused spies were innocent but because vengeance is unseemly. It was that simple, required that little ideological justification. Was Jean Harris, the Virginia girls' school headmistress, justified in shooting four bullets into her two-timing lover, Herman Tarnower, a.k.a. the "Scarsdale Diet" doctor? Outside the courthouse, Kempton shrugged. "Well, I was with her for the first three shots."

An unpopular cause is one thing, but it was the well and truly lost cause that brought out the unruliness, the mischief, of Kempton's compassion. By the end of his life, he could spare kind words not just for mafiosi but for that sovereign of twentieth-century American scoundrels, Richard Nixon. This is the Kempton who would apologize to his own muggers ("'Gentlemen,' I said at last, 'I feel like a shit.'"), who practiced "fairness up to the limits of the endurable," in the words of his colleague Les Payne. "Maybe it's not the scoundrel. Maybe it's the dignity I'm celebrating wherever it may happen to exist," Kempton said. Dignity is the cardinal value in his work. "It's how people act when the worst things happen to them."

It was a short list of people in whom he could find nothing to like whatsoever. Donald Trump was one ("dresses his hatred up as though it were a peacock's feathers"); Bill Clinton was another ("the mouth that refused to close even when he shut up"). He broke bread with many Communists, but "it's inconceivable to me that there would be a Nazi or fascist I could like." His regard for institutions, including political parties and newspapers, was not high. Of Columbia University, he wrote during the student takeover in 1968, "I have hated it as long as I can remember and am no fair judge of its agony." Go figure, even Columbia earned a kind of posthumous absolution: The archivists at the Butler Library are today the dutiful stewards of the Murray Kempton papers.

"What does it take to qualify for victimization—and the sympathy of Murray Kempton?" asked Buckley in the mid-fifties. (The *National Review* editor answered himself: It took being on the other side of "white supremacy, the Selective Service Act, and the Smith Act"). Besides Kempton's meandering grammar—try to diagram certain Kempton sentences, and before long you'll be staring at a spirograph—sentimentality was the most common complaint about him in his lifetime. He could be terribly sentimental; the pain at the end of many of his best columns is exquisite. Still, something more curious than compassion was at work in the temperament of a writer to whom respect flowed from so many disparate quarters: the liberals, his patrons; the conservatives, who came in time to be his flatterers; and the radicals, his shipmates, who usually hailed him even if they begrudged him light duty.

The journalism of Karl Marx was more vital to Kempton than the prophecy, he admitted. Reviewing Marx's *New-York Tribune* dispatches from the 1850s and '60s, he admired the way Marx, using only secondary sources, could see the iniquity of the British empire "as though he were Chinese watching the barbarian ships come up the river," as if he could see it from the victims' perspective. "Sympathy does not take him there; sympathy was not one of Marx's weaknesses; he is simply impelled to find the seat that affords the clearest point of view." Kempton knew enough about the trade by the time he wrote those words, at age forty-nine, to recognize the rub. Sympathy *was* one of his own weaknesses, but he joined it, as he joined his vast curiosity and fine manners, to considerations of craft.

"I was reminded of Kempton's courage as a street reporter while researching my biography of Malcolm X," remembered Les Payne, who worked alongside Kempton for years at *Newsday*. While interviewing Captain Joseph, a former commander of the Fruit of Islam, the Nation of Islam's security division, Payne listened as the enforcer "recalled Kempton with respect unheard of for a 'blue-eyed devil.'" When Malcolm X began at Mosque No. 7, in Harlem, Captain Joseph continued, "Mr. Kempton was the first white reporter to come around the temple." Cut to the night before the Ali–Liston fight, and there is Kempton up late at the Hampton House Motel, in Miami, drinking coffee with "Mr. Malcolm" and discussing the future of Black nationalism. The seat with the clearest point of view.

"I am a spectacularly bad interviewer," he once told David Remnick. "I usually make a twenty-minute speech, and then the interviewee says, 'Well, you may be right.'" For as much as Kempton epitomized the shoe-leather reporter, he did not pursue the sort of probing, thumbtack-and-string investigative projects favored by his friend and sometime competitor I. F. Stone. "I write every day for the next and walk wide of the cosmic and settle most happily for the local," he declared. But this might give a false impression: No one whose byline appeared in the *New York Post* and *The New York Review of Books* in the same week could be inattentive to the big questions.

Among Kempton's feats was to combine high and low, the street and the study. His references to history, literature, philosophy, and music were more than garnish; they thickened his stories, drew out their substance. His allusions were often arcane: It is hard to imagine a flitting comparison of Bobby Kennedy to Charles James Fox, eighteenth-century Whig parliamentarian, clarifying much at breakfast tables all across Queens (or Queens' College, Cambridge, for that matter). Even so, there was an egalitarianism to Kempton's regard for his readers' intelligence and curiosity. "The man is a marvel," Frank Sinatra once said of Kempton. "It's like listening to Louis Armstrong or Roy Eldridge: You don't know where the hell he is going, but somehow he gets there and it knocks your socks off."

To treat the people he covered as "characters" would have been an impropriety, but interior life interested Kempton greatly. He cared, as Irving Howe wrote of the revolutionary novelist Victor Serge, "about nuances, textures, and quirks of experience; he refused to dissolve men into historical forces." An elevated sensibility informed his reporting, while a life spent going around gave a certain authority—let's not call it street cred—to the essays and criticism he wrote for the *New York Review* and other publications. When Kempton rises to make a fine factual distinction in defense of his former editor, James Wechsler, remembered by the playwright Lillian Hellman as a friendly witness to the House Un-American Activities Committee, he does so on the authority, invoked almost apologetically in a footnote, that his was one of the names Wechsler named. Some petulant paleocon at *The American Spectator* or *The New Criterion* wants the mantle of H. L. Mencken? Senator, Murray Kempton served with Henry Mencken. He knew Henry Mencken. Henry Mencken was a friend of his. Etcetera.

Anathema to Kempton was the supposed value of "access." The reporter who strives to land the right interview or attend the right lunch, who wants to become an insider, is not much different from the blind man feeling his bit of the elephant, Kempton thought. You could do about as well from the outside. (On Marx again: "He is unchained from any notion of fixed place; he sits in his imagination wherever it would be most illuminating to sit.") Chumminess with the powerful was a related malady of his profession, because "it is next to impossible to judge any public figure with the proper detachment once you begin calling him by his first name." The conventions of journalistic style made most newspapers boring, he decided, but ultimately, "the disaster of American newspapers has been their continual reflection of the self-serving and incorrect judgments of events by those people who were responsible for them."

Kempton might also be remembered as one of the great general practitioners of "advocacy journalism." That term, so often deployed with condescension and coded derision, is a fair descriptor for much of his work. He had doubts about the crusading impulse, though, and the presumption that reporters themselves have much to do with changing the world. In his later years he was fond of quoting the last of the eleven *Theses on Feuerbach*, from 1845: "You know the wonderful thing Marx says—philosophers have described the world, but the point is to change it? Well, I think now the axiom's reversed—the world is changed, and the point is to describe it." The virtues of description were not to be underestimated. "I think the mind is really crying out for details," he said. "At least my mind is. What it is really crying out for is how the system works, what people say to each other, how they live. I don't mean what clothes they buy. The stuff you read that is really interesting draws a general conclusion from the particular. I mean, why do you read a story, except to be entertained and educated by it?"

The general from the particular: Edmund Burke (1729–97) knew how to get at that. Kempton loved Burke. Not Burke the philosopher, he said, "but Burke with the eye for the specific. I mean the Burke who knew that a government that cut off Marie Antoinette's head was not going to turn out all right."

James Murray Kempton was born in 1917, in Philadelphia, the son of a stockbroker, James Branson Kempton, and Sally Kempton née

Ambler, who came from an old Virginia dynasty transplanted to Baltimore. His parents' marriage was a union of losing sides, he wrote: "My mother's family had been beaten in the Civil War and my father's in some obscure skirmish of greed in the Gilded Age." To compound this unpropitious beginning, James Branson died of influenza during the 1918–1920 flu pandemic. His widow returned to Baltimore with her sons, William and Murray, ages four and three, respectively.

At the home of his grandfather, a former judge on the city's Supreme Bench, Kempton was raised by his mother and Aunt Virginia in circumstances he would describe so precisely as "shabby gentility." (Years later, he recognized the sediment of this stratum of Baltimore's down-at-heel aristocracy in Alger Hiss, the State Department official accused by Whittaker Chambers of loyalty to the Soviet Union. Another embarrassing personage, the Duchess of Windsor, had lived around the corner when she was still Bessie Wallis Warfield.) Materially, "shabby gentility" in a border Southern city meant a family that budgeted for the services of two Black servants but could not afford an automobile.

Their line included the Randolphs and Masons of Virginia, grand families who were supposed to have led the Confederate States of America. One ancestor was the Rev. Alfred Magill Randolph, Episcopal bishop of Northern Virginia and chaplain to Robert E. Lee; another, to the enduring embarrassment of his namesake, was Sen. James Murray Mason, author of the Fugitive Slave Law. By the 1920s, the family retained some pride of place, even as Sally Ambler Kempton took a job for wages at Hutzler Brothers department store. Murray was alone among his schoolmates, he realized, in having a mother who worked.

In the gothic details of Kempton's memory—of all the departments at Hutzler's, his mother was in bridal—there are shades of Dickens's Satis House and the hearth of Amanda Wingfield, the abandoned belle of Tennessee Williams's *The Glass Menagerie*, who instructs her children that the cultivation of charm is enough to correct for any inherited disadvantage. Kempton's upbringing was an education, then, in propriety, downward mobility, charm, and the self-delusion of white supremacy as codified in Jim Crow, whose dismantling at the hands of people like the servants he knew in childhood would so absorb him in years to come. It was the family's maid, Johanna Carter, who discovered Kempton passed out on the kitchen floor one morning in 1940 as gas filled the room from an oven jet—an absentminded accident, apparently, that surely would have been fatal.

Kempton's interest in newspapers was helped along by the fact that the most entertaining reporter in the country lived in town and wrote for *The Evening Sun*. The influence of H. L. Mencken is not hard to detect in Kempton's work, not least in his deflations of mountebanks from Davy Crockett to Donald Trump (who "demeans anything he touches, which is any place where he can leave his name permanently engraved"). Kempton's knack for distilling the menace and portent from a scene surely owes something to Mencken's reporting on the Scopes trial in Tennessee and the lynchings on Maryland's Eastern Shore; covering the trial of J. W. Milam and Roy Bryant for murdering Emmett Till, Kempton would inhale through gritted teeth the "fetid second-story courtroom, bulging to its dirty lime green walls with its all-white jury panel and with Bryants."

Kempton never wrote for the *Sunpapers*, as older Baltimoreans still call their flickering daily, but he caught a glimpse of Mencken at work during a summer job running telegraph copy at the 1936 Democratic National Convention in Philadelphia. There was Mencken in the press booth, years away from the stroke that consigned him to the writer's living death of silence, "weaving gold from the straw of the podium discourse while journalists at leisure craned over his shoulder to watch his next marvel clatter forth." Kempton would attend nearly every major party convention for the next sixty years, his own eminence and energy awing the press corps. He and Mencken shared notes at the 1948 convention of the Progressive Party, Mencken's last. The two of them understood what many correspondents never do: that a political convention, Kempton said, "is just not a place from which you can come away with any trace of faith in human nature."

If the Ambler home was an outpost of Richmond in the middle of Baltimore, Johns Hopkins, two miles north on Charles Street, looked from there like a satellite campus of Moscow State University.

The second half of the thirties was a time of unprecedented agitation on American college campuses, preserves of the elite though they remained. Against the backdrop of the Depression, Kempton and his fellows waged orderly but vehement protest against capitalism, rearmament, and the antique paternalism of the administration (which barred women and African Americans from matriculating, but not Jews, whose quotas came later. "I was the first campus radical they'd had who wasn't Jewish," Kempton recalled. "Therefore, I wasn't taken very seriously.") The professors who made the greatest impression on him were at odds with the university, including the philosopher Albert Blumberg, a logical positivist educated in Vienna who ran for mayor of Baltimore as a Communist, and Broadus Mitchell, a furious Kentuckian who resigned his post in the Department of Political Economy after failing in his campaign—supported by Kempton and friends—to force the school to admit its first Black student.

In this environment, there could be little pretense of journalistic detachment from politics. Kempton wrote his first columns for *The Johns Hopkins News-Letter* as a freshman and became editor-in-chief two years later, using his bully pulpit to galvanize the student body in support of petitions, strikes, and other importunities from below. He defended the right of campus Communists to hold their meetings and took a swipe at the *Sun* for red-baiting in its editorials on the New Deal—early instances of a lifelong tendency to shield the Left. For the hell of it, he welcomed a conservative classmate as a regular columnist ("Frankly, we believe that most of what he will have to say is pure hogwash").

Kempton was known to read a book a day at "the Hopkins," borrowing money from friends they assumed was going to a local bordello but was in fact for an evening's diversion with something like Harold Laski's *The State in Theory and Practice*. Still, he was hardly cloistered. He slummed along Pennsylvania Avenue, Baltimore's Black entertainment corridor, to hear jazz at the Royal, the Regent, and the New Albert. Before the U.S. Senate he testified in support of the unrealized American Youth Act, which would have allocated half a billion dollars to employment and education for young people—a good start, his comrades thought, to a society less reliant on its military. And when Kempton pitched in on the sailors' behalf during a strike at the Port of Baltimore, he found his solidarity rewarded with the offer of a summer job at sea. There was just one condition: membership in the Communist Party, such was the party's influence on the waterfront in those years. Kempton signed his card. "It's impossible to remember," he explained years later, with no trace of contrition, "there *was* a time in this country when you joined the Communist Party to advance your career."

Save for his affiliation with a vague network of underground couriers, Kempton's tenure as a Communist was unremarkable; these were Popular Front years, when it was possible to consider oneself a liberal and a Socialist and a Communist at almost the same time. He left the party following the Moscow show trials of alleged counterrevolutionaries, unsettled by a demand from on high for the addresses of Baltimore's Trotskyists, and alighted on the Socialist Party of Norman Thomas. (Fortunately for them, the Patapsco Trotskyists could not be found at home: They were all sailors.)

"My writing had already developed its style of windy preachment," Kempton said of his time at the Hopkins, "and I spent far too much time writing grand remonstrances to the dean." The student movement of the thirties amounted to little, he thought, but the themes of those early columns and the campaigns they stoked—the dignity of labor, the stakes of democracy, the rights of minorities, the cant of the establishment—he would write about for the rest of the century. The dean never died.

Kempton spent the early forties as a leftist of no fixed vocation, working as a relief investigator ("trying to steal enough for my clients, but there was never enough to steal") before moving to New York to join the floundering American Youth Congress, the student organization once favored by Eleanor Roosevelt whose membership split over the question of whether her husband was, in the final analysis, a damnable imperialist. Kempton became an organizer for the International Ladies' Garment Workers' Union, a publicist for the American Labor Party, and a writer of pamphlets for the Young People's Socialist League and the Workers Defense League. This last organization drew him to the case of Odell Waller, a Black sharecropper convicted of murdering his landlord by an all-white "poll-tax jury" in rural Virginia. With the law student Pauli Murray, whose intellect would move mountains in struggles for racial and gender equality to come, Kempton reported Waller's story for a pamphlet circulated as part of the national campaign to save his life. Appeals to Virginia's mercy failed, and Waller was executed in the summer of 1942.

Later that year, Kempton's credentials landed him a job on the labor desk of the *New York Post*, the paper where he would make his name. But not yet: He had barely spooled a typewriter ribbon when the Army called with orders to the Pacific. A series of reality checks—the Molotov–Ribbentrop Pact, Hitler at the Eiffel Tower, Pearl Harbor—had by this time disabused him of a "kind of silly, utopian, revolutionary view of the war," and the sworn pacifist went willingly with the Army to New Guinea and the Philippines. He led men in combat, including through an ambush north of Bataan that might have killed him had it not been for a cartridge clip in his pocket that stopped the bullet.

Kempton would make little of his military service in print; he did not trade on it even in cases when it might have certified the especially sharp indignation he could muster on the subjects of war and the government's treatment of veterans. At the time of the Gulf War, in 1990, he decried the lack of opportunities that led to a military with such a disproportionately high number of poor people of color among its recruits. It was the same argument, in essence, that he had made before Congress on behalf of the American Youth Act in 1938. The injustice of a nation where "winners preach war and losers fight it" never ceased to offend him. It was why, despite his revulsion to the Vietnam War and his own history in the pacifist movement, he resented the opportunism of privileged men who had avoided the draft.

After demobilization, Kempton worked briefly as an assignment reporter for the *Star* of Wilmington, North Carolina. This was the hometown of Mina Bluethenthal, his wife, who came from a family of progressive German Jews that included the suffragist and civil rights activist Gertrude Weil, an aunt. They had met as students in Baltimore—she was at Goucher—and married before Kempton went to the Pacific. The mundane stories from this period ("Fraternity Revives Ladies' Night") he pasted in a scrapbook and packed up with a young family to Princeton, New Jersey.

Kempton's career began in earnest once he returned to the *New York Post* in 1947 as apprentice to its labor columnist, Victor Riesel. Described by his own paper as a "glib, red-faced man," Riesel's three objectives, he said, were "to fight the crooks and Reds, to write colorfully, and to fight for the little guy." The late forties was an anxious time for organized labor: Union leaders were reeling from the passage of the calamitous Taft–Hartley Act, which rolled back the power they had accrued under the New Deal and triggered a kind of civil war over Communists in their ranks. Riesel's fixation on malfeasance made him a pest. Under his tutelage, Kempton learned to cover the labor movement critically but not crankishly—by the standards of what he understood to be its best democratic traditions. In time he developed a soft spot for "the crooks and Reds," as Riesel never could, and flowers from his bouquets to various unions can be found pressed in the pages of their digital newsletters to this day. The union, he once told an audience of AFL-CIO steelworkers, "is not property but mission. Anyone can belong to a union; but a union belongs to no one, and least of all to anyone who is ashamed of where he or she came from, and is indifferent to those he or she left behind."

The *New York Post* of the late forties was a liberal paper, its owner not a baleful conglomerate but a savvy former debutante and alumna of Bryn Mawr, Dorothy Schiff. Its typical readers, writes Schiff's biographer Marilyn Nissenson, were "people whose politics were Democratic-left, were likely to be Jewish, and were either members of the working class or intellectuals who sympathized with the proletariat and affected its style." In 1949, Schiff tapped Kempton to take over for the departing Riesel under a new executive editor, Paul Sann, and editor-in-chief, James Wechsler, a liberal anti-Communist who had been a leader of the thirties student movement at Columbia. (Riesel continued to make himself a nuisance at Hearst's *Daily Mirror* until an acid attack on the street left him blind in 1956, a crime traced eventually to the Mafia. "They should have gotten him in the hands," Teamsters president Jimmy Hoffa is reputed to have said.)

The turn toward national politics in Kempton's column came as Wechsler and Schiff established the *Post* as an antagonist of Sen. Joseph McCarthy. It bears remembrance that the *Post* and papers like it rooted their opposition to the witch hunt in its broad threat to civil liberties, not its specific injustice to American Communists, whom most liberals regarded as deceitful and dangerous. As the reporter Edwin R. Bayley once noted, the same week McCarthy announced to the Women's Republican Club of Wheeling, West Virginia, that he had "here in my hand" a list of subversives in the State Department, the *Post* ran a series by Kempton about perfidious maneuvering by Communists in the labor movement. But Kempton changed the more he saw of McCarthy and his allies' sordid tent show. By the mid-fifties, he distinguished himself not only as a critic of anti-Communist legislation but as an impassioned defender of Communists themselves. He wrote of the burial of Geraldine Lightfoot, on the South Side of Chicago, where the FBI could not seize the funeral director's guest book because the local Red Squad had beaten them to it. He got to know people like Victoria Wellman, the all-American teenager whose parents faced imprisonment and deportation, and Leona Thompson, who fought to have the ashes of her husband, a recipient of the Distinguished Service Cross and Communist Party official, interred at Arlington as he wished. "In the course of these efforts, I grew rather close to these victims," Kempton recalled, "and what surprised me most was how patriotic they were and how certain of the ultimate equity of American justice they remained."

For some American Communists, Kempton's sympathy was too little, too late. The John Birch Society, meanwhile, maligned him as an exemplar of "the Communist entrapment of a 'modern liberal.'" In fact, few if any liberals took as seriously the struggles of the country's "internal exiles," as Kempton called the beleaguered in his first book, *Part of Our Time: Some Ruins and Monuments of the Thirties* (1955). By insisting first that Communists were "more sinned against than sinning," and then, increasingly, that liberal Democrats bore greater responsibility for the witch hunt than they accepted, his columns anticipated revisionist histories of the era to come. It was very easy for those who had been radicals in the thirties to profit from their second thoughts about Communism, but Kempton's "second thoughts about second thoughts about second thoughts," as his *Newsday* colleague D. D. Guttenplan has said, set him apart. Of his peers in the press, Kempton remarked long after the fifties, "I think they were wrong, and that they neglected their education. All through that period, liberals were saying, 'I'm anti-Communist, but McCarthy has gone too far.' I think it was a failure of character. It's very American." His alienation from the political family of left-liberal anti-Communism matured his worldview, informing a sense of political homelessness that made him a more critical and idiosyncratic observer.

Kempton never appeared before the House Un-American Activities Committee or its Senate equivalent, the Permanent Subcommittee on Investigations, having assured McCarthy's henchman Roy Cohn in private that if summoned, he would offer no names. "I could give you a lot of high-minded reasons for it," he told Cohn, "but I'll give you a low-minded reason—I can't afford it commercially." His editor James Wechsler, however, agreed to testify after receiving a subpoena. Liberal anti-Communists should stand up to McCarthy on his own turf, Wechsler thought, dismissing Kempton's warning that he was sure to hurt himself more than he ever would the senator from Wisconsin. Asked by McCarthy for the record about Communists in his newsroom, Wechsler volunteered the name of a former communist: "I know of one. Mr. Cohn knows of him, too. He is a man named Kempton." This was no bombshell, but his reporter was right: Wechsler's testimony injured his reputation. "An editor who will inform on his own staff 'to keep the record straight' is an editor who has allowed himself to be degraded," remarked I. F. Stone.

Stool pigeons and other entrepreneurial experts in the conspiracy were frequent targets of Kempton's ridicule. In 1954, the McCarthyite journalist Victor Lasky brought a successful libel suit against Kempton for having suggested in a column that Lasky was hiding his own past in the Communist Party; Kempton wrote that he remembered "the man now known as Victor Lasky" handing out Trotskyist pamphlets at the Bowery YMCA in 1937. On appeal the court found in Kempton's favor, describing the column in question ("Comrade Victor") as "racy," "hyperbolic," "frequently cryptic in meaning, sometimes contradictory, and only dubiously suggestive of matters defaming plaintiff." Style, it seemed, saved the day.

Style had something to do also with the friendship Kempton began around this time with William F. Buckley Jr., who founded the conservative digest *National Review* in 1955. They were not such a strange pair. In Kempton, Buckley recognized a fellow dissenter from the liberal consensus, capable of field-dressing its contradictions with flourish even as he made his incision from the opposite side. It could be no coincidence either that each man had a reputation for mannered comportment and florid prose. ("It is my theory that Murray Kempton and William Buckley are the alternate signatures of the same infuriating man," wrote the journalist Mignon McLaughlin.) A few of the more worldly of Buckley's staff writers would take Kempton as an inspiration, none more than Garry Wills following his apostasy from the conservative movement. Kempton was Buckley's superior, Wills has written, and was perhaps the one writer on the Left that his old mentor really listened to: "This was a case of deep calling to semi-deep, and the semi-deep responded." Asked in old age about his attachment to Buckley, Kempton replied, "I've never thought of Bill as a serious man, which is a sort of compliment."

Having a couple of friends on the Right couldn't have hurt Kempton's safety in the fifties and sixties, he guessed. Even so, his FBI file grew steadily. The columns that passed the desk of J. Edgar Hoover got under the director's skin like nettles; he scribbled in their margins that Kempton was a "rat," a "jackal," a "snake," and "a real stinker." In a 1961 memo sent to Attorney General Robert F. Kennedy, Hoover complained that "Kempton has written many columns belittling me and criticizing my administration of the FBI." The director was unaware, apparently, that the president and his brother had read Murray Kempton for years.

Assessing the place of fairness in Kempton's work, Les Payne noted how easily his old colleague broadened a "fight for the underdog," from the plight of American Communists to the by-no-means-unconnected arena of the Civil Rights Movement. In the mid-fifties Kempton became one of the first white journalists to join "the race beat," traveling regularly to the South for a decade to report from schools, churches, courthouses, bus stations, and jails, little hamlets and hollows where country people would not bow. The power of these dispatches was immediate. "Murray Kempton's current articles in the *New York Post* on the Alabama situation are just about the most moving pieces of American reportage I've ever read," Langston Hughes wrote during the Montgomery bus boycott. (Hughes, a columnist himself, urged Simon & Schuster to commission a book from Kempton.) Editors from the New York *Amsterdam News*, *The Philadelphia Tribune*, and other papers of the Black press republished some of his stories ("From the gifted typewriter of Murray Kempton, *New York Post* columnist, has come one of the most touching accounts of the last week's carnival of sadism.").

Kempton's frequent traveling companion in the South was Ted Poston, the "Dean of Black Journalists," who had been writing for the *Post* for a decade when Kempton joined and was for years the only reporter of color there. As his white colleagues could not, Poston registered the paper's unique—and soon squandered—esteem among Black New Yorkers during what Bayard Rustin called the Civil Rights Movement's "classical phase." By his own industry and that of Kempton and others, Poston observed, "Negroes had come to believe that no matter where other Negroes were in trouble—Mississippi; Florida; Little Rock; Montgomery; New Orleans; Clinton, Tenn.; Cicero, Ill.; or New Rochelle, N.Y.—anywhere Negroes were up against it, they had only to buy *The Post* and find out what was really going on. Because *The Post* usually had somebody there to tell them about it."

A border Southerner with the ear of liberal New York, Kempton knew what to look for below the Mason–Dixon line and knew how to tell the things he saw there. Time in the trenches of the pacifist and labor movements made him a perceptive interlocutor with strategists like Bayard Rustin, Ella Baker, and A. Philip Randolph, whose Brotherhood of Sleeping Car Porters he revered. In 1956, Dr.

King wrote Kempton a letter of thanks for columns that "expressed the spirit of the movement," citing also the "contributions that have come into our office as the result of your articles." King and other leaders could not afford to be indifferent to the Northern white press; in their effort to appeal to white America's conscience, as such, they had an asset in a reporter who worked in sentiment the way a painter works in oil.

Beyond the South, and long after the passage of the 1965 Voting Rights Act, Kempton's attention to Black politics and the wider terrain of what historians call the Black freedom struggle was notable. Probably no American journalist of the twentieth century addressed a mostly white readership as often or with as much detail and direct testimony on matters of racial injustice, including in the areas of employment, education, policing, and housing. (With a map of New York City and a pen, Kempton once explained redlining to a white Alabama newspaper editor convinced there must be racial discrimination worth covering in the North too.) And yet the papers Kempton wrote for employed so few Black writers that he came to sit comfortably in the role of resident expert on "the Negro" in an era of much ponderous commentary by white intellectuals on this subject of subjects.

One of the few piercing criticisms of Kempton in print can be found in *The Omni-Americans*, the critic Albert Murray's 1970 polemic on the "folklore of white supremacy" and the "fakelore of black pathology." In a droll analysis of white intellectual presumption, Albert Murray didn't have to name his subject for readers to recognize a "well-known New York newspaper pundit, a somewhat reconstructed but somewhat sentimental Southerner out of Virginia through Maryland," a "well-meaning but sometimes condescending white maverick's maverick" who is "nice but proprietary." This description could still apply, years later, to a septuagenarian getting it all wrong in every way in a review of Spike Lee's *Do the Right Thing* in *The New York Review of Books*. (As James Baldwin wrote of an especially disembodied bit of *On the Road*: "I would hate to be in Kerouac's shoes if he should ever be mad enough to read this aloud from the stage of Harlem's Apollo Theater.") That Kempton reserved the vestiges of this particular proprietorship for so long had at least as much to do with the whiteness of the profession as it did his sincere ("well-meaning") belief as a first-draftsman of history that it is easier "to learn about America with an all-else-excluding concentration on the history of Afro-Americans than it has ever been to depend on histories that scarcely mention them." The volume and variety of his coverage of Black subjects is a testament to that concentration, but in the valuable archive he left behind—Hughes recommended Kempton's work for the "permanent record" of race relations—there are examples of when his liberty to write about Black America exceeded his insight. Ted Poston, who was not a columnist, simply didn't have the space or the time to work the same way.

In 1962, a restless middle period of Kempton's career began with his acceptance of an editorial position at *The New Republic*, in Washington. It was a bad fit, the town and the magazine. "I never knew what the hell I was supposed to do there," he said. After an eventful year and a half that included the March on Washington and the Kennedy assassination, he returned to New York for good, stopping over at the *World-Telegram and Sun* before taking his old desk back at the *Post* in 1966.

The reunion with Dorothy Schiff and James Wechsler was uneasy: He felt constrained, overedited, askew from his superiors over the Democratic president's handling of Vietnam, which he deplored. More and more, his column rankled the same readers who had written to Schiff that she should rehire him, and the tension reached a head in a series of controversies across the fateful year 1968. During the Ocean Hill–Brownsville teachers' strike, Kempton's sympathy for the Black and Puerto Rican "community-controlled" school board over the mostly white teachers union incensed the exact sort of New Yorker—left-leaning, lower- to middle-middle class, white-ethnic or Jewish—who liked to read Murray Kempton in the *Post*. "What happened to the Post's liberal stand for peace and understanding?" one reader wrote to Schiff. "And what has happened to Murray Kempton?"

Around the same time, he was rebuked by the AFL-CIO for a column blaming its national leadership's tolerance of racism for the inroads made by presidential candidate George Wallace into some of its locals. "The AFL-CIO," Kempton wrote, "has lived happily in a society which, more lavishly than any in history, has managed the care and feeding of incompetent white people." (Generations of historians would go on to cite this line, without context, as illustrative of the growing gulf between liberal intellectuals and the white working class.) That summer, sickened by Vietnam, he supported a political campaign for the first time in years by standing as a delegate for the antiwar challenger Eugene McCarthy at the Democratic National Convention in Chicago. There he was arrested by Mayor Richard Daley's police along with hundreds of others—a man of almost deviant propriety charged with and convicted of disorderly conduct. "I'm not sure newspapers are for me anymore," he told an interviewer the next year. He left the *Post*, again, to freelance and write books.

The sixties rattled many of the so-called New York Intellectuals ("The Family," Kempton nicknamed the *Commentary* crowd), clarifying their identification with the Right. To Kempton, the upheaval of those years was bracing; the sixties excited something anarchic in him. "I think you're going to have a series of revolts and withdrawals in this country," he said. "I think that a society which can wink at this war and act as though it didn't really exist, which I think the American Liberal Institutionalism has to a considerable extent, I think a society which has done that can expect, if not revolutions then ideological panty raids pretty frequently," he said. "I think it's a rotten country." He got himself arrested again, this time on purpose, at a draft board office on Varick Street. Around town he could be seen in the company of longhairs and Black Panthers. ("You're a cool mother-fucker, you know where it's at," *The East Village Other* once hailed him from its bekiefed and patchoulied offices above the Fillmore East.)

For the subject of his first book in fifteen years, Kempton chose the case of twenty-one Black Panthers charged in the spring of 1969 with plotting a series of terrorist attacks across New York City. Called *The Briar Patch* (a title inspired, incidentally, by Albert Murray's discussion of folklore in *The Omni-Americans*), the book's heroes included the young Afeni Shakur, pregnant with son Tupac during the trial. Kempton saw that the real conspiracy was the one set against the

Panthers by the New York City Police Department and its apparatus of political repression; the prosecution's case rested heavily on the testimony of taxpayer-funded provocateurs. This was not just the fifties all over again and the Panthers a new set of "internal exiles," but a case that seemed to contain the whole history of race and justice in the United States. With no employer to demand his detachment, Kempton spoke at rallies for the Panthers' defense, lent a typewriter to their support committee, and paid bail for Panther field marshal Don Cox before his flight to Algeria. "The Panthers are the bullseye but the black community is the target," he wrote. It was Kempton, in fact, who initiated the series of Upper Manhattan appeals that led to a fundraiser at the composer Leonard Bernstein's apartment, the "Party at Lenny's" sent up by Tom Wolfe in *New York* magazine as the risible crest of "radical chic."

The Panthers didn't know what to do with him, an informant told the FBI. The solidarity of an outlaw like Jean Genet was one thing, an ambassador from the pitiless white press quite another. Eventually the Panthers waved him away like an embarrassing uncle. There was some romantic adventurism to this chapter, to be sure, and traces too of midlife crisis. But "Murray Kempton was there every day in that courtroom," Shakur would remember to her biographer. "God bless him." The Panther 21 were all acquitted in 1971, and *The Briar Patch* won a National Book Award in 1974.

Kempton would never write another book, scuttling plans for a meditation on the fifties as debt—he was never rich—compelled him back to a day job. In 1977, he rejoined the *Post*, now the possession of one Rupert Murdoch. "Signing on with him was a bit like shipping out on the Staten Island ferry with, say, Long John Silver as captain," Kempton remarked. With this owner there could be no more formidable test of his suspicion, deduced from the career of the pugilist Westbrook Pegler, that reporters work better when they are at war with their employers. ("I'd chop all his sentences in two," Murdoch was overheard grousing.) They got on more or less in the event, but after five years Kempton sued Murdoch for peace by leaving the *Post* for the fourth and final time. He spent the rest of his career writing mostly for *The New York Review of Books* and *Newsday*, a "respectable tabloid" much as the *Post* had been under Dorothy Schiff. This seems to have been the happiest configuration of his working life: "going around" for columns, exegeting for Robert Silvers and Barbara Epstein at the *New York Review*, essaying here and there for publications like *House & Garden* and Ben Sonnenberg's literary magazine *Grand Street*.

An oft-told tale: Not long after Kempton won the Pulitzer Prize for Commentary, in 1985, he observed idly to a group of journalists that he had never won the Meyer Berger Award for human interest reporting. "You've just won the Pulitzer, Murray," someone said. Kempton demurred. "The Pulitzer is named for a publisher. The Meyer Berger is named for a reporter."

In "My Last Mugging," a 1971 essay written for *Playboy*, Kempton tells a dinner party story about getting robbed on the Upper West Side by a hapless duo he calls "Mutt and Jeff," after the comic strip. Almost robbed: He has nothing to hand over, just his regrets. All three of them are embarrassed (" 'Don't you think we feel like shits?' Mutt answered. 'We don't like to do this kind of thing.'"). Mutt and Jeff are already leaving, dejected, when Kempton discovers some change in his pocket and calls after them: "And Mutt came back and took it, and we said good night, and I went home with no sense that I had made it up to them."

"My Last Mugging" reads like a Manhattan set piece, a Murray Kempton comedy of manners, right up to the end, when Kempton reveals that he is the only one at his host's table, somewhere north of 59th Street and south of 110th, who is not laughing. Kempton has lost his mind, in fact, like the narrator of "The Tell-Tale Heart" ("Hearken! and observe how healthily, how calmly I can tell you the whole story"). He walks the streets in terror of being old and vulnerable to the city's underclass, he says, and of course it is about race—everywhere are "horrible shadows." The other day he forked over all the change he had to a Black teenager in the subway who only asked him for a dime. He could carry a heavy cane, he thinks, but there is the unbearable thought that he might find himself using it. In his shame, he writes, maybe he will leave the city for "some far place where a man can keep his mask and have no need to choose between wearing the face of the victim or the face of the beast."

But who, in this story, wears which face? A neoconservative, Irving Kristol wrote, "is a liberal who's been mugged by reality." So in Kempton's tale of horror, the hair-raising transformation is not into a wolf or a vampire but a contributing editor to *The Public Interest* or *Commentary*. His was not actual metamorphosis but nightmare or premonition. "Murray lives on the streets," Darryl Pinckney remembers their editor Barbara Epstein saying. Kempton knew perfectly well that hell is not getting mugged on the Upper West Side: Hell is conscription to the garrison state that is the New York Social Democrat's nightmare and the New York crypto-fascist's reverie—the Manhattan of Travis Bickle and Curtis Sliwa. After all, who are Mutt and Jeff if not the sort of "good men in the bad job" he loved to write about? For all his concern with personal conduct, the problem for Kempton is always poverty, not the poor. That is why, even at his weariest, he would never call himself a conservative, neo or otherwise. (Alfred Kazin would remember Kempton as "my only radical friend from the 1930s who never sold out.") In a city where violence and disregard circulate from the state on down—Mutt and Jeff must have learned their shakedown routine from the NYPD, Kempton thinks—the predicament of so many of his New York stories lies in how to salvage comity and comedy. The political alternative to this unhappy mansion, where some must mug and others must be mugged, was for the philosophers to decide; Kempton would stay on the ground, writing "each day for the next" against the design of Lucifer in the beast of "My Last Mugging," who begat Bernhard Goetz, who begat Daniel Penny. No doubt he had sat a while with George Orwell's description of his own poisoned soul as a colonial policeman in Burma, the anxious white oppressor of the 1936 essay "Shooting an Elephant," who "wears a mask, and his face grows to fit it."

Kempton's later columns provide an almost unbroken account of the city across the Koch, Dinkins, and Giuliani years. His attentions were prescient. Over the snickering of colleagues, he heard authentic wickedness in the prattle of local clown Donald Trump. With his ear to the street, he registered the dialectical emergence of an "all-but-universal public policy" against the poor, born of Reaganomics but coparented by a Democratic Party not much interested anymore in social welfare; we know it as neoliberalism. "What an interesting populace we have," he once wrote Kazin, years before mass incarceration was a subject for the bestseller list. "Nobody seems at all worried by the fact that we have the largest prison population and that it consists preponderantly of young blacks, a whole generation in jail." Little of what has come to pass in this country would surprise him. "One way of saying that we have been here before," observed Christopher Hitchens, "is to say that Murray Kempton was there before us."

So established was Kempton's prestige as "long-suffering watchman of the city's civic virtue," as the reporter Jim Sleeper put it, that his approval seemed to some like a municipal currency beyond value. If Murray Kempton had nothing nice to say about you, perhaps there was just nothing nice to be said. There is the famous story about Mario Cuomo when he was governor of New York: "How can I get Murray Kempton to love me," Cuomo asked the *Newsday* columnist Sydney Schanberg. A pause. "Why don't you try getting indicted, Governor?" Woody Allen still fumes that Kempton, who "had been an idol," took Mia Farrow's side after sitting in on their custody hearing. Kempton "made it sound like I was this rich, powerful guy with lots of money and many lawyers versus this poor, betrayed mother," Allen wrote in his memoir. If the director had been a closer reader he might have spared himself the disappointment—for in the jurisprudence of James Murray Kempton, aggrieved mothers are never at fault.

The valiant mother, especially with no man, was one woman to whose side Kempton could be counted on to rush; without resort to psychobiography, it stands to reason that having been raised by a misfortunate single mother himself was related to this tendency. The stories of other women and their claims—especially women together, not so many Joans of Arc—were only sometimes clear to him. Of all feminist writers it was his own daughter, Sally Kempton, who scrutinized his paternalism in a 1970 essay called "Cutting Loose," for *Esquire*. Her father, Sally wrote, nourished "a sort of eighteenth-century fantasy about our relationship, the one in which the count teaches his daughter to read Virgil and ride like a man." Kempton's old comrade Pauli Murray read it with interest, she wrote him, "and while I was amused at her rebellion against her perception of your attitudes on gender and applauded it, I could not help but reflect that you also gave her the gift of words with which to argue persuasively against your point of view." In time, they reconciled.

Today it would not be so unusual to hear it suggested, as Kempton did in a 1997 column about the sexual abuse of incarcerated women, that the second wave of feminism produced a politics more concerned with "prisoners chafing under glass ceilings than those sealed round with stone walls." But a raised consciousness did not take Kempton there any more than sympathy took the armchair correspondent Karl Marx to the banks of the Yangtze. It was beyond him to think all that seriously about feminism as a political project—or rather, it was always within his reach, had his conception of feminism not frozen around 1970 with his daughter's circle of sisters in the West Village, if it had not frozen already around 1940 with the "rebel girls" he admired in the CPUSA. Besides the quirk of his chivalry, his own sexual politics were marked by a certain rueful contrition. "Heterosexuality, being the most pervasive, is the most destructive of mankind's deviations," he once wrote. "It is a thing whose beauty cannot be mentioned without paying due respect to its terror."

Starting at least with the inspiration of the great labor journalist Mary Heaton Vorse, redoubtable women were important to Kempton's intellectual and professional life all along: Pauli Murray, Dorothy Schiff, the *New York Review* coterie of Susan Sontag, Elizabeth Hardwick, and Barbara Epstein, to name a few, and of course his wives, Mina Bluethenthal and Beverly Gary. The daily newsroom, however, was a man's man's man's world. His was one of so many intransigent guilds enjoined to tolerate members who were not white men, the class protected in their boorishness and license. ("I fought the challenge of middle age ridiculously drunk on the job," Kempton admitted openly, unremarkably.) When the conflict was between his "fellow workers" and management, his moral clarity was near crystalline—as when, during a stint with the CBS radio program *Spectrum* in the early seventies, he became the first of the network's on-air personalities to declare his refusal to cross a picket line of striking engineers. With conflict between fellow workers, though, solidarity could be fungible with the handshakes and passwords of the fraternal order of newspapermen.

So it was that Kempton closed ranks around his *Newsday* colleague Jimmy Breslin when, in 1990, the New York chapter of the Asian American Journalists Association demanded Breslin's resignation or termination following an atrocious newsroom tirade directed at Ji-Yeon Yuh, a young staffer who had criticized the sexism of one of his columns in an internal memorandum to their superiors. Breslin remained basically unrepentant and got a slap on the wrist. Yuh's job at *Newsday* simply ended there. (She is now a distinguished historian of Asian America.)

It is telling that in his own comments on the Breslin episode, Kempton accused Yuh of "finkery," a slight from the old union lexicon meaning an informer on the side of the bosses. In the precision of that epithet lay at once a catastrophic failure of sympathy by a writer renowned for that same faculty and a former labor columnist's perfect misapprehension of what was, among other breaches, a labor offense by Breslin. There was a story, too, about a woman's stand for dignity in the face of execrable male conduct and the complacency of her putative colleagues. That story included a dramatic mobilization of solidarity by Asian American journalists that put the "color-blind" liberalism of *Newsday* and papers like it to shame. It was a story, in other words, whose elements a reporter of Murray Kempton's sensitivities might have recognized, but the reporter Murray Kempton was missed it entirely.

From the choleric late career of Mencken, Kempton knew he was doomed to overstay his welcome. If Westbrook Pegler was right that in time the newspaper columnist becomes mere "packaged goods," Kempton figured, then the "dreary road to the wrapping and bundling counter is probably inescapable: there is the hunt for the discovery of what works, then the erosion of curiosity about what else might work, then the disappearance of all curiosity about anything unfamiliar, and at last the prison of the safety of one's own accepted manner." This depletion was a hazard of the profession, the columnist's black lung. It is a credit to Kempton's late style that he mostly avoided sounding brittle or imperious. He took his reputation as an eccentric in stride. Gibbon, Macaulay, Byron, Proust: these were his companions more than any literary clique. ("Live both in the future and the past," advised Lord Acton, whose essays Kempton kept on a shelf just above his typewriter.)

The years had not been weightless. His marriage to Mina Bluethenthal ended in divorce, and a second, to Beverly Gary, a reporter, also failed. In 1971, one of his four sons, James, died together with his wife in a car accident at age twenty-seven. The suburban house in Princeton was another lifetime; after the Pulitzer, an interviewer from the Johns Hopkins alumni magazine met him in a bachelor's apartment on West End Avenue, where he lived with jazz records and electric fans and kept a few bottles of beer in the refrigerator. His return to the Episcopal Church, to Saint Ignatius of Antioch on the Upper West Side, kept the Weltschmerz at bay. "You can, of course, understand that whatever meager disposition I have to glory in my past is quite displaced by my unease about the future," he wrote Buckley at the beginning of the nineties. "My present work seems somehow to have misplaced, if not quite lost the joys of the day; and I've been working with too gloomy a desperation to relocate them. They will return."

So they did. Kempton wrote many of his most trenchant and amusing columns in the last years of his life. A collection, published in 1994, announced the marvel of his long career and brought him laurels to pad his pallet on the floor. Here, wrote David Remnick, was "the one true original in the business."

It was around this time that Brian Lamb, gentleman-inquisitor of C-Span, asked Kempton where he stood, politically, at age seventy-six. From below tortoiseshell glasses came a contemplative frown, the lower lip drawn back and puckered quite like the twenty-year-old whose picture had appeared on the front page of the *Baltimore Sun* in 1938, next to the headline reading "Low Education Makes Soldiers, J.H.U. Student Tells Senators."

"I think I'm a sort of Tory or anarchist, I suppose," he told Lamb, adding, as if to clarify: "I don't know what the word means, but I think of myself as a radical."

What did the word mean, after sixty years? After Burke–Wadsworth,

Taft–Hartley, and Ocean Hill–Brownsville? After the National Maritime Union and *National Review* and the Philippines? After Odell Waller, the Hollywood 10, and the Panther 21? Eight hundred pages passed across the desk of J. Edgar Hoover and a sympathy card, when his son and daughter-in-law died, from the desk of Richard Nixon? After one Pulitzer, two Polks, and too many bills to pay?

Perhaps "radical" meant what Orwell, in his essay on *Gulliver's Travels*, decided about the satirist and pamphleteer Jonathan Swift: "He is a Tory anarchist, despising authority while disbelieving in liberty, and preserving the aristocratic outlook while seeing clearly that the existing aristocracy is degenerate and contemptible." Kempton's distaste for the two parties and for "abstract political thinking," he told Lamb, grew more pronounced with time. In his later columns, especially, the lucid melancholy of the old Tory before the coarseness of his age is joined with the anarchist's hope against hope in the emancipatory potential of "fellow feeling." Essential to his egalitarianism was the leveling notion of sin. To have a sense of sin is to recognize one's own fallibility and that of others, which might, if you see it Murray Kempton's way, conduce relations of affinity, empathy, and even solidarity. Sin is why he celebrated the scoundrel's display of dignity or admission of shame and not scoundrelhood itself. "I never wonder to see men wicked," Swift wrote three hundred years ago, "but I often wonder to see them not ashamed."

Eminent journalists, critics, and politicians filled the pews of Saint Ignatius of Antioch for Kempton's funeral in May 1997. He had planned the ceremony in advance to follow the Church of England's Order for the Burial of the Dead, with the name of the deceased spoken just one time, no eulogies, and a bit of singing by the congregants. This was nothing so vulgar as a "celebration of life." What it was like was a Murray Kempton column, said Robert Silvers. The Rev. Gaylord Hitchcock, rector of Saint Ignatius, explained to a reporter there: "The service is typically Anglican. At this particular point, the focus is upon God and His mercy and His love, and not the American obsession with self and lionization of the individual. It is deliciously Kemptonian countercultural. He keeps us honest even from the grave."

✧ ✧ ✧

Of the thousands of columns, reports, essays, reviews, appeals, and miscellaneous articles written by Murray Kempton, relatively few have ever been published more than once. A 1963 collection, *America Comes of Middle Age*, culled some of the best of his first dozen years as a *Post* columnist. Thirty years later, he struggled, with help from the writer Darryl Pinckney and the editor Steve Wasserman, to draw a line around all the intervening history and experience for a retrospective collection, *Rebellions, Perversities, and Main Events*, funded by the largesse of William F. Buckley Jr. It is difficult to distill so much writing across so many decades into a single book. The omissions could have easily filled a second volume, Buckley thought.

This new collection has benefited from the discernment of an editor who understood Kempton's quality better than any. Barbara Epstein, cofounder and coeditor of *The New York Review of Books*, was Kempton's companion in the eighties and nineties. When he died she became his literary executor, responsible for settling the business of his career and finding a repository for his bushels of clippings. "Some of these columns are in a yellowing and frail condition, dating as they do from the Forties," she wrote one archivist. "Preserving them is one of my main concerns, since they present a brilliant and virtually daily chronicle of over fifty years of history." There was something else, too: "At the moment, I'm concerned with organizing the material in an effort to collect some of his uncollected pieces in a posthumous book, or perhaps two books."

This was obviously a personal project as well as a literary one; editing Murray Kempton was a way of spending time with Murray Kempton. Barbara Epstein found a home for his papers, but the book never came together before her death, in 2006, her hopes having been dampened, perhaps, by the suggestion of at least one apologetic publisher that it would be a hard book to sell. A box containing her work on it lived in storage with her daughter, the writer and teacher of public health Helen Epstein, for years.

The present volume, enriched by Barbara Epstein's file, presumes to take up where she left off. Included here are pieces from every period of Kempton's career, the earliest written when he was eighteen and the latest when he was nearly eighty. It contains the best of his work in different forms, long and short, and shows the breadth of his interests and the scope of his witness in the twentieth century, including dispatches from a hardscrabble coal town in western Maryland, a bus carrying Freedom Riders through Mississippi, an Iowa cornfield with Nikita Khrushchev, an encampment of guerrillas in El Salvador, and Moscow at the end of the Soviet Union (these last two assignments filed by a reporter in his seventies). If initiated readers find a favorite piece missing, there is bound to be another in these pages to surprise them, at least, and to affirm the critic Wilfrid Sheed's observation that "after a thousand or more Kempton columns, I have no idea what the man will say next about anything."

There is an element here too of what literary scholars call "vicarious autobiography." The contents are presented in order of publication to locate Kempton in the history of his times, and the arc of his life might be traced across these writings to an extent. Kempton was less inclined to self-disclosure than many of his peers, which is not to say he avoided self-examination. From Mencken, a *Harper's* editorial noted in 1956, he received the wisdom that a reporter could be "the central character in a drama of his own contriving," but his was a lighter touch than the New Journalists who followed. His pose was that of the "bemused naif" (said Molly Ivins), "a lean grey keen man" (Stephen Spender) perambulating through the world, "costumed for, perhaps, some minor but consoling corporate position" (Elizabeth Hardwick). About the closest Kempton gets to Hunter S. Thompson in these stories is the recollection of smoking "reefer" at a Count Basie show during the Roosevelt administration. He did finally have something to say about his life, a memoir begun much too late. What he wrote of that book, to be called *Once Ain't for Always*, after a line in Bessie Smith's "Lost Your Head Blues," appears in this collection: a chapter about his ambush during the war, published posthumously in the *New York Review*, and a reminiscence of his childhood in Baltimore that is printed here for the first time in edited form.

Despite the occasional glossy magazine feature and column syndicated in Washington or Los Angeles—despite the Pulitzer, even—Kempton was never well-known outside of New York ("which is to New York's credit," said Buckley). He wrote no definitive document of the zeitgeist, like Joan Didion or James Baldwin, nor did he possess the requisite narcissism to cultivate a public profile on the level of Norman Mailer or Gore Vidal. If Kempton was in fact the "real founder of the New Journalism," as the investigative reporter David Halberstam believed, he never accrued vacation property and film options like Tom Wolfe, the writer whose clothes, prose, and politics all suggested a lurid, Bizarro World doppelgänger of Murray Kempton. (While not a full-fledged literary antagonism, Wolfe and Kempton seem to have held each other in special disregard. Wolfe was "a fashion writer," Kempton thought, who "has no social purpose in his writing"; Kempton, wrote Wolfe, "used so many elegant British double and triple negatives, half the time you couldn't figure out what he was saying.")

On television, Kempton could be charming but hopelessly digressive, careening through precious airtime in a voice that still held the brackish tannins of shabby genteel Bawlmerese. Listening to Kempton hold forth, recalled one junior reporter, "was kind of like tuning in the dial on someone who was talking about life and reality and class guys against bums and the New York Giants, and the *New York Post* against the *Times*, only there was really no order, except that Kempton kept interrupting himself, to try and answer practically unanswerable questions." In column inches, this conversation with himself cohered. It was as if "he thought naturally in thousand-word boxes," *Harper's* said, "and could think no other way." It is no wonder, then, that his reputation as the reporter's reporter endures among those remaining acolytes of what Molly Ivins called the "Murray Kempton cult in this country," whose youngest initiates are themselves now gray.

Disinterments like this book always carry the risk of accidental defilement. It is also the case, as Kempton confessed of his own regard for Mencken, that "the idolator molds his idol from the clay of his personal prejudices." Among the prejudices of this editor is that to leave Murray Kempton half-remembered as paragon of the late, lamented American newsroom of Nescafé and aspirin tablets is rather to flatten the writer he was and risk deadening the insight he might render us today. He belongs to whatever is noble in the tradition of American newspapers ("St. Murray of the Tabloids," *The New York Times* once called him), but from this vantage he looks to have been more inspiration than influence—a front-bencher of journalism's loyal opposition, who wrote in a mode that was more textured and more generous and so often just stranger than daily newspapers then or now could quite reconcile. "The grudge, the storehouse of rancor," wrote his friend Elizabeth Hardwick, "was not his style and perhaps in that way he was a little out-of-date in the present hyperbolic atmosphere." Hardwick meant the 1990s, so how out-of-date does that make him now? Kempton "understood 'reporting' in the deepest sense of that debauched word," noted Alexander Cockburn. "He leaves no heir."

Newspaper columnists today seem a bit like the remaining handloom weavers at the time of the industrial revolution, incredulous before the satanic mills of online opinion platforms. At least the handloom weavers had a durable claim to artisanship. Few columnists today go around. Too many are concerned with being the adult in the room, with "just asking questions," concurring with management. If they ever wanted to be reporters, they do not want to be anymore; instead, they want to be like the dean at Johns Hopkins in 1938. "Kempton still goes everywhere to see for himself and to ask his own questions," the reporter Earl Caldwell told his readers. "In the world of newspaper columnists, that makes you special." Jon-Henri Damski, the long-running gay press columnist, once ventured that in opinion writing, laziness finds a corollary in prejudice. Did anyone else notice, Damski wondered, that the homophobia of Mike Royko, Kempton's Chicago analogue, became more conspicuous as his columns more often betrayed the signs of one who had forgotten the value of leaving his desk? "Top-class journalists, like Murray Kempton," Damski wrote, "listen to the street sounds of the many voices in America, which make their columns click, sound alive and real." No research assistant or composite character can go around for you.

Of reporters, Kempton said, "I think it's our job to describe the little piece of the world that we know." In these pieces he takes you with him as he goes around, to the seat with the clearest point of view. He is not all that interested in debate. Description is the essence of the job, the part that cannot be fudged, and it demands humility from the reporter. If there is a lesson in Kempton's avowals of error and sin, it may be that the familiar intellectual conceits—moralism, contrarianism, even the posture of civility—will come up short. More dependable is the ethic of work, the discipline that keeps the writer out in the world, with others, rather than beside or above it. For Kempton it was fidelity to the ideal not of being right but of being there, away from the trough of punditry, where abstraction evaporates and in its place is an actual person to help you take the measure of things.

In a column written in 1951, with over four decades of work ahead of him, Kempton admitted that "even the social value of what I am doing—if anybody really does things for their social utility—seems to me a debatable business. Who am I to preach to people?" He wrote to the end as if he never closed that question. It is not just Kempton's style that makes him so hard to emulate: Few writers are so honest as to remain so unassured.

Among the papers in Barbara Epstein's file is an inventory of clothing donated to Housing Works: a lined raincoat, gray flannel trousers, the handsome suits Kempton wore even at the height of summer. His bicycle, whose periodic theft amused him, wound up somewhere; perhaps it was stolen from its new owner and then stolen again from the thief. At Saint Ignatius of Antioch there is a niche for him at the columbarium whose plaque is inscribed with nothing besides his name and dates, "December 16, 1917–May 5, 1997." The draft copy contains a copy edit, "~~Dec.~~ *December* 16," from Barbara Epstein's pen.

Here is a sampling of so many days spent going around. What general conclusions may be drawn from their particulars are hard to predict. It would be enough for Murray Kempton just to be read. "The only final importance of newspapers may very well be that people leave them on subways," he said,

> and, on the lonely morose grumble of the Rockaway Line, some Richard Wright, some James T. Farrell, some Hart Crane, some Norman Mailer, some Grace Paley—in the disguise of an ado-

lescent with his time to come—may pick you up and by heaven you have a duty to be ready for cross-examination. It is a heady—even an arrogant—thought that there might be a moment when you were read; and a great part of the joy of residence in the province of those who go around is the fleeting hope of such a moment whenever you begin a morning there.

I

LOSING-SIDE CONSCIOUSNESS

For those who looked further than the mere form of the *News-Letter* there were the improved editorial columns controlled by the embroiled, busy, idealistic, but always guiding hand of Editor J. M. Kempton. New life appeared in the usually most-ignored two columns of the newspaper; all are convinced: Mr. Kempton did a good job.

—Johns Hopkins University yearbook, 1939

I'll Still Take Roosevelt

10 • 6 • 36

After four years of it, I'll still take Roosevelt.

Such a position is, I suppose, an indication of the most arrant stupidity. Kindlier critics might call it divine madness. For a few have had so many opportunities to see the light as have been granted me. Embryonic captains of industry, rich in the expediencies of two summers of bank-running, have taken me aside to lay bare, in all their horror, the mysteries of New Deal finance. Alcoholic viewers-with-alarm have backed me into corners and have raked me fore and aft as a betrayer of the Flag, the Bible, and the Founding Fathers. And yet here I am, with our civilization crumbling into dust, sitting, as in the ivory tower, still peacefully surveying the desolation wrought by Tugwell, Ickes and Frankfurter.

It is a good thing to sit down and take stock of one's opinions every once in a while. I suppose it is a good thing even when one's opinion is really an emotion. For any opinion grounded on an ideal rather than a business index is, in our time, really an emotion.

As a matter of fact, I think the Roosevelt case is pretty strong even statistically. The latest indices form a fair sample of the results of "fumbling with recovery." And those who talk so glibly of the coming inflation and national bankruptcy would profit from the works of such able New Deal apologists as Chester Crowell and Joseph P. Kennedy.

But, for myself as well as the Baltimore *Sun* there is "little satisfaction in a merely frugal Roosevelt." I'd probably be for him if he were as wasteful as his critics contend.

For there are two kinds of waste—the waste of money and the waste of human resources. Through the last half-century we have been piling up for our posterity a heavier load than any debt Roosevelt can create. Our waste of material resources is reflected in the shifting sands of the great agricultural Middle West, our waste of human resources in the faces of the men who file by the office of the National Reemployment Service. Some call any desire to better such conditions Communism. Personally I prefer to call it common decency.

The New Deal represents the first attempt of an enlightened liberalism to deal with these problems. The attempt has often been a faltering one, but, in any aspect, it is a thousand times better than what went before.

And that's why I'm still for Roosevelt. We did not secure the blessings of Utopia for ourselves and our posterity by his election in 1932, and we will hardly secure them this time. What we will and have had is a progressively liberal government, recognizing and in some measure facing our present problems. And that, in a major crisis of world democracy, is about the best we can reasonably expect.

People are constantly telling me about the "purge" of the Republican party. The Old Guard, hitherto unrecognized, was, according to their account, off its collective feet and carried away by a new (Republican) liberalism, nurtured and brought to flower in Topeka and personified in the sturdy figure of Alf Landon.

The Kansas gang seems to have turned an ordinary Republican wake into a colossal evangelical orgy, beside which the services held under the auspices of the late Billy Sunday take on the color of Witches' Holidays.

It is a glorious picture, and we can almost see Abraham Lincoln and Theodore Roosevelt beaming paternally in the background.

Now I am not one of those who hold to polemic as the sole weapon of debate. I hope I will never be one of those who thinks all the sheep are on my side and all the goats on yours. This is not intended as an *apologia* for Joe Robinson and Paul McNutt. Nevertheless, I feel that it is important to examine the present state of Republican morality.

There are men—and Al Smith is one of them—of whose honesty and sincerity I have no doubt, who have set their faces against the New Deal. For many of them the stand has been a painful one, and they should be honored by all parties for taking it.

But there are other men, still sitting in the high councils of the Republican party and still heavy contributors to its war chest, who have fought with every resource at their command, every attempt at social legislation in the last decade. They are the men to whom the eight-hour day was a Communistic plot, and to whom any form of social security is a reflection on the individualism and self-reliance of the American worker and his employer. For the last four years, they have been roaring down Franklin Roosevelt in every Union League Club in the land. I am not naive enough to believe that these men are now apostles of the "New Freedom."

In spite of every effort on the part of Mr. Landon and the ridiculous Frank ("Turn The Scoundrels Out") Knox, the Republican party has failed to rid itself of the incubus of the support of practically every outstanding American reactionary. Landon says that Roosevelt is fostering Monopoly; yet the Iron and Steel Institute is solidly Republican. Knox says that Roosevelt has attacked the civil liberty of the individual; yet William Randolph Hearst is Landon's most conspicuous supporter. And Landon says that, under Roosevelt, the rich grow richer and the poor grow poorer. I submit this astounding statement as needing no comment. No, the facts are too inescapable, the line between progressive and reactionary too clearly drawn.

I spoke a while ago of "a crisis in world democracy." By the time these words appear in print, the liberal popular government of Spain—which Mr. Hamilton calls "Communist"—may have fallen before the combined onslaught of the Fascist powers. The inevitable capitulation of Madrid will leave England and France as the only major democratically constituted nations in Europe.

At such a time, a clear-cut victory over the forces that make for reaction in America will be of incalculable importance. The repudiation of these men and their philosophy cannot be too overwhelming. I am hoping with all my heart for that repudiation. As one who calls himself a liberal, I couldn't hope for anything else.

Last Boat for Jerusalem

1941

We have talked a long time about democratic disasters.

And you can stack the facts any way you choose; they still add up to final defeat if we accept the philosophy under which the United States government proposes to fight the Nazis.

The current drive to militarize America cannot be confused with real anti-fascism. Those who now press it look forward to an empire built on the hunger and repression inherent in an economy of armaments and extending its control deep into Latin America. They work with desperate speed to save the privileges of a society in decline with a new model fascist army.

These people must and can be checked. The great mass of ordinary Americans is still torn between its hatred of the Nazis and the war dictatorship which is the only alternative the rulers of their country can offer.

There is just one program which can fulfill their aspirations.

First of all, an end must be made to the mockery of starvation and unemployment in the richest country in the world. Hitler has no greater ally than the vast impersonal fact of factories idle while millions of Americans need their productions desperately.

There is no real national unity which is not based on plenty for all. Just as we recognize that resistance to fascism is hopeless so long as the rulers of industry control our defense program, so we must conclude that the motive of private profit stands as the chief bar to the truly democratic world which alone makes war against Hitler worth the fighting and sure in its victory.

For us in America, there yet remains a choice between an enforced and a democratic collectivism. We can guarantee our defense against Fascism here and abroad only through the institution of Socialist planned production under democratic controls. Such a system alone can eradicate the causes of native reaction and provide the economy of plenty which could rally the enthusiastic support of the masses of Americans to its defense.

And, in the Europe of the Nazis as well, whatever hope there is for the anti-Fascist movement is bound up with the aspirations of revolutionary Socialism. Whatever temporary successes he may achieve through his policy of repression and conquest, Hitler is unable to provide a final solution for the basic causes of popular discontent. His civil war on the continent did not come to an end with the capitulation of France. It goes on in new and as yet under-developed forms all over the occupied areas; and the crushing weight of German imperialism will serve only to heighten its intensity. The underground forces upon which the final victory over Nazism depends might struggle as successfully for the revival of the Holy Roman Empire as for the reconstruction of German capitalism. For them Socialism stands first on the order of the day.

An American military state dedicated to the preservation of an obsolete social order is actually the deadly enemy of European anti-fascism. Should the United States go to war against Hitler, our own labor and Socialist movement would fall as first victims, and the anti-Nazis would lose the single effective force which might halt the intervention of American reaction against a German workers' republic.

A Socialist America would represent a defeat for Hitler far outweighing his present triumph. It would raise again the torch of liberty in a world which has almost forgotten the sight of the flame. It would rally and inspire men of good will in every country around a concept of progress which challenges the very fundamentals of Nazism and war.

For, in the last analysis, there is no anti-Fascism but Socialism. At this moment, as the old order lies dying, the ideal of a classless society stands forth as the one clear symbol of the centuries-old battle of the little people of this earth for a measure of freedom, justice and economic security.

All for Mr. Davis: The Story of Sharecropper Odell Waller

(with Pauli Murray)

1941

"Gretna, Virginia," writes Jonathan Daniels, "is an inconsiderable community on that U.S. Route 29 which runs through the heart of the country of textile mills from Virginia through the Carolinas to Georgia. North of it is the little town of Alta Vista, which makes rayons and cedar chests. Not far below it is Chatham where well-to-do girls, many of them from the North, learn the lessons and ride the horses of the Episcopal Church's excellent and fashionable Chatham Hall. Little Virginia boys march there in the uniform of the Hargrave Military Academy. In the same section lived long ago Colonel Charles Lynch, who according to Virginia tradition, gave his name to Lynch law."

It certainly isn't the kind of country Erskine Caldwell would pick to write a book about. The sky is too smooth; the little shoots on the tobacco hills look too green in the sunshine and the people are too sure in their manners and too rich in their laughter.

Yet, as you ride the bus from Danville, you're likely to hear hot painful words through the darkness:

"An' then Ah went in the white section to get a drink an' this big white man says so meanlike, 'Git back on your own side, sister,' an' it was dirty an' they had a little ole hole to pass the water through."

Or, "Looks like there's nothing a colored man can do down here to git justice. I've never run into no trouble myself but I've had to take plenty to keep out. I reckon I'll jes' go on takin' it."

Or they turn to you in their cars and say:

"Lissen, mister, I've lived in this country thirty-eight years an' if you find an honrable darky, there ain't nobody better, but what you get a mean one, there's nothing else to do but shoot him."

They're not very bitter about these things down here. It's been a long time since anybody got lynched, but color is not the only bar to a full enjoyment of Pittsylvania County's blessings. This is no country of rich men. Tobacco is the chief cash crop, and what with federal crop curtailment and the winter blight, there isn't the money there used to be here.

"Sure, it's a pretty country," they will tell you, "but it's been hit here."

Almost everyone around Chatham lives off the land, with debt always stalking at his back. Most people work on shares, and even the landlord is likely to be himself a tenant or a mortgage-ridden farm owner.

December 8, 1940, the Pittsylvania County New Citizens League held a big meeting for seven hundred first voters and recent high school graduates. The president of Washington and Lee University was down to sing the glories of the American system of equality and justice. He was too tactful to take public notice of the fact that there were no Negroes in his audience.

There are 61,000 people in the county. Of these, 36,000 are white and 25,000 colored. The last time anyone counted, there were only 6,000 white people and 200 Negroes eligible to vote.

It costs a man $1.50 a year to vote in Virginia. And unless the court records show the poll tax to be paid up at least three years back, you can't elect your judges, and you have little or no chance of sitting on juries.

On Saturday nights the Chatham streets are filled with brown farmers from the hills. The boys outside the Main Street diner are a delight in themselves; no one could flash a wider smile or a richer laugh. Here they forget the long slow days in the tobacco fields; no thin-lipped deputies, no Jim Crow laws to irritate; no forced sales or road-gangs—just a race of happy people on a well-earned holiday.

As likely as not, there is not even a word of their neighbor, Odell Waller, who is scheduled to die in a Richmond electric chair, nor of Oscar Davis, the landlord he killed in self-defense. Yet the story of

Odell Waller and Oscar Davis is as native to Pittsylvania County as the green tobacco leaves and the Georgian front of Chatham Hall and the soft laughter by the Main Street diner on a clear Saturday night.

Odell had his brief thrust of fame, to be sure. But after they brought him into Chatham, dragging him by the belt as if it were a dog-collar; after the witnesses and the Commonwealth's attorney had spoken their pieces, he was found guilty of first-degree murder and sent up to Richmond to die. People got worked up for a while over how Waller shot and the angle of his bullets; one or two white men said, "That nigger ought to be lynched," but no one cared very much about hearing the story of the life which he and Oscar Davis had lived before their final quarrel. Perhaps this was because it wasn't a very exciting story and was all too common in Pittsylvania County.

But if you ask them, they'll tell you about Odell Waller. White men will tell you that his parents, Willis and Annie Waller, had farmed their own land around here for years, and were "as honorable Nigrahs as you could want." They've heard tell, of course, the boy turned out mean, but they'd never heard anything against him before this.

The colored people will tell you that Odell was a good boy, who worked hard and was more cool and levelheaded than the general run of young folks. He had need of these qualities. Even though his father owned his own farm and a half-interest in a wheat binder, meeting the mortgage payments and the taxes was never an easy job; by the time Odell was twenty, it had become pretty near impossible.

Stocky little Odell will tell you, as he grips the bars of his cell in the Richmond death house, pressing his face forward with the intensity of a man whose hours are numbered, "My father was a po' man what believed in hard work. He made everybody aroun' him work. I didn't have no school at all to atten' when I was small. Later, for three years I walked ten miles a day to school."

Willis and Annie Waller were heartbroken when Odell had to stop school and go to work in the fields at sixteen. The boy had done well in his studies. Willis Waller's death in 1938 brought an end to one phase of the family's independence. The bank moved in, and within two months Odell and his mother saw their land sold out beneath them.

They didn't give up. Odell was now twenty-two, a strong, willing boy—Annie Waller will tell you that, as she holds her withered hands two or three feet above the ground to show how small he was when he first went behind the mules. She will tell you, "That boy is all I got. 'Course he's my sister's child, but I caught him when he draped—he jes' same as mine, and I raised him."

Odell wanted to give up farming and get public work. He saw his young life being frittered away in the blind alley of toil and debt, but his mother thought the farm was the only place she could make a living. For her sake, Odell stayed on the land. He got married and went to farming on shares, helped by Annie, his mother, and Mollie, his wife.

They took the two hogs, the fertilizer, and the wheat binder and went to work on Oscar Davis' land. They never had an easy time. For every four sacks of wheat they harvested, three went into the Davis barn; for every six bundles of tobacco they harvested, three went to Davis. Their own wheat went into bread, and the cash from their share of the tobacco crop, along with the products of the little house garden, didn't provide any luxuries. They killed one of the hogs and salted it down when the first cold weather came. They ate the sausage, the chitterlings and some of the bacon, but they sold most of the meat to make a little cash. Even so, money was so scarce Annie Waller didn't have shoes half the time.

There isn't much agreement about Oscar Davis around Gretna. Some white people say there wasn't a better man in the county. He taught Sunday School at the Methodist Church, and in all his life he never spared himself or his two strapping sons at the farm work. He lived and died, they say, as a good Christian and an honored citizen.

But the Negroes who knew him saw that side of Oscar Davis which tells of the two-sided character of many Southerners. Those who worked his crops speak of Oscar Davis with something close to hatred. They tell stories about the time when he and his son, Edgar, had such a falling out that for weeks afterwards Mr. Davis carried a gun. They speak of the hard words he was quick to give the man who worked for him.

"He was one," as an old hand put it, "who liked to dawg the colored man. He wanted you to do all the work while he did all the ridin' 'round."

Maybe that wasn't Oscar Davis' fault: He had worked so hard for such small rewards all his life that there was little time to learn the social graces that characterize Virginia aristocracy. In his last years, he found himself an old man with his third wife, a frail and sickly woman, two sons who proclaimed to the countryside their dislike for farming, and not even riches to comfort him. He had lost his private holdings and sunk into tenancy years ago. He was a renter now from a Mr. Shields and was beginning to feel the full weight of the general depression, which hit Chatham when the tobacco market fell off. He had even tried to hold off his creditors and the sheriff with a little bootlegging on the side.

Pressed from above by his landlord, he took it out on the poverty-stricken colored people who worked for him. After Odell's first sharecropping year with him, Davis began to take his trouble out on him. The two had been friends until that time, as good friends, that is, as a white man and a Negro can be when one works all day to see more than half of his crop fall to the other.

Their first open difference came when government agents assigned his spring tobacco allotment to Oscar Davis in 1939. He cut down Odell's land to four thousand hills, less than two acres, and pocketed the cash benefits paid for the reduction. With their cash crop thus eliminated, the Wallers faced a desperate winter.

A year and a half later, Odell was to review the story as he faced a jury fighting for his life. He was steady, and calm; he told it as if he were reading from the pages of a book. And indeed his humble life was being summed up in a trial court record.

"I moved onto Mr. Davis' 'long 'bout January 2, 1939. I sowed a crop of corn, tobacco, and wheat. I was supposed to get one-fou'th the corn crop; Mr. Davis was to help work one-fou'th the wheat crop. I had a tobacco crop which Mr. Davis received one-half of, also Mr. Davis had a tobacco crop and his sons had a crop. After we got to working Mr. Davis' crop, all hands would get in and work, but whenever it come to my crop, wouldn't be nobody helpin' but jes' me and mine.

"We got along all right, didn't have no trouble along during the year 1939—but Mr. Davis was mighty crabby anyway, didn't bother me none at all, but would jump on the boys for the least thing. He carried a pistol and his oldest son threatened to kill him.

"Edgar told him, 'You can have the farm after this year; I wouldn't fool any more time.' Frank Davis decided he wouldn't farm either.

"During the fall of 1939, wheat-sowing time, I fixed the wheat land, getting it into shape. Mr. Davis would be hilling tobacco for other people and won't paying me.

"He was going back and fo'th to see his wife in the hospital. After I got the wheat land fixed, I holped him strip the tobacco. Then the acreage come on in 1940 and the government people cut the tobacco crop down. They allowed six acres and three-tenths. Mr. Davis says that's enough for us. I lit in then, and during the fall of 1939, Mr. Davis, his sons Edgar and Frank, and myself began to be whiskey dealers: We dealt in that along, and then started in to make ready for the 1940 crop.

"First I went to cut wood, I split up wood as hired labor for to holp us. Well, I holped him break up his 1940 tobacco land, corn land, run his pasture, everything. I even took money out my pocket—didn't pay as much as Mr. Davis, only about fifty cents or seventy-five cents out my pocket,—but I paid that.

"During this time, come on spring, after I got the land into shape—everything in, Frank Davis 'llowed to his father he was going to get Henry Davis."

Henry was an eighteen-year-old colored boy who worked for the Davis boys and carried the same surname. The colored folk around Gretna didn't know so much about Henry—where he came from, who his friends were, or what he was like. He didn't know anybody around the county, and he stayed too close to the Davis huskies for the colored folk to like him much. Odell had a quiet independence that was disconcerting to white men. They didn't know how to take him. Henry Davis was more pliable. He scared easily, and was grateful for small favors. Six months later he was to turn against Odell, as the State's only eyewitness to the shooting.

Odell went on with his testimony. "That suited Mr. Davis. He brought him there and distributed the whiskey—"

Odell paused. Once he might not have admitted he was bootlegging with a white man, but now deeper forces were at work in him, he must tell everything. He must make the jury understand what bread means to a man.

The jury was a white blur, their faces never changing expression. Did it matter that Odell needed a chance to explain? Can any black man break through the impenetrable white wall?

"Then one day we went on by the barn and he said, 'This will be your crop, about four thousand hills.'

"I asked him, 'Can't you give me as much as two acres of tobacco? If you do that, I can give you ha'f and have one acre for myself.' But, no, he wouldn't do that. I went on disgusted."

At first, Mr. Davis was polite to the Waller family. He pointed out that things weren't too easy for anybody in Pittsylvania County, and that Odell was free to go where he could do better. If he didn't like his house, the landlord was always ready to take it back. But where could Odell go with a wife and mother to support? Besides, what about all the labor he had put into Mr. Davis' crop for nothing?

"I said no more crop for Mr. Davis if he can't give me any more. I was jes' getting into debt everywhere. I saw Mr. Davis, and told him that if he would let me work my crop of four thousand hills, I would tend to his. But, no, he wouldn't do that. He wanted to get me taxed into working the whole crop. After he wouldn't agree to let me to tend my crop, he 'llowed if I want any more'n this four thousand, I wouldn't tend to none. I told him, 'If you give me two acres, I would tend it all together.'

"But he wouldn't agree to that. Said I'd better find something else. I said, 'You could let me have the house for part of my work and maybe I could get off even. He 'llowed he'd let me know about that."

Here is the whole sorry picture—no written contract with the landlord—just a casual agreement that could be broken at the landlord's will. To city folk, the pattern becomes more familiar now—a northern contractor looking for cheap labor, a farm boy fighting off debt and needing a little cash to care for his family.

"I waited a week or so, working on a job or two; Mr. Percy Dance, a contractor, I told him about it and he said—I been working for this man off and on for ten years—he had a contract in Maryland and would I go with him? I come on back down the road. Mr. Davis was over there on the road. This boy, Henry Davis, was in the field harrowing. Mr. Davis hollered to me to come on by there. He wanted me to do work.

"Mr. Davis hollered, 'Where you been?'

"I told him I been up to Gretna to see Mr. Percy Dance.

"He said, 'You going with him?'

"I told him, 'Yes sir, I could go with him.'

"He said, 'Well, you will have to give me my house.'

"I said, 'I can give you the house tomorrow.' Then I said, 'You ought to pay me something for working, don't you think? I deserve something for my work.'

"He 'llowed, 'Naw, I ain't going to pay you none.'

"I 'llowed, 'Naw, I ain't going to move either.'

"He said, 'The only thing I will pay you, I will see you when the crop is finished.'

"He hollered and told me to get his cow; it don't graze enough in here. I went on to the house, I didn't bother about getting the cow. I didn't say anything the next day or the day after that. Then Mr. Davis said he was going to get rid of the cow, and he got rid of the cow.

"Then I reckon there was about a week before Mr. Percy Dance come and asked me was I ready to go to Maryland, and I went with Mr. Percy to Maryland to work then. It was 'long the middle of April."

Odell was worried about Mr. Davis even while he was in Baltimore. He wrote his mother asking her to have Robert Waller, a cousin, work in his place to save their share of the wheat crop and he kept sending money home to pay the cousin. He told her to help Mr. Davis with the tobacco crop and to let the Davis family use the Wallers' binder when wheat-harvesting time came.

Annie Waller is a small Negro woman, so small in fact, that when she sits on the bed, her full-buttoned shoes dangle nearly a foot above the floor. When she walks, she is humped with a stoop which long days in the tobacco fields make habitual to the ancient. She is shrunken and wrinkled, only her hands are full-sized. After one glance at Annie Waller, you can see nothing but her hands. They are purple and ashy-bald with the crop blight. They are raw from years of handling cow teats and dry tobacco leaves. They are the spades with which the earth-bound grub in the ground for their food.

Annie didn't even know her age. She got little further than looking at pictures in newspapers. She had no glasses and depended mostly on the children to read letters to her. She counted on her fingers, and it took her nearly a half hour to "back" (address) an envelope; but she could work hard, and she could figure. Until Odell got into trouble, she had never been fifty miles from the place where she was born, and she had never even heard of Niagara Falls; but she knew her rights.

Annie had done housework for Mrs. Davis while she was ill in the hospital. They were to pay her at the rate of $2.50 a week. When Mrs. Davis came home, Annie toiled about the house, waiting on her until she was strong enough to do her own work again. Annie was a good worker. Small as she was, and given to few words unless it was to children, she could move through a house like a fresh wind, With a brown paper bag turned upside down on her sparse hair and narrow forehead, she went from one task to another until everything shone spick and span. You didn't have to tell Annie what to do or follow behind her. She never asked questions.

The Davises still owed Annie $7.50 for her services. Mr. Davis kept promising he was going to pay her when the crop came in, but somehow he had never gotten around to it. It's so easy for white men to string colored folk along. Promises made are lightly broken; like promises to children or to animals, there's little honor in them. Annie accepted this with the calm dignity of those who have come to realize that trouble is their portion of life.

Now Odell had told her to help Mr. Davis plant and work his tobacco so he would "plough her up" some sweet potato land.

"Long 'bout the fou'th Friday and Sad'day in May, 1940," she will tell you, "when it was cold, and rainin', and so raw no 'oman oughter been outdoors, there I was in Mr. Davis' fields a-plantin' terbacker. There waren't another 'oman out there 'sides me—jes' a whole gang o' min and boys. I was workin' up to my ankles in that red mud in the rain till it was so dark I couldn't even see the rows before me. I holped Mr. Davis plant that terbacker and I holped him hill it. Mollie was smarter'n me. She didn't do no work and she didn't get nothin'. I did all the work, an' I still didn't get nothin'.

"Then it come on time to work that terbacker. One Sad'day I was goin' to the mailbox, and Mr. Davis, he was goin' to the barn.

"He called me, 'Come on down by the barn, Aunt Annie—' they call me Aunt Annie, you know—

"I went on down by the barn. He says, 'You goin' to help me work that terbacker today?'

"I commenced to thinkin' jes' as hard and fast as I could.

"I said, 'I don't know, Mr. Davis. I bin workin' an' workin' around here, and it seems like everything goes to Mr. Davis. It's all for Mr. Davis; I don't see nothin' in the ground for Annie.'

"Mr. Davis says, 'I told you if you'd get a sack of fertilizer, I'd fix you up some sweet pertater land.'

"I says, 'But I told *you*, Mr. Davis, you owed me seven dollars an' a ha'f, an' if you'd let me have a ha'f a sack of fertilizer for that, I could get some sweet pertater land.'

"Mr. Davis. says, 'Hell naw, I ain't let you have none, an' I ain't agoin' to let you have none.'

"I says, 'Well, that settles it.'"

Annie Waller had reached the end of her rope. She wasn't going to work any longer for nothing.

At this, Mr. Davis lost his temper. These Wallers were too damn uppity for niggers. They were always wanting something and you couldn't boss 'em around like you could most sharecroppers. Ragged and poverty-ridden as they were, they had the nerve to be independent. He told Annie he wanted his house back—the little shack she and her daughter-in-law lived in. She supposes she might have gone to the law; but she didn't think much about it, and "it probably wouldn't have done much good no-how."

In three days, the law came to her. She and Mollie were ordered to move. The sheriff's deputy wasn't given to long explanations or to courtesies. Odell didn't have a written contract and that was enough to put him at his landlord's mercy. The sheriff's deputy told them,

"Mr. Davis wants his house, an' if you're not out of here by next Thursday, I'm gonna come back here and throw you out, an' sell some of your things to pay the cost of moving you."

"I was outdoors then—only thing I jes' hadn't moved," Annie will tell you. "I put on my bonnet and went down the road to my neighbors, I told them, and some of my church folks got together to holp me. Everybody flocked to me—some buildin' pig pens, some fixin' a place for my chickens."

They went dumbly, poorer than they came. They did not owe Oscar Davis one cent; they had paid for their fertilizer under the ground and the "top-dressing" over the ground. They had one hog left. The colored minister let them stay in his little cabin just outside of Gretna. They had to leave behind the garden of "greens" they planted that spring.

Today, it is this eviction which Annie Waller feels most keenly. When she reaches this point in her story, she stops and runs it over in her mind and has to be prodded to go on, as if anything else would be an anticlimax.

In spite of the eviction, however, Odell's share of the wheat must be saved. Mr. Davis had told her she could come on the place and get things out of her garden. She didn't write Odell what had happened. When wheat-harvesting time came a few weeks later she did as he had asked her. She let Mr. Davis use the binder, and put her "man" in the field to help with the harvest. She put in "fifty for fifty," bringing her own food over to the Davis house and helping to cook and feed the men while they worked. They threshed out the grain in two-bushel bags; Robert Waller lined them up in rows—three for the landlord on one side and one bag for Odell on the other. But Mr. Davis wasn't sharing that day.

"What you settin' out that wheat like that for?" he asked Robert.

"Everybody takes out the fourth at the thrash-box, don't they? That's the ways they been doin' it everywhere I been helpin' out."

"All that wheat's goin' down in my barn," said Mr. Davis. The bags were lumped together, carried down to his barn and locked up.

Robert didn't say too much at the time. He went on counting the bushels as they came through the funnel. To this day he will tell you the total—208 bags and one picked up from the leavings.

"Mr. Davis," he said later, "was the first man I know who didn't take out the shares at the thrash-box."

Odell came home bright and early one Sunday morning—the 14th of July. The day before was his birthday and he thought he would run down home for the weekend. It took a little while for him to find his family in their new place.

Annie and Mollie were up in the loft shucking some corn they had saved for the hog, when they saw someone coming around the yard and into the front door.

"Lawd, Mollie, there's Odell." Annie could tell him by his pants legs as they looked out of the loft window.

If Odell had heard the story from the neighbors, he said nothing, but listened to his mother tell it through. People who were there will tell you he remained as cool and calm as you want.

He went to church that morning, spent the afternoon at his mother's shack, and went with her and Mollie to the little Fairview Chapel that evening. Once a week the colored folk around Gretna get together at Fairview and pass the time of day. Odell stood around on the outside with the young fellows and talked while his mother and wife visited with the women inside. Thomas Younger, who owned a truck, was there. Odell asked him if he would take him over to Davis' the next morning to get his wheat. Thomas said he had to go to Chatham on Monday, but he promised to take Odell if he went early in the morning. The deal was closed, and Odell went on home with his family.

Odell was up at dawn on Monday. It was a cloudless blue morning.

He called his mother. "Momma, I'm goin' to get my wheat this mornin', cause I got to go back to Baltimore."

Annie took a little white potato sack and a knife from the kitchen table.

"I b'lieve I'll go with you an' get some things from my garden." She wanted to cut some greens, pick some string beans, and dig up the "Ahrish" potatoes they had left when they moved.

Mollie Waller testified later at the trial that Odell told her he was going to get part of his wheat, and asked her to cook breakfast and have it ready by the time he got back.

Thomas Younger and a young boy, Buck Fitzgerald, came along with the truck and Annie and Odell climbed in. They stopped off at Robert and Archie Waller's little farmhouse. Archie, an old man, was sitting down at the breakfast table.

"Archie, come on holp me a while," Odell called out. "I got a lot o' wheat."

Archie was helping to thresh wheat at Mr. Johnson's place, but it was early and he could help Odell for a little while. He got on the truck and rode with them to the Davis place. He said later that Odell smiled and never said a hard word all the way up.

Mr. Davis was standing in the yard talking to Henry Davis. Two months later in Chatham court, Odell was to tell the story this way:

"When I walked up in the yard, I said, 'Good morning.' I said, 'Mr. Davis, I come here to get my wheat.'

"Before he said anything Henry Davis spoke up and said, 'What you gonna carry that wheat on? You can't carry it all on one trip.'

"Mr. Davis said I won't gonna get that damn wheat away from here. I said, 'I got a truck.'

"He said, 'I told you you won't go carry it away from here.'

"He used some dirty words, and from one word to another, and he usually carried a gun and run his hand into his pocket like he was trying to pull out something. I had my gun and out with it. I opened my pistol and commenced to shoot at him—I don't know how many times. I didn't look at it. Mr. Davis hollered and fell. I went down by the barn by the woods and stayed down there until in the evening. Then I come up to Joe Allen's house that night and his wife, she come to the window. I said, 'Where's Thomas at? Tell Thomas to come here.' She sent over to get him. He was all scared and said, 'Odell might as well go on and give up—four or five in a male posse with pistols are after him.' I turned and went through a corn field . . . I left to get out of the way and keep 'em from stretching me up."

When Odell started for the woods his last words to Annie were, "Momma, get the wheat." Annie, who had been sitting in the truck and heard the first shot, told the boy, "Turn this truck 'round and le's get out of here."

They streaked for home. She was not to see Odell again until they brought him back to Chatham jail. She admits she was pretty scared for the next week or two. Men were out in the woods with guns and dogs, hunting Odell "like he was a rabbit." Someone broke into her little shack twice looking for photographs or letters. Mollie was so frightened, she refused to live in the shack any longer, and finally Annie had to lock the door at night and stay with neighbors.

They took Oscar Davis to Memorial Hospital at Lynchburg, where he died two days later with four bullet wounds in him. Authorities in Columbus, Ohio, picked up Odell the first week in August.

At the trial Henry Davis, the colored boy, stammered out the incredible story that his boss was unarmed and that Odell just up and shot Mr. Davis four times *without a cross word passing between them.* Two Negroes, Thomas Younger and John Curtis Williams, both testified that Odell had threatened on Sunday to kill Mr. Davis.

Mrs. Oscar Davis testified that when she heard the shooting she ran out and led Oscar to the house and helped him get his pants off. She claimed he had nothing in his pockets except his pocketbook. Under cross examination, she said the pocketbook was a bill folder and that she thought he had it in his right pocket.

Nineteen-year-old Frank Davis told the Court his father's dying words were, "Frank, I am going to die. Odell shot me without any cause. He shot me four times, twice after I fell." It developed in the cross examination that when Frank Davis had testified at the preliminary hearings several weeks earlier he had said nothing about his father being shot twice after he fell.

Edgar Davis admitted that he had once had an argument with his father in the presence of Odell and others.

Archie Waller, Mollie, and Annie Waller were the only witnesses for Odell. Because she couldn't walk "so good" and Chatham was ten miles away, it was hard for Annie to get to the trial. Judge Clements was patient with her rambling on the witness stand. Annie didn't know anything about rules of evidence. She only knew that she wasn't allowed to explain many things that to her were important. "I said just a few words, and I was getting so far down to what really happened that the jedge set me down."

Probably the evidence didn't make much difference anyway. Ten of the twelve poll-tax payers on the jury were farmers, and most of them hired sharecroppers themselves. The Commonwealth's attorney didn't have much trouble convincing them.

The trial was ended in two days. Mrs. Waller was shocked to think everything could be over so soon. It seemed as though everybody was in a hurry to get it over and done with. The white people were sorry, but the pattern of caste had been violated. A Negro had killed a white man, and the law must take its course. It didn't matter what anybody might have to say to explain the background.

Nevertheless, the Negroes aren't satisfied. Over and over Odell will tell you if you speak to him in the Richmond death house, "I didn't aim to kill Mr. Davis. I was jes' aiming to keep him from killing me." And those who knew Oscar Davis best think Odell shot to save his life. Those who believe the State's evidence say, "Mister, you can push us colored folks just so far."

But what is strange, the Davis boys finally brought Annie Waller her share of the wheat—after the trial, they left her fifty bags. That three humble people might have their bread, one man was killed, another was sentenced to die, the Waller family without their chief breadwinner were left objects of charity, the Davis family was sold out for debt and scattered through the county; and Henry Davis, the only eyewitness for the State, an outcast among the colored folk of Gretna, is now forced to live only with white people.

In considering Waller's case, it is important to understand certain psychological factors. Rigid barriers of caste and class produce fear and suspicion, and the caste system itself is perpetuated by mob violence, coercion, and a die-hard tradition. It is a bitter commentary on the nature of race relations in this region that black men and white approach their differences within a framework of violence. Countless Negroes will admit openly that any one of their group who seeks an accounting with a white man may expect to be cursed, beaten or killed. Others will say privately, and some even publicly, that, in certain sections of the South, a Negro's life is worth nothing unless he is armed. It is this primitive emotion of fear, intensified by keen economic competition and insecurity, which produces lynch mobs on the one hand and on the other an Odell Waller who said, "I had my gun and out with it."

It is difficult to believe that a man with the intention of premeditated murder would ask his wife to cook breakfast for him during his absence, and would take witnesses along with him to the scene of the killing. Jonathan Daniels put his finger on the crux of the problem: "It does not seem to me strange to suppose that the white man was trying to cheat the Negro. It does not seem to me difficult to believe that the young Negro went to demand his rights more in terror than in murderousness. My observation is that more scared men kill than brutal ones: I can understand the contention that poor little Waller was the product—as Bigger Thomas was—of a whole system of racial suppression, of racial fear."

It is a whole way of life for a disinherited people that flings its challenge to us, daring us to practice democracy as well as to preach it. The story of Odell Waller exposes some of the great injustices which exist in our United States, and shows out of what hidden depths of fear and insecurity those injustices arise.

The Wobblies and Tom Clark

8 • 2 • 49

What the wobblies had the most of was laughter.

Their leader was a big bull named Bill Haywood, who opened his one good eye with double hookers in Greenwich Village apartments and roared his credo that "the workers and the employers have nothing in common" on open-air platforms from Los Angeles to Lawrence, Massachusetts.

Their folk hero was a Scandinavian songwriter named Joe Hill, who was executed for murder by a Butte, Montana, firing squad. The wobblies tell you still that Hill was framed because he carried an Industrial Workers of the World (IWW) card. And they say he had a perfect alibi he couldn't use because it would have compromised the name of a lady.

That was the wobblies—defeated but gallant. The strikes they ran were heroic sorties against misery. They customarily tore a town wide open for a few weeks, and then departed with no traces but a glorious memory.

But for all the red roses in the strikers' funerals and the pitched battles with the State Guard, the wobblies never stopped laughing.

The songs they sang "to fan the flames of discontent" were comic as often as not and there was a schoolboy's imagination behind a lot of their agitational tactics.

In Spokane, when one of their speakers was arrested, every wobbly in the state of Washington set up his soapbox in the streets. Within a few hours, the Spokane jailhouse was so crowded with improvised revolutionaries that the sheriff had to let them out to avoid a ruinous food bill.

More than 1.5 million men—and a smattering of their "rebel girls"—have belonged to the wobblies in some past time. Maybe 20,000 still hold cards.

Most of them joined when their hearts were young and hopeful; they were copper miners, sailors, loggers and itinerants who rode boxcars and looked out every morning bleary-eyed and somewhat surprised not to see the Red Dawn come up like thunder.

Now for most of us the IWW lives, if at all, with the memories that have to come back whenever the CIO autoworkers rise to sing "Solidarity Forever," the anthem they borrowed from the wobblies and with words like "working stiff" and "scissor bill."

As the wobblies have grown older, they've mellowed, and their harsh words about our homegrown "exploiters" have paled beside the things they say now about the Russian Utopia. Nobody, you'd say, has any reason to be afraid of them.

Yet this museum piece is a labor story again—because Attorney General Tom Clark has made the IWW the first union to be placed on his list of subversive organizations.

Clark didn't exactly call the wobblies "subversive"; for purposes of the loyalty check, he placed them in a special category of "organizations which seek to alter the form of government by unconstitutional means."

The wobblies immediately sent Clark a protest. They reminded him that the Supreme Court, to which President Truman has just appointed him, had in 1927 found that the IWW does not advocate "unlawful acts or methods." And they asked him to give the reasons for his order.

To all this, they got a reply which said in effect that Executive Order 9835, under which the wobblies got their black eye, does not require disclosure of the grounds upon which the decision was reached.

Tom Clark will thus ascend the Supreme Court with two peculiar distinctions. As an Attorney General he has plainly acted contrary to at least one court decision.

And he and the President have disregarded that amendment to the

Constitution which says that "the accused shall have the right to be informed of the nature and cause of the accusation."

And, in all this story, there are questions of more than theoretical justice. For the IWW has union contracts for 1,500 workers in two Cleveland plants; this month Fortune magazine raises the question of whether the Clark order would bar the IWW from an NLRB ballot or the workers in those two plants from work on government contracts.

And once we concede that a union as such can be labeled subversive, what happens to the pro-Communist outfits in the CIO?

Christmas in Shallmar, Maryland

12 • 22 • 49

The little boy at the plate hit a high fly that should have been out, but the left fielder came in too far and let it roll past him. That was all the kid needed. He scooted around the bases like the ghost of a jackrabbit and was home safe well ahead of the throw-in.

"Oh, he can run fast all right," the shortstop said, without animus. "But he's been eating good. His daddy's been scabbin' in one of them nonunion mines."

In every congregation there is a backslider, so Shallmar isn't being hard on that kid or his mother and sister. The father is home only on weekends, and his wife sits in her kitchen and talks a little ruefully about his fall.

"He's been a good union man all his life, and we hate to have him do this, but he got a chance to dig fire coal in that nonunion mine over in the western part of the state." She gestured toward her little boy. "The kids tell him his daddy's a scab, but I say it's better than starving to death."

The nonunion mines are John Lewis' soft underbelly. They're growing every day. During the last strike there were enough of them to keep coal output at a fourth of normal.

The fifty men here who haven't dug an ounce of coal since their mine closed last March could probably find work in an unorganized pit if they wanted to. But so far only one of them has broken down.

Two weeks ago John Crouse was very close to starvation. His 6-year-old son, Billy, had lost the sole of his shoe so irrevocably that he could go back to school only after teacher Paul Andrick had given him a pair of his own son's to wear.

Now the Crouses are eating again, but there's still no chance that he can work soon. But, if you mention the possibility of going to a nonunion mine, his wife says:

"I'd rather go hungry than him go down in one of them things."

And John Crouse adds, without apology: "I'll never work where there's no union. I remember what things were like before we had a union. And you got to understand that if we go into them nonunion mines, pretty soon the union will be broken and there won't be any more jobs than there are now, anyway."

John Crouse and Albert Males, financial secretary of the United Mine Workers here, are both fifty-two. Both talk about nonunion coal miners as if they had some unmentionable disease.

That almost religious approach to the UMW may burn highest among the old miners. It's possible to find among the younger men here just a little less conviction that the union is always and irrevocably right, but not enough to say that John Lewis' hold is detectably weaker. A town where kids know words like "scab" is a pretty solid union fortress.

To the old miners, Lewis still has the limbs and bearing of someone from Olympus. Albert Males tells you how he was "that" close to Lewis when the union's western Maryland district had a banquet for him at the 1944 UMW convention in Cincinnati.

"When you get him at a party like that, he's as jolly as everyone," Males says. "Of course, at the convention he was all business. But at the banquet, John Jones, our district president, told a couple of stories and John L. Lewis laughed real loud."

The memory of the great man laughing must have been something you could take back with you to remember always.

And to the old miners again, Lewis is right even now in the confusion when the industry is sagging and his strike goes badly.

The adjective for the operators is still "God-damned," and the smoothest press agent on earth isn't going to get the men who say it to change it.

Women Pickets Only 'Floozies' to Tennessee Troops

6 • 7 • 50

Morristown, Tenn.—As these posts go, American Enka was a good place for maneuvers. It took a day and a night to quiet the populace; by Friday, the Guardsmen had rolled up to their shelter halves and moved into the plant so they wouldn't have to sleep in the mud.

On Saturday, a captain in charge of the guard mount said you could hold a Sunday School picnic on the CIO textile workers' picket line. On Saturday night, there were moves of University of Tennessee football games, the winning ones.

The Guard officers sat in their orderly room and talked labor relations before their recall today. The Dixie Division has a fine war record—Anzio, France, Germany; and most of these men had been combat officers in it. Most of them too had been in armies of occupation before.

The middle-aged among them are a little fat now and very glad to leave their shirt necks open. Their colonel had glasses and a sandy mustache and looked more like a civilian in uniform than he could have in 1945.

But, when the girls went by on the plant walk, the things that were said about them were the things that must have been said about the frauleins at Wiesbaden.

And the things that were said about the picket tent across the road were the things that soldiers have said about hostile civilians in an enemy country since Caesar landed in Britain.

There was a Negro in the picket line, and the fat major spread his hands and pointed to the line.

"You see that Nigger," he said. "I'd like to know where he comes from. The company said they haven't hired a black here since the plant opened."

This had to be an enemy country, and the enemy had to be something strange and alien and from far away.

"It looks quiet over there now, but you should have seen it when we come in," a captain said.

"One of our boys said he'd been called everything but no one ever called him a scab off a monkey before," the captain said. "We told them to button their lip and they just had to stand there and take it.

"Them girls—they weren't no more than floozies—just stuck their faces up to ours and taunted us. Some woman there told her kid that I was a pretty tin soldier and wouldn't he like to take me home for a doll."

I said that, with provocations like that, you could understand why some of the boys might have slipped out at night and dusted up a few strikers.

"You could, but none of them did," the colonel said. "What those strikers don't realize is that if the people in the plant came over there and started beating up the pickets, we'd protect the strikers just the way we're protecting the company now. We don't take sides."

"And before long," a lieutenant said, "there's gonna be as many people in the plant as there are on strike. Then you gonna see something."

Whatever they may or may not have done with their hands, the officers of the Guard couldn't say they hadn't taken sides in their hearts.

"We all feel the same way about this thing," the captain said.

And, you can get an argument about the hands of a few of the Guards. Tommy Jinks, a striker, swears he was picked up by three highway patrolmen and two MP officers in Morristown on the afternoon of Memorial Day.

They stuck pistols in his ribs, he swears, and one of them said, "You're going back to work, you ... ...," and they called him other and worse things. When he went to jail, there were no charges and they let him off.

That same afternoon, some more guards are said to have stood and watched the cellblock clubbing of Blackie Warwick, a CIO textile striker.

"Oh, hell, that Warwick's an agitator. The people in town told me he spent three years in Russia. Look how dark he is; he don't come from here," a guard lieutenant said.

Blackie Warwick was born fifteen miles from Morristown, and—while he was supposed to be in Russia—he was working on the atom bomb in Oak Ridge.

When Warwick was in the hospital, MP Captain Edward Hunter and Lieutenant H. B. Bracey got into an argument with the two CIO officials who had taken him to the doctor.

Robert Cahoon, a textile workers' lawyer, charges Bracey hit him with a pistol butt across the lip and jaw—the gash is still there. And Bracey and Hunter worked over Silas Switzer, the local business agent, and when they had finished, they carried him off to jail.

Sheriff Bo Medlin said first that Cahoon had tried to rescue Warwick from the police and that Switzer had knocked a guardsman down. Since there were witnesses at the hospital, that was a thin claim and the charges have been altered to resisting arrest. But the officers in the orderly room still believe them.

"Where does this Cahoon come from, New York?" a lieutenant said. "Anyway he ought to know better than to try and rescue a client."

When they got Switzer to jail, they threw him in a cell. And, for a time thereafter, the guards taunted him. It is not a story a man makes up about himself. In its details, which I won't print, it reminds you of the sport the Nazis played with the Jews in Vienna.

Gov. Gordon Browning sent an Assistant Attorney General to investigate these charges and he came out with a full clearance of the guard, the sheriff and the highway patrol. In that entire investigation, he never talked to a union man.

You can count the guilty guardsmen on your fingers. Most of them believed they were doing their duty and keeping the peace.

When you went to England during the war, they used to give you a little book on the customs of the country. But no one oriented these boys.

No one told them that American Enka had agreed not to resume production during the strike and then had torn up the treaty. No one explained that the "floozies" and "the sneaky boys from Newport" and the rest of their neighbors on the picket line were people watching strikebreakers come in and take their jobs.

And so they believed every wild story the company told them. That is why, no matter how hard they try, soldiers cannot really be peace officers.

II

"FROM THE GIFTED TYPEWRITER OF MURRAY KEMPTON"

He would appear to have a passion for the defense of civil liberties and to be definitely unsympathetic to legal restrictions on communists.

—FBI memorandum, 1962

Huntsman, What Quarry?

4 • 29 • 53

Thad Mason, a cadaverous and doubtlessly authentic waif from the Communist storm, was here yesterday on a one-day contract at the tent show of the Honorable Bill Jenner, chairman of the Internal Security Committee of the United States Senate.

Joe McCarthy was brooding in the shadows and Mason had the field to himself—a full bag of Senators, the television cameras and the high school students.

Mason had been born the son of an Ohio Polish steelworker; he had joined the Communist Party in 1936, and served it thereafter in a dozen menial capacities until he broke in Poland in 1950. His high moment as a Bolshevik had been in Detroit in 1943 when, as factory inspector, he had stolen the blueprints of a General Motors landing craft for transmission to the Soviets.

In those days he had served what we might call the greasy-thumb espionage center, since its two major figures were a short-order cook and a third assistant dishwasher in the GM cafeteria. It was a story of overwhelming artistic plausibility, the Communist conspiracy having always been a dank and gloomy affair whose deeds of darkness are performed much more often by short-order cooks than by career diplomats, the steam table being far more conducive to discontent than the tea table.

Mason spent the usual time sketching the reasons for his fall from the path of the true grace. Liberal education, he said, matter of leaving *Das Kapital* around loose on the bookshelves at Ohio State. His first misstep had been joining the Liberal Club.

Pat McCarran opened the eyes of a Gila monster and said, "Did you say Liberal Club?" Mason said he had, and Old Pat snorted, "We have a lot of those around here still."

But nothing McCarran or Mason could say really brought the show alive. A schoolteacher sitting in the first row suddenly asked whether any of the Senators present was McCarthy. A reporter answered no, but there were some pretty gamy specimens. Before he could roll off their names, the teacher said that in such case there was little purpose in staying and rose and departed, her little charges trailing behind her.

For the tourists come to see McCarthy as they have come to see no other Senator since Huey Long. He is an enormous, burgeoning phenomenon, blotting out all competition even in absentia. By the time it adjourns, this session of Congress will have achieved just two things: It will have made Hawaii a state and Joe McCarthy a colossus.

His contempt for the rules of political behavior is matched only by his contempt for decency. Last night, the Wisconsin Chamber of Commerce set forth a buffet at the Hotel Shoreham; it is the kind of occasion no normal politician would dare to miss. Alexander Wiley, who is a very important Senator, was on hand until the last drop of whiskey and the last chorus of "On Wisconsin" had been expended.

McCarthy sent one of the girls from his office staff. His absence was a source of dreadful pain; a number of guests chafed at being neglected, and one or two went so far as to say that Joe just doesn't function when it comes to representing his constituents. No one, of course, talked one-tenth as much about poor Wiley.

No man looks less like a Senator. McCarthy's unbuttoned double-breasted suit looks as though it had been washed in clam chowder; he might have been sitting up all night filing the points of his teeth; his eyes are dripping red. Every day his power grows and every day he looks more uneasy, like one of those great Victorian swindlers waiting for the bubble to burst.

Just to think of him unsettled normal men. A Wisconsin businessman was talking about him last night at the bereft buffet of his

Chamber of Commerce. "Joe," he said, "has the eye on just one thing in life." There was a silence as his auditors waited for the ultimate answer.

"I wish I knew what it was," he said at last. "I wish I knew."

A Night Thought

6 • 11 • 53

This is an abuse of my function, and I do not see how it can do any good, but I would like to say a word in favor of commuting Julius and Ethel Rosenberg's death sentences to life imprisonment.

It would be nice if it were an easy, sharp and clear defense of the innocent. There seems no reasonable doubt that the Rosenbergs are guilty. I did not attend their trial; I can claim no basis for contesting the judgment of the jury or the wisdom of Judge Jerome Frank, who made the most detailed evaluation of any of their appeals.

To say that the Rosenbergs are guilty may be a service to truth. But to stop there is not a service to mercy.

I am not even against the electric chair; there are a number of people walking around who belong there. But capital punishment can be justified only as a deterrent to future offenders. In the case of the Rosenbergs, the chair can only be an instrument of vengeance.

The crime of the Rosenbergs is basically a political one. They were Communists acting for the Soviet Union. Their defense committee has just read a collection of their Sing Sing correspondence, which is an unashamedly dehumanized mess of left-wing gook right down to the moment when Ethel expresses her eternal fealty to the Dodgers because "it is chiefly in their outstanding contribution to the eradication of racial prejudice that they have covered themselves with glory."

It is precisely because the Rosenbergs are the kind of people they are that electrocution is so inadequate an appeal against the kind of thing they represent. Any potential spy reading those letters could well see in them a shining example; to the dedicated Bolshevik there are no terrors in the distant prospect of a death like this one.

There is in clemency the ultimate hope of repentance, but I would not argue that very seriously. The notion of commutation for policy is an unattractive one anyway. I have heard it argued that, if we electrocute them, the Communists will make them martyrs, and I have heard it argued that, if we commute their sentences, they will say we acted out of bad conscience. Isn't it time that Americans stopped worrying about what Communists say, and, in the words of Walt Kelly, "acted like themselves 'stead of like other folks"?

For the basic argument for executing the Rosenbergs is the argument of vengeance. We are today in full cry for blood and vengeance, and it is a very popular cry. I am sure Judge Kaufman's death sentence was a very popular decision. If it were left to the Gallup Poll, the Rosenbergs would be hanged feet up in Times Square.

All I know is that it is a very refreshing thing to hear Judge Dimock remind a United States Attorney that Elizabeth Gurley Flynn was guilty of a crime somewhat less heinous than murder or arson. It is very refreshing to walk into Learned Hand's court and hear the old judge discuss the Rosenbergs as the human beings which they and everyone else seem determined to forget they are.

It was also a very refreshing thing the other day to hear Frank Hogan plead for the right even of a gangster to refuse to testify against himself, whatever a prosecutor's temptation to cut corners. For there is in all these men the sense that justice is a thing above the passions of the hour and that its mission is to correct, not to avenge.

This is not my province because I have very few claims to being a serious fellow. There are a lot of other things I would rather have written; believe me I would have written them and gone home if I could get rid of this uneasy sense that it is somehow wrong to do unto the Rosenbergs the thing they may well have done unto some of us. It is a cardinal tenet of the Soviet Union that man can live without pity. I do not yet think that it is an American dogma. Can't someone besides the Commies write the President?

Bad Day at the Track

3 • 11 • 54

One of Washington's premature springs, false and treacherous enough, no doubt, to need all the protection of the Fifth Amendment but delightful in its way, suffused the Capitol yesterday afternoon. Joe McCarthy slouched off the Senate subway, like a wounded fox with the press pack close on his unshined shoes.

His eyes dripped, his bald spot glowed with humid phosphorescence, the gasping tick in his throat sank from its normal pulse of hysteria and softened to sound like the hart panting for some running stream. Joe McCarthy had spring fever.

"It is a crime," he said, "to be inside on a day like this." He was a-weary, and he wanted to lie somewhere safe in the shade.

As he lingered beside the elevator, Sen. Flanders (R-Vt.) came walking toward him without a moment's unease. Joe McCarthy said, "Hi Ralph" and threw a blue-serge arm around the shoulder of this old man who had accused him of trying to wreck the Republican Party and had been commended by the President of the United States for same. Flanders giggled a little and said he was glad to see Joe, and they rode up together and McCarthy said, with a smile and a trickle in his throat, that he'd been looking up Flanders' record.

It was not one of Joe McCarthy's good days. The President slapped him, the normally quiescent members of his investigating committee spat at him, the wind was rising and the track had come up mud. This race had been run, and Joe McCarthy was tearing up his mutuel tickets. He'll be back at the $50 window with a big bundle as soon as he can find a scratch sheet.

No day when Washington is obsessed with conversation about

Joe McCarthy could ever be considered a total loss by Joe McCarthy, but there were signs yesterday that the new turn in the discussion sat heavy on him. As he walked into his committee hearings he looked no more swarm-haunted than usual. But, before very long, his wounds began to ache, and he was railing at the absent Sen. Jackson (D-Wash.) because some friend of the Republic had heard Jackson speak at a club and had reported a heretic observation that McCarthy's detectives hadn't come up with much but "warmed-over biscuits." Sen. Symington (D-Mo.) intervened on Jackson's side and, in a moment, McCarthy was pounding his ashtray like a gavel and shouting that he was sick and tired.

The hearing, thereafter, became the usual shambles; Roy Cohn made a handsome effort to inject Albert Einstein into the Federal Communications Laboratory; but McCarthy's own boredom hung over it all like the raven over the infected house. Someone had slipped him a note about President Eisenhower's press conference. This meeting adjourned; he began the wearisome daylong process of "no comment" on the President's statement. He ran into Jackson on the elevator and said, "Hi Scoop," with that delinquent choirboy's smile. There would be no great confrontations this day.

He went to the Pentagon and lunch with C. E. Wilson, coming out to announce that what he had called twenty years of treason in the Army had only been twenty years of softness; the adjectives were paling in the spring. He returned to the Senate to confront a rumor that Sen. Potter (R-Michigan) was demanding that Roy Cohn be served up as a human sacrifice to the gods of mischance. McCarthy and Potter left Symington alone to conduct their hearing and spent forty-five minutes in Joe's office and came out to say (Potter) that nothing would happen today and (McCarthy) that Roy Cohn's future was as "counsel to my committee."

While they talked, McCarthy sent a message to Symington to keep the hearing going as long as he could and that as a reward Joe would guarantee him the Wisconsin delegates to the next Democrat convention. It was a day for rare public distemper and consistent private accommodation.

His bad day at the track ended, McCarthy sat in his office talking to the reporters, wearily, abstractedly, like a loser on election night, not so much grim as drained of his emotional capital, half wondering if it is all worth it. It is not a sensation likely to survive the night; tomorrow the scratch sheets will come up, the mutuel window will open, and Joe will be standing there ready to shoot the roll again.

The Real Davy

6 • 21 • 55

Born on a mountaintop in Tennessee
Greenest state in the land of the free
Raised in the woods so he knew every tree
Killed him a b'ar when he was only three.

Wasn't. Not precisely. The real Davy Crockett was the son of a saloon-keeper. And all his life, whenever he heard the word "bar" he never waited to ask "Liquid or solid?" Just went hunting.

He never was much for chores. He preferred to sneak off to hunt for squirrels. He met his first bear at the age of eight and took off like the tail of a comet, even as you and I and Hemingway's Francis Macomber.

When he was twelve, his father sent him to school. Davy played hooky for the first three days until the schoolmaster caught him and chased him with a hickory stick. So Davy ran away from home. He wasn't the slave of duty, wasn't Davy; but no man could say that in his later years he didn't do his utmost for his father's ghost by chipping in for the support of every saloonkeeper he met.

Davy grew up to be a very brave young man, who would bear any hardship to escape a routine day's work. He married his Polly after a woodlands courtship which was, to be charitable, unconventional. Then he took off to join Andrew Jackson in the Indian wars. After two months of those, he took off from Jackson and went home to Polly.

Crockett's biographers, who seldom let him give himself the worst even on those few occasions when he consents to, say he may have been on a secret mission. He, himself, says that he and his company of de-volunteers almost had to shoot their way out of Jackson's camp. Anyway, anything was better than home, so he came back and pulled his time as a private.

Then he came back to settle in a place seven miles from the nearest dwelling. (The latter was, as you might expect, a grog shop.) There he pursued bear and public office with evenhanded ferocity. He was elected a colonel in the state militia, and then a justice of the peace and learned to write, and then to the legislature and then to Congress as a Jackson man.

When he got to the House of Representatives, he did not stand up and introduce himself as "fresh from the backwoods, half horse, half alligator, a little touched with snapping turtle." The snapping turtle routine was an invention of the Eastern yellow prints, and Crockett was alleged to have introduced it in a Baltimore saloon. He admitted the locale but repudiated the dialogue as beneath his dignity.

A reputation for being undignified was the plague of Congressman Crockett's career; he once wrote his constituents to shoot down a canard about his bad table manners at dinner with President Adams. He wore his coonskins only at campaign time; his Washington portraits all show him in the black coat and the high collar which was the uniform of the Congressional Bar, a rostrum more familiar to him than the well of the House.

In that cool retreat, spinning his memories, the call to quorum very seldom sounded insistent. One reason Crockett finally lost his seat was an absentee record which showed him missing 63 roll calls in two years.

As a Congressman, Crockett's great project was a $60,000 appropriation to deepen the Fork Creek River in his home district; he is hardly the only legislator—but he must be the only one not forgotten—who did not raise his voice except during debate on the rivers and harbors bill.

But as time went on, Congressman Crockett's consuming passion was his war on President Jackson, a subject upon which he became so local a bore that Congressional Debate reporters took to recording only the entry that "Mr. Crockett made some desultory remarks in opposition to the executive government."

Like it says, Crockett first broke with the President, and commendably so, over Jackson's mistreatment of the Indians. But Davy only spoke once on the Indians and thereafter left their salvation to John Quincy Adams and went off to relieve that other sufferer, the Bank of the United States.

And so Crockett became the only friend of Nicholas Biddle and the money power west of the Alleghenies. This made him a kind of Arthur Godfrey of the Eastern fat cats, and it is to that fortunate fall that we owe the legend.

Jackson's enemies had a surplus of ruffles already; they needed some coonskin; the Republican search for the common man as a symbol is 120 years old. And so, while Crockett carried his bear hunts and japes through their nth adornment in the Congressional Bar, the Whig ghostwriters took over his heavier duties and managed the miracle of breaking his rich and gamey tongue to the cadences of a premature John W. Bricker. They also wrote most of the legends about his prowess, seasoning them with attacks on the Democrats.

For what chewed at Davy was a sharper-toothed assailant than any bear; he had the presidential bug. His autobiography, which appears to be the only authentic work among the multitude of memoirs his hacks fabricated over his name, suggests five times that he would be an adornment to the White House.

In 1835, in pursuit of this most dangerous of game, Davy Crockett took a tour of the Northern states where he freeloaded splendidly off the local Liberty Leagues. He saw the textile mills in Lowell, Massachusetts: "I went among the many young girls and . . . no one expressed herself as tired of her employment or oppressed with work; all talked well and look healthy." These symbols of the loom, he said, made $1.90 a week and put most of it in the bank.

He ended his tour of Eastern civilization in Philadelphia, where who could have greeted him but Joe Grundy? Here a Philadelphia arms manufacturer gave him a new rifle as a reward for his bloody campaign for the Bank of the United States. He called it Betsey, after his second wife. That's the Betsey of the ballad—a Republican campaign contribution.

When poor Colonel Crockett got back to Tennessee and opened his patriotic assault upon the good sense of the voters, he ran into trouble at once. He struggled back into his buckskins; he told his jokes and bought whiskey like forked lightning, but it didn't wash. Jackson was a vengeful man, and Davy got whupped by 235 votes.

In the summer of 1835, during John Marshall's funeral in Philadelphia, the Liberty Bell cracked; but Davy Crockett never got back to the Congressional Bar to fix old Liberty or even strike a blow for her.

He went instead to Texas, leaving behind him a poem called "Farewell," which reflects with a certain lack of resignation on the ungrateful character of the Tennessee voter. (This is the song on the other side of the "Davy Crockett" record; and is thus a bestseller; the historians of the Disney Research Center were too tactful to include the last stanza, which, set to music by Fred Waring, would have served the Willkie campaign well.)

He went off to the Alamo. His memoirs of that journey, which make up the end of the legend, are generally considered to be a forgery made up by some hack seeking a buck. They include, among other things, an account of Crockett cheating at a turkey-shoot. The prevailing version of his end is that he did not die fighting at the Alamo but surrendered and later fell victim to the cruelty of Santa Anna.

Nothing of the aforegoing can wipe out the fact that Davy Crockett was a brave and gallant fellow, who profited far less than other promoters from the fraudulent character of his legend, and who certainly, in life as he has in death, served American industry well.

Intruder in the Dust

11 • 1 • 55

Moses Wright has been a fieldhand in the Mississippi Delta for as many of his sixty-four years as he has been able to walk. For the last nine of them, he has cropped shares for G. C. Frederick, a planter near Money, Mississippi.

Before his troubles came, he was as much of a success as a field Negro could hope to be in the Delta. He even owned a narrow corner of land outright; with cotton at $175 a bale, he could expect this year to make a little more than $2,000 from the land he farms for Frederick.

It is the essence of the Mississippi Delta that white people live off Negroes. This month, in Sumner, the Negro picked cotton and the white man loafed open-mouthed around the county courthouse. The prime economic law is that the Negro owns nothing. He cannot even be a bootlegger for Negroes; Leroy Collins, a Negro, appears to have made his living selling sneaky pete to other Negroes; but he acted only as agent for J. W. Milam, a white storekeeper. By these standards, Moses Wright was almost a man of substance. Around Money, Negroes and whites alike called him "Preacher," an honorary title for good Negroes as "Judge" is for white lawyers who have escaped disbarment for twenty years.

Moses Wright was not a man with much impulse to escape Mississippi. Once every three or four years, he and his wife Elizabeth would travel North on the Illinois Central—W. C. Handy's tives. To the Mississippi white, who regards his Negroes with a mixture of fear and guilt, Chicago is a kind of Sodom of corruption, and Moses Wright's relatives were an astronomical distance removed from him.

The farthest away seems to have been Mamie Bradley, Elizabeth

Wright's niece, a $3,600-a-year federal worker living in a lower middle class section of South Chicago. She had been born Mamie Carthan in Webb, Miss., and been taken North when she was two. She was the widow of Louis Till, who had been killed in the war; their son Emmett was now fourteen.

Emmett Till was an average schoolboy who seems to have had most of the ambitions of the new Negro: he planned to go to college and learn a skilled trade, both expectations far above the cotton fields which were Moses Wright's destiny. One day, early in August, Elizabeth Wright suggested that Mrs. Bradley give Emmett a vacation in Mississippi. She was very happy with the invitation. On August 18 she went home early to help Emmett pack. While he was getting his clothes ready, she says she explained to him that Mississippi was not like Chicago, and that he must be especially polite to any white man he met and, in any crisis, be ready to go down on his knees.

Emmett appears to have been quite gay about the approaching adventure. As he was leaving, he picked up his father's old beat-silver ring, with its initials "L.T."; it had always been too big for him; he showed his mother that his finger was now large enough to wear it.

"Gee," she said to him, "you're getting to be a big boy now."

There were six boys at the Wright house in Mississippi. Their life appears to have been narrow enough to make any relief exciting. On Wednesday night, August 25, Moses Wright took them to church according to custom; he had hardly bowed his head there when the boys had sneaked out and taken his old car.

They rode up to Money, which is a row of stores and filling stations along the railroad track in the dust and there Emmett Till went into a store to buy a few cents worth of bubblegum. The store he chose was not one frequented by the Wrights; it was owned by Roy Bryant, a smoky-eyed young paratrooper, and the son of a fecund clan with a reputation for brawling, whose chief was his huge, balding thirty-six-year-old half-brother J. W. Milam. Bryant was an ill-tempered, edgy man and a merchant with small appeal to quiet customers like Moses Wright.

The night Emmett Till went there for his bubble gum, Roy Bryant was out of town, and the store was tended by his wife, Caroline, a high school beauty already chipping and fading at twenty-one. She and Emmett were alone in the store for a few minutes, and she is the last surviving witness to his conduct. With the Bryants in crisis, Caroline testified that Emmett, whom she described as a man, made her an indecent proposal. The only undisputed fact seems to be that he left the store with a suggestive "Goodbye" and that, when he was in the car and she came out, he emitted a woo-woo whistle.

It was a very small gesture, but one which Emmett's country cousins failed to report to Moses Wright, if only because it was part of an escapade which would have brought his wrath upon all of them. Moses Wright got his official notice of Emmett's capital crime at two o'clock the next Saturday morning. He had come home from an evening at Greenwood and had been asleep an hour when he was awakened by a voice outside his cabin shouting, "Preacher, Preacher!"

He arose to answer the summons; as he was going to his door, the voice went on:

"It's Mr. Bryant. I've come for the boy that did the talking at Money."

When he opened the door, there was J. W. Milam standing with a flashlight and a pistol. "I'd know Mr. Milam if I seen him in Texas," said Moses Wright afterward. "I want the boy from Chicago," Milam said. Moses Wright took the invaders back to the bedroom where Emmett Till was sleeping with Moses Wright's son Simeon. J. W. Milam shook him awake and asked if he was the boy from Chicago. Emmett Till answered "Yes," and J. W. Milam said, "Don't say 'yes' to me or I'll whup hell out of you."

At the door, Elizabeth Wright pleaded for Emmett; she promised to give Mr. Milam any money he wanted. Moses Wright stood on the porch; there was a third man out there in the column of blackness. Afterward, out of six decades of training as a field Negro, Moses Wright said that it seemed to him that the two raiders treated the third companion as though he "were a colored man." They did not know Moses Wright; they did not even know Emmett Till's name; they were to learn it from the newspapers later; they had been led to their objective by a Negro. In the Delta, even the night riders have their body-servants.

And then Moses Wright entered a plea for Emmett that was rooted in his sense of place and tradition. He asked Milam just to take Emmett out and whip him. "The boy don't look like he's got good sense," he said. But Milam pushed Emmett out on the porch; as he went off, he turned and asked Moses Wright how old he was. Moses Wright said sixty-four; and Milam asked him if he knew anybody present. " 'No,'" he said, " 'I don't know nobody' and they said I'd better not or I wouldn't live to be sixty-five."

They took Emmett out in the dark; J. W. Milam flashed his light on the boy's face out by the car. Moses Wright, standing on the porch, heard a "light" voice from the rear of the car say, yes, that was the boy; and then the car, with lights out, was gone down the road to Money. Moses Wright went back in his house, and the boys told him what had happened in Money on Wednesday night. By now, Elizabeth Wright was hysterical; Wright drove her to Sumner for the Chicago train. Every day, for the next two weeks, she would write and tell him to concede defeat and come North.

But Emmett was gone and Moses Wright had to stay to find him. Afterward, alone in his house with his gun, waiting for his crop to come in, he would explain his revolt only by saying that, if he had kept quiet, "They'd think I done it."

And so, that same Sunday afternoon, Moses Wright drove to Greenwood and told the story of Emmett Till's abduction to Sheriff George Smith. Bryant was a friend of Smith's; and, as a friend, Smith drove out to Bryant to ask him about the old Negro's complaint. Smith found Bryant asleep in the back of the store on the hot Sunday afternoon which had followed his long Saturday night. They talked as friends in the sheriff's car; Smith asked Bryant whether he had taken a colored boy out of one of the cabins the night before. Bryant answered that he had brought a boy back to his store, decided that he was the wrong boy, and then turned him loose to find his way home. Thereafter, said Roy Bryant, the outraged husband, he had played cards all night with his kin.

The sheriff could do nothing but arrest J. W. Milam and Roy Bryant for kidnapping. They sat in Greenwood jail for three days while the rain came driving down. Moses Wright clung to his cabin; around noon Wednesday, Deputy Sheriff John Ed Cothran came there to report that a body which could be Emmett Till's had been found in the Tallahatchie River.

Moses Wright went out to the muddy Tallahatchie and was shown a body lying face down in a boat with its head beaten in. A sheriff's deputy turned it over, and Moses Wright saw it was Emmett. The ring the boy brought down from Chicago was still on the body's finger; the Negro undertaker pulled it off and gave it to Moses Wright.

The body lay on a slab in Greenwood for a day. A policeman took its picture, and the print was buried somewhere in the city files. Dr. L. D. Otken, a local pathologist, came to certify death; he testified with considerable vehemence later that he hadn't touched it and had no views as to the cause of death. That was the closest the county came to an inquest; then the body was turned over to Moses Wright with the understanding that it would be buried at once in the graveyard at Money.

But then Mrs. Bradley called to tell him to ship the body to Chicago. He sent it off and went back to his cotton, seemingly unaware that, by now, Emmett Till's name cried out in every newspaper and that, just because he had gone to the sheriff to clear himself with Mamie Bradley, his life could never be what it had been.

Milam and Bryant were moved to the Tallahatchie County jail; their trial was set for September 19 in Sumner, a dusty old village with five hundred residents and the metropolis of a plantation county with a population of thirty thousand, two-thirds of them Negroes.

Governor Hugh White rasped in Jackson that Mississippi must prove to the world that its system of justice was capable of revenging the murder of a Negro boy by white men. To Hugh White the stake was Mississippi's old claim that it could deny the Negro property, the vote, and equality of education, and still grant him the equal protection of the criminal code. On almost the same day that he approved a legislative program to freeze segregation in the schools and make agitation for Negro rights a criminal offense, White appointed Robert B. Smith, a former FBI agent, to direct the state's case against J. W. Milam and Roy Bryant. He had been telling Tallahatchie County for years that the Negro was an object of fear and contempt; now he would try to persuade twelve of its white citizens that it was a capital crime to murder a Negro boy.

He had to take Smith, an alien from Ripley, which is two hundred miles from the Tallahatchie, because no Sumner lawyer was available as special prosecutor. All five members of the Sumner bar had joined the defense; the friends of Bryant and Milam put glass jars in the stores and raised $10,000 to finance their case.

By now, the white minority which clutches the Delta had found the story it needed to believe: Emmett Till had been murdered and it was a good thing, because he had tried to ravish Caroline Bryant. And then again, he had not been murdered at all; he had been smuggled back North by the National Association for the Advancement of Colored People, and a fake body, with the Till ring on its finger, had been thrown in the Tallahatchie. County Sheriff H. C. Strider, who had seen the body and turned it over to Moses Wright as Emmett Till's, sat in his tax collector's office and talked and talked and finally decided that it had not been Emmett Till at all and might even have been a white man. All of a sudden, there were no witnesses for the state who were not Negroes.

There was, of course, Moses Wright alone in his cabin; he had sent his boys away and slept there near his cotton with a rifle under his pillow. Sheriff Smith had given him permission to defend himself, but no one bothered him. There was an assumption that, in the crisis, the tradition would triumph and he would collapse too. Sidney Carlton, of defense counsel, summed up the community view when he said: "Mose will tell one story in the cotton field, and quite another story on the stand."

J. W. Milam and Roy Bryant came to trial on Monday, September 19, in Sumner's fetid second-floor courtroom, bulging to its dirty lime-green walls with its all-white jury panel and with Bryants. They came with their little boys, who babbled and tottered and tugged at their daddies and from time to time aimed their empty water pistols at deputy sheriffs and went "boom-boom." It was so hot that J. W. Milam said once that it was hard not to feel mean on a day like this one; but he is an indulgent father, and, from time to time, he would tickle his son Billy and both would laugh.

The courtroom was so crowded that there was no room for Moses Wright to sit down; he stood in the back, a thin old man, in a tieless shirt and his galluses and old, cracked shoes. There was a concerted, metronomic ballet of waving fans between him and the judge's desk before which Smith and District Attorney Gerald Chatham struggled to pick a jury which might, by some thin chance, believe Moses Wright.

On Wednesday morning, Moses Wright was called to the stand. He sat in that squeaking old chair and told the prosecutor, who kept calling him "Uncle Mose," what had happened on that Saturday night hardly three weeks before.

The moment came when he was asked to point out J. W. Milam as the man who came to get Emmett Till. Moses Wright stood up; he raised himself on his tiptoes, thrust out a skinny finger, and looked full into the heavy, violent face before him and said, "There he is." And, for good measure, as if to compound his crime, he turned a little and threw out the finger again and said, "There's Mr. Bryant." He seemed almost jaunty about it, but he sat down and thrust his body against the chair back, as though his conditioned flesh was rebelling against his new brave spirit; and then it was possible to understand that he was defying not just Milam but his own oldest habits.

Then he was offered up to Sidney Carlton for bulldozing, and the voice of the defense attorney was the voice of every white overseer that Moses Wright has heard since boyhood. Carlton roared and Moses Wright's rebellious flesh shrank back from habit, but his tongue forced him to the wildest piece of defiance a Delta Negro can accomplish; he stopped saying "Sir," and began answering Carlton's every lash with a "That's right" which was naked at the end. He ran the hardest half hour of the hardest life possible for an American, and in the end he clung to his story. Carlton let him up, and he went back to the witness room where at least there was a seat for him.

For the next two days, the state of Mississippi labored to convict two white men on the testimony of Negroes like Moses Wright. Emmett Till's mother came to the stand carrying a fan; it seemed almost an affront to the spectators that she could thus imply that a Negro felt the heat as much as a white. She was very calm and quiet, holding herself in check, as though from some desperate sense that, if she remained contained, the jury might see her as a mother and not as a Negro. The defense began a chain of questions designed to prove that she was from Chicago and a race inciter; very coldly Judge Curtis Swango ruled it out. In this courtroom, she would be called "Mamie," but just this once, in Mississippi, the judge and not Chicago would try a murder case.

She was excused, and the trial went on; the state put on another Negro witness, a stammering eighteen-year-old fieldhand named Willie Reed who swore that he had seen J. W. Milam and Emmett Till together the morning after the boy disappeared. While Willie Reed fought to sustain his story, Mrs. Bradley and Moses Wright sat in the courtyard outside—she by herself and he with the other field Negroes in their appointed place around Sumner's Confederate monument. Out there she talked about the books she reads and the job she holds and it was plain that white Sumner should fear her more than it did Emmett's whistle. For this is a county of courthouse loafers living off another people, of storekeepers with an all Negro custom, of plantation owners with air-conditioned homes and swimming pools who pay their hands $3.50 a day, of county payroll riders and tax collectors. Mrs. Bradley is a civil servant paid more than a Tallahatchie sheriff's deputy; the notion of a Negro competing for a public job is as outrageous as miscegenation.

In the courtyard Moses Wright was saying that he'd try to hang on in Mississippi: "I'm so scrounged down in this country that I hate to leave it." Upstairs the defense was putting on three white witnesses, including the sheriff who had turned the body over to Moses Wright, all loudly swearing that it couldn't have been Emmett Till's body.

On Friday morning, Chatham and Smith fought without hope to persuade the jury that Bryant and Milam deserved to die for the murder of Emmett Till. The defense was more restrained; it had, after all, very little to worry about. There was only the detail of the ring on the body, and this was explained, very sedately, to the jury by J. W. Whitten, of defense counsel, a thin young man of infinite delicacy, who under ordinary circumstances wouldn't spit on the peckerwoods before him.

Whitten said his theory was that Bryant and Milam had sent the Till boy home just as they said they had. Moses Wright had driven down the road and met Emmett coming back. He had picked him up and gone in search of one of those enemies of good race relations who abound in Mississippi as they do in Chicago. And these people had planted an old corpse in the river with Emmett's ring on its finger.

The Delta Negro must have a kind of chemical sense of danger; there could be no other reason why, while the genteel young Mr. Whitten was thus putting the finger on him, Moses Wright went into the sheriff's office, collected his witness fee, and walked down the road, across the bridge that leads out of town.

The jury was out an hour and eight minutes and came back with the appointed not guilty verdict. Bryant and Milam heard it with cigars in their mouths, and thereafter luxuriated twenty minutes in the courtroom for the news cameras. There was no demonstration, partly because Judge Swango forbade it and partly perhaps because everyone except J. W. Milam was a little ashamed of himself.

Willie Reed and Mrs. Bradley went North the next day. Both were empty-handed; Willie Reed is without property by definition, and Emmett Till is so entirely obliterated by act of the jury that his mother cannot even collect his $400 insurance policy.

Moses Wright went back to his cabin; he still hoped to gather his crop. A few days after the trial, when all the reporters had gone and the television cameramen with them, five carloads of white men drove down the road from Money and stopped at his cabin and raised the old cry of "Preacher, Preacher." Moses Wright hid in the fields; the next day he went to Chicago for whatever the city holds for a man whose hands know nothing but cotton. His crop appears to be a dead loss.

Sumner has shuddered and recovered; it has lost no one but Emmett Till, who was a stranger; Mamie Bradley, who was an expatriate; Willie Reed, who can hardly be listed in the census, and Moses Wright. And yet whatever history Tallahatchie County can have for this decade is the history of these rejected people. Who would have thought that four poor Negroes had so much blood in them? Who, most of all, would have thought that Moses Wright could be trained so long to bend his knee and then, worn down at sixty-four, raise his head and leave white Mississippi with the uneasy sense that it had impoverished him and cast him forth, but that it has lost more than he has, because he carried with him the only intact piece of pride in all their state?

The Way It's Got to Be

2 • 9 • 56

Autherine Juanita Lucy is not really Autherine Lucy—except to strangers to whom she is a symbol. To her family and to her friends, she has always been Juanita Lucy.

She appears to have been less afraid than most persons in authority were on Monday when a mob seized the campus of the University of Alabama and stoned not just her but, deplorable as it is, two white people as well. The mob was shouting, "Autherine's got to go!" They were shouting about a stranger and not about Juanita Lucy. She may owe some of the glory of her posture to a sense that, when they howled at Autherine, they were howling at a symbol and not the name of a real woman who is Juanita.

She started on the road which brought her to where she and all the South stand today very casually in the summer of 1952. Polly Myers Hudson, who was her classmate at Alabama's Miles College, called her up and said:

"Juanita, how would you like to go to the University of Alabama?"

"I said I'd like to very much, and we got all the forms and filled them out and went to the university and applied in person—me for library science and her for journalism. We were refused and then we went to court."

In the beginning, she did not tell her family: "They would have opposed it to the nth degree." They believed—who can find a Negro in Alabama who doesn't?—that Negroes should go to State University.

"But they would say and did, 'Why does it have to be you, Juanita?'" Why should she go through this? "My sister still says that. If she were Juanita, she wouldn't be in the University of Alabama."

When she began, Ruby Hurley, the Southern field secretary of the National Association for the Advancement of Colored People, wondered whether she was really a good choice. She seemed, as she seems still, so quiet and reserved that Ruby Hurley was inclined to doubt that she could run her appointed course.

Polly Myers Hudson had been NAACP president at Miles and seemed of stronger cast. Now Polly Myers Hudson has been shunted aside; it was Juanita who went into the bearpit; it was Juanita who was stoned; and it is Juanita—why Juanita of all people?—who has run the course.

She was admitted after the courts gave the university no other choice. The first two days at the school were the lonely days that every new student has, but they were calmer than she expected.

"In the history of education class, I asked a young lady what the name of our professor was and she told me. As I was coming out, a young lady said 'How do you do?' and I answered 'How do you do?'"

The name of the girl who spoke to a lonely student on her first day in school is not known to any human record, but it must be written somewhere.

"I saw a boy in the bookstore make a funny face at me, but that was all." The first two days were more normal than she could have hoped. Her instructors were especially courteous; there was only one who paid no attention to her at all. He was Charles Farris, who taught her American Government. "He didn't notice me."

She wondered at the time if this was a snub and only found out yesterday that Charles Farris, more than any man on the university faculty, had risen in public to speak for her rights as a student. ("I went to bed," he told his class the next day, "as an employee of the trustees of the University of Alabama and I awake today the employee of a mob.") When she read that, she understood the special courtesy he had shown in simply taking her for granted.

"I guess that is the way it should be." The name of Autherine yesterday brought reporters from London and offers of scholarships from the University of Copenhagen; but the heart of Juanita understood that the only victory would come on that day when she walks unnoticed and taken for granted on the campus of the University of Alabama.

She sat yesterday in Birmingham's colored Masonic building—this is a town where everything is black or white—in a powder-blue suit, a mystery to all who came to talk to her. Someone desperately seeking asked her how she would feel if she got into the women's dormitory and was coldly treated. She answered:

"If I go into a dormitory and there are people I cannot reach, I'll just have to remain what you call nonchalant."

He asked her if she was just a young woman who wanted the best education available in the state of Alabama or whether she considered herself a pioneer for her people. And was she proud of her glory, or did she sometimes wonder too why it had to be Juanita?

"I guess," she said almost in apology, "that I do consider myself something of a pioneer. I wish these cameras would go away. I can't be haughty or proud just because everybody seems to know me now." She opened a sheaf of roses from the New York Dress Pressers Union, and rendered by request of the photographer a pose which conveyed with infinite subtlety how ridiculous this all was. "It just seems that it was put in my lap."

There were scareheads in the papers outside Birmingham that she had fled her home in fear for her life. But she spent Tuesday night in her house as she always has; all night the telephone rang with obscenities and every time it rang it was answered.

"Perhaps," she said, "I need a gun but I carry none."

She is the daughter of an Alabama farmer, at twenty-six the baby of nine children. Her family has dispersed all over America; she has brothers in Detroit and Chicago. She lived a while in Detroit, and she was very happy there, because it is easier than Alabama.

"But this is my home and I must stay here. The Negro must stay in the South because he's needed here. If he must do something new and different, he must do it here."

And what does she want?

"I have a combination of desires," she said. "I would like to go to the university in peace and quiet and have friends there."

And when that is over, she would like to be a librarian at the high school two blocks from her house. That is the wild dream for which Juanita Lucy reaches: peace with dignity.

When the riots came, she had not felt their terror directly; and she had been frightened first because the university officials who came to her geography class to protect her had been so frightened. "I kept asking them what was happening."

The university officials asked afterward where she could have found her calm; they assumed that she must have had training somewhere, and must be paid a great deal; as one of the girls said, where could she have found those lovely shoes?

Why you all of persons, Juanita? What is this extraordinary resource of this otherwise unhappy country that it breeds such dignity in its victims? Why is it, in every great tragedy there is some poor Negro you can prod and push and never hear say the wrong thing? Where, as a matter of fact, did those white students come from who were elected as leaders of their university and, in their test for which no one could have trained them, stood up as no grownup did for the dignity of the human person?

This is what William Faulkner was talking about when he said of the Delta Negro that he endured. Through poverty, shame and degradation he endured.

You push and drive Juanita Lucy, tired and holding, so terribly tired and so totally contained, about why of all people she runs her course the way she has and neither of you can answer. This side of God, every observer can only wonder at the resources of the human spirit.

All the Saints

3·7·56

The poverty of the Bethel Baptist Church, colored, cannot be measured by visiting strangers. It can only be hinted at by mentioning its windows, which are cheap, opaque glass paid for in every case by a contribution which would not be more than $10.

A Bethel church parishioner aims at some kind of immortality—as though his face were in stained glass at Chartres Cathedral—by buying or having bought for him a window and having his name painted upon it: "Brother A. E. Jenkins, clerk since 1941; Brother Sylvester Taylor, president of the Senior Usher Board, or Sister Duanunimi Sanders, Sunday school teacher for 51 years."

It fell upon Brothers Jenkins and Taylor and Sister Sanders in Bethel Baptist last night to mark the third month of the Negro bus boycott of Montgomery's segregated buses, for which, as someone said, their children's children's children will some day remember them.

Their meeting was supposed to begin at seven: most of the seats were filled three hours early; when the appointed hour came, they choked Bethel's corridors and bulged its walls, and they had been singing for two hours. There must have been 1,200 of them, mostly cooks and maids and almost entirely the kind of Negroes whom the White Citizens Council loves and commends to the attention of the inquiring outside observers.

The Rev. L. Roy Bennett read to them the 13th Chapter of the First Epistle of St. Paul's to the Corinthians: "If I have not charity, I am nothing. . . . Charity vaunteth not itself and is not evilly provoked and thinketh no evil." Then he began to shout the ancient cadence and they stirred and shouted with him while he pushed and drove the beat: "We pray tonight that You may bless each one who may go weak and teach him that we must keep marching in Thy name. . . . We can't make the journey except that we go with You. . . . Sometimes the mountains gonna be high, well, Jesus, O Jesus, sometimes we don't know where we go. . . . When we've done walking and our feet are tired will You meet us somewhere, maybe on the roadside or on some hard pavement?"

Roy Bennett has been indicted for criminal conspiracy and will be tried here next March 19 with 114 other Negroes—30 of them ministers of the gospel—for his part in the Montgomery bus boycott. And last night he and a united congregation prayed for the time when "there's no more 'I'm right' and 'you're wrong'" and all men are brothers.

They sang "I Need Thee Every Hour," and the Rev. Martin Luther King, also indicted as a felon, rose and told them that all over the world people are talking about them . . . "No one else in the world could have done what we have done." He was talking about these, the ordinary Negroes of Montgomery. Perhaps, said Martin Luther King, he would go to jail: "You know, we'd be in jail, all of us, but tonight we wear the whole armor of God and we carry the ammunition of love. Love is our ideal and resistance is our message. We're gonna love everybody and we're just gonna stay off the buses."

These are the poorest and the simplest people, singing about the tie that binds and they shall not be moved and he was telling them about Mahatma Gandhi. "All of us have come together," said the Rev. Mr. King, "the PhDs and NoDs, just remember that Aunt Jane who knows not the difference between 'you does and you doesn't' is no different than any PhD in England.

"The white man should love the Negro and the Negro should love the white man because God loves them both."

No stranger could look upon them unmoved and unawed by their unchanging faith that love can rescue Alabama. It is the Alabama in which they will endure out their lives; as one of them said last night, the White Citizens Councils don't have enough money to pay them to move out from this their home.

And, waiting here, they reach out to the tender of love and forgiveness to any white visitor who walks among them. It cost them $2,000 a week to keep their bus boycott going; last night they took in more than a week's budget; all but $1 came from Negroes, but the Rev. Mr. Bennett was proudest to report that a white friend from Baltimore had sent that. They cheered that widow's mite as though it were some great treasure; they overlooked the thousand just men and rejoiced for one poor redeemed sinner.

The Montgomery Negro bus boycott goes on and may go on forever because it cannot be settled short of an unthinkable apology from white to black Alabama. And the strikers sit and radiate love, this ragged band of brothers, and they endure and cannot be moved.

They come and they sit in sparse barns like Bethel Baptist Church, with signs of their poverty and weakness all around them and they sing the assurance of ultimate peace in victory. The most hostile white man who came to watch them had to confess that they are better led and surer of the end than he is. The deep South has come face to face with the cruel fact that one side possesses all the privileges and the other all the saints.

And nights like this at Bethel Church leave every Southern white man, no matter what he says in public, with the uneasy sense, that if Christ were born again he would be born in Alabama, poor, menial and black.

Buckley's National Bore

July 1956

William F. Buckley's *National Review* has used up nine months of life and presumably settled into its desired mold as expression of conservative dissent from the liberal rhetoric which dominates our time. Under this theory, the Editor of *The Progressive* has sent along its first twenty-seven issues with a request for an extended analysis of its content and tendency.

Textual analysis is a high art, and one which is probably beyond me when I care and certainly unapproachable when I am only bored. It is a hard thing to read twenty-seven numbers of *National Review*; but then I think it is a rather hard thing to have read 552 pages of anything purporting to be an American journal of ideas. Very few Americans handle this sort of thing persuasively, although we do have some talent for going out in the street and looking at people. I concede that Buckley could catch me up if I went so far as to say that nobody on *National Review* has yet felt the compulsion to go out and look at the face of, say, George Meany or Walter Reuther; yet the effect is compellingly as though no one had. It all seems to have been sweated from obscure segments of *The New York Times*.

I think I know Buckley well enough to feel that I could pronounce to him nothing crueler than the judgment that his magazine is a bore. He is a young man capable of considerable *esprit*; as a companion, he can be preferable to the average assistant professor of political science who regards him as an enemy of the light. I do not wish him to fail, except in the superficial sense of dying an old man without ever seeing the kind of America he thinks he wants; and, if I did, I could not wish him the emptiness of this particular failure.

It is a disaster when men plan and dream and find themselves still in a locked room. I have known too many of the sort of women who are intense about their membership in Americans for Democratic Action not to feel some bond with almost anyone they hate. They can tell me that John Chamberlain is a servant of the Black Hundreds; I know him only as man who left *Life* to go straight on *The Freeman.* I remember James Burnham when Trotsky condemned him to the dustbin of history; we are all the losers if any man who dares to announce so outrageous a judgment is proven right. Willy Schlamm was once only a boy who hoped to lead the Austrian revolutionary movement; now he has settled here trying this one last go; has anyone the heart to wish him confronted again by the fact of fresh defeat?

These editors of *National Review* think of themselves as alone and outnumbered by the herd. There is a virtue in isolation; to secede can mean to gain detachment; but you somehow settle *National Review* when you say that it has taken this natural advantage by the scruff of the neck and thrown it away.

For Buckley cannot bear to be alone. For that reason, he will always be cursed by the liberals because he once loved and may still love Joseph R. McCarthy. I hope I am not being unfair to this commitment when I summarize it by saying that Buckley appears to have judged McCarthy as an instrument which was delicate but which appeared to work. Those who dislike the people make a great mistake when they entertain the illusion that they know what the people like.

I think that misconception might explain the worst aesthetic feature of *National Review*, which is that it is so badly orchestrated. I do not think Buckley would permit it to be scored this way if he so truly loved his audience as to feel that no piece of really bad taste would escape it. As an instance, he employs as his political analyst one Sam M. Jones, whose credentials in this line have not before come to my attention. Jones' product is presented in the sort of print in which it came off the typewriter, a device designed by editorial custom to indicate that it is served so fresh and hot that there is no time either to composite it with care or to set it in normal typeface.

Jones is the kind of analyst who can offer his readers the hope that a deadlocked Democratic convention will turn to Lewis O. Douglas.

He is also accustomed to describing the governor of New York, the senior senator from Tennessee, and the titular head of the Democratic Party as "Ave," "Estes," and "Adlai," a vulgarism only to be explained as the sort of thing Buckley thinks one has to give one's troops.

And I hardly think he would permit one style to grate so painfully upon another in the same pages if he were not possessed of the illusion that *National Review* is a sort of popular front. He struggles across a field made perilous by souvenirs left behind by his sacred cows. Jones, as an instance, is assisted in his peerings by W. Brent Bozell, who between evenings of ineffable gentility spends his days writing speeches for Sen. McCarthy. There is an aspect of Buckley and Bozell which gives any reader the hallucination that the editors of *Partisan Review* have entered into partnership with the editors of the *Chicago Tribune*. It is as though they had decided to detest only half the Philistines.

Last November, one Robert Phelps contributed a review of Ilya Ehrenburg's *The Thaw*. He began: "*The Thaw* may be called a novel only in the sense in which a prefabricated dwelling may be called a home." Now this seems to me in the full, proper, meaningless spirit of the hinder *avant-garde*. But *National Review's* audience consists substantially of persons who live in prefabricated dwellings and infest cocktail parties and talk about the "so-called liberals"; I know their sort because I inhabit a prefabricated dwelling myself. I do not mention this association because I am reacting to any slur against ratepayers of my class, but only because it seems to me a sentence without any consideration of true meaning. A prefabricated dwelling is a home if there is love in it and nothing if there is not.

National Review has this side dedicated to the snubbing of upper-middle-brow culture; as drama critic, Schlamm delights in the destruction of Arthur Miller and Clifford Odets and Brooks Atkinson of *The New York Times*. Alienation can be of great assistance in dealing with what passes for culture and enlightenment in a period like this one: *National Review* deserves to exist if only because there are so few organs in this country impatient with the sort of people who have made shrines of the Actors Studio, the Child Study Association, and the Psycho-Analytical Institute.

But this wonderful animus against the hardening institution of mechanistic liberalism has all too little room to breathe. Professor John Abbot Clark can frame a heavy but somehow affecting piece about the decline of humanism in the United States, which Buckley will accept gratefully and then surround with quotations from Sens. Bricker and Knowland and Jones' pilgrimages to Georgia to examine the promise of Herman Talmadge or to Arizona to witness the achievement of J. Bracken Lee. To be touched by a call for a return to style in our national life and then be offered John Bricker is to lay down one's standard in the moment one picks it up.

I have no right to enforce upon *National Review* my own peculiar notions of what is the stuff of journalism; but it is saddest of all to read five-hundred-odd pages of commentary on American life and find that so little happened with any juice and blood in it. It can't have been that dull a six months. Adlai Stevenson fought and hardly appears to have decisively won a terrible battle to preserve his own high concept of public purpose against the reality of American political habit. Autherine Lucy was stoned from the campus of the University of Alabama. Each was a person caught in an extraordinary situation; by itself, ideology does not debar a journal from having something of interest to say about their confrontation and their test. But persons possessed by ideology are simply uninterested in that sort of thing: to them there are only ideas and no conflicts of the heart. So Buckley left the handling of Stevenson to his hacks; about Autherine Lucy, he could find nothing more revealing than the report that her lawyer had sent a message of greetings to the convention of the National Lawyers Guild, which is about to be placed on the Attorney General's list of Communist fronts.

In all this period, the only event involving a human being and not some piece of paper which appears to have moved the editors of *National Review* was the death of Henry Mencken, for whom both Schlamm and Clark wrote obituaries. Their burden was that one reason for the desperation of our present pass is our shortage of Menckens. This is certainly true; I have no time to quarrel with ideologues over the possession of the dead; it is hardly as obscene for *National Review* to appropriate Mencken as it was for the Communists to co-opt Lincoln to their national committee. Mencken certainly hated everything the state has done for the last twenty-five years; in all that was nonessential, *National Review* can claim his bones. In what was essential, I can only offer the image of Henry Mencken displaying sample copies of the *American Mercury* to a gathering of the Minute Women of America or dispatching his political correspondent to "a motor court in Arizona" for a raptured confrontation of Gov. J. Bracken Lee.

But I think the essential Mencken has something to say about the swamp to which *National Review* has come so soon. It was his great strength that he revered no human being since Johann Sebastian Bach and that he has no hostages anywhere. Schlamm can quote with approval Mencken's dictum, "A government is at bottom nothing more than a gang of men, and as a practical matter, most of them are inferior men." (As I recall it, Mencken's solitary declared exception was Henry Cabot Lodge I.) Now this may not be a totally accurate estimate; but a man who holds it can function with it. What cannot function is a magazine which approves the notion and then offers J. Bracken Lee for our study and admiration.

The essential weakness, I'm afraid, is in Buckley himself. The gentleman who detests gentility has a hard road at best; and Buckley has obvious difficulties reconciling William the well-bred with Bill the mucker. He is most at ease as William the well-bred; in the gray patches of *National Review* there are occasional pebbles with a certain shine, and most of them are left by Buckley himself in those moments when his sense of irony breaks its conscious check.

He can discover, as an instance, that, to encourage free discussion, a New York private school for young ladies invited its inmates to a debate on the topic: "Resolved, that Senator McCarthy's Un-American Activities are justified." He can read a brochure from *The Nation* announcing that its new publisher will "continue to side with the intellectual and social non-conformist" and note that the accompanying brochure carries testimonials from "such reckless non-conformists as Arthur Hays Sulzberger, Helen Rogers Reif, Felix Frankfurter, Dag Hammarskjold, and Harry S. Truman—brothers all, in martyrdom, as a result of their lifetime refusal to conform."

There must be a certain pleasure in discovering bits like this and allowing one's fancy to gambol as one pleases; but there is something in Buckley which shrinks from the intrusion of irony into any discussion of the high serious purpose of his side. Thus George Meany is "a man of raw courage and superior intelligence" when he deals with the Communist issue, and a creature of the "professional left" when he attacks Adlai Stevenson for insufficient passion about civil rights. Buckley is reduced to summarizing the struggle of that wonderful, stubborn old man Syngman Rhee to cling to the presidency of Korea unto his death this way: "The contest was ideologically uninteresting, for both major parties are anti-Communist and anti-Socialist."

He can, when the fit is on him, write and feel no compulsion to rewrite so awful an affront to his own literary sensibilities as this paragraph:

"What besides deploring phrases about the fix we are in do Mssrs. Stevenson and Harriman have to suggest? They say not a word about the axioms and premises—which were of course their own—on the basis of which we flew to the trap at Geneva. Their positive proposals are, as always, for more negotiations, billions more dollars spent with no idea of what it will bring, 'moderation' (Stevenson) and God save the mark, Harriman's ideological rabbit—the Democratic party's 'understanding of people—not only at home but around the world.'"

As an editor, he has a high seriousness about the intellectual process and dares to subject those of his readers who are happiest picketing the UN building to the contributions of serious voices from the academies like those of Wilhelm Roepke, Russell Kirk, and Professor John Abbot Clark. Yet, when Dean Acheson wrote a book, Buckley selected to review it Joseph R. McCarthy, who is so contemptuous of formal scholarship that he never appears to have found out that Lenin's first name was not Nikolai. And a few weeks later, he printed a letter from a New Jersey lady reporting her joy at finding that: "Senator McCarthy writes forcefully and wittily, and has given the most quotable line of the year. 'For the worst Secretary of State in American history, it [his book] is only a minor failure.'"

It is somehow idle to ask whether this sort of thing is or is not the Lord's work; it is so obviously below the standard of Buckley or anyone else with a sense of craft. It is somehow unfair that a man could arouse so many passions and have so little passion within himself. No one who knows the persons he and his associates write about—whether with affection or distaste—could recognize any of them in its pages; what is wanting is their intricate humanity. It is as though even the paper in their lives had been transcribed by an interior carbon; India is only Nehru; Georgia is only Talmadge; Arizona is only a motor court that is a way station for J. Bracken Lee.

Journalism is a sullen and hopeless art, whose practitioners are doomed to oblivion at the end and to expire by boredom long before that unless they are sustained by the surprises and shocks and ambiguities in the persons they are assigned to cover. Certain notions of faith and charity, if not of hope, are essential to it. It would have spoken to Oswald Garrison Villard exalting William Jennings Bryan and said that this was marvelous but not Bryan; it would have spoken to Bill Buckley damning Dean Acheson and said that this was infamous but it was not Acheson. Never to have known passion and bereavement, like Bill Buckley, would have been as fatal to it as to have left all true passion behind like so many of the poor ruins who have chosen their last site with him.

I remember—and hope it no breach of trust and taste to say so—one evening I tarried with Buckley at the home of J. B. Matthews, who is the doyen of professional anti-Communists. I was arguing that there are moments in the memory of all men which have to do with the faces and the fates of other men and nothing to do with their labels and that these are the realities of experience. In a desperate essay at my point, I asked Matthews where he was the night Sacco and Vanzetti died. He answered that he had been in Times Square and had seen the flash of their execution in the lights around the building that was the first and one of very few times he had ever gotten drunk.

The scar of that moment had never left him; he was back as he was that night—so many changes before—feeling again all its agony and despair. To travel with passions like that is a heavy burden for any man; but *National Review* is a lesson in the perils of traveling otherwise.

I have come this far, and I have failed in my assignment; I have not explained what a deplorably unenlightened view Buckley takes of, say, the World Health Organization. Somehow that has seemed to me beside the point. What is the point is a letter by William Butler Yeats, who was a certified fascist in the thirties and would have been assured a wreath from Prof. Clark had he died last week. Yeats wrote a friend that he naturally hoped Franco would win in Spain, but God help him when the Irish volunteers in Franco's army came home victorious.

"I am convinced," he wrote, "that if the Spanish war goes on, or if [it] ceases and O'Duffy's volunteers return heroes, my 'pagan' institutions, the Theatre, the Academy, will be fighting for their lives against bigotry."

If only all of us could understand that way to just how much of the essential part of ourselves our allies are enemies.

Daughter of the Furies

1 • 29 • 57

Victoria Wellman is the fourteen-year-old daughter of Saul Wellman, a leader of the Detroit Communist Party, and of his wife, Peggy, whom the government is trying to deport to Canada.

Last week Vicky Wellman was graduated from Hutchins Junior High School in Detroit wearing the Bronze Medal for Americanism awarded by the American Legion. The medal cited her for: "Courage, Leadership, Honor, Service and Scholarship."

Vicky's more-than-ordinary piquancy was compounded in this case by the circumstances of her father's business, and Detroit is very proud of itself, of the Legion, of its school system and of all concerned except, of course, her parents, who, after all, only brought her up.

The Detroit Free Press commented: "In spite of the home influence to which she must have been exposed, Vicki obviously acquired a deep sense of understanding of what it means to be an American citizen . . . [this] is a tribute to [the Legion's] sense of fairness which enabled it to judge Vicki's qualification on their own merits."

It is things like this which long ago made most civilized persons understand that, if there is a God in heaven, the average editorial writer in the average newspaper had better get to his knees and beg His compassion as fast as he can. I don't think anyone but an editorial writer would suggest that we are a great people because the American Legion abstains from demanding that children name names.

Vicky answered the telephone last night at her home, where, let us all hope, she was womanfully resisting the dreadful influence of her mother and father.

She is in high school studying dress design. "I want to be a hair stylist, but they don't have that course there." She has no particular favorite subject, and she supposes that swimming is her favorite pursuit. She likes Elvis Presley and Sammy Davis, Jr.

She had been quoted in the Free Press as saying: "I'm real happy that Daddy is proud of me." "Oh," she said last night, "they made that up, but I am real glad."

Was she in her turn proud of her father and mother? The answer was the obvious one that this was a silly question.

"I agree with them," she said. "I mean I think they're right, although I don't really care much about these things."

She said the excitement was "fun while it lasted." "I've put the medal away with my brother's." Her brother David won the Legion Americanism award at Hutchins in 1955, shortly after his father was convicted of conspiring to advocate the violent overthrow of our society.

Peggy Wellman was saying that, come spring, Vicky and David may face a pretty serious test of the qualities of courage and honor the Legion has certified in them. Saul Wellman could be in prison; and Peggy Wellman could be deported by then. Once sent to Canada, under the Walter–McCarran Act, she is forever barred from returning.

"They may have to decide whether to go with me or stay here and visit their father in prison."

It is strange, as I have said all too often, how humanity tricks and taunts us. We write laws which are aimed at declaring that Communists are not people, and they bedevil us with the faces of children like Vicky who was ten years old when her father was first arrested, and who thinks he is right, and who wants to be a hair stylist.

Medals aren't for fourteen-year-old girls anyway. They are for grown men fighting for their country. We owe Vicky something much more important than a medal—the home she grew up in and the mother who raised her.

The Inheritance

6 • 19 • 57

When they ask you what labor unions have meant to America, set down this:

In the Teens of this century, Philip Murray was fired for hitting the weighmasters who cheated him on his tonnage, and he walked back from the mine, up a hill, into the torches held against the night by the other miners, and listened to the speaker talking about the United Mine Workers of America.

In the twenties of this century, the miners struck in West Virginia and were thrown into the state prison. They looked out their jail window at the state capitol and laughed and laughed every time a visiting intellectual translated the inscription on that edifice. It was: "The Men of the Mountains Are Free."

In the thirties, the auto workers won their strike at General Motors, and streamed down the streets of Flint, their beards wild in the auto lights, the conquerors and the liberators of the earth.

And for the fifties, set down this:

Last March 6, James G. Cross, president of the Bakery Workers Union, which is almost as old as the Knights of Labor, was put on trial before the executive board of his international union on charges of corruption. His accuser said that there was $29,000 missing from one local union fund and that some of it had gone for a Cadillac for Cross. In his own defense, Cross answered:

He had a Cadillac. It had been given to him under these perfectly reasonable circumstances: The Chicago Bakers locals had wanted to give him a Christmas party, but he couldn't come.

"Then a man who I figure is smart said, 'Jimmy, if we give you a party, half the money will go to a hotel, so why don't we present you with something that will be worthwhile and you won't have to split the money with a hotel?'"

That something, said James Cross, was a Cadillac. This version of events appears on the evidence to have been a lie; you can judge a man by the sort of lie he considers an account of justifiable conduct.

His accuser said that Jimmy Cross had wasted union funds on his expense account. Jimmy Cross replied that his duties had been heavy and the burden onerous:

"Almost every night we were in Miami Beach, from the Fontainebleau Hotel to the Eden Roc, the Americana, the Cotton Club, Dorio's restaurant."

His accuser said that Jimmy Cross had spent union funds to call his girlfriend. Cross answered that the union was supposed to pay his phone bills, and it didn't make any real difference if they were $2 or $10,000. The general executive board heard these charges and this defense and it voted in a very few minutes to clear James Cross and continue him in his stewardship. It then moved unanimously to suspend Curtis Sims, the secretary-treasurer who had brought the charges.

The general executive board of the Bakers Union consists in the main of pie-cards, appointed and removed at the will of James G. Cross. No reasonable man could think of any cause, except simple economic necessity, which would make them look at this image of the labor leader of the fifties and find it good. I think, in making this judgment, most of all of Herman E. Cooper, general counsel for the union, who took away $81,000 in legal fees last year.

Cooper told the Senate Committee on Improper Labor-Management Practices yesterday that it is impossible to measure the value of a lawyer's services. I certainly cannot measure it; I can only say that $81,000 is more than the lifetime income of Wolfgang Amadeus Mozart. By that standard, it may be enough to justify Cooper's sitting at that meeting, hearing Cross thus describe himself, and going out into the streets to fight with passion to help him keep his job.

It is not the cash or the skills it brought which disturbs me; it is rather the passion with which Herman Cooper accepted the assignment. He is, by the way, general counsel for my own union; to the extent to which I contribute to his retainer, I too am a sinner, and I apologize.

James Cross needed money for a house in Washington. The union was supposed to pay for it, but the money was slow in coming. So he borrowed the $56,000 from an employer with whom the union dealt. The evidence indicates that the employer had no reason to be dissatisfied with the investment. Cross then needed—or thought his status required—a house in Palm Springs, Florida, and he borrowed $40,000 from the same employer for that.

Cross was accused of cuffing around five persons who opposed him at the union's last convention. One of them was a grandmother. In this gallant exercise of his decision for democratic centralism, Cross is alleged to have employed the assistance of a vice president of the union who pulled a gun on one of the recalcitrants.

Cross is now before the Senate of the United States and charged with explaining himself. The horror of the condition into which circumstance has brought American labor in the year 1957 is that he will try to make the case for himself without either denying or apologizing for these facts: (1) An employer helped him buy his house. (2) His duties required a tab at the Americana. (3) He charged the union for his fights and his frolics.

He proposes to stand before us all and proclaim himself innocent of any sin except these inconsequential ones. Let us, when we judge him, remember that the leaders of his union knew everything we know now more than three months ago, and refused to act against him.

We should remember that last fact when anyone says that the unions can cleanse themselves as they are now constituted. We should also remember Philip Murray and the West Virginia miners and the Flint strikers and the dream to which they gave their lives, and the terrible, empty world in which James Cross is their heir.

Loyalty

8 • 14 • 57

Alene Austin, a maid-of-all-work, boarded one of Paul Knight's buses to go home late Monday afternoon last July 16. She found it full except for one seat half occupied by a white passenger, her name unknown.

It is Alene Austin's recollection that the white passenger suggested that she sit down beside her. She did so and rode that way for two blocks until driver B. T. Fundabark ordered her to the back of the bus. After some dispute as to his rights and hers, Mrs. Austin got off and walked and has not boarded a bus since; and now no Rock Hill Negro rides that way to work.

Alene Austin will not talk to reporters about this action whose consequences are so disturbing to Rock Hill. "It's not because I'd lose my job," she says. "I'm a good worker and I'll never need a job. It's because the lady I work for has been good to me, and I trust her, and she says I shouldn't talk about it."

Her employer drives her to and from work every day. It is her employer's fear her neighbors will therefore think she is giving comfort to the boycott, and Mrs. Austin therefore feels it best that, on her side, she keep quiet.

Rock Hill, or any Southern town, is, I suppose, about these two women, one white and one Negro, one servant and one mistress, and the divided loyalties which each one feels. It is that division of loyalties which makes Cecil Ivory, chairman of the bus boycott, insist that Rock Hill is a good town, and explains why Thomas Murdoch, a volunteer driver in the boycott, left Detroit, where he was an Auto Workers organizer—"I tell these people they haven't seen strikes"—and came home to live.

It is this division of loyalties which afflicts the life of Mayor Emmett Jerome as he gropes for some solution to this, the latest of the troubles which have shadowed his administration. Mayor Jerome is at once conscious of the Negro's grievance and conscious that Paul Knight gave the city of Rock Hill bus service when nobody else would take it over. "That was big of Paul; he said he'd do it even though there wasn't any money in it." Now Paul Knight says that he will never restore bus service except on the fundament of segregation. "Paul's a country boy," says Mayor Jerome sadly, "and he feels too deep about this thing to talk about it."

The boycott is the latest in a series of troubles which have been the burden of Emmett Jerome's last year in office: the long losing CIO Textile Workers' strike at the bleachery, the burgeoning of the Klan, the immolation of the moderates. In the spring of 1956, Emmett Jerome was proud because he had brought Rock Hill's Negroes and whites together in a Council of Human Relations to discuss gradual solution of their mutual problems; the council withered away against the first hot breath of an issue.

One of the issues which destroyed it was the Nature Museum in Rock Hill's Fewell Park, a handsome brick structure from which Negro children have always been barred. It is a place not without reverence for persons of color; Rock Hill is very proud of the Indians who lived there in 1700, and has a birchbark diorama of the tribes then extant on the Nature Museum's face. A visitor who went by after closing hours looked in to see the image of a brown body in loincloth spearing a fish. The Nature Museum is a sort of zoo of native fauna; the voice of a captive mockingbird could be heard from inside, its lightness, its ease and its irony reminding the ear of nothing so much as the voices of the Negroes of Rock Hill relaxed at their meetings in their churches.

It is not good or evil but only tragic that men should cease to communicate because they cannot agree as to the rules of admission to a building dedicated to children.

The Klan, the National Association for the Advancement of Colored People, the CIO Textile Workers—these are the disparate bodies symbolizing the troubles of Emmett Jerome. And there too loyalties conflict and are divided; there are estimates that 20 percent of the Textile Workers in Rock Hill are or have been members of the Klan. There were fistfights at Klan meetings because the speaker criticized the union; Ray Berthiaume, the Textile union's director here, says that dozens of his members left the Klan because it was against the AFL-CIO. "I've got members who still go to meetings and believe in everything they say, but call me up and tell me what the Klan says about us."

Ray Berthiaume has sinned not once but twice: he is not only a CIO organizer but he sends his son to St. Anne's Parochial School, the only one in South Carolina where Negro children and whites study and play together. The Klan has twice burned a cross outside St. Anne's; Ray Berthiaume's name and his sin and the name and sin of all the other white parents with children at St. Anne's are read out at every Klan meeting.

"Our union members who are Klansmen say lay me off," Berthiaume says. "I'm wrong but I'm theirs."

Mayor Emmett Jerome is one of a dozen white South Carolinians who took part in a symposium gathered by two young Episcopal ministers calling for moderation and understanding on the race issue. His message then was that there can be no segregation at the foot of the cross. This sort of proposition, which hardly seems debatable to civilized men, has cost him a great part of his popularity; he will not run again—the sophisticated view is that he would be unlikely to win. He goes out of office in February, and he feels himself a failure.

"I'm not looking for sympathy," he said yesterday. "I know I can find it in the dictionary. But I had hoped when I began that, as mayor, I could do something to bring people together. And now it seems worse than ever." It seemed beside the point to suggest that he would not have ended much worse for being bolder. It seemed more important, but hopeless, to suggest that merely by standing there, a symbol of divided man, he had held up what little light remains for the children of South Carolina.

The Wrong Man

8 • 15 • 57

Claud Cruell and Sherwood Turner did not know each other very well, even as a Negro knows a white man. Claud Cruell was old enough, for one thing, to be Sherwood Turner's father. He had, in fact, known Sherwood Turner's father; they had grown up together in these hills near the North Carolina border.

No one prospers to excess in that country. Claud Cruell was thirty-three years old twenty-five years ago when he got the $500 it cost him to buy the fifty-two acres which form the basis of his one-hundred-acre farm tract.

"They gave it to me," he says, "because nobody else wanted it." He and his brothers farmed it and worked it over mostly for corn; they were Negroes surrounded by white neighbors. The size of his acreage is no measure of wealth; he and his wife, Fanny, made most of their cash income taking in laundry from ten white families in their neighborhood, carrying it down the hill to a stream below their house and beating it clean on rocks with sticks.

Six years ago, Claud Cruell began building his house. It took him five years; when he had finished he and his wife moved from their old cabin into this brick house with its wide porch and its square columns which has almost too much room for a couple in their fifties without children. Still, life had been kinder and more peaceful for Claud Cruell, an old Negro, than for Sherwood Turner, a young white man. Sherwood Turner had stomach trouble; he worked on the rarest of occasions; he was on what passes for public relief in Greenville County. The children kept coming; about a year ago, there were seven when the landlord told Sherwood Turner he would have to move out.

That afternoon he met Claud Cruell and asked if he could rent the old cabin.

"I told him," says Claud Cruell, "that it wasn't worth living in. But he said he had to have something, so I let him have it for $5 a month, which wasn't too little for what it was worth."

"I think," says Sherwood Turner still, "that he's as good a colored man as I've ever seen in my life. I hate to say this, but he's holped me when none of my brothers would holp me.

"I remember once I came out of the hospital and we didn't have food in the house, and Claud put me and Goldie and the children in his car and took us down to the store and bought us $15 worth of groceries."

It may have been putting them in the car and carrying them down to buy them groceries which started the rumors about Claud Cruell. That, and the Turner children playing on the Cruells' large and empty porch. "Claud thought the world of the kids, and they think the world of him," says Sherwood Turner now.

The Klan is far away from the hills, at least thirteen miles away to the south in Greenville. There are perhaps twenty active Klansmen, truck drivers most of them, with Elvis Presley haircuts. On Saturday night, July 20, they met and elected young Marshall Rochester, a sash-and-door factory hand, as their president. Rochester said that something had to be done. Someone present had a dim recollection that there was something about a Negro man and a white woman having an affair in Travelers Rest.

Two Klansmen with their wives and their children went berry picking to look the terrain over the following afternoon. Sherwood Turner passed them as he was driving Goldie down the hill to the Greenville Hospital for a kidney operation. He left the children alone in their cabin, in the care of Marie, the oldest of them, who is eleven. As the sun went down, Marie grew lonely, and went to the Cruells' house to ask if they could sleep there. They were asleep when there was a rattling at the door, and Claud Cruell looked up to see the avenging army of the Klan around him.

They put a chain around his arm and beat him. He kept saying that he was the wrong one, and they went on beating him. At last they left him and took his wife and put her in the car and rode her around, cursing her and telling her to stop mixing with white people, and dumped her out. While they were hitting Claud Cruell, little Marie got up with the gun her father had left her, and they took it away, and wanted to know why she had so few clothes on around these niggers. In her statement to the police, Marie Turner referred over and over to Daddy Claud.

Fannie Cruell walked home to find her husband sitting outside in the car, bowed over. He had sent the children home. He says he didn't see much sense in calling the police. But Sherwood Turner called Sheriff Bob Martin and the deputies came out and took the depositions. Sheriff Martin talked to the neighbors and satisfied himself that the Klan had picked the wrong man.

A visitor drove by Marshall Rochester's dirty red house on a rutty dirt road; it was dark at 9:30. He and the Klan seemed somehow irrelevant; what was relevant and unanswerable was the question of the dark passion that moves a man to use up his weekend avenging a rumor in a strange county thirteen miles away.

The Cruells have suspended their laundry business until they get their morale back. The Turners, upon the sheriff's advice, moved away last week. Claud Cruell sat on his porch in the dark glasses his eye doctor prescribed. "Yes, sir," he said, "I miss the children. A fellow can't help but miss children for a while."

Goldie Turner, returned from the hospital, was away from her new home. "She went out to see if she could pick a few beans and get us some money," said her husband. "I didn't want to move out of there, but if a bunch would get up there and start shooting these kids, it would be terrible." He said again that Claud Cruell had been kind when nobody else was. There was about the children the awful stale smell of unwiped, unwashed vomit. Little Marie, her shoulder pulled up against the weight, was carrying a huge pail of water into the house.

It cannot be counted among the least of the South's sorrows that she and her brothers and sisters have been parted from the best and kindest friends not of their blood that they have ever had.

The Big Cheese

4 • 2 • 58

Joseph Profaci, the *principe* of olive oil, was observed yesterday wandering, a plucked owl among the television cables, at the Senate Mafia hearing, in search of an audience with Robert Kennedy.

"I got to get home," he said. "I pray to God that the sickness that's happening to my kid should not happen to yours. Do you want to see their pictures?"

He reached into his back pocket and took out a vast display of his six children, sleek, plump, rosy and lovely as six pimientos. Joseph Profaci is billed here as a member of the grand council of the Mafia, and he is certainly the oldest surviving delegate to its convention in 1928.

"Mafia, Mafia," said Joe Profaci, "it's a fantastica storia. They say I was in Cleveland, because they arrest me there in a card game. I coulda been in the Mafia. In my village in Sicily, when I was thirteen years old, I didn't even belong to the Knights."

Instead, Joe Profaci became a grocer in Palermo, and then in Chicago; he was twenty-seven years old when he came here from Sicily loosely pursued by its *carabinieri*.

He settled in Brooklyn, and since then his troubles with the terror of the total state have been those to be expected by any simple businessman, the conviction for adulterating the olive oil and for dodging his taxes. He looks like what he is, a squat Sicilian grocer, harried by, but resistant to, the importunities of the starving; he was our largest importer of olive oil, and his grip on tomato paste was so universal that wholesale grocers, faced with the choice between their love of country and their sense of civic virtue, began buying the stuff in Hungary, where it was cheaper.

"How do I know they were labeling my olive oil wrong?" said Joe Profaci. "I never bought any olive oil in my life in my own name. I don't even know the name of the ship. It was the broker. He put it in barrels. I didn't know whether it was 75 percent or 25 percent oil; it was olive oil, wasn't it?

"Now they close down fifty-two of my businesses. They took my home. I live on rent. In Bath Beach. I got nothing.

"And what do they say about me? Cocaine." Joe Profaci pulled at his nose and sniffed. "What I know about cocaine? I hope a man should die if he messes with cocaine. It's dishonest.

"And look what they say about me. After the war, I send $3,000 over to Italy to bring five nuns over here. Now they say it was for cocaine. And one of the five nuns was my niece. Look, you go to Italy; you ask the secretary to the Pope. I give you a letter."

He believes in the saints and he believes in the Mafia, being a simple man, large of hope at night, mean of spirit by day. Even when he owned the mass of the provolone on the Brooklyn docks, Joe Profaci lived in Bath Beach in Brooklyn. The brigands of the Internal Revenue Service took away his house and the farm in Hightstown; he moved down the street to a rented apartment. "Heroin," he says to curious strangers, "I don't know what heroin is. Don't they call it cocaine?"

Joe Profaci's day away from his children had been spent largely watching his social inferiors. The Senate Rackets Committee has been studying the mob's Apalachin conference; in deference to its jurisdiction, most of the delegates it canvassed were labor skates, with a corresponding lack of social stature.

There may not be a Mafia, but there is an America, and it is divided on class lines. There were labor delegates to Apalachin and there were employer delegates; the difference between them, in our affluent society, is indicated by the fact that the labor delegates served most often as chauffeurs for the employer delegates.

Rosario Mancuso, one such chauffeur, was described as a former official of the Utica hod carriers union who had occupied those hours free of commitment to the toilers as a bouncer in a gambling house. I cannot say, on the basis of observation, whether Rosario Mancuso is a steward I would approach with less confidence as a dues-payer seeking enforcement of my rights or as an oppressed plunger questioning the absolute fidelity of the wheel. He looks like a man who, in either case, would be working for the house.

There was also John Charles Montana, delegate to the New York State constitutional convention in 1937, president of the Van Dyke Taxi Co., and member of the Buffalo Zoning Commission, who brought considerable pain to the committee of citizens who had named him Buffalo man of the year in 1956 by being caught in the Apalachin house of Joseph Barbara last November when the state police descended upon Barbara's fifty-eight guests. Montana explained his presence on this melancholy occasion in a fashion which I will summarize because it is entirely logical and might have happened to you and me:

Montana was driving his three-month-old Cadillac to Pittston when the brakes failed because it was raining and he bethought himself of his old friend Joe Barbara who has fifteen mechanics who hang around the house for just such emergencies as this, so he drove to Barbara's house and he was wet from fixing the windshield wipers which had also broken down, and Mrs. Barbara made him a cup of tea to take the chill off his bones and then Joe Barbara came in and said there was a roadblock outside, so John Montana did what any respectable citizen would do and cut out to the woods and that was absolutely all there was to it.

For some reason or other, after this description of a routine moment in the life of an honest enterpriser, John Montana was dismissed by his interrogators with a noticeable sniff, and was free to go back to Buffalo and service as a director of the Erie County ASPCA. He left with a few ill-chosen Anglo-Saxon words about the witnesses against him. He couldn't be a member of the Mafia. Joe Profaci wouldn't use words like that.

Ten Days That Shook

9 • 24 • 59

This was the night and this the place where they closed the show. The wagons trail home to Pittsburgh and then to Washington. But no one day will ever again be the length of a man's life. The future can only be unlikely; the impossible belongs to the past. There is a little madness to come, but it will be a madness henceforth controlled by James C. Hagerty.

The white lights of the million rockets are going out in the night of the Iowa sky. The sound of the million voices singing a dozen different Handel oratorios at once is dying, although no one can say how long the memory of those lights will blind our eyes and the echo of those noises will deafen our ears.

But they are only memory and echo. We shall not ever see again the scenes of a single yesterday; in a week, we shall have begun to doubt we ever saw them:

Nikita Khrushchev, heir of Lenin, Stalin and Peter the Great, standing, his ventilated shoes encased in silage, in a field of beheaded sorghum, watching his host, Bob Garst, go down to the earth to pick up handfuls of the infinite essence of the droppings of generations of prize cattle and throw them in the face of a banzai charge of cameramen.

Henry Cabot Lodge, American Ambassador to the United Nations, Brahmin-born and schooled for command, bending over to ask the Chairman of the Council of Soviets if he hadn't seen enough. "See," said the Chairman, "the capitalist is trying to hide things from me."

"This will be a jovial day," said Lodge. He spent it handling the microphone for interpreters, a grand duke become overnight a Paris doorman.

Khrushchev and Lodge walking through the Department of Swine Nutrition of Iowa State University. Khrushchev observed with satisfaction that the sows were standing up in their lying-in rooms "at attention for me." The air was filled with the bursting smells of excess animal vitamin. "In all his life," said Khrushchev, "Mr. Lodge didn't take in as many smells as he did today." Their trip completed, the Chairman of the Soviets said: "It's too late for me to enroll here in your school. But, if you have a Chair of Pork Chop, Mr. Lodge and I may be useful there."

Khrushchev looking at a machine which is a pride of Bob Garst's farm, although it seemed at the moment to exercise no visible function except to pick up two hundred pounds of chopped sorghum and dump it on the heads of the photographers. A television man stuck a microphone next to the Chairman to catch his reactions. There was a pregnant silence; it was ended for national consumption by the voice of a State Department security man reaching for the intruder. "Throw the SOB out on his head."

Now they are over, those ten days of voyaging into astral reaches beyond prior limit of the imagination. How can we measure the distance we have traveled or the time we need to recover from it? Will life ever be the same for any of us again? And will not Moscow seem just as gray to Nikita Khrushchev as Pittsburgh or Washington or New York to us his fellow travelers?

Adlai Stevenson had lunch with Khrushchev and Bob Garst yesterday. (It is the measure of this epic that even Adlai Stevenson becomes a parenthesis in it, although it is the measure of Adlai Stevenson that he offered the presence of a shining and honorable parenthesis.) Stevenson was saying afterwards that he found Khrushchev a man changed since he saw him in Moscow a year ago; he could not define the change very well, except to say that it seemed to be a matter of education. I think we have changed him, although I can define it no better than Stevenson could.

The memory he takes home is not just the color of the country, or the richness of its earth, or the luxury of its appointments. For the gaudiest image he has seen is of our fools, our vast national surplus of the comic and the excessive. We tend to think of our country as having become gray and characterless; but Nikita Khrushchev comes here and who does he meet in quick succession but Spyros Skouras, a drunken CIO vice president, Bob Garst and the American photographer, all abounding with idiot delight?

It was a trip which might have been planned by a committee of trained Bolsheviks to show him America in its least respectable aspects.

Yet has anybody on earth ever had as much fun as Nikita Khrushchev has had for the last ten days? We can never put mankind back into its old sober mold again. Nikita Khrushchev may very well go home and be his old self in a few days, but he will miss us as long as he lives. He knows now that no place on earth is as much fun as America.

What will happen—and I am quite serious—to the Soviet state when Nikita Khrushchev wakes up back in a country where all day long nobody laughs but him?

Let Me Off Uptown

9 • 21 • 60

Upon this note, let us cease all debates about the national purpose. It is simply this:

Love B. Woods was born in Columbia, South Carolina, ages ago. When he was young, he was so religious that he considered it a sin to read a newspaper. After graduation from the Negro college in Columbia, he took a job as a waiter, as a bridge to the higher life. He wanted to save enough money to go to Palestine and walk in the steps of Saint Paul.

After that pilgrimage, he went back to being a waiter; the vocation of Christ slipped away, but the faith remained. Love B. Woods became a Harlem real estate man.

He owned the old Woodside Hotel, which is engraved in the cultural history of the United States because it was there that Count Basie wrote "Jumping at the Woodside." Basie went downtown; the Woodside is forgotten; but Love B. Woods stayed on in Harlem.

He came to the peak of his life when he bought the Hotel Theresa at 125th Street and Seventh Avenue. The Theresa was where the Negro entertainers stayed in the thirties; it was, like most Harlem property, owned by white people in those days. After the war, the downtown hotels began taking Negro guests; the Negro entertainers went downtown, and the Theresa drooped, victim of the first stages of integration. Then, since it was no longer a profitable property, the white people sold the Theresa to Love B. Woods.

It was a sign and symbol of pride with him. He is an old man, and he remembers a time when a Negro had as much chance to own the Theresa as he does now to be United States Senator from Mississippi.

Since the Theresa was at last the property of Negroes, he wanted it to be a model of Christian conduct. He closed the bar because he did not like the class of girls who came there, and he caused to be put in the lobby a sign courteously requesting that the tenants not congregate at the door and inspect the sidewalks because women prefer not to be stared at when they are passing a hotel.

I should strongly doubt, having seen the manager of the Shelburne, that he operates an establishment morally superior to Love B. Woods'. But, as the manager of the Shelburne knows, the rewards of purity are not excessive; Sunday, as on most days, the Theresa was far from filled.

When Love B. Woods came home from church on Sunday, he had a call from a man asking if he might have forty rooms for Fidel Castro in case of an emergency. Love B. Woods answered that it was the policy of the house to take any guest who sought admittance.

The next day, shortly after noon, two Cubans came to see Love B. Woods.

"They had a conference with me for half an hour," the old man said. "I gave them the rates of the rooms, $20 a day. They offered me a check. I figured I better call the Police Department about them before I took their check, because it is not our policy here. So I went around to the precinct to ask the sergeant what he thought, and he said that I should use my own judgment, but if I had any trouble, call them. After that, I thought I better ask for cash.

"So they went downtown and got me the cash for one day, and I told them that today at two o'clock, I had to have the rest of the cash for ten days' worth of rent. But you know, I've never had a more orderly group of people. And they're such good tippers that I don't think I'll press my point about the cash this afternoon."

So the Theresa yesterday was the capital of the revolutionary tide. Outside on the sidewalk the black nationalists walked around and argued respectfully with Jackie Robinson, who explained that he was an American and that whenever Castro attacked America, he attacked all of us.

America had suddenly absorbed Fidel Castro; we were in a Southern town standing on the corner, quietly intimate, human again. No pickets, no wild cries. Jackie Robinson was saying that he was devoted to Love B. Woods, but even so, he waved at the heap of the Theresa and asked the group: "Would Castro stay in a place like that except for purposes of propaganda?"

And then there was scream of siren and gang-shag of cops, and a black Cadillac and Nikita Khrushchev in a blue suit and the Order of Lenin embracing a barbudo on the sidewalk.

Love B. Woods stayed in the kitchen instructing the waitresses not to forget to hand the guests in his Gold Room the menu.

Khrushchev was forty minutes with the maximum leader of the revolution—the conjunction of the unlikely with the impossible and, of course, in Harlem. In our time, the field of the cloth of gold is 125th Street and Seventh Avenue.

Knock our country, tear it down, call it what you will—and I shall call it worse—but name me one other piece of real estate under the eye of God where a man can be born a Negro in South Carolina and grow up to possess the summit where Fidel Castro and Nikita Khrushchev, after so long a climb, finally pause and wrap their arms around one another.

A Seat on the Bus

3 • 25 • 61

Three country boys with tickets for Meridian, Mississippi, stood ringed round by bayonets and waited for the 7 a.m. Trailways bus out of Montgomery.

"I don't care," said Jack L. Kelly, of Orangeburg, Mississippi, "I immigrated with 'em in the Army; I don't care if I immigrate with 'em on a bus."

The line of Guardsmen opened a passage by the terminal, and six cars led by a proud People's Cab and filled with Negroes came through and stopped by the white waiting room. Martin Luther King Jr. pushed open the door and the Negroes filled that sacred precinct. The clerk began stamping the tickets.

Six Freedom Riders sat down at the lunch counter, ordered coffee and were served. All the customs for whose sake Montgomery had come close to murder were suspended yesterday for the higher purpose of getting the plague out of town.

By now the three country boys had been swept away, to get to Meridian who knows when. The National Guard of Alabama had commandeered the 7 a.m. bus to Jackson. There climbed aboard, in mixed and irregular array, eight Jim Crow college students, two of them girls, three Nashville Negro ministers, and a white companion, Paul Dietrich, a Washington office worker.

Also sixteen communications specialists, three out of Luce, and six Alabama National Guardsmen and last of all, Major General Henry Graham, Adjutant General of the state of Alabama.

"We wish you sincerely a good trip," he said, and sent on its way the bus and its forty-two-car escort with the three search planes sweeping back and forth over its head.

A reporter told Paul Dietrich that he had guts. "I hope I have them tonight," Dietrich answered in a soft voice.

The children were tired, no one had slept much the night before. They began singing their calypso song, which cries brightly out: "Come on Mr. Kenn-ee-dee, Take Me Out of my Miseree."

THE PASSING SCENE

They began to drowse, looking out the windows at the flat country of their great-grandfathers' childhood. Every now and then, they would pass a car with silent white men lined up at a crossroad, once or twice a Negro cabin with its tenants standing expressionless on the porch, only watching, most of the time; occasionally, in places safely isolated, managing a sudden, momentary wave.

Past Selma, where the Alabama Citizens Councils were born; past a road gang whose white-jacketed Negro prisoners stood lined up, wondering; past Femopolis, where a truck driver threw some unknown object and slapped the side of the bus loud enough to wake a sleeping student.

The Rev. James Lawson, of Nashville, teacher-in-charge of this field trip, was sadly reading his Methodist prayer book. He said that they had hoped to come here as ordinary Negroes must, testing and meeting all the hazards. Now they were extraordinary Negroes sealed off from the reality of the sullen, watching clumps of whites, and the occasional expressionless Negroes on their way.

These laden hours might not shine, but they should not pass unimproved. He called his students back, and began once more to go over with them the endless questions and judgments about specific incidents of the test.

He asked the reporters and cameramen to move up front; the students sat in the back, cut off, by coincidence. Except for Dietrich, the Freedom Ride was segregated.

The reporters talked about other times and other places. Once or twice a voice came up from the back. "We should stand," the voice said, "and wait for the violence and, if the violence breaks our ranks, we should join our hands and hold together as long as we can."

After three hours and a half, General Graham ordered a rest stop. These were captured invaders being carried out of Alabama; they could not disembark within sight of an Alabama citizen. They stopped by an empty field. Lawson stood behind the bus—the Guardsmen lined up, their backs to him, their bayonets fixed against some invisible hazard—and Lawson explained that this was not the normal course he and the students were committed to run.

"We are a nonviolent force and we are protected by the instruments of violence. We should prefer not having this protection. We are not seeking violence, but, if it is coming, we must accept it as other Negroes have to."

The prisoners went back to their internment. They rode on to Scratch Hill; it was the border of Mississippi. One of Governor Ross Barnett's helicopters came down in a field beside the road. It had come up rain. The Guardsmen with their bayonets stood at the ready, the rain soaking their fatigues.

Julia Aaron of New Orleans, who is just twenty, looked out from the bus at them, and said: "That's terrible. Those poor men having to stand there and getting wet."

STATE LINE

The ear listened for the note of mockery. It did not come; Julia Aaron's voice was all concern.

The thought of Mississippi, dark and swarm-haunted, worked its mysterious chemistry. General Graham was scouting ahead. The reporters were once more in front; the students in the back. A white man catching himself sitting automatically next to a white man thought of all the acceptances the name and memory and custom of Mississippi had laid upon him, and he began talking to another white man about the all the little nonsenses and silences one must endure—petty but prideful—and suddenly they both understood at just the same time how wonderful these students are—bravely and casually walking straight through everything as far as their bodies will take them.

It rained on, Julia Aaron was saying that she had heard that Mississippi is a beautiful state. The tensions of the prospect otherwise sat even on those who had no sensible reason to feel tension. Most of all, perhaps, only on those. All over the bus, softly, slowly, oddly sweet, the voices of the students began to sing "Go Down, Moses, Away Down in Egypt Land."

After an infinity, General Graham came back and the convoy rolled to the rendezvous with the Mississippi National Guard—a garage at a crossroad—and Alabama got off with a cursory farewell and Mississippi got on without a greeting.

Mississippi turned out to be Lieutenant Colonel "Sunny" Montgomery, a State Senator from Meridian, a captain and six Guardsmen with bayonets; two fat sergeants stood in the aisles (to sit would be to integrate), the hard faces like the heavy clouds above.

Mississippi's orders were to scuttle westward, the colonel said he knew not where. A student started a question; another student said "play it cool," and they sang a while, "Black and White Together We Shall Not Be Moved," and Colonel Montgomery squared the shoulders of his back.

There were two hours and a half left. The silence of imprisonment fell. The students looked out the windows through streets dotted with clumps of white citizens, offering a silent, obscene gesture of derision.

A REQUEST

Thus came Khrushchev to Iowa, or candidate Kennedy to Indiana. But they represented great physical forces tolerating unfriendly lands; they had other places to go. This rolling, shuddering paddy wagon was alone in the world.

There had passed six and a half hours without food or respite. The Rev. Corty T. Vivian, a Nashville minister, got up and asked the colonel to stop the bus and let some of the passengers off to go to the bathroom. He was suffering a condition thought of as comic and certainly not dignified, but still the most painful known to a man of good conscience. The poor man fought for his dignity until his hands were gray around the rail in front of him and his face was the face of a deep interior wound. He went to "Sunny" Montgomery again and "Sunny" Montgomery told him to get back in the bus. The Rev. Mr.

Vivian stood arguing and the colonel said to the trooper, "Put him back; there'll be a stop before too long," and the Rev. Mr. Vivian sat back down again and through his teeth and in the agony of his body said, "May you come to the point when you can ask His forgiveness for these animal acts. Not to allow a man common decency. What do you tell your children when we go home? What do you say to tell God when you pray in church, or do you pray?"

The colonel looked out on the road, his back to that voice, his shoulders stiffening, but with a neck that never reddened. Thus, in military glory, Colonel Montgomery brought the inmates in to Jackson.

DESTINATION: JAIL

Jackson was ready, the Trailways station surrounded by policemen, the crowds sparse and at a distance, a path cleared to the colored waiting room. The Rev. Mr. Vivian sat and fought the needs of his body until he could get off with the other Freedom Riders.

They came in silence and were met in silence, and walked in silence into the white waiting room. The two girls and Paul Dietrich and Matthew Walker, a thin Fisk boy, stood in front of the white restaurant. A policeman said in flat tones that they would have to move on; then he took out his book and wrote their names and they marched to the police wagon already installed and off to the new-model, separate and equal city jail. They were guarded from the strangers on the sidewalk by Jackson's famous separate and equal police dogs.

Paul Dietrich and Matthew Walker walked to the wagon together; Matthew Walker put an arm around Paul Dietrich's back. It had all been done correctly. It was done correctly with the second bus from Montgomery sealed and guarded by air and land like the first (altogether, there were twenty-seven riders arrested) in a total of six silent minutes, a record for tidy dispatch.

Later on, Chief of Detectives Meade Pierce met the reporters, and reminded them that "We haven't mentioned segregation; the charge is not moving on."

The students, he said, are just as polite as they can be. He hoped they would be comfortable; Jackson is proud of its jail. It has its custom, of course. He had asked them not to sing. He closed by extending the visiting press all possible courtesies and hoped it would respond by telling the North how cordial Jackson's response had been.

A small section of the North is hereby informed that Jackson at least defends itself against the future under the auspices of its Chamber of Commerce.

The Saddest Story

6 • 5 • 62

Geraldine Gray was born in Mississippi and her mother brought her north to Chicago just after the First World War when the great migration began.

She became a Young Communist on the South Side in 1938, and after a year she married Claude Lightfoot, who was a comrade and has now become the Chicago leader of the Communist Party. Last month she died of cancer.

The saddest stories an American could read, if they were printed outside the Communist press, are the accounts of the funerals of American Communists.

I did not know Mrs. Claude Lightfoot, and I cannot report whether she was a good woman. In any case, one would think that those who hated her most, since they hated a Communist stranger more than a real person anyway, might suspend any judgment upon her the day she died.

Geraldine Lightfoot lived all her adult life in South Side Chicago, which is a Southern city. She was a regular communicant of the Mount Hebron Missionary Baptist Church and was buried according to its ritual. Four Negro ministers spoke, along with Benjamin Davis and William Patterson of the American Communist Party. The ministers reported her a good Christian and the party speakers reported her a good Communist. It was an odd mixture, and, at the present stage of our civilization, it may seem impossible that a woman could consider herself a good Christian and a good Communist. Persons expert in the conspiracy may assume that she joined the church as a Communist tactic to fool the South Side. But the South Side is not that easy to fool: she was always a public Communist, and she must have earned the friends who came to her funeral.

Some, of course, were Communists. But most of them seem to have been neighbors and fellow church members. There were three guest books at the funeral parlor and 696 visitors signed their names.

George O. Jones, the funeral director, reported afterwards that a young man, properly identifying himself as a member of the FBI, came to his establishment and asked to see the guest books. As a good citizen, George Jones was anxious to cooperate with generous and majestic government, but he could not. The Chicago police had already picked them up at closing time the night before.

We are all safer today because the Department of Justice has in its files a sheaf of photostats, labeled: "Guests at the wake of one Geraldine Lightfoot." It is not so precious as a Communist Party petition from 1941, but it has its uses.

The FBI and the Chicago police came to the funeral, of course, and took notes while the leader of the church choir gave her testament to Geraldine Lightfoot's virtues. Mrs. Lightfoot was buried in the village of Forest Park; a motorcycle policeman stood at the gate and copied down the license plate of each car that entered. "Maybe," said village Police Chief Joseph L. Cortino, "the FBI and the Chicago Police Department want them." Then Chief Cortino stood at the graveside, his revolver on, and heard the minister's final words and watched the coffin lowered and went back to lesser duties of law enforcement.

And that was a Christian burial in the United States of America, the great bastion of Christianity. In death as in life, a Communist is merely an object for police routine. And just what had that woman done that she and her friends should deserve this at the end? And what have we all done to make it possible for our country not to feel the shame it deserves at this moment?

"I would like to talk to you tonight quite personally . . ."

7·7·62

I would like to talk to you tonight quite personally. I come to you as a very safe man—and a very secure one and one who is in no danger. I am an exceptional figure on this platform. I regret to say that there are more victims on this platform than there are bystanders. In fact, I think I am the single bystander. I would hope that if you struggle on another year that the bystanders will outnumber the victims next year. I speak tonight as best I can for all the people who I think would like to be here and are not here because of difficulties and confusions and troubles.

The point about which we should all think, I think was rather well made by Eugene Victor Debs when he said, "While there is a soul left in prison, none of us is free." I cannot stand before you today and tell you in all honesty that I believe that the Communist Party has totally served the Debs tradition. I cannot say that I, myself, and my Socialist Party have totally served the Debs tradition. I can say that there has been in the history of the United States, along with Lincoln and along with Washington, only one Eugene Victor Debs, and I hope that for those of you who have fought to keep this door open as long and as well as you have, out of all of this there will come one child from one of us who will be another Eugene Victor Debs.

I am really here because of people rather than notions and ideas of the national safety or the national law. I heard a great deal about the Federal Bureau of Investigation, but I cannot ever forget poor Michael who served his country so well in the F.B.I. that he turned his wife in to the F.B.I. while he was courting her—don't laugh, there might be an F.B.I. man sitting here—turned his wife in to the F.B.I. while he was courting her and after they were married he went on turning her in and he might be turning her in still today except that one afternoon she was packing his shirts and their three-year-old daughter came upon his F.B.I. report naming her, her father and her brother. An old Irishman once told William Butler Yeats that there are things you cannot do even to save a country. I think, too, of the McCarran Act in quite personal terms, because I think that in a sense it represents the final arrival in our nation of the final denial that the objects of its outrage are human beings.

I know the son of a Communist who has lost two jobs for no apparent reason except that his father continues with his party activities. I know a great many others, and I would like to end by talking very briefly about them as people, and about my gratitude to them as people. And I will try to be brief and as honest as I can in saying this. I think that the Communist movement through my lifetime, with all its sins and all its terrible troubles, has represented a great ideal. I think America, with all its sins and all its troubles, has represented a great ideal. I think tonight is a night which should be a reconciliation for all of us. And I think of all the people that I have known who have been Communists and who this movement transcended and brought to witness for all mankind in many ways. I think of Pasternak, Djilas; I think of Earl Browder—I think of Gurley Flynn—I think of all those who've endured and fought and kept their faith in a common conception.

I have known many Communists in my life. I have not known them as criminals. I knew them once as activists—and we had our quarrels. Someday, if you're ever put back on your feet again, I hope we may quarrel again. But in the interim I would like to say this: This country has not been kind to you, but this country has been fortunate in having you. You have been treated as people should not be treated in a civilized society. You have been arrested, you have been followed, you have had your phones bugged, you have had your children fired, you have had everything that can be done to make life as difficult as possible. Throughout this, I can think of numbers of you that I have known who have remained gallant, and pleasant and unbroken. I think your association with those who are victims of trouble and bore their troubles, will someday come to give you a place in history—very unlike the one perhaps that you expected, but not the one that you've been given today.

I will define it by saying our children's children will someday walk together in the light and they will do it—because numbers of you have done what you could to keep your courage and your patience. And oddly enough, I don't assign that courage and that patience to the Marxist-Leninist doctrine quite so much as to the fact that you are Americans—that you feel that America is part of your heritage, and you feel that America will do right by you and your children as human beings. I salute you and I hope for times to better. There is one more thing I'd like to say about why I am here and then I will leave you. I think particularly about Mrs. Claude Lightfoot who died last May, last month, was buried at a ceremony openly attended by the F.B.I. in a Christian church in this Christian country, whose funeral car was followed by state policemen who took down license numbers, and from whose wake the guestbook was taken home for scrutiny and photostating by the Federal Bureau of Investigation. I would like to say at the end—and this, I think, is really how I feel about the McCarran Act and about what it really means to all of us—I think that as long as the F.B.I. goes to funerals and takes down the names of mourners, that all Americans belong at meetings like this.

Visiting Hours

8 • 6 • 62

Mrs. Martin Luther King brought her children, Yolanda, six, Martin Luther III, four, and Dexter Scott, eighteen months, to the city jail to visit their father a little after noon yesterday.

They had never seen their father in jail before; and he, rather than Mrs. King, had suggested that it would be better if they did not see him behind bars.

"They're so active," she said. "And the cell's so narrow." She and they waited outside the chief's office while the Albany police arranged for King to receive his family in the narrow hall between the cells and the booking desk.

Someone asked how long she thought her husband would stay there. Her face was suddenly painful and she said she didn't know, but she hopes very much that it might be coming to a close. She and he are essentially such reserved people, and to be conspicuous is such an embarrassment to them, and the police court so alien. They are actors with a particular talent for reconciliation; yet they have been assigned the part of active resistance; it is one of the strangest twists of this strange country that Martin and Coretta King, of all people, should have become symbols of militant disturbance to the official South.

The children had precisely fifteen minutes. They came out to play in the lobby through which so many children, not really much older, have marched off to jail in the past six months. They asked for Cokes and were firmly overruled; Martin III reached up to try the water fountain.

Mrs. King was undisguisedly relieved that it had all been so easy. "I told Martin," she said later, "that if you stay away much longer the baby won't know you." But that worry, like so many others, had not come true. Yolanda, she said, was the only one of the children who was beginning to ask the sort of questions to which fruitful answers can be given.

"I told her and Marty too this time that Daddy had gone to jail to help the poor people, that there are people different from ourselves who don't have good homes to live in or enough food to eat.

"The first time Martin went to jail in Atlanta, Yolanda heard about it on television. She started crying. I told her, 'Yorky, Daddy's gone to help the people. He's already helped some people; he has to help some more. He'll be back.' And then she stopped crying."

She has tried, as mothers must, to protect Yolanda as long as she could. "When they built Fun Town for children in Atlanta, she was after me to take her there. I put her off as long as I could and finally I had to tell her that some of the people who built Fun Town are not nice Christian people and unfortunately they didn't want colored children. She started crying. And I told her: 'It won't be long before Fun Town is open to all the people. That's what your Daddy's working for.'

"And this time Yolanda said, 'I want Daddy to come home.' And then, 'Tell him to stay until he fixes it up so I can go to Fun Town.'"

Fun Town had been the first time Mrs. King had to tell Yolanda. "I want her to have a healthy attitude toward white people. She will have her bitter time, but I think that we have protected her enough so it will pass."

But Yolanda hears things, as children will. One of their friends told her that there were people who hated her father. "You wonder why people say things. She went to Martin and he told her, 'I don't think a lot of people hate me. But a lot of people don't like what I'm trying to do.'"

But young Martin is four, and cannot see enough of his father. "Boys are different; he needs that firm hand." A visitor asked just how many more times her husband would have to go to jail and for how many more years they would live as they do now.

"I think five years," she said with that familiar sudden sadness. "After that, it will not be all perfect but it will be different." Her largest hope is that the term to which they have been called will only be five years. They are five years to be accepted as prescribed and to be endured in infrequently broken measures of pain and worry.

Back at the Polo Grounds

August 1962

The return of the Polo Grounds to the National League was like the raising of a sunken cathedral. It is a place sacred in history and hallowed in the memory. Christy Mathewson used to make his home on the bluff above the Polo Grounds. When he was working, Mrs. Mathewson could look out her window at the scoreboard and, when the seventh inning came, put the roast in the oven secure in the knowledge that her husband would be finished and showered and home from the plough in an hour.

When the Mets brought the National League, or anyway its shadow, back to New York, there was no place for them except this old shrine. The Mets' permanent stadium at Flushing Meadows is a year from completion; and the City of New York had long ago leveled Ebbets Field and sowed a housing project on its site.

So George Weiss, the Mets' new president, took the Polo Grounds from necessity more than sentiment. Weiss, of course, is the deposed general manager of the Yankees; and the Yankees are the authors of that age of elegance and class distinction in baseball which really began with their Stadium Club, a response to the corporate expense account.

Weiss' prospectus for Flushing Meadows would be garish for a trotting track: "The stadium will be triple-tiered with twenty-one escalators to speed fans to and from their seats. . . . A 1,500-seat, comfortably decorated main dining room will be available to season box holders. . . . There are fifty-four public rest room installations conveniently located on all three levels: twenty-seven for women, twenty-seven for men. Each women's rest room has its own lounge or powder room."

But all is a total affront to the tradition of the National League in New York, where Ladies Day was never for ladies and where there was absolute democracy in the affliction of misery upon rich and poor alike. Dodger fans had every vulgarity but the vulgarity of wealth; Giant fans had no vulgarity at all. The mere age and squalor of the Polo Grounds comforted its customers; you could as easily catch some bronchial disease in its dank recesses as you used to be able to catch malaria at night in the Roman Colosseum, and both contagions earned the romance of history.

The New York of the Giants, Dodgers and Yankees was an annual re-evocation of the War between the States. The Yankees were the North, if you could conceive a North grinding along with wealth and weight and without the excuse of Lincoln. The Giants and Dodgers were the Confederacy, often undermanned and underequipped and running then because it could not hit. You went to Yankee Stadium if you were the kind of man who enjoyed yelling for Grant at Richmond; you went to the National League parks to see Pickett's charge. George Weiss, a displaced quartermaster general of the Union Army, does not understand that persons committed to endure losing causes do not care about escalators.

The old Dodger fans were the kind of people who picket. The old Giant fans would be embarrassed to do anything so conspicuous, but they were the kind of people who refuse to cross picket lines. Yankee fans are the kind of people who think they own the company the picket line is thrown around. It is impossible for anyone who does not live in New York to know what it truly is to hate the Yankees. As writer Leonard Koppett has said: "The residents of other cities who hate the Yankees really only hate New York." He has noticed they even hate the Knicks, the most underprivileged established team in the National Basketball Association. But, if you live in New York and you're not a Yankee fan, you hate them the way you hate Consolidated Edison or your friendly bank.

George Weiss, being insensitive to these nuances, could not, even for one year as tenant, let the Polo Grounds rest as the raddled, gray, pigeon-speckled old rookery its mourners had left, for what everyone assumed was the last time, after sacking and looting it after the Giants lost their last game there in 1957.

Weiss has in Mrs. Joan Whitney Payson, the Mets' owner, the most generous of patronesses. He had spent $450,000 of her money decking the Polo Grounds in orange, blue and green paint and ornamenting its walls with faintly abstract advertisements for cigars, Scotch, pomades, salamis and breath sweeteners. As a woman, Mrs. Payson may have been enchanted at first glance; but, as a sport, she must have been saddened to see that Weiss had painted out the numbers which used to remind all present of the distance to the foul poles and which were so much the controlling mathematics of its epic history at the Polo Grounds.

It is 257 feet to the stands in right field; and, for its prior active years, the Polo Grounds had proclaimed that terrible statistic unashamedly on its fence. Bobby Thomson's home run against the Dodgers in 1951, the most famous in baseball, traveled barely 300 feet to left. Hitting in the Polo Grounds is like playing a pinball machine. Those numbers were symbols reminding us how in life we are in the midst of death and that the afternoon could end, as so many uncertain struggles had ended before it, with the ridiculous accident of a high fly 260 feet to the wrong field.

Carl Hubbell once pitched forty-six straight scoreless innings as a Giant and this string remains a National League record. Sal Maglie, a Giant almost as sacred in the memory as Hubbell himself, came closer than any other National League pitcher to breaking that record. Maglie was in the Polo Grounds one August afternoon in 1950, two-thirds of an inning away from Hubbell's scoreless total when a young Pirate outfielder named Gus Bell hit a line drive that traveled 257 feet to the foul pole for a home run. The devils who tenant the Polo Grounds had punished Maglie for affronting Hubbell; being long in memory, they have now punished Maglie for affronting Hubbell; being long in memory, they have now punished Bell by bringing him back here to finish his career as a Met. For the Polo Grounds, being storied and ancient, is also cursed.

That curse was upon the Mets on opening day in the Polo Grounds. It had rained much of the morning; there was the chill of old night in the air. An usher pulled the collar of his new orange windbreaker up around his chin. "You better watch out," said a colleague. "Mr. Weiss wants our collars down at all times." Casey Stengel was in the dugout with photographers, reporters, and the withdrawn and brooding eminence of Rogers Hornsby, who has been hired to coach hitters who either already know how to hit but no longer can, or, if they learn how, are unlikely to be able to.

Stengel complained that his arm was still sore from throwing plastic baseballs at the lower Broadway crowd which had welcomed the Mets to New York. Behind him, Dan Topping of the Yankees was sitting in a box; you thought of Khrushchev on a state visit to Bulgaria and there was a sudden, useless urge for Casey's Mets to get fifty runs. The Mets came out running earnestly and heavily on a wet track; they were loudly cheered by a cluster of children in right field, an odd demonstration of the persistence of buried tradition, since none of these greeters could have been older than 6 when the National League fled New York.

George Weiss was suffering in Mrs. Payson's box behind the Met dugout. The devils of the Polo Grounds had devised for him a special torment. The groundskeepers, in their spring cleaning, had come upon two rusted iron chairs and, presumably to save the long walk to the scrap heap, had thrown them into Mrs. Payson's box, like dead rats in a garden. When he owned the New York Giants, Horace Stoneham would have sat unprotesting, ankle deep in coffee cups and hot-dog wrappers because he took it for granted that this was the normal environment of his playground. Weiss waved a pallid hand, a fear-stricken smile upon his pallid face. "Please," he said to one of the special guards, "this is Mrs. Payson's box. Can't you do something about it?'"

Down below, Stengel thrust his head through a floral horseshoe, clowning for the photographers. He rarely spoke with his players. Instead he capered and tested the rain and always posed, a reminder that he had been hired as much for his showmanship as for his managing skill; perhaps more. Showmanship and salesmanship are important to the Mets, who have more television sponsors than Jack Paar had. We describe the future they represent when we remember they started the season with one tested and still possible major-league pitcher—Roger Craig—and three tested major-league announcers.

Weiss had bet his future more on memory than on hope. Only

Sherman Jones, the pitcher in his first home lineup, bore a name not indented in the memory of the customers. Six of the starters against the Pittsburgh Pirates had played in the Polo Grounds in its last prior season five years earlier. Gil Hodges, a fifteen-year man, would certainly have started if he had been able to walk; and Joe Ginsberg, Stengel's catcher, was no less pickled with brine than his colleagues and would certainly have qualified as a Polo Grounds initiate if he had not spent most of his eleven major-league years in the low-rent district of the American League.

A visitor went down to inspect the Met Lounge, which is reserved for season ticket holders only and where "gentlemen must wear coats, ladies, inclusive of girls twelve years of age and over, will not be permitted to wear slacks of any type or abbreviated clothing." There he was first inspected for dress and credentials by a pretty girl in a pinstripe jacket and with eyes like a house detective. This ordeal entitles the elite to a fifty-cent hot dog.

Stengel's old horses took the field with heartbreaking determination of stride and common impression of haunch. The noise was suddenly immense, almost a profanation at the Polo Grounds, which was always a cloister. It was also unexpected from a crowd of twelve thousand; we were back at Ebbets Field where six thousand customers used to maintain a roar in an ordinary game against the Cubs, which always left any outlander with the suspicion that the management had installed a record player that was blasting "Crowd noise–Dempsey-Firpo 1923" somewhere in the stands. So this was a Dodger crowd; Weiss had staked his appeal there, with Hodges, Craig, Don Zimmer, and Charlie Neal. Bobby Thomson was absent; but Ralph Branca was there, with an abject grin, to be photographed pointing to the fatal spot in left field and to explain again that it would have been a home run nowhere else.

Still, an inning and two-thirds had to go by before everyone was carried back to that lost time in the mid-fifties when the Giants were sixth. Smoky Burgess got the Pirates' first hit, and then Don Hoak sliced a fly 270 feet to the wrong field, off the wall for a double to score Burgess. Jones had been introduced to that curse of the Polo Grounds, and Hoak, who knew it of old, may be excused for the indignant reflection that he had been cheated of a home run. Then Bill Mazeroski hit a drive well over 370 feet to tight center, the afternoon's first evidence of lust but normally an out in the Polo Grounds, the tallest and thinnest park in the big leagues. Richie Ashburn and Gus Bell ploughed and floundered and waved under it, and before Bell could complete the salvage, Mazeroski was on third and Hoak was home. Jones had been introduced to his outfield and was two runs down and innocent.

In the third inning Jim Marshall entered history by walking, the first Met to reach base safely. The first Met hit had to wait until the next inning and belonged to the pitcher. The first Met extra-base hit—a double—came in the fifth and could be credited more to mud than to muscle; Marshall lifted a fly near third; Dick Groat fell chasing it. After two outs it came Jones' turn, and Stengel had to dispense with this young man, already so much more sinned against than sinning. A claque behind first base began crying for Hodges; Stengel sent up Ed Bouchee instead and was rewarded with an honest single to center and a run. It was the old man's first trip to his bench, a thing of tatters; for one brief and wonderful moment, the devils had suspended their curse for Stengel's first command decision.

In the end the Mets lost 4 to 3. The first two of those four runs were tawdry; the third was the comparatively honest consequence of two singles and a wild pitch; and the last the direct result of two wild pitches. That is the balance of their dreary future; and it was underlined by the reflection that, in two of the three Pirate scoring innings, the Met pitcher had stopped the first two batters.

Groat finished the game caked with mud to his hips, from the occasions when he had fallen down, going first to his right and then to his left. But he had made plays he had had to make. The new uniforms of the Met infielders were immaculate as they dragged home to the clubhouse; none of them fallen down, not because they do not have desire but they no longer have possibility. They cannot get close enough anymore to the doubtful chance to make use of the desperate dive. People are always saying that one-eighth of an inch is the difference between winning and losing baseball. With the Mets, it is three inches. No one could count the afternoons there would be like this one.

But the first day had been distorted by climate and the illusion of accident. The following Monday, the Mets greeted the new Houston Colt .45s. Hodges was at first; the sun was out; the cries from the stands were faint and infrequent; there were only three thousand customers, the Dodger fans having already struck the colors. We were back on one of those long slow afternoons remembered from sixth place at the Polo Grounds in 1956.

The Mets went on to tie the Colts in the ninth and lose in the eleventh, a pattern picked up from the 1955–57 Giants. Those Giants were the subject of the only baseball short story written in the fifties with a legitimate claim to a place in the canon of that art form. Called "Seven Steps to Heaven," after the beer commercial, its author was E. B. White, and it was about what baseball has become in the electronic age, since its hero never went to the park but watched the disasters of the Giants as shadows on his television screen. But the Mets are not those Giants.

Those old Giants had Dusty Rhodes or Hank Sauer in left, and neither had ever pretended to be a fielder. Rhodes departed cursed and cherished. But who has a right to curse Frank Thomas? Weiss wanted to assault the sentiment of New Yorkers with what would have been a respectable, if Mays-less, All-Star National League outfield in 1954—Thomas in left, Richie Ashburn in center, and Gus Bell in right. But it does not make you feel sentimental to see Ashburn thrown out on a deep grounder to third when he would have been safe just two years ago. It only makes you feel sad. It makes you sad, too, to see Hodges stand at the plate, trying to chip to the wrong field, a device of shortstops. These are men of great personal class; no one can enjoy seeing that what is hard for them now is what used to be precisely the easiest thing.

More than anything else, this condition must account for the brooding sorrow which chokes the Mets' dressing room after every defeat. The atmosphere has been compared to the dressing room of a team that has lost the World Series. Still a World Series is a transient thing; for those losers, there is always next year. But for the old men on the Mets, there will be no next year; this is where it ends; every afternoon is a reminder that the flesh is grass.

But then Weiss has always had a colder attitude toward old ballplayers than the rest of us do. The Met customers in left field occasionally express that difference by bringing along a banner painted "Rod Kanehl fan Club." Rod Kanehl is a thirty-two-year-old outfielder-infielder who had never appeared in a big-league game before this year. His future is dim, but then so is his past. He carries no memory of departed glory for any spectator to regret; and this demand that he play every day is in some way a protest for the dignity of greater names. These fans would rather look at a faint hope than suffer with a damaged memory.

The Clarity of A. Philip Randolph

7 • 6 • 63

It is not Asa Philip Randolph's style to embarrass presidents of the United States in large assemblies; and so, when he came as a vice president of the AFL-CIO to the White House along with three hundred other labor leaders, Mr. Randolph's brief comment on the President's televised speech on civil rights two nights before was at once a stately compliment and a measured reminder: "It was a magnificent speech, but it was, unfortunately, made rather late."

When the President had left the room and his audience was moving toward the outer air, a southern brother approached Philip Randolph and asked where he could find someone from the Labor Department. "I got a problem to tell him about," he said. "The colored people are doing all right in my state. It's the white people I'm worried about. They're being discriminated against."

Randolph gravely escorted this stray over to the nearest Labor Department official and went away. He returned to Harlem amused but unsurprised; he is the only figure in the American labor movement who has, for twenty years, been able continually to surprise his country, but nothing surprises him.

His Brotherhood of Sleeping Car Porters is aged and fading; it never had more than fifteen thousand members and no more than five thousand of these are working now. Porters with thirty years of service endlessly deal the brittle old playing cards in their recreation room on 125th Street in New York, awaiting their chance for an infrequent extra run. The porters may strike any day for the forty-hour work week which they alone among the operating railroad crafts have not achieved. They can expect the other unions to support their picket lines; this little group of old men could produce a national railroad strike. Nothing is new about their headquarters except the fresh picket signs.

The porter has always been poor and a menial; segregation created his job; the Pullman Company hired Negroes as porters because Negroes were inexpensive. And for most of the thirty-seven years of their union's history, the porters have taxed themselves for campaigns to destroy segregation on the railroads, but they seem to have been defeated by economic history. Their union has raised their pay scale to a basic $436 a month, which has made a porter's job one fit for white men, so fit in fact that occasionally a white youth comes to the Brotherhood in search of a union card; it cannot be given him, because there are not enough jobs for the old members, let alone new ones. There will be no white porters, and there will be no Negro engineers; the rule for employment on the railroads is not opportunity but seniority.

World War II was the best time they have known as workers. They used its rewards to finance Randolph's March on Washington movement, whose threat in 1943 won from Franklin D. Roosevelt the executive order which set up the wartime Fair Employment Practices Committee.

The first Freedom Rides into North and South Carolina and Tennessee were planned in Randolph's office in 1946. Bayard Rustin, a veteran of that first adventure into jail, remembers that everyone else had discouraged him until he came to Randolph. "It doesn't matter if you only get eighteen people," Randolph said then. "If you go down there, other people will rise and follow." He was looking seventeen years ahead as though they were the next day.

Ralph Bunche remembers traveling to Atlanta on the Seaboard line in 1947. South of Washington he went to the diner and was shown a table behind a partition. He looked at it, announced that he had not lived quite long enough yet to accept segregation, and went back to his room.

"About half an hour later, my door buzzer buzzed. I opened it and there were two sleeping-car porters and a waiter from the dining car with trays neatly covered and they told me that they had decided to bring me this food, because no Negro, in their view, who refused to eat at that Jim Crow table would ever grow hungry on a train where they served. They didn't mention it, but I took it that the food was with the compliments of the company."

The Brotherhood Building on 125th Street was headquarters for Thomas Patterson, Eastern Supervisor of the Sleeping Car Porters Union, who once traveled to Wilmington, North Carolina, to negotiate with the Atlantic Coast Line. He was ejected from its dining car for refusing to sit at the segregated table. The next morning, Patterson completed his union business with a Coast Line lawyer; that afternoon, he sued the Line for his humiliation on the diner. The railroad settled out of court, and its Jim Crow partition was removed for all time; Patterson gave his award to the Brotherhood.

In 1955, Edward D. Nixon, a Pullman porter, summoned the Negro community of Montgomery, Alabama, to boycott its buses. Nixon knew that it would be politic to choose one of the Negro ministers as leader of the boycott. The youngest, and a stranger among them, was Martin Luther King, Jr., of the Dexter Street Baptist Church.

"He didn't say much, and I didn't know whether to trust him. But he had the richest church and he could hurt us," Nixon remembered. "So then and there, I nominated him to head our committee. I figured on pushing him out so far that he couldn't run away. And, with that bad guess, we got Moses."

Such is the history that suffuses this old command post set away in a Harlem that has changed hardly at all. Three floors down are the displays of studios that offer tap, ballet and other lessons in how to escape to the great world, and the advertisements of employment offices that offer jobs for maids in New Jersey.

"What was your class at Harvard, Phil?" Franklin D. Roosevelt asked once, bemused by the massively cultivated tone of a man whose only degree was from Cookman College, a Negro high school in Florida. "Who is Randolph?" a World War II government lawyer asked as he brought in draft after draft of an FEPC order in 1943, only to be told that "Randolph" was not yet satisfied that any of them went far enough.

"I wish you hadn't said that, Mr. Randolph," Harry Truman answered when Randolph told him in 1948 that he would advise every young Negro to refuse to serve in the Army so long as it was segregated. Randolph answered that he was sorry to have to say it; and, when President Truman was restored to calm, he signed the order which integrated the armed forces.

In 1951, William Mills, a Pullman porter, escorted a detachment of American soldiers into his car at Spartanburg, South Carolina. The sergeant was a Negro; most of the men in his command were white. One of the white boys put his head out of the window and asked in the accent of the South, "Sergeant, what time we supposed to get off?" The sergeant answered, and turned to see William Mills looking at him. "Yes," the sergeant said. "It's true. It's true."

Randolph is seventy-four, thinner than he used to be. Men who have worked with him for thirty years call him "Chief" and treat him like a piece of old china; he tires more than he used to and lies down for a nap in the afternoon, like any country lawyer.

His only vanity is his manners. He has lived all his life in Harlem; he travels to the outside world as the ambassador of a Negro union. He carries a courtesy so old-fashioned that the white men with whom he negotiates are sometimes driven to outsized rage by the shock that anyone so polite could stick so stubbornly to what he believes; it was from such a shock presumably that George Meany breached the customary decorum of an AFL-CIO convention in 1959 by rasping, "Just who elected you, Phil, to represent all the American Negroes?" Randolph, almost alone on the convention floor, had been persisting in his insistence that the AFL-CIO had been derelict in its promises about civil rights.

"Every now and then," says Bayard Rustin, "I think he permits good manners to get in the way and that he even prefers them to sound tactics. Once I complained about that and he answered, 'Bayard, we must with good manners accept everyone. Now is the time for us to learn good manners. We will need them when this is over, because we must show good manners after we have won.'"

Yet the Black Muslims trust Randolph more than they do any other Negro leader. When he organized a neighborhood committee on Harlem's economic problems, he invited Malcolm X, the local Muslim prophet, to join. There were objections from the respectable. Randolph replied that when any group of citizens offered a representative, it "would be most improper not to recognize him, even though it will, of course, be most unfortunate if some of the ministers decide they can't go along."

Malcolm X came to his office. Randolph patiently explained how the Negro and the white will have to live together and how wrong he thought the Muslims were not to think so. Then he congratulated the Muslims on their campaign against whiskey and narcotics. "That," he said gravely, "may be the greatest contribution any of us have ever made," and arose to help Malcolm X on with his coat and see him to the door. Malcolm X has said since that all Negro leaders are confused, but that Randolph is less confused than any of them. Last spring the Muslims put a picture of this pacifist on the cover of their weekly journal.

"When Randolph began," says Bayard Rustin, "the Negro leader had the terrible problem of living by his wits. It was very important that there be one man who could not be corrupted. That man was Randolph. Even now, any time you have a plan and don't quite trust yourself, you go to Randolph and, if you are fooling yourself morally, you can trust him to point it out."

Randolph suddenly appears as the only figure who can reconcile the painful personal differences that have fallen upon the Negro protest movement at the height of its sweep and its fashion. We confront one of those occasions familiar in all revolutionary movements when doctrinal differences pass over into personal quarrels. Its moment of revelation came just after the murder of Medgar Evers, Mississippi secretary of the NAACP. Martin Luther King, Jr., called an NAACP official to suggest that together they proclaim a day of national mourning and self-examination and was told that he was always rushing into cases where he had no place or business.

The alliance between King and the NAACP has always been uneasy. They have moved by different roads in the same direction, King mainly in the streets, the NAACP in the courts. King's young can seem irresponsible to the NAACP's middle-aged; and the NAACP's middle-aged can seem stodgy to King's young.

Randolph is alone among these leaders because he neither feels nor incites hostility. He is a pacifist in a Native American tradition; before most members of King's nonviolent army were born, he was reminding the Negro of Thoreau's prescription to cast the total vote with feet and voice along with the ballot. He has a natural sympathy for King. Still, there are ways in which he is more moderate than the NAACP. While the association has been in open war with the AFL-CIO, Randolph has kept his friends there, offending them only on matters of principle. The porters remain as they have always been, moderate in the particular that involves manners, and radical in the general that involves principle.

Not even a malignant imagination could assign Randolph one side or another in the quarrel between King and the NAACP. King he judges to be not just a modest man but a humble one, which, for him, disposes of the NAACP's complaint. On the other side, he reminds the radical young how important it is to respect the association, and Roy Wilkins, its executive secretary. "We must cultivate Roy," he tells them. "The association is the most important of all our organizations." He respects King because he has roused the poor Negro with results more consequential than any leader before him; and he respects the NAACP because it reaches the Negro middle class and can call upon its local chapters for hundreds of thousands of dollars in crisis; there is no other resource like this one.

Two months ago, Randolph had announced that he would call one hundred thousand Negroes to Washington to demonstrate against unemployment in October; it had seemed then just an echo of his 1943 march on Washington and scarcely relevant. Wilkins and King had different concerns and higher priorities, and without them, Randolph seemed reduced to the depleted resources of the porters. But then President Kennedy introduced his civil rights bill; Washington had again become the center and Randolph's march the critical item on the movement's agenda this summer. Randolph moved his march to August; he and King agreed to widen its scope to cover the civil rights bill. There was suddenly the surprising prospect that Congress would debate these bills with thousands of Negroes standing outside the Capitol.

Randolph and others were called again to the White House on June 22, just before the President was to leave for Europe. Mr. Kennedy said that he hoped that it wouldn't be necessary for Negroes to come to Washington in great groups while the debate was going on. Philip Randolph answered that he was afraid the choice was no longer whether Negroes came to Washington or not. "The choice, Mr. President, is between a controlled and nonviolent demonstration and an uncontrolled and violent one."

Mr. Kennedy answered that a president had many responsibilities and he wanted it made clear that he was not inviting them. Randolph's manners instructed Mr. Kennedy that he was talking for the record.

Randolph returned to plan a march that would be unlimited in aim, and that would remember above all the needs of all the poor and displaced, whatever their color.

"The Negro people are just one other depressed area," he said the other day. "As long as there is unemployment, it's going to hit us. The Negro is in the position of the white hod carrier and the white longshoreman. I should like all the unemployed to come with us. We complain because the building trades have no room for Negroes, but the real trouble now is that these unions are designed for profit through scarcity. If the crafts were open to us, that could not, in the present economy, create more than forty thousand jobs.

"When we have won, there will remain the Negro sharecropper. We shall end, great as this is, with a very sharp disillusionment when the great rallies are over. We had this experience with sit-downs in the thirties. We are basically a working-class group; we will not move unless we move with the rest of the working class."

More than anything else, Philip Randolph said, he would like to bring the displaced miners of Hazard, Kentucky, to Washington with him. He was silent just a moment, contemplating what all this sudden energy could mean, not just to the Negro, but to the whole United States. His secretary came in and reminded him that it was time for his afternoon nap. The Pullman porter, weary and depleted, has raised himself for just this one last effort to redeem his country.

The March on Washington

9·4·63

The most consistent quality of white America's experience with the Negro is that almost nothing happens that we—or perhaps even he—expects to have happen. Faithful to that tradition, Washington waited most of the summer for the avenging Negro army to march on Washington for Jobs and Freedom; what came was the largest religious pilgrimage of Americans that any of us is ever likely to see.

When it was over, Malcolm X, the Muslim, was observed in the lobby of the Statler. It had, he conceded, been something of a show. "Kennedy," said Malcolm X, "should win the Academy Award—for direction." Yet while the President may have triumphed as director-manipulator, he was also deftly manipulated by those whom he strove to direct. "When the Negro leaders announced the march, the President asked them to call it off," Bayard Rustin, its manager, remembered the next day. "When they thumbed—when they told him they wouldn't—he almost smothered us. We had to keep raising our demands . . . to keep him from getting ahead of us."

Rustin and A. Philip Randolph are men who had to learn long ago that in order to handle they must first permit themselves to be handled. The moment in that afternoon which most strained belief was near its end, when Rustin led the assemblage in a mass pledge never to cease until they had won their demands. A radical pacifist, every sentence punctuated by his upraised hand, was calling for a $2-an-hour minimum wage. Every television camera at the disposal of the networks was upon him. No expression one-tenth so radical has ever been seen or heard by so many Americans.

To produce this scene had taken some delicate maneuvering. Randolph called the march last spring at a moment when the civil rights groups had fallen into a particularly painful season of personal rancor. Randolph is unique because he accepts everyone in a movement whose members do not always accept one another. His first support came from the nonviolent actionists; they hoped for passionate protest. That prospect was Randolph's weapon; the moderates had to come in or be defenseless against embarrassing disorder. Randolph welcomed them not just with benevolence but with genuine gratitude. When President Kennedy expressed his doubts, Randolph answered that some demonstration was unavoidable and that what had to be done was to make it orderly.

It was the best appeal that feeling could make to calculation. The White House knew that the ordinary Negro cherishes the Kennedy brothers and that the larger the assemblage the better disposed it would be not to embarrass them. When the President finally mentioned the march in public, he issued something as close as possible to a social invitation.

No labor leader since John L. Lewis in 1933 has succeeded in employing the President of the United States as an organizer. Even Lewis only sent his organizers about the pits telling the miners that the President wanted them to join the union, and was careful never to tell Mr. Roosevelt about it. Randolph got his President live, whole and direct.

If the march was important, it was because it represented an acceptance of the Negro revolt as part of the American myth, and so an acceptance of the revolutionaries into the American establishment. That acceptance, of course, carries the hope that the Negro revolt will stop where it is. Yet that acceptance is also the most powerful incentive and assurance that the revolt will continue. The children from Wilmington, North Carolina, climbed back on their buses with the shining memory of a moment when they marched with all America—a memory to sustain them when they return to march alone. So it was, too, for all the others who came from Birmingham, Montgomery, Danville, Gadsden and Jackson—places whose very names evoke not only the cause but the way it is being won.

The result of such support—the limits it placed on the spectacle—was illustrated by the experience of John Lewis, chairman of the Student Nonviolent Coordinating Committee. Lewis is only twenty-five; his only credential for being there was combat experience; he has been arrested twenty-two times and beaten half as often. The Student Nonviolent Coordinating Committee is a tiny battalion, its members gray from jail and exhausted from tension. They have the gallant cynicism of troops of the line; they revere Martin Luther King (some of them) as a captain who has faced the dogs with them and they call him with affectionate irreverence, "De Lawd." We could hardly have had this afternoon without them.

Lewis, in their spirit, had prepared a speech full of temerities about how useless the civil rights bill is and what frauds the Democrats and Republicans are. Three of the white speakers told Randolph that they could not appear at a platform where such sedition was pronounced, and John Lewis had to soften his words in deference to elders. Equal rights for the young to say their say may, perhaps, come later.

Yet Lewis' speech, even as laundered, remained discomfiting enough to produce a significant tableau at its end. "My friends," he said, "let us not forget that we are engaged in a significant social revolution. By and large American politics is dominated by politicians who build their careers on immoral compromising and ally themselves with open forums of political, economic and social exploitation." When he had finished, every Negro on the speakers' row pumped his hand and patted his back; and every white one looked out into the distance.

So even in the middle of this ceremony of reconciliation, the void between the Negro American and a white one remained. Or rather, it did and it didn't. At one point, Martin King mentioned with gratitude the great number of white people (about forty thousand to fifty thousand out of an estimated two hundred thousand) who had joined the march. There was little response from the platform—where it must have seemed formal courtesy—but as the sound of those words moved across the great spaces between King and the visitors from the Southern towns, there was the sudden sight and sound of Negroes cheering far away. Nothing all afternoon was quite so moving as the sight of these people, whose trust has been violated so often in the particular, proclaiming it so touchingly intact in the general.

We do not move the Negro often, it would seem, and we do it

only when we are silent and just standing there. On the speakers' stand there was the inevitable Protestant, Catholic and Jew without which no national ceremony can be certified. Is it hopeless to long for a day when the white brother will just once accept the duty to march, and forego the privilege to preach? Dr. Eugene Carson Blake of the National Council of Churches told the audience that the Protestants were coming and "late we come." It was the rarest blessing—an apology. We have begun to stoop a little; and yet it is so hard for us to leave off condescending.

We cannot move the Negro by speaking, because the public white America seems to know no words except the ones worn out from having been so long unmeant. Even if they are meant now, they have been empty too long not to sound empty still; whatever our desires, our language calls up only the memory of the long years when just the same language served only to convey indifference.

Yet the Negro moves us most when he touches our memory, even as we chill him most when we touch his. August 28 was to many whites only a demonstration of power and importance until Mahalia Jackson arose to sing the old song about having been rebuked and scorned and going home. Then King near the end began working as country preachers do, the words for the first time not as to listeners but as to participants, the intimate private conversation of invocation and response. For just those few minutes, we were back where this movement began and has endured older than the language of the society which was taking these pilgrims in, but still fresh where the newer language was threadbare.

The Negro comes from a time the rest of us have forgotten; he seems new and complicated only because he represents something so old and simple. He reminds us that the new, after which we have run so long, was back there all the time. Something new will someday be said, and it will be something permanent, if it starts from such a memory.

Romans

(with James Ridgeway)

12 • 7 • 63

> *"Robert Frost wrote fifty years ago, 'Nothing is true except as a man or men adhere to it—to live for it, to spend themselves on it, to die for it.' We need this spirit even more than money or institutions or agreements."*
>
> —JOHN F. KENNEDY, November 18, 1963

By Saturday night, even the television seemed worn out by attempt and failure and ceased to comment and gave over to a succession of photographs of the columns and the windows and the corners of the White House and of the shadows of the great Lincoln head in Springfield and to a voice reciting "Oh, Captain, My Captain." It is to be, then, the grand style. But the ship has not weathered every storm; Mr. Kennedy is not Abraham Lincoln; not because he is more or less, but because he is a remembered physical presence and Mr. Lincoln an image of the plastic arts. One's own time is personal, not historical. Just how long will it be before many of us will want to read a book about the day Mr. Kennedy was shot?

The news of the President's assassination was given by a taxi driver to three gentlemen as they left a hotel on Arlington Street in Boston. They turned right around and hurried back inside to attend to their investments. Packed with students and businessmen a shuttle plane from Boston to Washington waited for permission to take off when the captain came on the intercom: "Folks, up here on the flight deck we've been listening to the news and the President is dead." There was only time to hear one woman say "How dreadful" before three men went back to discussing plan specifications. A college student reading *Agamemnon* paid no visible attention. One of his notes read, "love-in-hate." The plane took off, the stewardess collected the money and started to serve drinks. Then the captain was back again. They had been listening to more news, that is trying to listen to news because their real job was to hear flight control. There had been a gun battle in Dallas; a patrolman was killed; the police had taken a man in a movie theater. Vice President Johnson was now the President. The talk of business went on through this, and stopped only when the captain again interrupted to say that the new President had been sworn in aboard an aircraft. A few laughed.

They ask too much of us when they ask us to act up to the grand style. We are not an emotionally affluent people. And yet some of us always complained that Mr. Kennedy did not seem quite emotionally committed enough. But now someone remembered with special affection a moment late in the 1960 campaign. Mr. Kennedy was in a motorcade and the Democratic governor who was with him said how wonderful it was to feel the love with which these crowds pressed forward to feel the touch of their candidate. "Oh, dry up," Mr. Kennedy said. It seemed now somehow a special grace in him that he used only the real in emotion and abstained from fabricating the expected. He had too much respect for the grand style to counterfeit it; how much truer to him might we have been if we had come down in scale and if the many of us who must have remembered the lines from Cymbeline had thought them proper to speak:

> *Fear no more the heat of the sun /Nor the furious winter's rages.*
> *Thou thy worldly task hast done /Home art thousand ta'en thy wages.*
> *Golden lads and girls all must /As chimney sweepers come to dust.*

Cymbeline is a Roman play. The Kennedys are a Roman family; America seems only a Roman crowd. For us alone in it, there is only a terrible irritation with God and with self and with every other face that is left.

Friday night caught most of the President's Cabinet away from the city. All that could be collected from his official establishment came to Andrews Air Force base to meet the dead man come back from Dallas.

Everything mechanical intruded as it would intrude all weekend. The lights were vagrant, savage and aimless; the planes came and went on distracting, irrelevant missions. The face of Undersecretary of Commerce Roosevelt seemed the ruin of his father's. Every uncared-for lank of Sen. Dirksen's hair, every fold under every chin, seemed for the moment our own fault.

For we had lost in the instant the hope of beginning again. Reason might argue that the sense of a new start was already gone. The main story in the morning's *Washington Post* had detailed the exculpations of a congressman who had made a 1,000 percent profit from the stock of a company which had enjoyed his good offices with the Internal Revenue Service. The very Senate which dissipated in shock at the news from Texas had just before been waspishly disputing the privileges and emoluments of elective office. For weeks it had been hard to remember anyone in Washington talking about anything except who was getting what from whom. Mr. Kennedy seemed to be wasting in his city and to be nourished only by the great crowds in the countryside. The films from Dallas, painful as they were, reinforced the feeling that he was his old self only away from Washington. It could be argued then that we would see a time when we recognized that all that promise had been an illusion; but you need only look at hope lain dead to know how easy it is to look forward to regret. It had been less than three years since Mr. Kennedy had announced that a new generation was taking up the torch; now old General de Gaulle and old Mr. Mikoyan were coming to see the young man buried.

The great red and white plane of the President of the United States came to Andrews at last bearing all the transition in one horrid, large, economy-size package. There was a portable yellow elevator to bring Mrs. Kennedy and Attorney General Kennedy down with a casket that looked like a ship's chest. Half of Lyndon Johnson could be seen waiting in the open door behind them. Mrs. Kennedy's weeds as a widow had to be what some said was a strawberry and some said was a raspberry-colored campaign suit. Everything mechanical that did not intrude functioned badly; the elevator seemed to stall; Mrs. Kennedy tried a door of the ambulance, which did not work, and the attorney general, with a deliberation unbroken as hers was, found one which did and she was gone at last, the high Roman figure that she would be all weekend.

So Mr. Johnson came on, tall as ever but wearing the glasses which his image of himself has always thought unsuitable to state occasions, emptied by his misfortune of all his vanity, small and large, and of almost everything else. His lips seemed wet, his chin uncertain; there was a fear that he might be a man who would cry in public and who there was enough his better to blame him? He said something into the microphones that was identifiable only as being hoarse, broken and undeservedly apologetic, and then his new household gathered around him. And the eye as cruel to everyone else as the heart was cruel to self, focused and saw only the hearing aid of an undersecretary. The next morning, Mr. Johnson had repaired his interior and left off resenting himself, as all of us had better do if we are to get about our business.

As the people waited the passing of the cortege on Sunday some of them squabbled over who was to stand on the stepladder and shoot the first pictures and at what speed and at what lens opening. A mother trying to tune up a transistor radio said to a pouting child, "I want you to understand one thing. This is very important to me." Amidst the people came a teenager with a portable tape recorder. He stuck out a microphone and said, "Sir, on this day of national mourning how do you feel?" Coming away from the Capitol after viewing the bier, a man with a camera slung over his head said to another man with a camera, "Did you get any good pictures?"

One sat in the Senate press room away from the rotunda on Sunday night and read a wire service report on the tributes paid to the patriotism of Jack Ruby by the master of ceremonies of Mr. Ruby's strip parlor. There was a story about the good fortune of the Dallas citizen who had been in at the death with his movie camera and had sold the films to Life for $40,000. The National Football League had played its full Sunday schedule; every seat in Yankee Stadium was filled with mourners. One thought with respect—it was not possible to be grateful to anyone—of Randall Jarrell for having known enough soon enough to have written a book and called it *A Sad Heart at the Supermarket.*

Then a man spoke up and said:

"She came in with the children this afternoon when the rotunda was first opened and she was standing and waiting and the kid looked up at the dome and began to walk around, and she bent over and touched him and he looked up and she straightened her shoulders to show him how to stand at attention, and he did it for about ten seconds. You know, I wish it was a dynasty and the kid was taking over and she was the regent."

Monday was sunny and for those to whom life is a picture, the Capitol was the best and largest color television screen anyone could hope for. A boy sat on his father's shoulders and his father told him to use the number one setting. The band began "Hail to the Chief," the boy raised his camera and instructed his father not to move. Behind them a woman put a child on her shoulders; the child must have tickled her because she kept laughing, comfortably, and this pleasant distraction continued until the coffin could be detected from its flag to be coming out and she left off and pointed her finger and said with undiminished gaiety, "See, there he is." One left and walked past a girl clutching a paperback. Then suddenly there was one man kneeling with his hands over his eyes and his hat on the sidewalk, and it was impossible not to stop and put a hand upon his shoulder and not to begin to hope that a chain might be put together again.

In front of St. Matthew's the crowd was quieter.

The bands and the soldiers went by, the pipers last; and then, like thunder, there was Mrs. Kennedy with the senator on one side and the attorney general on the other and ramrods up their spines. And behind them, the powers and potentates of the earth; the Kennedys were marching with all of Madame Tussaud's in their train, as though Charles de Gaulle had been created a Marshal of France and Haile Selassie I the Lion of Judah only for this last concentrated moment. The powers and potentates waited; Mrs. Kennedy, for the moment made flesh again, gathered her children. Cardinal Cushing came down, under his miter, looking, to his credit, a trifle irritated with God; we could be grateful for the Catholics and grateful to them for providing one cardinal who looked like a Prince of the Church.

And the children in their sunny pale blue coats began walking with their mother up the stairs, the little boy stumbling only at the vestibule and then they were gone. We had lived awhile with old Romans; now the doors were closing and we must make do with ourselves.

The Champ and the Chump

3·7·64

Just before the bell for the seventh round, Cassius Clay got up to go about his job. Suddenly, he thrust his arms straight up in the air in the signal with which boxers are accustomed to treat victory and you laughed at his arrogance. No man could have seen Clay that morning at the weigh-in and believed that he could stay on his feet three minutes that night. He had come in pounding the cane Malcolm X had given him for spiritual support, chanting "I am the greatest, I am the champ, he is a chump." Ray Robinson, that picture of grace who is Clay's ideal as a fighter, pushed him against the wall and tried to calm him, and this hysterical child turned and shouted at him, "I am a great *performer*, I am a great *performer*."

Suddenly almost everyone in the room hated Cassius Clay. Sonny Liston just looked at him. Liston used to be a hoodlum; now he was our cop; he was the big Negro we pay to keep sassy Negroes in line and he was just waiting until his boss told him it was time to throw this kid out.

British journalists who were present remembered with comfort how helpful beaters like Liston had been to Sanders of the River; Northern Italian journalists were comforted to see on Liston's face the look that mafiosi use to control peasants in Sicily; promoters and fight managers saw in Clay one of their animals utterly out of control and were glad to know that soon he would be not just back in line but out of the business. There were two Catholic priests in attendance whose vocation it is to teach Sonny Liston the values of organized Christianity, and one said to the other: "Do you see Sonny's face? You know what he's going to do to this fellow."

The great legends of boxing are of managers like Jack Hurley, who had taken incompetent fighters and just by shouting their merits, against all reason built them up for one big payday at which they disgraced themselves and were never heard from again. Clay had created himself the way Hurley created his paper tigers. His most conspicuous public appearance in the week before he was to fight had been a press conference with the Beatles. They were all very much alike—sweet and gay. He was an amateur Olympic champion who had fought twenty professional fights, some of them unimpressive; and he had clowned and blustered about how great he was until he earned his chance from a Liston who, if he could not respect him as an opponent, could recognize him as a propagandist skilled enough to fool the public. A reporter had asked Liston if he thought the seven-to-one odds against Clay were too long, and he answered: "I don't know. I'm not a bookmaker. I'm a fighter." But there was no hope Clay could win; there was barely the hope that he could go like a gentleman. Even Norman Mailer settled in this case for organized society. Suppose Clay won the heavyweight championship, he asked; it would mean that every loudmouth on a street corner could swagger and be believed. But if he lay down the first time Liston hit him, he would be a joke and a shame all his life. He carried, by every evidence unfit, the dignity of every adolescent with him. To an adult a million dollars may be worth the endurance of being clubbed by Sonny Liston; but nothing could pay an adolescent for just being picked up by the bouncer and thrown out.

On the night, Clay was late getting to the dressing room and he came to stand in back of the arena to watch his younger brother fight one of the preliminaries. He spoke no word and seemed to look, if those blank eyes could be said to look, not at the fighters but at the lights above them. There was a sudden horrid notion that just before the main event, when the distinguished visitors were announced, Cassius Clay in his dinner jacket might bounce into the ring, shout one more time that he was the greatest, and go down the steps and out of the arena and out of the sight of man forever. Bystanders yelled insults at him; his handlers pushed him toward his dressing room, stiff, his steps hesitant. One had thought him hysterical in the morning; now one thought him catatonic.

He came into the ring long before Liston and danced with the mechanical melancholy of a marathon dancer; it was hard to believe that he had slept in forty-eight hours. Liston came in; they met in the ring center with Clay looking over the head of that brooding presence; then Clay went back and put in his mouthpiece clumsily like an amateur and shadowboxed like a man before a mirror and turned around, still catatonic and the bell rang and Cassius Clay went forward to meet the toughest man alive. He fought the first round as though without plan, running and slipping and sneaking punches, like someone killing time in a poolroom. But it was his rhythm and not Liston's; second by slow second, he was taking away the big bouncer's dignity. Once Liston had him close to the ropes—where fighters kill boxers—and Clay, very slowly, slipped sideways from a left hook and under the right and away, just grazing the ropes all in one motion, and cut Liston in the eye. For the first time there was the suspicion that he might know something about the trade.

Clay was a little ahead when they stopped it. Liston had seemed about to fall on him once; Clay was caught in a corner early in the fifth and worked over with the kind of sullen viciousness one cannot imagine a fighter sustaining more than four or five times in one night. He seemed to be hurt and walked back, being stalked, and offering only a left hand listlessly and unimpressively extended in Liston's face. We thought that he was done and asking for mercy, and then that he was tapping Liston to ask him to quiet down a moment and give the greatest a chance to speak, and then we saw that Clay's legs were as close together as they had been before the round started and that he was unhurt and Liston just wasn't coming to him. It ended there, of course, although we did not know it.

"I told ye'," Cassius Clay cried to all of us who had laughed at him. "I told ye'. I just played with him. I whipped him so bad and wasn't that good. And look at me: I'm still pretty."

An hour later he came out dressed; a friend stopped him and the heavyweight champion of the world smiled and said he would be available in the morning. His eyes were wise and canny, like Ray Robinson's.

The Meritocracy of Labor

2 • 2 • 65

The most public life Ernest Green is ever likely to know is now not quite seven years back in his past. He is only twenty-three now. Ernest Green was the first Negro to be graduated from Central High School in Little Rock, Arkansas. He was for a while a subject for all the news photos, a thin child with glasses walking through the crowds in the fall of 1957, and then still a thin child in a black robe with his classmates in the spring of 1958, a graduate, thanks to the protection of federal troops.

He was one of 601 seniors at Central High School. Just fourteen of them wrote their good wishes in his class yearbook.

"I really admire you, Ernest," the secretary of Central High's student government wrote under her picture. "I doubt if I could have done half so much if our positions were reversed. May you achieve all your goals and they be the best."

The fifties focused on the special Negro, and his story was always inspiriting. Now the sixties are confronted with the ordinary Negro and he has almost no story at all.

Ernest Green departed the South to complete his education at Michigan State University; and few of the strangers who saw him in his singular high school year can have thought much about him since. The other day I went to Brooklyn, from some small curiosity about the ordinary Negro, and came upon Ernest Green. He has found his goal in the Bedford-Stuyvesant area, which is Brooklyn's Harlem. He spends his days trying to find jobs for young Negroes as plumbers, electricians and carpenters.

It would be too much to say that it is as hard for an ordinary young Negro in New York to be taken on as an apprentice in a skilled trade as it is for an extraordinary young Negro to be admitted to a Southern university. But it would not be a great deal too much to say.

In 1958, the year of Ernest Green's high school graduation, the New York State Commission Against Discrimination made an ethnic survey of the apprentices in the state's construction industry. Apprentice training is the only means of entry into those building crafts which have always been the best general opportunity for comfort and pride available to the young whose education ends with high school. In 1958, the State Commission Against Discrimination estimated that perhaps 2 percent of New York's fifteen thousand construction apprentices in training were Negroes.

That estimate may have been generous. We have lived since through seven years of innumerable protest demonstrations by Negroes and frequent if seldom effectual responses in plea and intervention by government. And after all these efforts at remonstrance and conciliation, no responsible agency can yet assert that more than 12 percent of the construction apprentices now in training are Negroes.

The skilled-job market has, of course, always been controlled by a company of trade unions which have been the only medieval institutions in the city, being hierarchic, feudal and frequently consanguine. Apprentices, more often than not, have been connected by blood or friendship with full members of these guilds. The tradition of the job as property to be bequeathed or given away has done as much to bar the Negro as any lively prejudice against his color. There were three thousand union plumbers in Brooklyn a year ago last August; nine of them were Negroes, none of whom held the "A" membership card and earned the $4.10 an hour wage that rewards survivors of the apprenticeship stage.

Last spring the State Commission for Human Rights found Local 28 of the Sheet Metal Workers Union guilty of discriminating against Negro applicants. Local 28 had and has 3,300 members, none of whom was or is a Negro. Some twenty-six of the thirty applicants accepted for the local's apprenticeship program in July 1963 were related to union members. A journeyman fitting the standards of this guild earns up to $6.15 an hour. Under pressure of court orders, Local 28 has agreed to give up selecting its apprentices by family bond and to subject all applicants to an aptitude test supervised by New York University next month.

A construction worker's certificate as a skilled craftsman may at last be coming to depend less on favor and more on objective standards. Last year, the Taconic Foundation made a grant to the Workers Defense League to seek out young Negroes to take these tests. The League set up its apprenticeship program headquarters in the most impressive building on its shabby block on Fulton Street. Ray Murphy, holder of the master's degree in clinical psychology, which is so much easier for a Negro than a plumbers union work permit, is its director and Ernest Green is his assistant.

They have perhaps 150 young Negroes on their rolls as prospective applicants to any apprenticeship class a union opens up. None of them can remember schools remotely as good as Central High in Little Rock. They had no chance against the barriers of custom; and now they do not have a greatly improved chance under the test of merit.

Their common problem is illustrated in the case of Arthur Harris, nineteen, a graduate of Thomas Edison Vocational High School in Queens, where he was selected above all his fellow seniors as laureate in the plumbing award of the ladies auxiliary of the Master Plumbers Association. In April 1964, Arthur Harris tried to follow the bent indicated for the best plumber in his class by applying to the apprenticeship training program sponsored by Brooklyn Plumbers Local Number One. Local One did not answer his letter; Ray Murphy intervened and in October the education committee of Local One agreed to let Arthur Harris take its aptitude examination.

The new merit system for neophyte plumbers administered by New York University is not one of rigid intellectual standards. An applicant, to be eligible for apprentice training, need only show himself above the level of the bottom quarter of the average American high school senior class. Arthur Harris could, then, have passed with a score of 100 out of a possible 400. He scored a 63; and, at that, may have done no worse than a majority of the other applicants, all of them white graduates of New York City schools. No more than twenty of the sixty testees seem to have achieved what is no more than a 25 percent passing grade.

Arthur Harris scored 5 out of a possible 100 in the category of "mental alertness"; 7 out of a possible 100 in mechanical reasoning; and 5 out of a possible 100 in numerical ability.

Ray Murphy guesses that a young man who had mastered the elements of the ninth grade would pass this test. There can be no sensible quarrel with the honesty of the academicians who conducted it. We can only conclude then that the best prospective plumber in a New York City vocational school had been equipped by his teachers to rank less than a point above the lowest 5 percent of American high school graduates in alertness, mechanical capacity and skill with numbers.

Arthur Harris has dropped from sight since this disaster; Ernest Green is afraid that he has given up. Most of the young Negroes who sit in Bedford-Stuyvesant are like Arthur Harris and other graduates of vocational high schools, which means that they belong to a category of persons trained for no vocation at all.

We can assume, however, that if the Taconic Foundation and Ray Murphy and Ernest Green are patient enough, the building trades unions will have to yield their privileges and accept their apprentices on objective merit. But even that surrender is by no means imminent; most of Ray Murphy's day is spent in the continual interventions necessary to persuade or press union officials to give his charges a chance just to take their tests.

There is the case of Emmett Washington, a member of the maintenance division of Local Three of the International Brotherhood of Electrical Workers. In June of 1964, Local Three sent out letters to its members asking if they had any sons who might like to be apprentices to its construction division. Emmett Washington wrote back that he had no son but that he himself was a member of the union still young enough to be an apprentice. He got no answer; Murphy inquired further on his behalf and was told that the local had decided not to hold a class this year.

"I took one kid down to Local Two of the plumbers union to see a man named Kearns who is secretary of their joint apprenticeship committee," Murphy said. "When we got there Kearns came out and said that Kearns wasn't in. We had to go back again before he'd give him an application. I'm still not sure when he will take a test.

"I took two kids to Local 40 of the ironworkers last October and they told us they weren't interviewing applicants unless they were accompanied by two sponsors who were union members. They had promised two years ago that they would no longer require sponsors. I got in touch with the secretary-treasurer and reminded him of some of these things and he called back to say that it had all been a mistake and we should apply again.

"We went back down and while we were waiting, one of the white applicants said we could go in first because his sponsors hadn't gotten there yet. Anyway, we were finally able to make an application ten days ago."

Still, the tests are coming; the problems that cannot be righted by any pressure at Murphy's command still have much to do with the unreadiness of the tested. When we think of the ordinary Negro, we recognize that the New York school system has settled into a mold as segregated in class as anything we have deplored in European education. The South, of course, traditionally drew the distinction of race; the academic public high school was for white children; the industrial or vocational school was for Negroes. New York has unconsciously drifted into a system which, in essentials, ends with the same result.

A child's pattern is set when he is thirteen and ready to enter the complex of city high schools. He may, if he can pass its tests, enter an academic high school and hope to go on to a municipal college, where the tuition is still free and open to any high school graduate with an average of 85 in his academic subjects. Short of that, he can try for a technical high school, where the academic standards are also excluding and where he can learn a trade. Failing all tests, there is no place for him except the vocational school that teaches almost nothing and serves no purpose beyond the requirements of compulsory school education.

On the bulletin board in Ernest Green's office, there is a clipping from *The New York Times* telling the story of Michael Stewart, the first Negro apprentice to be accepted by Local 40 of the ironworkers union. "'His father, Malcolm Stewart, writes technical manuals for Sperry Rand,'" Ernest Green read from the *Times*. "Now there's a working-class background."

Sheet Metal Workers Local 28 sent out word last week that on February 13, it would conduct its objective test for apprentice applicants as prescribed by court order. Murphy and Green think they might have as many as sixty candidates; Dr. Kenneth Clark has agreed to hold classes for them at the Northside Center for Child Development and, in the little time remaining, do whatever private tutoring can to repair the damage public education has done.

"You know, five of our kids did pass the electricians' apprenticeship tests on Long Island," Ernest Green said. "Of course, three of them were college students. They were overqualified. Maybe I'll take the sheet metal test myself."

He is the graduate of a Southern high school and a Midwestern university. It does not seem that attainments significantly less impressive will soon give a Negro a chance to work at a skilled trade in New York.

Robert George Thompson: American

1 • 26 • 66

"The cremated remains of Robert George Thompson will not be interred in Arlington Cemetery."
—The Department of Defense, January 27, 1966

Buna was a long time ago. It had become a part of history three months after the battle for it was over; it was a rest area by the spring of 1943; and those who had been there before you were proud because they had seen the last time that the Aussies had charged with the bayonet in their shined shoes and because you never could.

Buna was the Aussies' last great battle in World War II and it was the Americans' first in New Guinea. The Aussies had begun it marching over the Kokoda Trail from Port Moresby and coming down in parade formation to the coast, singing "Waltzing Matilda," the legend insisted, until the Japanese began to fire. The 127th Infantry Regiment of our great 32nd Division came with them; Robert George Thompson was a staff sergeant in Company C of its 1st Battalion.

And there at the Monombi River, as his company commander later put it, Robert Thompson, "voluntarily led a patrol of five men in a successful attack and the establishment of a bridgehead . . . in broad daylight against a heavily fortified position, this patrol swam a heavily swollen and rapidly flowing river. ... Clad only in shorts and with utter disregard for his own safety, Sgt. Thompson not only directed the crossing of his platoon but led them in a successful attack against two dominating pillboxes, thereby securing a small bridgehead."

These five soldiers held that patch of ground all day, and, when it was over, what they had done was thought to be one of the balances of the battle for Buna. Robert Thompson was awarded the Distinguished Service Cross and recommended for promotion to captain. A United Press correspondent asked who he was; and he smiled in the shy way he would never lose and answered, "Maybe you won't believe me, but I was a Young Communist League organizer in Ohio." He was sick by then and came home very soon with tuberculosis and malaria.

He stayed in the Communist party all his life. He paid more for that than for any sin there may be in that choice; all in all, he spent five years in prison; once, while he was waiting in the chow line in the West Street jail, an anti-Communist hit him over the head with a hammer, and he lived on a very narrow edge ever after. When he died last spring, he was only fifty and was national secretary of the American Communist party.

This was a soldier. A soldier is not merely a man with a gun; he is a man who follows his commitments with that utter disregard for his personal safety which is the memory enshrined in Robert Thompson's citation. If he is in a war, he is in the infantry; if he is against a war, he is in the resistance. His choices are never for comfort; to live is for him to be a target.

It is not curious but natural that, dying, Robert Thompson should have wanted to be buried, not as the exile that civilians had tried to make him, but together with other soldiers in Arlington National Cemetery.

The Army could think of no way to deny his widow his wish; and his ashes were delivered the other day to Arlington for a military interment next Tuesday. The protests began to come in from the places from which protests always come, and the Army bucked the problem to the Justice Department, which came through yesterday with a finding that the Army did not have to bury Robert Thompson if it would be inconvenient.

And so an American who was brave has been judged and disposed of by Americans who are cowards of the least excusable sort, cowards who have very little to fear. Yesterday, the Army called Robert Thompson's widow and said that it would send his ashes wherever she wished.

Wherever those ashes go, the glory of America goes with them. They belong to every soldier. They are all that remains of that afternoon at Buna, the guns in front and the vulnerable, half-naked body swimming to engage them. Those ashes had done everything for us but disgrace us; and now, by our treatment of them, we have disgraced ourselves.

Four Days in Mississippi

7·1·66

Thursday, Canton.

From a distance there had been the prejudice that this affair was of no importance; on the scene there was only the conviction.

Just 143 of these wanderers were still afoot on the road between Benton and Canton when one found them in the morning. At their front walked Martin Luther King and Stokely Carmichael of the Student Nonviolent Coordinating Committee, an NBC announcer between them, to whom they delivered variant points of view on black power.

It rained, off and on, in Canton that afternoon and Stokely Carmichael ran among the crowds of local Negroes on the sidewalks crying out "Black Power," "Black Power"; they were not looking at him.

There was one of those emergencies which the movement, because it has lost the public's attention, seemed now to need to invent; the County of Madison had refused the marchers permission to erect their tents on the grounds of the Negro school. They went to the courthouse first and sang their songs and, under the delusion of that moment without inhibition by the establishment, the local Negroes joined the march to the school grounds to put up the tents.

Suddenly there were no more state policemen in sight. Stokely Carmichael and Martin Luther King stood on the moving truck which carried the tents of the marchers and Stokely Carmichael put his long arm in the air and said he understood that the troopers thought they could come and take the school. "Let us show them," he said, "that all the scared niggers are dead."

Then the eye wandered and one understood where the state police had gone; they were lined up fifty yards away in their gas masks, their carbines at the ready. Someone counted sixty of them. "This," said Stokely Carmichael, "is when we separate the men from the mice." And then there fell upon the Madison County Negroes the silence born of an understanding how brief had been their moment of mockery and affirmation, and they began to drift away from the truck. The marchers were alone again; they started to put up their tents.

The troopers came down and stood waiting until as much of the game as wished came down into their hunting preserve. And then the march's crew raised their arms and held the tent edges aloft and the troopers threw their gas canisters. The wind was perfect for the attack. Men lay down in the smoke and it blew through them sluggishly. Then men and girls began to run. "Don't stop them. Leave them an escape route," a troop commander called. And, behind, with the cold malice of a man who has hated them and their company for three weeks, a trooper threw a canister at each coughing beaten figure as it passed.

There were perhaps a dozen resisters left to be cleared. Three troopers had a youth with a football sweater on the ground and they were kicking him into the road. One understood then that there had been orders for no arrests, just a beating from the field.

"Get up," a trooper said to the youth he was kicking. The voice came hollow and impersonal through the gas mask; the reality of power had no face except the long snout and the plastic eyes. At the other end of the ground, two troopers had a white man down; one of them hit him three times in the face with the butt of his carbine; one could hear the bolt bounce and the wood crack. He rose at last outside on the road, one side of his face pushed in and the other swollen out, and went away—on his back a patch with the inking "Medical Assistant."

The Attorney General of the United States said late at night that he was confident that law and order were being maintained. The Governor of Mississippi announced that the marchers had attacked his state police. None of the Attorney General's representatives on the spot seemed in a position to say what every witness knew, that this statement was a lie. It is, of course, law and order when everyone who hits anyone else is wearing a uniform.

Friday, Philadelphia

The marchers had almost been driven from Philadelphia here, four days ago; according to their nature and their commitment, they had to return today.

The coming back to Neshoba County began with the sight of those persons who had never left it, of the cars with the rebel flags around the courthouse, and of the Baptist church on the hill above Philadelphia, where perhaps two hundred of the county's Negroes sat and waited for what they knew they would have to endure, at worst to be hit, at best to be scorned. They sang a long time about how they were ready to do what the spirit says they have to do. It was more a prayer than a song: their leader made no effort to increase their beat; they knew and yet they were ready and they had earned the right to be a little sad about the moment before them. Then the marchers came out of their cars and the beat increased. It is the point of their mission to tell the county Negroes that they have nothing to be afraid of; that is, of course, not true, but it is in the small lies to self that real self-respect begins. The marchers have earned their right, too.

The march back was over Negro gravel and came at last to white pavements and its course was being directed by the sheriff's deputy, Cecil Price, charged by the federal government with having conspired to abridge the civil rights of James Chaney, Mickey Schwerner and Andrew Goodman by assisting in their murder and burial in a red river bank.

In the square, the marchers lined up faithful to their agreement to keep off the courthouse lawn, separated from those who hate them by troopers who also hate them and by two thin pieces of string and perhaps twenty feet of roadway on each side. The Rev. Clinton Collier, leader of the Neshoba County Freedom Democratic Party, stood on the steps and, as he began to speak, the howls of the spectators began and a few bottles were thrown, harmlessly. It was the first time in Clinton Collier's life—and the next could hardly be close—that he could speak his mind to all of Neshoba County.

He used it in a way that ought to have made everyone present wonder how he would use his own one chance. He had known more comfortable places, he said. "But I don't much care as long as I can be here and declare our rightful place in Neshoba County. ... We have been dictated to long enough. You can tell about these people who are yelling at us because, if they had decent things to do, they would be home tending to their own business. We are here to help this county. And we will come back until we can declare that every bit of a man everywhere in the world is like everyone else."

Oddly enough, the horrible crowd around the courthouse was listening; it heard every sentence through and then spat it out of its mind with a howl of hatred. It went on like that all through this special half hour of these county Negroes until King's turn came and the crowd spat out each of his sentences with special disgust until he arrived at his peroration: "We're gonna win because, though the arc of the moral universe is immense, it bends towards justice. We're gonna win because there standeth God in the shadows protecting his children." Then suddenly, almost harsh: "We're gonna win because the Bible is right when it says, 'You shall reap what you sow.'"

And he stopped and just as suddenly there was silence all about. It lasted just long enough for nothing to be heard until the beginning of the applause of the marchers.

So this whole day was perhaps half a second when Martin Luther King enforced upon us the reflection that what you sow you shall reap, and the ten seconds when a Negro preacher could look upon white people and tell them that, if they had decent things to do, they'd mind their own business.

Sunday, Jackson.

And now the poor 143 of Thursday come down from Tougaloo for the last eight miles, 8,000 by now and another 6,000 waiting to join them at points along the way and all singing about the light of freedom.

The march had been slow on Thursday from the mere need to endure. It was as slow now from the congestion of triumphant wake and when it came, after an eternity, to the state capital, the few white teenagers who had come to scoff were quite invisible behind the incredible file of black faces. There seemed, indeed, more white marchers than there were white protesters.

The day after James Meredith had been shot, someone said, the march had begun not just without money but without the promise even of food. "And so we sent word down the road that these are black folk and they are coming down the line and, where we went, you were there to feed us." And he looked at all these people he had never known before and said, "It was what you did, what you did."

So these men, Meredith, King and Carmichael, have done all the things they have done because they have refused to accept what everyone else knows to be the reality of existence. Now they had been rescued by the poor Negroes who had refused to accept the harshest reality in their country. No one thanked anyone else. Thanks are for distinguished visitors. Members of families do not owe it to one another.

III

DISILLUSION, REVISION, COMEDY

Defendant Kempton, also a delegate, joined the march near Grant Park and continued on to 18th and Michigan. He too was told that if he went south of the "line" he would be arrested. He walked through the line and was placed under arrest.

—*City of Chicago v. Weiss*, 1972

K. Marx: Reporter

6 • 15 • 67

Dr. Charles Blitzer's Introduction to *The American Journalism of Marx and Engels*, a selection of thirty-three of the more than five hundred dispatches which Marx and Engels composed for Greeley and Dana's *New-York Daily Tribune*, is so exemplary a work of information without intrusion that it is embarrassing to begin by finding fault with its conclusion. If Marx seems "less striking and original today" than he must have seemed in the mid-nineteenth century, this is because, Dr. Blitzer says,

> the general approach to political history and analysis that he invented has been almost universally adopted in our time. If a preoccupation with the social and economic background of politics, and a determination to uncover the real motives that lie behind the words of politicians and governments are the hallmarks of modern political journalism, then Karl Marx may properly be said to be its father.

But these dispatches are striking and original, it seems to me, just because they have so little to do with most of the journalism I read or, for that matter, construct myself. The best of Marx's descendants are no closer to him than collateral. There is a puzzle here rather like that which arises when one confronts the early Carlyle: One sees at once that here is the way to get at the thing, and wonders why, with the sign painted this plain, the road has been so seldom followed.

That Greeley and Dana exploited Marx (and, without knowing it, Engels) is a piece of anecdote so familiar that President Kennedy sought to amuse the American Newspaper Publishers Association with the notion that the revolutionary specter might never have arisen had the *Tribune* not beggared its correspondents. Marx's contempt for Greeley had its side of self-disgust for having fallen so low in trade: "grinding bones and making soup of them like the paupers in a workhouse." "Mere pot boiling," Engels said long afterward. "It doesn't matter if they are never read again." Indeed Marx and Engels were not the unconscious future of daily journalism. They are only a sport in its past; and the conditions which have permitted their interlude were passing even while they grumbled at how trivial was the work which, as serious men, they never succeeded in trivializing. Greeley had his side; he was also cutting his own wage and Dana's, because early in the 1850s there had begun the process by which the *Times* slowly ground down the *Tribune*. "The *Times* was crowding us too hard . . ." Greeley wrote in 1852. "It is conducted with the most policy and the least principle of any paper ever started. It is ever watching for the popular side of any question that turns up, and has made lots of friends by ultra abuse of Abolitionists, Women's Rights, Spirit Rappers, etc., which I cannot do. Besides it has had the most room for reading matter the past winter . . ." That great instrument of collectivist progress, the journalism of accommodation had arrived.

"I have written nothing for Dana because I've not had the money to buy newspapers," Marx wrote Engels that same year. That remark is instructive, not for what it says about Marx's poverty but for what it tells us about his method. He was the journalist of the most despised credentials, the one who does not have access. Circumstance condemned him, of course, to be an outsider; but one comes to doubt that easier circumstance would have altered the method. Marx seems to have been incurious even about what was convenient to hand.

Did he ever visit the Crystal Palace? If he did, there is no evidence that this visual experience worked in any way upon his imagination. The most "unabashed hymn to industrial progress under capitalism" George Lichtheim has found in Marx and Engels is their vivid conjuration of the immense shift that would come in the locus and proportion of commercial power with the discovery of gold at Sutter's Mill.

Marx had no use for the tactile and no infirmity of distraction by it. At the center of his imagination was the document from whose pages the historical moment jumped only for him. The successive lodgings in Soho, the British Museum, and Hampstead Heath are the only London places where Mehring sets him. It cannot be argued that direct observation would have been of no use to him whatever. If *The Eighteenth Brumaire* remains on a plane above even the best of this work, the difference, along with its higher passion, must be his direct experience with its events; he was acquainted with some of its personages and had at least seen many of the others. Even so, intimacy could never have been so important as the method itself. *The Eighteenth Brumaire* might be just as unique a piece of historical specification if Marx had got it up from nothing except the files of the *Moniteur*. The problem with any such surmise is that the *Moniteur*, superior though it might otherwise be to the run of the Parisian press, was inadequately stocked with the raw material of fact upon which the historical imagination depends for stimulus. A journalist whose needs and disposition confined him to the study of paper could hardly have worked, however uncommon his genius, anywhere except in the London of the 1850s. Periodicals embodying a special national idiocy can be found anywhere of course; but the British had those and something more. Their journalism was free and lively enough to provide a rich ration of revelatory anecdote. And what was more consequential, the British were the only social statisticians in Europe, which meant that they counted their sins along with everything else; Great Britain was the only European nation that bothered to compute its deaths during the 1848 epidemic. This material, primitive as it was, was all Marx needed; what is embarrassing, one hundred years and megatons of documentation later, is how much more he did with such treasures then than our journalism does now.

There were no limits of time and distance to the range of his mind. The House of Commons debates the British rule of India, "in the usual dull manner," and Marx is off on an examination of the question, impossible of course without a long consideration of the origins and the destruction of the Indian village system. The Duchess of Sutherland attacks slavery in America; and Marx notes the event as a definition of the "class of British philanthropy which chooses its subjects as far distant from home as possible and rather on that than on this side of the ocean." The definition would not, of course, be complete without a full account of the rapacities of the Staffords in Scotland since the end of the seventeenth century.

He notices points that appear to have escaped all public debaters, whatever their side; he even wonders—as no mere ideologue could have—whether India has not cost Britain more than it has been worth to her. Most of all, he is unchained from any notion of fixed place; he sits in his imagination wherever it would be most illuminating to sit. When he writes of the opium war, it is as though he were Chinese watching the barbarian ships come up the river; when he unearths the bluebook that describes revenue methods in India, he is the Brahman being tortured for his taxes. Sympathy does not take him there; sympathy was not one of Marx's weaknesses; he is simply impelled to find the seat that affords the clearest point of view.

There are none of the rewards of access in these dispatches. They are faintly suggested only by Engels in his sketch of Lord John Russell, where there is some of the small change of gossip we have got used to in journalism. But a man who rode the hunts might have picked that up, from the tone horsemen have always used about any Bedford, whether he was Tory, Whig or philosopher. Engels does Palmerston from Hansard and the Foreign Office blue books, the documents in this case being quite enough even for lesser men. For Palmerston is one of those parliamentary men who leap up at us, dancing and dodging, from the official page:

> If not a good statesman of all work, he is a good actor of all work. He succeeds in the comic as in the heroic, in pathos as in familiarity, in tragedy as in farce, although the latter may be more congenial to his feelings. . . . Being an exceedingly happy joker, he ingratiates himself with everybody. Never losing his temper, he imposes on passionate antagonists. If unable to master a subject, he knows how to play with it.

Of all the illusions we bring young to journalism, the one most useful to lose is the illusion of access to sources. To take two cases, I. F. Stone gets along splendidly by avoiding it, and Walter Lippmann gets on no less splendidly by having it and throwing it away before settling down to make up his mind. Persons privy to events either do not know what is important about them or, when they do, generally lie, as even Lincoln lied to Greeley for purposes of seduction. Marx had neither temptation nor opportunity of access; even so, his judgment again and again fits very closely the private observations of those persons safe inside the closed society that he speculated upon from across the moat.

By 1852, he had barely learned enough English to do the *Tribune* chores, which Engels had, until then, been composing under his name; yet he was already able to dismiss that summer's parliamentary elections:

> The bribery and intimidation practiced by the Tories were, then, merely violent experiments for bringing back to life dying electoral bodies which have been incapable of production, and which can no longer achieve decisive electoral results and really national Parliaments. And the results? The old Parliament was dissolved, because at the end it had dissolved into sections which brought each other to a complete standstill. The new Parliament began where the old one ended; it is paralytic from the hour of its birth.

In that same month, James Graham was writing Gladstone: "It will be an impossible Parliament. Parties will be found too nicely balanced to render a new line of policy practicable without a fresh appeal to the electors." In 1855, even Disraeli, in a letter to a friend, embroidered for Palmerston a metaphor very like Engels', seeing the Prime Minister designate as "utterly exhausted and now an old pantaloon, very deaf, very blind and with false teeth, which would fall out of his mouth when speaking, if he did not hesitate so in his talk."

In Marx's journalism, then, we read dispatches which come as close as contemporary publication ever could to the journals the shrewder members of a ruling caste keep for themselves and the letters they write their friends. There the Outsider meets the Insider: Marx makes himself in his own work the embodiment of the Hegelian principle of the contact of extremes.* His intimacy with persons never seen extends as easily to ground never walked upon. When Marx deals with the Indian village system, there is the impression—he was not above cultivating it—that we look upon the distillation of long years of experience in the East set down by a man whose command of every possible detail of the picturesque is controlled by his determination not to let it distract our attention from his hypothesis. Yet all of it is the work of the historical imagination; it is difficult to think of anyone who approached its achievement except the Burke of Macaulay's grand compliment:

> His knowledge of India was such as few, even of those Europeans who have passed many years in that country, have attained, and such as certainly was never attained by any public man who had not quitted Europe. He had studied the history, the laws, the usages of the East with an industry such as is seldom found united to so much genius and so much sensibility. Others have perhaps been equally laborious, and have collected an equal mass of materials. But the manner in which Burke brought his higher powers of intellect to work on statements of facts, and on tables of figures, was peculiar to himself. In every part of those huge bales of Indian information which repelled almost all other readers, his mind, at once philosophical and poetical, found something to instruct or to delight. His reason analyzed and digested these vast and shapeless masses: his imagination animated and colored them. . . . He had in the highest degree that noble faculty whereby man is able to live in the past and in the future, in the distant and in the unreal. . . .

---

* "A most profound yet fantastic speculator on the principles which govern the movements of humanity" Marx begins his dispatch of June 14, 1853. "[Hegel] was wont to extol as one of the ruling secrets of nature what he called the law of contact of extremes. The homely proverb that 'extremes meet' was, in his view, a grand and potent truth in every sphere of life, an axiom with which the philosopher could as little dispense as the astronomer with the laws of Kepler or the great discovery of Newton."

But, aesthetic homage aside, these dispatches deserve that special praise reserved for works whose rediscovery makes us doubt every succeeding work that has neglected them. After Marx and Engels, even such an excellent model of the energetic and the curious as Asa Briggs seems disturbingly insular. I do not mean just that Briggs is philistine; Marx was pretty philistine himself. It was nearly impossible for a Victorian not to be, and it probably remains unavoidable when one has been long engaged with Victorian studies. But these occasional pieces by Marx and Engels leave you with the feeling that all general histories of the 1850s are incomplete, an impression which makes dubious Dr. Blitzer's assertion that the Marxist attack has been almost universally adopted in our time. For there is a sense that Marx's method is now never put to more than half its use: that Briggs understood the materialism without appreciating the dialectic; and that G. M. Young appreciated the dialectic without understanding the materialism; and that both travel Macauley's upward road past setbacks overcome and in progress ever ascending.

To read Marx is to commence to suspect that a great deal of what was to happen to Great Britain was determined by the forces which developed the nineteenth century's solutions, and thereby fixed their limitations. It has become, for example, almost automatic for even the soberest historians of the early Victorian period, when they come to the Ten Hours Act, to be carried away by the spectacle of an aroused national conscience. But Marx noticed even then how contained and confined that conscience has always been: The Established Church, having watched the Enclosures without protest, was suddenly aroused at the sufferings of the victims in the cities. The difference in response had an obvious root for Marx: The Church got its living from the landlords; the mills were owned by Dissenters.

We have grown used to dismissing the Marxist assessment of motive as simpleminded: Still, if this shot were wide of the mark, would there have been as much cant in the Victorian conscience as there was, could there indeed have been that indifference to all humans who were not Western Europeans? One reads all the way through *The Age of Improvement* without being reminded that Great Britain and France invaded China for no other reason than to force the opium trade upon her: It is an event described only in histories of China, and in the irony of Marx:`

> While the semi-barbarian stood on the principle of morality, the civilized opposed to him the principle of self.

For the decay of Britain probably began, not so late as we usually set it, but in the years of Palmerston and Russell, who seemed far-sighted when they were only indifferent; the one the most insular of foreign adventurers, the other the reformer who changed almost nothing. Great Britain, more lastingly even than France, established government as the theatrical art from which we suffer still. Its invention defeated Marx; one of his mistakes was his failure to recognize that no one is a fitter instrument for resisting history than the mime. England's lasting educational impress on the Indian subcontinent was not the railroad from which Marx expected so much, nor the English verse from which Macaulay hoped for so much. It was instead the mummery that has produced the Pakistan whose official lies are so like Sir Douglas Haig's and the India that lies in the cadences of the *New Statesman*. The post-Marxian world is an international of the insular.

Still one arises from this hack work of Marx's and thinks of him, defeated, in the heroic form Isaiah Berlin evokes during those years in Soho:

> The task of preparing the workers for the revolution was for him a scientific task, a routine occupation, something to be performed as solidly and efficiently as possible, and not as a direct means of personal self-expression. The external circumstances of his life are therefore as monotonous as those of any other devoted expert, as those of Darwin or Pasteur, and offer the sharpest possible contrast to the restless, emotionally involved, lives of other revolutionaries of his time.

Journalism is certainly the less important of the two vocations that have forgotten his example of how a job of work should be done.

The Underestimation of Dwight D. Eisenhower

September 1967

The full moment of revelation about the great captains may be possible only for one of the casualties they leave behind them. Richard Nixon was writing in hospital: Just once, the resentment whose suppression is the great discipline of his life breaks through and is taken back with that saving clause about the best sense of the word, of course. Yea, though He slay me yet must I depend on Him.

Dwight Eisenhower was as indifferent as Calvin Coolidge, as absolute as Abraham Lincoln, more contained than John Kennedy, more serpentine than Lyndon Johnson, as hard to work for as Andrew Johnson. Historians seem to accept most of these qualities as necessary for greatness: certainly none of them diminish it. But, then, most are accounted sinister by the great mass of civilians, and to confuse civilians and to keep them off his back is the soldier's art. Eisenhower, who understood everything, seems to have decided very early that life is nothing unless it is convenient; to show the living flesh of greatness to one's contemporaries means to show one's face in combat and to be argued about: The only convenient greatness is to appear as a monument.

The most precise description of Eisenhower was rendered in another connection by Edward Lear:

On the top of the Crumpetty Tree
The Quangle Wangle sat.
But his face you could not see,
On account of his Beaver Hat

For his Hat was a hundred and
two feet wide,
With ribbons and bibbons on
every side
And bells, and buttons, and loops,
and lace,
So that nobody ever could see the face
Of the Quangle Wangle Quee.

Innocence was Eisenhower's beaver hat, and the ribbons grew longer and more numerous until his true lines were almost invisible. It took a very long watch indeed to catch the smallest glimpse.

"He told Nixon and others, including myself, that he was well aware that somebody had to do the hard-hitting infighting,* and he had no objections to it as long as no one expected *him* to do it," Sherman Adams says.

It was the purpose of his existence never to be seen in what he did. When he fired Sherman Adams, his chief of staff, as a political liability in 1958, Adams thought it was Nixon's doing. While he was coldly measuring the gain or loss from dropping Nixon as his 1952 vice-presidential candidate, Nixon thought it was Thomas E. Dewey's doing.

When this gesture proved insufficient, Eisenhower accommodated to what was inevitable, if transient, and even offered himself up as battle trophy for Goldwater's brief triumph at the San Francisco convention. It was a situation where, the surreptitiously neat having failed, the heroically messy could hardly succeed. The useless employment of further resources would have been an affront to that superb sense of economy which made Eisenhower a soldier successful just for being so immune to notions of glory and to pleasurable anticipations of bleeding.

"He is the most immoral man I have ever known,'" one of Nelson Rockefeller's captains said not long ago. He was probably wrong: There is always the danger of going overboard in moments when the watcher thinks he has found Eisenhower out. To be absolutely immoral is a

* Definable to the Democrats as the dirty work.

perilous excess: Being moderate in all things means, after all, being moderate in the expenditure of immorality.

No thought was to be uttered undisguised: The face had as many ranges, indeed as many roles as there are sins to commit, because it was an instrument for hinting without ever quite saying. Even the syntax was an instrument. When things were at their stickiest in the Formosa Strait, James Hagerty, his press secretary, told the President that the best course would be to refuse to answer any questions at all on the subject if it came up at his press conference.

"'Don't worry, Jim,' I told him as we went out the door. 'If that question comes up, I'll just confuse them.'"

Those press conferences, his highest achievements as craftsman in masks, seem certain to be half the sport and half the despair of historians; they will give up, one has to assume, and settle for the judgment that he was a man hopelessly confused, it being so difficult to confess that anyone, across so many years, could still so superbly confuse you. The mask he contrived for his comfort has already become the reputation. Generals like MacArthur and Montgomery, as proud of their intelligence as he was appalled by their weakness for theater, seem to have thought him stupid, as he certainly thought them a little dippy. The other presidents already evoked most often for comparison with him are General Grant and James Buchanan. But still there abides the mystery of why he never left the country ruined by his laziness, as Buchanan did, or himself ruined by his friends, as Grant did.

The difference in both cases was partly Eisenhower's intelligence, partly his appreciation of those occasions when self-indulgence can produce worse inconveniences, and partly that chilliness of his nature which protected him from ever indulging others.

"I could understand it if he played golf all the time with old Army friends, but no man is less loyal to his old friends than Eisenhower," John Kennedy observed when he was a senator. "He is a terribly cold man. All his golfing pals are rich men he has met since 1945."

"In the evenings when he had no official engagements or on weekends," says Adams, "the President liked to spend his time with old friends whose faces were often seen at Gettysburg—Bill Robinson, the entertaining George Allen, Cliff Roberts, Pete Jones, Bob Woodruff, Al Gruenther, Slats Slater, Freeman Gosden ['Amos' of the famous radio team of Amos and Andy], Sig Larmon."

These Sigs and Petes and Slatses could hardly have been more stimulating than his old Army comrades—of whose intelligence he does seem to have entertained the lowest opinion—and, when one member of a salon is granted special distinction as "entertaining," his fellow inmates must be dreary indeed.

But the Sigs and Petes had one substantial advantage: They earned his affection as Casanova made *his* conquests: They were men who paid.

Once, Eisenhower remembers, he had a few days' rest in Scotland on a state trip; and someone, thinking he might be lonely, suggested that he call a few friends to fly over for golf and bridge.

"The idea," he says, "struck me as intriguing, in certain respects the brightest I had heard during the entire trip. Forgetting the time differential, I picked up the telephone and within minutes was talking to Bill Robinson in New York. My call got him out of bed: In New York it was two o'clock in the morning. Without a moment's hesitation he accepted my invitation and a few hours later he and 'Pete' Jones were on their way. I was indeed fortunate to have friends who were such light sleepers."

He lived among strangers; his protective coloration was the appearance of being amiable and innocent. Very seldom does he give himself away: Once he said that, when he was president of Columbia, he never went for a walk at night without carrying his service revolver with him. There is surprising hauteur in this image of the most eminent neighbor at large in Morningside Heights; but there is also the grandeur of a man whose dedication it was never to experience a moment of confrontation without the proper weight of means; to him all life was a matter of logistics.

He is revealed best, if only occasionally, in the vast and dreary acreage of his memoirs of the White House years. There he could feel safe in an occasional lapse of guard. For one thing, political history is the opiate of Democrats and he had spent eight years grandly erasing any suggestion from the minds of anyone else that anything he might ever say could be remotely interesting. He had concealed his marvelous intelligence from admirer and critic alike; by now, there was little danger of its being noticed even if confessed; he could be as secure in his memoirs as in his private diary.

The Eisenhower who emerges here intermittently free from his habitual veils is the President most superbly equipped for truly consequential decision we may ever have had, a mind neither rash nor hesitant, free of the slightest concern for how things might look, indifferent to any sentiment, as calm when he was demonstrating the wisdom of leaving a bad situation alone as when he was moving to meet it on those occasions when he absolutely had to.

Of course, we think: That is the way he wants us to see him; he is still trying to fool us; but he won't get away with it this time. And so he has fooled us again, for the Eisenhower who tells us that he never makes an important mistake is telling us for the first time about the real Eisenhower.

There is the sound of trumpets, the fog of rhetoric, then for just a moment the focus of the cold intelligence.

The President-elect goes to Korea.

"We used light airplanes to fly along the front and were impressed by the rapidity with which wounded were being brought back for treatment; evacuation was almost completely by helicopter since there were no landing fields for conventional planes in the mountains. Except for sporadic artillery fire and sniping there was little action at the moment, *but in view of the strength of the positions the enemy had developed, it was obvious that any frontal attack would present great difficulties.*"

All else would be conversation; one look had decided Eisenhower to fold the war.

Iraq's monarchy has been overthrown, Lebanon's government is collapsing, the British are otherwise committed; President Eisenhower will have to send the Marines.

> The basic mission of United States forces in Lebanon was not primarily to fight. Every effort was made to have our landing be as much of a garrison move as possible. In my address I had been

> careful to use the term 'stationed in' Lebanon. . . . If it had been prudent, I would have preferred that the first battalion ashore disembark at a dock rather than across the beaches. However, the attitude of the Lebanese army was at that moment unknown, and it was obviously wise to disembark in deployed formation ready for any emergency. As it turned out, there was no resistance; the Lebanese along the beaches welcomed our troops. The geographic objectives of the landings included only the city of Beirut and the adjoining airfield.

And, thereunder, he appends this note of explanation:

> The decision to occupy only the airfield and capital was a political one which I adhered to over the recommendations of some of the military. If the Lebanese army were unable to subdue the rebels when we had secured their capital and protected their government, I felt, we were backing up a government with so little popular support that we probably should not be there.

There was French Indochina, now of course Vietnam, and this cold intelligence looks upon the French with all the remote distance it would always feel from the romantic poetry of war:

The President is told that the French propose to put ten thousand troops in Dien Bien Phu.

> I said, "You cannot do this."
>
> "This will bring the enemy into the open," he said. "We cannot find them in the jungle, and this will draw them out where we can then win."
>
> "The French know military history," I said. "They are smart enough to know the outcome of becoming firmly emplaced and then besieged in an exposed position with poor means of supply and reinforcements."

Never thereafter could he contemplate the war in Indochina except in the frozen tones of a war college report on a maneuver by officers who can henceforth abandon all hope of promotion. The French, he instructs Foster Dulles, have committed the classic military blunder. In Geneva, Dulles is said to have hinted that the United States might use the atom bomb to save the French; there is no evidence that he would have dared transmit that suggestion to a President who plainly would not have trusted him with a stick of dynamite to blow up a fishpond.

Dulles, unhopefully, does pass on a French plea for United States bomber support of the Dien Bien Phu garrison; Eisenhower does not even seem to have noticed it. He had already made up his mind about that:

> There were grave doubts in my mind about the effectiveness of such air strikes on deployed troops where good cover was plentiful. Employment of air strikes alone to support French troops in the jungle would create a double jeopardy: it would comprise an act of war and would also entail the risk of having intervened and lost. [Sitting with Undersecretary of State Bedell Smith,] I remarked that, if the United States were, unilaterally, to permit its forces to be drawn into conflict in Indochina, and in a succession of Asian wars, the end result would be to drain off our resources and to weaken our overall defensive position.

The French went down; Eisenhower blamed them and the British, who, of course, blamed Dulles.

Then, in his utmost refinement, there is the Eisenhower who supervised the CIA's U-2 reconnaissance flights over the Soviet Union:

> A final important characteristic of the plane was its fragile construction. This led to the assumption (insisted upon by the C.I.A. and the Joint Chiefs) that in the event of mishap the plane would virtually disintegrate. It would be impossible, if things should go wrong, they said, for the Soviets to come into possession of the equipment intact—or, unfortunately, of a live pilot. This was a cruel assumption, but I was assured that the young pilots undertaking these missions were doing so with their eyes wide open

> and motivated by a high degree of patriotism, a swashbuckling bravado, and certain material inducements.*

Then Francis Powers' U-2 was shot down, and Eisenhower, of course, ordered the announcement of the "previously designed 'cover story.'"

Upon which, "Mr. Khrushchev, appearing before the Supreme Soviet once more, announced what to me was unbelievable. The uninjured pilot of our reconnaissance plane, along with much of his equipment intact, was in Soviet hands."

The State Department was still lamely adhering to the cover story. That seemed totally irrational to Eisenhower, who at once ordered a full confession, altering its draft "to eliminate any phrase that seemed to me to be defensive in tone.

"In the diplomatic field," he explained, "it was routine practice to deny responsibility for an embarrassing occurrence when there is even a 1 percent chance of being believed, but when the world can entertain not the slightest doubt of the facts, there is no point in trying to evade the issue."

And there we have, in Dwight Eisenhower of all unexpected persons, the model of that perfect statesman of Voltaire's ironic dream, the one who could learn nothing from Machiavelli except to denounce Machiavelli.

The precepts are plain to see:

1. Always pretend to be stupid; then when you have to show yourself smart, the display has the additional effect of surprise.
2. Taking the blame is a function of servants. When the orange is squeezed, throw it away.

---

* One of the confusions making difficult the full appreciation of Eisenhower's subtlety is the condition that he seems to explain himself in anticlimactic series. For example: "As president of Columbia, I became deeply interested in the educational, financial and public relations aspects of the job." Normally one would expect a college president to be more interested in education than in public relations, and the succession seems anticlimactic. But, with a little thought, one understands that Eisenhower knew he was at Columbia as a public-relations man. In the same way, normal rhetoric would assign the climactic role in the readiness of a soldier to sacrifice his life to "high degree of patriotism": Eisenhower, with perfect understanding, gives the emphasis to "certain material inducements."

3. When a situation is hopeless, never listen to counsels of hope. Fold the enterprise.
4. Do nothing unless you know exactly what you will do if it turns out to have been the wrong thing. Walk not one inch forward onto ground which has not been painfully tested by someone else.
5. Never forget the conversation you had with Zhukov about how the Russian army clears mine fields. "We march through them," Zhukov had said. It is a useful instruction if applied with the proper economy. Keep Nixon and Dulles around for marching through mine fields.
6. Always give an enemy an exit.
7. Never give an ally his head.
8. Assume that your enemies are just as sensible as you are. ("Personally I had always discounted the probability of the Soviets doing anything as 'reaction.' Communists do little on impulse; rather their aggressive moves are invariably the result of deliberate decision.")
9. Lie whenever it seems useful, but stop lying the moment 99 percent of the audience ceases to believe you.
10. Respond only when there is some gain besides honor in meeting the challenge or some serious loss from disregarding it. For example, when Eisenhower was the first candidate for President in memory who indicated that he was unable to pronounce the word "injunction" when discussing the labor problem, I suggested to one of his admirers that he seemed extraordinarily dumb.

"If he's so dumb," was the reply, "why is he such a good bridge player?"

Like all defenses of Dwight Eisenhower, it seemed silly at first; but, with thought one understood its force. Eisenhower spent the twenties as an officer in garrison; his friends were civilians in towns like Leavenworth, Kansas. He learned to play bridge well because his pay did not cover losing money to civilians. He is equipped to respond to any challenge which seems to him sensible.

He was the great tortoise upon whose back the world sat for eight years. We laughed at him; we talked wistfully about moving; and all the while we never knew the cunning beneath the shell.

I talked to him just once. He was in Denver, getting ready for the 1952 campaign when he would have to run with Republicans like Sen. Jenner who had called General Marshall, the chief agent of Eisenhower's promotion, "a living lie." I had thought that anyone so innocent as Eisenhower would be embarrassed by this comrade and proposed to ask what he thought about what Jenner had said. It seemed cruel to spring any such trap to anyone this innocent, so I told Hagerty that I intended to ask the question.

The time came and I asked, "General, what do you think of those people who call General Marshall a living lie?"

He leaped to his feet and contrived the purpling of his face. How dare anyone say that about the greatest man who walks in America? He shook his finger in marvelous counterfeit of the palsy of outrage.

He would die for George Marshall. He could barely stand to be in the room with anyone who would utter such a profanation. The moment passed while the enlisted man in garrison endured his ordeal as example to the rest of the troops; and suddenly I realized that in his magnificent rage at me, he had been careful not to mention Sen. Jenner at all.

Afterward Hagerty took me aside and the General offered the sunshine of his smile; there was not the slightest indication that he was thinking that there was anything for him to forgive or me either. It had simply been the appointed ceremony. I was too dumb to understand him then. It would take ten years before I looked at his picture and realized that the smile was always a grin.

Responses to "Liberal Anti-Communism Revisited"

September 1967

[Ed. note: The following are Kempton's answers to a symposium questionnaire circulated by Commentary *magazine; they appeared in print together with responses by Daniel Bell, Irving Howe, Robert Lowell, Dwight Macdonald, and others.]*

1. It has recently been charged that the anti-Communism of the Left was in some measure responsible for, or helped to create a climate of opinion favorable to, the war in Vietnam. What justification, if any, do you find in that charge? As someone whose name has been associated with the anti-Communist Left, do you feel in any way responsible for American policies in Vietnam?
2. Would you call yourself an anti-Communist today? If so, are you still willing to support a policy of containing the spread of Communism? If not, why have you changed? Assuming that you once supported containment because you were opposed on moral rather than narrowly political grounds to the spread of a totalitarian system, why do you think it wrong to apply the same principle to Vietnam?
3. Do the recent revelations concerning covert CIA backing of projects, some of which you probably sympathized with, or may perhaps have been involved in yourself, prove that liberal anti-Communism has been a dupe of, or a slave to, the darker impulses of American foreign policy?

1. I should hope more than anything else that this discussion will proceed without the spite and rancor which afflicted so much of the Communism of the thirties and the anti-Communism of the fifties. In deference to that dream of fraternity, I must beg off attempting to assay the responsibility of the "anti-Communist Left" for Vietnam. Abstract designations (this one covers Jay Lovestone *and* Norman Thomas) are of very little use for description and almost none for judgment. Guilt is, after all, personal. If we have been taught nothing else, I hope to have learned that you have said very little about a man when you have put a label on him.

Fifteen years ago, to be a member of the anti-Communist Left meant generally to accept historical American liberalism as the alternative to the Soviets. To the degree we made this acceptance, it is hard to argue that most of us can disclaim any contribution to the climate which has ended with Vietnam.

Vietnam is a liberal's war. Mr. Johnson summed up the image appointed for it when he described General Westmoreland as possessed of a soldier's head and a social worker's heart. Mary McCarthy has noticed how much the rhetoric of our pacification campaign sounds like everything that has been taught in political-science departments of American universities for the last twenty years.

No member of the Left could have been employed by the government of this country unless he had been certifiably anti-Communist. Even those of us who had no aspirations for such service found it useful to describe ourselves as anti-Communist. I do not mean to exaggerate the McCarthy terror; still, to enter at all seriously into the American debate, some security clearance was needed, even if you had to proclaim it yourself. I am not saying that we were insincere in accepting this description of ourselves but rather that we accepted it without thinking it through. For twenty years now, the foreign policy of the United States has been conducted in the language which religions evoke for the struggle between our light and your darkness.

To call oneself a member of the anti-Communist Left was, I'm afraid, to speak in some of the tones of religious incantation and to feel oneself as part of a holy war. Now that Vietnam has brought us to that turn at which holy wars generally arrive at one time or another,

I do not think many of us can disclaim some responsibility—even if only for pronouncing the litany—for the atmosphere which so overbore our prudence and our tolerance as to bring us to the bombing of farmers in villages.

In fairness to others, I should talk of my own part. So far as other Americans are concerned, I long ago stopped thinking of myself as an anti-Communist. For quite a while, though, I retained some prejudice against alien Communists at war with the United States.

Part of the reason for this prejudice was that I had been a soldier myself under remarkably amusing circumstances. I identified with our soldiers. What gradually became an enraged distaste for domestic anti-Communism began, in fact, with annoyance at the way this government treated former soldiers who happened to be Communists. I have always thought of myself as a nationalist if not a patriot; it would be embarrassing to me to think myself a supporter of the enemies of my country.

It will be noticed that, in taking this attitude, I was entrusting the definition of the enemies of my country to a government which I knew from direct experience could not even be trusted not to interfere with the liberties of its own citizens.

The only value of the Vietnam experience has been educational. If it had not lasted so long, we should not, I think, with quite the same certainty, have been able to understand how much of the history of the United States in the world for twenty years now has been, as was said of Turkish history, "entirely military and entirely mendacious." We have now been watching Vietnam for two years; the Bay of Pigs lasted three days and Guatemala three weeks. Vietnam works on the understanding as a slow-motion film does; here we can follow actions which at all other times have simply flashed by. There can now be no excuse for us not to know what our leaders are like.

I come now to an interior quarrel whose exposition may disqualify me from any part in this symposium at all. I want to know why it is so hard for me to express the sympathy which, in logic, I should feel for the Vietcong. I am, after all, not a pacifist. The genuine pacifists have had, all in all, the most honorable record of any group of Americans over the last twenty years. But, unless it is genuine, that position seems to me a dishonorable disguise. It would be convenient to be able to say that the enemy is war itself and not the government of the United States. But I am not used to being neutral. It is already painful enough to notice how obviously more attractive Ho Chi Minh is than General Ky. Will the time not come when, in our hearts, we shall have to choose between them?

We are unready for that choice, for a reason which seems to me more relevant than the words we still use about being of the Left or of the Right. Our trouble is that, as Americans, we do not have the habit of being in the opposition. We do not have Burkes and Foxes. That is why it is possible to read a work condescending to Burke from the pen of a member of the political-science department of a university whose international-relations department may have a subsidy from the CIA and whose biology department is assisting the Defense Department in germ-warfare research. A man in the real world must be able to say, when he has to, that his government is the enemy.

2. No, in sorrow, because I wish real life were simple enough so that one could feel that one had said something when one called oneself an anti-Communist. To say so is immediately to have to take most of it back.

"Are you still willing to support a policy of containing the spread of Communism?" I assume the questioner is talking about real toads in real gardens. If so, what policy of containing Communism am I being asked to support? That of the government of the United States, I assume again.

Arthur Schlesinger's *A Thousand Days* contains one superlative *précis* of that policy. When Trujillo was assassinated, Schlesinger says, "Kennedy examined the situation realistically:

'There are three possibilities,' he said, 'in descending order of preference: a decent democratic regime, a continuation of the Trujillo regime or a Castro regime. We ought to aim at the first, but we really can't renounce the second until we are sure we can avoid the third.'

The most temperate and sophisticated man to be President of the United States in our lifetime thus accepted the "policy of containing

Communism" as leading to the conclusion that Trujillo was preferable to Castro. Forget the dubious assumption that I "once supported containment because [I was] opposed on *moral* rather than narrowly political grounds to the spread of a totalitarian system." Ask yourself whether the government of the United States has ever been so opposed; that is the policy of containment we are talking about.

3. I caught myself the other day reading the names of the Board of Directors of the Carnegie Endowment for International Peace, and trying to guess CIA affiliations. There is a little of J. B. Matthews in us all. I should like to govern this impulse; to call a friend "a dupe of, or a slave to, the darker impulses of American foreign policy" sounds to me like language we ought to get out of our systems.

We are fortunate to have Thomas Braden's memoirs of his career as the CIA's paymaster to the anti-Communist Left because otherwise it would be hard to appreciate the mindless vulgarity of this operation. You pity anyone who had dealings with this sort of man as you ought to pity the Hollywood Communists for the former taxi driver who was their district organizer. Braden's assertion that an editor of *Encounter* was "an agent of ours" is the language of an *apparatchik*; and our experience with the House Un-American Activities Committee ought by now to have made us thoroughly suspicious of these confessions which are also boastings.

The CIA experience, for most of my friends who engaged in it directly, was, I suspect, very like what the experience of being a Communist must have been for many other Americans. That is, there were in it no very large sins. There are, however, certain affronts to one's domestic sense. When an apparatus tells a man that reasons of state make it necessary for him to conceal his affiliation, it may or may not have harmed his character but it has certainly damaged his capacity to function as a friend. An Englishman who was being paid by *Encounter* had, for example, a clear right to know whether he was being paid by CIA funds, because, if there is one thing that ought to be a conscious act, it is the decision as to whether you will enter the paid service of a foreign government. An Englishman who wondered and asked an American friend had a right, assuming that the friend knew, to a frank and honest answer. I have always thought that E. M. Forster's statement that he would sooner betray his country than betray a friend was deficient in logic. Still, in the real world the issue is generally presented as a real betrayal of one's friend as against a fancied betrayal of one's country; and Forster's is quite a good rule in practice, just as any society whose rules make it impossible for one single man to trust another is a very bad society in practice.

My own mind, I'm afraid, is quite divorced from the politics of Right or Left, which will not, I hope, be taken to mean that I want it to be divorced from political responsibility. The most substantial lesson to me from the CIA experience has come from the realization that Ignazio Silone was the editor of a magazine which would very probably never have been published without a CIA subsidy. The lesson seems to me neither that the CIA was so wicked that it even corrupted Silone nor that the CIA was so high-minded that it even helped Silone. The lesson is in the figure of Silone himself. For he is a man who could have this experience, suffer, if you choose, this suspicion and remain absolutely beyond our criticism. Because we know him, we know that he could not do the low or dishonorable thing. We think of Silone as we always have because we know what he has always been. The resource of a man, as of a movement, is not the intellectual but the moral capital. There are not many of us who have earned that automatic trust; and that is perhaps the worst thing that can be said of the anti-Communist Left.

Still, we are not as old as we sometimes think we are; and, if we have the sense detachedly and forgivingly to learn from what has happened to us, there remains a way to go and work to be done.

Thoughts on Columbia

4 • 30 • 68

I have hated it as long as I can remember and am no fair judge of its agony. After all, an institution which has had on its Board of Trustees at the same time the publisher of *The New York Times* and the District Attorney of New York County can get away with pretty much anything in the way of lies and swindles in this town. These things are not really Columbia's fault, since it has never learned those inhibitions—public opinion and the force of law.

So I am a man whose dream for Columbia is that it fall into ruin like the Roman Forum, in the eighteenth century, with the Church putting a cross over it, the grass growing, the peasants tethering their goats and an occasional traveler musing over the vanity of worldly pride.

Still it does have inhabitants. And what must it be like to teach political science at Columbia? Your theme is presumed to include the normal means by which citizens impress their will on the agencies of government. And you teach against the background of your university's decision to build a gymnasium in Morningside Park. That is hardly as bad an example of Columbia's attitude toward its neighbors as was the outright contempt expressed for them by Jacques Barzun when he was Columbia's Provost three years ago; still it is a fair sample of its normal indifference. Harlem's politicians protested; Mayor Lindsay had doubts; Columbia went ahead.

So then a few hundred students went on a sit-down strike; and, as one of the fantasies which afflict institutions with the garrison mentality, there arose a rumor that Harlem might invade the campus. Then and only then, Columbia decided to halt construction of the gymnasium. Peaceful objections failed; direct action and the rumor of riot may have succeeded. It is difficult to envy the political scientist who, after that experience, has to go on explaining to the resources of the orderly processes of democratic debate our system offers the poor and the powerless.

Yet you commence after a day or two to feel a curious affection for the faculty. What President Kirk abandoned, these men in their poor confused way have defended.

They are faintly ridiculous, of course. You have to look and sound ridiculous when the representatives of order have scuttled and you are brave enough to step in and try to do their job, with no loftier credential than is encompassed by the phrase *ad hoc*. On the one side you have student rebels whose prime demand was that they be guaranteed immunity from any punishment for what they had done and thus recognized as still members of our great untorturable middle class. On the other you have anti-rebel students whose only demand was for punishment.

Across from you is Mathematics Hall where Tom Hayden commands a college repertory company doing *Marat-Sade*; behind you is Hamilton Hall, now Malcolm X University, Stokely Carmichael declared president. Before you is the terrible muddle around Low Library, where students punched one another yesterday and where the motorcycle cops waited to be unchained.

The faculty did not meet the occasion with very impressive rhetoric. Its conversation sounded too much like the cartoons of Jules Feiffer or the letters in the *New York Review of Books*.

Its members do not always conduct themselves with a proper sense of their own dignity. Since Friday they had cordoned off Low Library, because anti-rebel students threatened to riot unless the demonstrators were stopped from going in and out of there.

Yesterday afternoon, the demonstrators outside began throwing food at the demonstrators inside. Every now and then, they would fire too low—Columbia has a deplorable record for completing passes—and a broken piece of citrus would fall on some professor with tenure.

Still they stood, with accepted loss of dignity, and tried to uphold the honor of their university. Nowhere, in these melancholy scenes, was president Grayson Kirk visible. Whether by fair means or foul, this poor man will do nothing for his honor. His suit will be free of stain and his record free of nobility to the end.

Illusion to Reality

1968

I am not entirely sure whether the worst aspect of the Democratic National Convention was the contempt Mayor Daley held for us as delegates or whether it was the contempt we held for ourselves.

We were prodded, pushed, and frisked by Andy Frain's guards—which means the Mayor's—and we almost never protested, being no more than the Mayor able to recognize ourselves as members of a parliament, a curious parliament to be sure, but enough of one to render our persons, if not sacred, at least above continual stoppage by the king's men. The Mayor had chosen pretty girls and college boys to do a job which should belong to police matrons and they did it both incompetently and nastily. The Mayor's contempt for us had led him to assume that we would not care how we were treated so long as we were treated that way by outwardly ornamental children. And in most cases he was correct in that judgment; to object to the violations of one's humanity became to confess oneself a raging crank. A few of the objections expressed were almost without exception founded on dissent less from the Mayor's manners than from the Mayor's choice of a candidate. His goon-bunnies, for example, stopped lady delegates and searched their handbags whenever the fancy seized. I never saw a lady with a Humphrey button object to this humiliation. So we should hardly be surprised at Vice President Humphrey defending Mayor Daley against his detractors; the Mayor is part of the package a Democratic nominee takes with the prize.

A mayor of Chicago packed the galleries for President Roosevelt in 1940. A mayor's boss, Jake Arvey, did the same job for Adlai Stevenson in 1952.

I pray, with no great assurance, that if the Mayor had supported Sen. McCarthy, all of us McCarthy delegates would have been at least half as outraged at the way he treated us and innumerable private citizens in the streets as we were. But until now most Democratic liberals have lived without complaint with the dark side of their party; to have been thrown out on the street by Mayor Daley means then that we have lost the illusion of power and can hope to have gained some sense of reality.

I happen to have been arrested by Mayor Daley's police—or more precisely the Mayor's governor's National Guard—on the last night of the Convention. That constitutes my only direct experience with his peace forces that week. My treatment was comparatively pleasant; I met about three markedly courteous policemen for every two beasts. What surprised me about the Mayor's police force was that it has no general standard of conduct. A Chicago cop does pretty much what he pleases, being pleasant or nasty according to his nature. This, I suppose, is that permissive society which, in editorial complaints, is generally cited for blame only for the conduct of the young.

What surprised me even more was the sort of persons who got arrested with me that night. They ran to an unusual proportion of first- and I suspect last-timers, including as they did, the personnel director of a hospital, the president of a state college, a Rockefeller campaign manager from Kentucky, a book editor, and a reporter from *The New York Times*. These, I think, are persons who had never before imagined themselves getting arrested, having been until now careful about personal containment and acceptance of order. What the Mayor had done to make them feel that to get arrested was the only respectable thing a quiet man could do in Chicago that night is detailed earlier in these pages; I can only testify that whatever it was, it was terrible enough to make men careful about appearances prefer the Mayor's jail to his face on television or his company in the Convention Hall. And that was the judgment not just on Mayor Daley but on what their country had become. The Mayor is not Bull Connor, who could be blamed just upon a section of the country. He is Chicago and that is the heart of the country. For these quiet and sober persons to have sought arrest to be rid of him that night was not just a decision about the Mayor; it was an act of revolt against the government. Mayor Daley has taught us all a great lesson about this country. Having learned from him, we will never be the same. Anyhow, I hope not.

A Victory for Proper Manners

3·7·70

The conviction of those disturbers of the peace known even to their enemies as "the Chicago seven" was a victory for those Americans who are more shocked by unsightly deportment than by cruelty. There will, we are afraid, be others: the jury which voted to send them to prison shared its jury service with another jury which acquitted three Detroit policemen charged with "executing" three Negroes during that city's 1967 riots.

It becomes, then, very hard to believe that a man in uniform will readily be punished for shooting a private citizen, or that a private citizen will readily be set free if there is evidence that he aroused a man in uniform. Official America is sullen, bored, affronted by hair, obscenity and the contumely of the young. Mr. Agnew's popularity may be overestimated, but this message does seem widely accepted as the voice of middle America, and it reaches the highest pitch of acrimony when it confronts bad manners in anyone except himself.

The Vice President's hotel was picketed, as it generally is, when he spoke in Chicago on the birthday of President Lincoln. The protesters, thin as to numbers but diverse as to variety of outrage—they ran from the homosexuals to the Revolutionary Youth movement—walked around chanting "F— Agnew" (raising in one witness certain thoughts of having reached a terminus of rhetoric; it must be hard to think of tomorrow's slogan after crying out this one today). "Did you hear that?," a voice said in the cold. "That's *brutal*." It was the voice of a Chicago policeman; in official America, for the moment at least, an atrocity is words. That reaction defines the depth the Vice President has touched in his constituency. To hear him is to be struck very soon by a curious displacement in the object of shock: ". . . disruptive demonstrations aimed at *bludgeoning* the unconvinced into action . . ." "The Vietnam Moratorium . . . is not only negative in concept but *brutally* counter-productive." "It appears that by slaughtering a sacred cow, I triggered a holy war."

A "slaughter," then, is what one does to a sacred cow; a "trigger" is what sets off loud public discussion. The only bludgeon is the larynx. To be brutal is not to do what we, or even the Vietcong, do to Asian farmers; to be brutal is to be Dr. Benjamin Spock speaking to a lunchtime crowd in the Federal Triangle. The epithets we wore out on real horrors are confined now to mere annoyances.

The judgment in the "Chicago seven" case suggests the prevalence of this displacement of normal outrage; one day's exposure to the trial sustained it. At one point near the end, defense counsel William Kunstler approached the bench with perhaps a shade more flamboyance than restrained theatrical convention might approve. Judge Julius Hoffman sat his ground as though it were really threatened. "Stand back, sir," he said, his heroism suppressing his quaver. What electricity was left in the great case had come down to the person of this old man and the thrill he felt at confronting the peril of people he held in his power.

After the conviction and confinement, the Sheriff of Cook County enforced haircuts on the defendants and then carried pictures of them shorn for triumphant display at a meeting of local Republicans. United States Attorney Thomas Foran told the parents of a Catholic high school class that all the defendants were "fags" and that "we've lost our kids to the freaking fag revolution."

It does not seem at this juncture to occur to enough Americans that the language and conduct of this description are far worse from quasi-judicial officials than any similar excess from a private citizen. It can, of course, sensibly be argued that the "Chicago seven," in the ferocity of their attack on the dignity of their judge and their prosecutor, destroyed any chance they had of communicating their own dignity. The posttrial statements of their jurors certainly suggest that they were convicted not for what they did in the streets of Chicago in the summer of 1968 but for their behavior in Judge Hoffman's court over the last four months, behavior which certainly made the prosecution's description of their conduct and intentions more persuasive than any evidence at the prosecution's command.

What is more depressing is the apparent incapacity of whatever is "established" in the country, even its liberalism, to understand that private citizens ought not to be sent to prison for five years on no showing of anything except bad manners. There can be noticed, for example, in *The New York Times*, which ought to be the repository of whatever conscience and curiosity we have left, a tendency to make its own the official definition of the responsibility of the public man as against that of the private citizen. In essence, it seems that *The New York Times* has ceased to resist as the television networks have; the *Times*, having been unable to be fair to Vice President Agnew until he threatened it with reprisals quite beyond his power, has now been rendered incapable of treating him as open either to present or future criticism. He has enforced for himself the respect owed to a national symbol.

There is no way of estimating the end of what is a thoroughly depressing state of things. The President's appointments to the Supreme Court indicate that he wants judges who are taut, gloomy and anxious to punish; and the liberals cannot deny them their chance unless some evidence can be adduced that they are also crooked. The President is not a vindictive man; but his experience and his constituency are very much on the side that wants to restrain rather than that which aims to liberate. He is uncomfortable with noisy persons of any sort; and the blacks and the young *are* noisy; in these circumstances, they are not likely soon to be weighed with much delicacy in court.

The source of malady may, of course, also be the cause of its cure. The malignity of the Chicago verdict is something quite bad enough by itself; but one aspect of Mr. Nixon's government argues against a spread of the spirit it represents into disciplined repression. Persons subject to outrage by spectacles of evil which are entirely rhetorical are given to remedies which are rather rhetorical too. The administration is niggardly, and the logical extension of its principles much too expensive. Crime control, whether it attacks a social pathology or merely suppresses its symptoms, is a costly business; and Mr. Nixon does not like to spend money.

Moreover, the Chicago defendants represent a view of America accepted by a great many persons who, although quieter, are numerous enough to constitute a point of resistance which could give pause to persons of tougher kidney than Mr. Nixon. With all their departures from gentility, they managed somehow to divide a jury and almost to bring it to hopeless disagreement. Their message then would seem to have a force quite beyond the imagination of their judge and their prosecutor; the Vietnam war, diminishing though it is, remains a wound on the conscience of many of our citizens; they sit on juries and, in greater numbers than ever before, distrust our government. It is hard to believe that Mr. Nixon will serve himself well if he moves on without regard for their sensibilities.

The Panthers on Trial

5·7·70

Twenty-one members of the Black Panther Party were indicted a year ago last April for having conspired to blow up five New York department stores, a police station, the New Haven Railroad's right of way, and the Bronx Botanical Gardens. One of them was Lee Berry, who is twenty-four and was under treatment for epilepsy at the Manhattan Veterans' Hospital on the day of his indictment. He telephoned the police department to say where he was and report himself available for inquiry. There followed a descent in force and Berry's summary removal to the Manhattan House of Detention, where he was held under $100,000 bail.

He endured the next seven months in surroundings whose amenities have been certified by the New York City Department of Correction: "Over-crowding has resulted in two or three men being assigned to a cell intended to accommodate a single man." His attorneys very early began to complain that he was an invalid in a condition of casual neglect.

After three months, Assistant District Attorney Joseph Phillips responded with an affidavit from the Deputy Commissioner of Corrections, which, he said, "effectively refutes these complaints." Even so, State Supreme Court Justice John M. Murtagh ordered Berry's case "marked for medical attention," not, he explained, because he gave credence to the contentions of defense counsel but simply "as a precautionary measure."

In July, Berry's counsel returned with a claim that Berry had been beaten by a guard. Commissioner of Corrections George F. McGrath has since, effectively so far as any action is concerned, refuted this complaint by swearing that,

> The report of the institutional physician on duty at the time, Dr. Collins, indicates that Berry had a small laceration on his left eye which was treated by applying a band-aid. . . . [Dr. Collins] suspected epileptic seizure because of the findings of post epileptic shock at the time of the examination. . . . It is submitted that if plaintiff Berry was assaulted as he asserts with a blackjack there would be more substantial evidence of injury than found by Dr. Collins.

Epileptic seizure could serve the Corrections Department to explain Lee Berry's abrasions; it was, of course, of no use to him in avoiding five days in solitary confinement for insulting the guard he had accused of beating him. His diet throughout that period of treatment was bread and tea. Somewhere, in the confusion of these disputes, his regular medication was withdrawn. His counsel consumed the summer and most of the fall urging writs to have him removed to a hospital. The hearings were put off again and again because Assistant District Attorney Phillips did not have time to attend them.

It was November before Judge Murtagh ordered Berry to Bellevue Hospital for observation. There he seems to have collapsed. He was operated on for appendicitis; the pathologist found that the hospital had removed a normal appendix. He developed pneumonia; the doctors operated again for a clotting of the blood vessels in the groin. In January, the hospital discovered a hole or an abscess in his lung. In February, when the Panther indictments finally came to trial, Lee Berry was too sick to come to court; and Judge Murtagh, with the consent of Assistant District Attorney Phillips, severed his case from that of his thirteen codefendants. There was no show of embarrassment for all the months when complaints of his treatment had been dismissed as vaporings in the cause of a malingerer.

There was, indeed, no thought of reparation or even of indulgence. Judge Murtagh, not needing the degree of reflection which would have gone into composing an opinion, refused a request that Berry's bail be reduced to make possible his hospitalization somewhere except in a prison ward. He was then forgotten. The thirteen Panthers went to trial; and thereafter every noticed affront to the public conscience came from the manners of the defendants rather than the methods of their prosecutors.

The contumely of the defendants in the first weeks of the proceedings drove Judge Murtagh to suspend their trial and order them from the court until they would swear themselves as "prepared to participate in a trial according to the American system of justice." Judge Murtagh became then the first generally recognized victim of unfair treatment by any party associated with the New York Panther case, a curious eminence indeed since the only proven, let alone suggested, crime which might justifiably be described as mayhem was visited by the city upon Lee Berry rather than by Lee Berry or any of his codefendants upon anyone else. But that has been described in detail in no respectable precinct except the women's page of *The New York Times*, whose city desk has persistently regarded it as unworthy of attention, except in one case where Berry's complaint was given summary notice followed by an extensive rebuttal from the Commissioner of Corrections.

It was the last of Lee Berry's misfortunes that the Corrections Department should suddenly have remembered him at a juncture when the general sympathy with the suffering of Judge Murtagh had established the Panthers as "the vicious criminals and hooligans" Assistant District Attorney Phillips describes when his solicitude for the proprieties of language expected in an American courtroom has been especially wounded. On March 11, Commissioner McGrath removed Berry from the inadequate attention of Bellevue to the thorough inattention of the Rikers Island infirmary. His lawyers were not told of the transfer; his medical records were not sent along with him. Four days afterward a private physician retained by his wife obtained a court order to visit him and found that all "medical management had been discontinued" and that his condition had already begun further to deteriorate. After a week, the Corrections Department consented to his return to the hospital.

As there is then no enormity which our institutions cannot imagine from a Panther, there is no malignity which a Panther cannot expect from our institutions.

The month of alarm that the conduct of the defendants might deny the state an orderly trial followed almost a year of indifference by the state over whether the defendants would have a fair one. That imbalance would be curious if it were not our habit to mark what a man says and assume that we have thereby described what he does. The *Times,* to take a case, adorns its index every morning with an italic box labeled "Quotation of the Day," and the day's happenings are listed less conspicuously below.

So then, when the Black Panthers profess to live by the gun, we assume that they are murderers; and, when the Assistant District Attorney cries out that "justice has been trammeled by these defendants," we assume that we are listening to the outrage of a man concerned with justice.

When the defendants were indicted on April 1, 1969, District Attorney Frank Hogan announced the charges at one of those televised press conferences of his whose rarity makes certain the pervasiveness of their notice. He made only a single addition to the allegations of the indictment, but that was more striking and more immediate than anything else in the text before him. The defendants, he said, had planned to bomb Macy's, Korvette's, Bloomingdale's, Abercrombie and Fitch, and Alexander's *that very day.*

It would be a while before the police department's list of deadly weapons seized in the arrests became available as basis for quiet judgment of the imminence of the peril averted. The only potential explosives which seemed practical for carrying into the stores in a woman's handbag—the alleged technique of the *attentat*—turned out to be three pieces of pipe, suitable for arming as bombs but not so armed. Assistant District Attorney Phillips occasionally displayed one of these samples in court as dramatic evidence of the heinous intent of the defendants. But he does not appear to have come up with anything more impressive, and little else is suggested in the counts of the indictment. No one can in fairness assert that these defendants had not intended violence at some future time; but we have to say, on the weight of the District Attorney's own evidence, that we know now and he ought to have known then that they had not equipped themselves for the huge coordinated assault imputed to them in the clangor of his proclamation of their crimes.

For the next ten months there would exist for the public no image of these otherwise invisible persons except the description provided by the District Attorney who indicted them. It was the description accepted by every agency that dealt with them thereafter; Supreme Court Justice Marks set their bail at $100,000 before their indictment was available for inspection by their counsel. The arraignment of Lee Berry was processed with such desperation that there was no time to inform his lawyer, a condition descriptive of an atmosphere rather than any substantial defect of appointed justice, since he could have appeared surrounded by a cloud of counsel and the finding would have been no different.

At one point in the proceeding, William Kunstler protested for the defense that District Attorney Hogan's public outcry had already made a fair trial impossible. Justice Marks replied severely, "I don't think Mr. Hogan's office needs anyone to defend him."

The defendants passed then to the supervision of the Department of Corrections. They entered, of course, as detainees awaiting trial, a category rather different from that of persons already judged guilty; they were received as convicts. "There is reason to believe that they are extremely dangerous," the Deputy Commissioner directed his staff, ". . . and they shall be kept separate and apart from each other at all times." In accordance with this procedure of treating the Corrections Department's wards under no definition of their characters except the District Attorney's, they were scattered over seven different institutions. There were complaints that these conditions of isolation placed too heavy a burden on lawyers struggling to prepare a case for clients with whom they were barely acquainted. Assistant District Attorney Phillips dismissed them with this reply:

> I have . . . assisted the defense on two occasions in holding joint conferences with all their clients at a centrally located place. *Those meetings for the convenience of defense counsel are expensive for the Corrections Department.* [my italics]

It would take five months of argument before Justice Murtagh agreed to order weekly meetings of one and one-half hours' duration of the defendants together with their lawyers. By then, to be sure, the defense was pressing in Federal Court for some improvement in the conditions of detention. Mayor Lindsay's Corporation Counsel offered a strenuous resistance founded almost entirely on testimony by Commissioner McGrath, which the innocent might be surprised to find put forward as its philosophy of law by a city government often noticed for its enlightenment.

His treatment of the Panthers, Commissioner McGrath attested, was "not based on the premise that [they] are guilty as charged . . . but rather it is intended to ensure the greatest likelihood of success in maintaining the order and discipline of the given institution."

He progressed through a series of distinctions which never established any visible difference in their treatment as persons living under a presumption of innocence from that appointed for persons sentenced for guilt.

They were, he noted for example, "exponents of a political philosophy over which there is considerable controversy." They must then be kept apart for their own safety. "The danger is greater if contact is permitted between plaintiffs housed in the same institution, for through such contact the likelihood of open discussion and attendant public reaction is greater."

These were, Commissioner McGrath insisted in his oral testimony, dangerous, obdurate, and untrustworthy prisoners. His written affidavit cites the enormities of only one of these hard cases: "The plaintiff [Lumumba] Shakur was disciplined on July 8, 1969, for possession of a ball-point pen and a Black Panther newspaper."

Beyond this and the adoption as his own of the District Attorney's description of his wards, Commissioner McGrath defended himself by certifying the uniform degradation of all the prisons under his care. The defense complained that some of its clients had been denied mattresses: "In respect to the assertion that on occasion plaintiffs have been without a mattress, the department, during the last two years, has been purchasing specially covered mattresses for all its cells. Prior thereto, the incontinency of some of the inmates prevented the use of regular mattresses. However there has been no policy to deprive plaintiffs of a mattress. Almost all of the cells in the Manhattan House of Detention are equipped with mattresses."

And, further, "In respect to the assertion that plaintiffs have been denied access to the institution's library, the library has been closed for approximately seven months prior to the commencement of this action."

While the defendants thus struggled to establish their rights as having some weight when balanced against the convenience of their jailers, District Attorney Hogan was selecting the judge who would try them. It is an assumption prevalent in the criminal courts that Mr. Hogan picks his judges in cases really consequential to him. In this case, rather by accident, the operations of this custom were made publicly more manifest than they normally are. The ideal trial judge aspired to in our criminal system is supposed to come to his case looking upon defendants as unfamiliar to him as they are to the jury.

In deference to this conception, the courts prefer to have the parties argue their pretrial motions before a judge other than the one who will preside over the trial itself. That is the theory of Special Part 30, where judges hear and rule on motions in cases they will never try; pretrial motions often require the ruling judge to read the grand jury minutes in the case, a possible taint of the mind from which the theory at least prefers to protect the trial judge.

Still, throughout last fall's preliminaries, wherever they turned with their motions, the Panther lawyers never encountered a Criminal Judge except Justice Murtagh. At length Panther attorney Gerald Lefcourt wondered if he might somehow take his plea to Part 30. That recourse, Judge Murtagh replied, would not be possible, because the New York State Appellate Division had assigned him permanent custody of the case in all its aspects. Lefcourt inquired of the Appellate Division and received the reply that Judge Murtagh was incorrect.

There followed a complaint and this explanation:

Justice Murtagh had been assigned full command of the case by Justice Mitchell Schweitzer as administrative judge of the criminal courts. Justice Schweitzer said that last summer he and the District Attorney had been struggling as always with the clutter of the calendar. Mr. Hogan had observed that the Panther trial would be immensely complicated: Couldn't matters be eased if one judge were assigned to preside over the case all the way through? He suggested Justice Murtagh and Justice Schweitzer agreed. The explanation, then, was what it generally is when a question is raised about some incident in society's treatment of the New York Panthers: the convenience of an institution transcends whatever shadow of the rights of the defendants might lie across its path.

The result, whatever the excuse, was for the judge who would try the Panthers to be selected by the District Attorney who would prosecute them. It was to this assemblage of so many familiars that these defendants were brought still strangers from their isolation to trial at the beginning of February.

The dignity normal in the court they entered could not, for the next month, be remembered except on those Monday mornings when Judge Murtagh had them wait while he disposed of the morning calendar, a parade of criminal cases lending themselves to summary action, either for judgment or postponement. Judge Murtagh sits in a brown courtroom. All last fall and into the spring, there remained unrepaired on the wall a hole—the shape and size of a large map of Norway—left behind by falling plaster. If a defendant can hardly expect a jury of persons with a background like his own, we have assured him a trial in surroundings very like his home.

On one of those Mondays Justice Murtagh had before him a building inspector believed to have taken bribes for passing defective fill and convicted of contempt for failure to cooperate with the Grand Jury. Assistant District Attorney Jeffrey Weinfield, curiously slack to those who knew him otherwise only as a sword unsheathed and ready at the Panther hearings, desultorily urged some vague term in prison. "I am loath," Justice Murtagh replied, "to impose sentence in this case." A watcher reflected, without vengeful animus, that on some summer's day the whole East Bronx will sink from sight upon fill of the sort approved by the man before him. No matter; Justice Murtagh understood that a building inspector who takes a bribe could no more understand the social consequences of the act than a young man who signs on as an assistant district attorney. Go, he said, cooperate with the Grand Jury, avoid evil companions.

There stood up a Negro, his defeats much easier than his age to count on his face; a woman from Legal Aid stood by his side. They were plainly strangers to each other. He had been convicted. It was Justice Murtagh's duty to pronounce sentence. The proceedings were inaudible: the Assistant District Attorney said something, the defendant said nothing, and the Legal Aid lawyer barely anything, and the judge gave him a year. He did not seem sure that he had heard what had happened: a year seemed longer than he had expected. The Legal Aid lawyer explained, not coolly annoyed but plainly under pressure for time, that this was as good as they could have gotten.

Legal Aid functions by accommodation of this sort; it is not frequently enough able to offer the defendant services assuring him anything but the sentence the District Attorney appoints for him. It is another assumption of the criminal bar that no attorney in charge of Legal Aid's criminal division is ever appointed without prior solicitation of the District Attorney's opinion of his capacities.

Then Justice Murtagh abandoned the comfort of having defendants who are accustomed to be humble and turned to their disconcerting opposites in front of him. Their difference from the usual defendants was most noticeable during the month of their outcries; but those, while seldom irrelevant, were not always apposite, not invariably reflecting the dignity of revolutionaries. They produced more laughter than they ought to have. One felt that, if these fluid improvisations continued too long, we would arrive at a certain failure of seriousness from men and women in a tragic circumstance.

The lines, even for persons implacably defense-minded, were not clearly enough drawn; some part of almost everyone has to go out to a judge who is being called a pig. There was too much of the coarseness, not enough of the kindness, too much of the impudence, and not enough of the simple bravery some of us have come to admire in the Panthers. One could not say that it did not work but, inescapably, it would not work for long; the defendants had chosen the resource of the night-club insult, and that is a well where the bucket hits the bottom very soon.

But that something more which might reward a patient wait upon them was suggested just once that month when the defendant Michael Tabor gave his witness. The defense had been contesting the scope of the police search on the arrest night; and Michael Tabor had been called to describe the morning hours when they came for him. His opening reminiscence was of coming home after midnight and of talking to his wife before they went to sleep:

"We discussed our coming child," he said, "and the ways and means the party can serve the needs of the people, specifically the free breakfast program."

The elevation of this tone ought to have been ridiculous; but it was everything except that. The voice enforced a majesty to which Michael Tabor's past troubles of drug addiction and present circumstance of imprisonment could assert no formal claim. It was the voice of the organ in the cathedral. The same god that had granted him this instrument had added the most perfect instinct for its employment. No sentence departed from the cadence of the litany; the chosen word was always the stately as against the common one. (Wouldn't we say "help the people" where Michael Tabor says "serve"?) And as he had found the precise tone, archaic without ever being primitive, for this old-fashioned instrument, he had found its most proper theme: for the next two days we would listen to a nineteenth-century man explaining his salvation by Grace.

He was yielded up to Assistant District Attorney Phillips who approached him with the assurance, the coldness, the contempt of that rectitude which is armed with the criminal record of the witness.

Michael Tabor conceded the record. He is twenty-three now and had been a narcotics addict from the time he was thirteen until he was nineteen; and he had stolen to "secure funds for my habit."

"Is it fair," the Assistant District Attorney pursued, "to say that you would lie, cheat, steal, or kill to get narcotics?"

"I have lied, stolen, cheated to get narcotics," Tabor amended, "I would not kill."

"When did you become truthful, Mr. Tabor?" Phillips asked.

"When I liberated my soul and body from the plague of hair-o-wine," Tabor answered.

It went on that way, the District Attorney leaping, the witness pulling him gravely, even sardonically, to earth, until a moment when there came a defense suggestion of a recess. "A recess," Phillips protested, "gives the defendant an opportunity to be coached." He remained possessed of the caricature he had brought with him; he could still imagine no source except coaching for a performance of this quality from a person so contemptible. How little of life the criminal prosecutor knows. Joseph Phillips must have processed a thousand felons, most of them black and all of them too full of common sense to risk talking back to him; he had never had a chance to know that the Street, for a thoughtful pupil, is our one best school for counterpunchers.

Yielded at last back to Crain, one of his defense lawyers, Michael Tabor explained his struggle with heroin:

"I began with hair-o-wine at the age of thirteen. I thought it something slick, something sly. Then, after a while I did not feel my nauseous and disgusting reality. I did not smell the rancid stench of the urine-soaked tenement dungeons. I did not hear the wailing sirens of the police cars. I did not feel the uncollected garbage underneath my feet. I sank deeper and deeper into the pit of degradation."

And then, just when he had begun to recover, he had met "a piece of literature, *The Autobiography of Malcolm X*. It gave me a new purpose in life." There had come over the courtroom a silence rather like awe; the organ had struck the key in its audience. We were listening, with no visible intrusion of irony noticeable on the faces even of his prosecutors, to a man on trial for arson and attempted murder telling us how his soul had been saved. He had arrived, he carried us, to an understanding through an investigation of himself and of the system and he had learned:

"Heroin addicts and alcoholics are all woven from the same fabric. It's just that their disease manifests itself in different forms. The only way the various psychological diseases can be overcome is by effecting a radical overall change in the social system."

And at that, the spell over Judge Murtagh seemed to break. The cure of alcoholism is one of his several good works; and there intruded upon him Michael Tabor's equation of the Irish curse with the black one—of the drunk with the addict. The identification could not be made. He roused himself, the gap between them opened again, and he said, "Counsel, don't you think we had better get back to the issues before the court."

So then, the once-born are trying the twice-born. Phillips recognizes that. Whenever he rises before some judge to whom the defense lawyers have hopelessly repaired, he justifies his treatment of these prisoners by imagining the infamy of their characters, and reaches for the worst thing he can say about them. It always is,

"They are terrorists rather than ordinary criminals-for-profit."

They are then, for their prosecutor, simply the kind of ruffians society cannot employ or forgive—the over-principled kind. The defendants understand that special mark upon them; even Richard Moore, the Panther who was the lord of their misrule in Justice Murtagh's courtroom, does not mock when he comes to contemplate what for him is plainly his redemption. He, more than all the others, is of the Street. He went to prison after a gang fight when he was seventeen and stayed there to the end of his five-year term, adamant against the acquisition of one day's good time.

"I didn't do time like everyone else," he says. "The average blood upstate does it nice. The guards used to say to me, 'Why do you do your time so hard? Every other dude up here tries to smile.' But, when I came out, I asked myself why should I ever go back for nothing, like stealing a pocketbook. Why shouldn't I go for trying to change things, for trying to deal everybody a brand new deck?"

Most of the hearings have been given over to the testimony of policemen on the conduct of the arrest and search of various defendants. It is Justice Murtagh's task to assay their probity; his bearing at this assignment was a reminder of how early he found his church and how secure he is in its assumptions. In the forties, when he was Mayor O'Dwyer's Commissioner of Investigations, he was indicted for a failure of zeal in pursuing his inquiries into a police department which had sold itself intact to a bookie.

The indictment had no basis except political spite. In February the *Times* had the bad grace to mention it and occasionally thereafter some defendant or other would shout at Justice Murtagh, "You're a bandit judge; you been indicted." But that was unfair. Justice Murtagh was then, as now, incapable of corruption; he was also unfortunately then, as now, incapable of imagining that policemen could lie. That incapacity may explain his rise in the courts. There are very few people who do not know that policemen lie by now; and district attorneys are dependent enough on those lies to cherish any judge innocent enough to believe them.

Policemen have to lie, if only because they are incurable slovens at record-keeping and must invent explanations to take care of the pedantries of constitutional prejudice. These hearings, for example, have been a series of revelations of warrants missing, official reports unfiled, memo books lost. Beyond those minor lapses in procedure, there were no search warrants in this case, a lack which cast a shadow over the rights of the arresting officers to seize any objects not in plain sight. As a result they were forced to conjure up for Judge Murtagh vistas of rifle stocks protruding from beneath mattresses and gun butts falling out of closets and other prodigies, making it necessary for them to soil the Constitution while protecting the public by rummaging through anyone's bureau drawers. No one except Justice Murtagh could have believed any of it.

The defense had no recourse except to probe for evidence of some special zeal which these policemen may have brought to this assignment from their hatred of the Panthers. Success, for what it might be worth, was available to them only on the first day: Detective Joseph Coffey reported that he had found Tabor "most docile" when he was finally brought to earth. There was enough malice in his satisfaction to encourage Lefcourt to press on in the afternoon:

Defense Counsel: Have you said that the Black Panthers should be eliminated?

Coffey: Yes, sir.

Nightfall seems to have been a time for Mr. Phillips to make sure that no future witness allow himself a show of emotion even this inconsequential; everyone who followed Coffey had that suavity and disinterest in matters of public controversy we generally see in policemen on the witness stand, if not nearly so often on the street.

The defendants appeared incensed when Coffey described Tabor as docile under custody. They seem in general rather embarrassed at having been taken without firing back, as though anyone who had observed their exuberance after ten months in prison could question their courage or doubt the dignity of Michael Tabor's containment under any circumstances.

Yet they have been brought here at least as much for what they said as for anything they may have planned to do; and it would seem very much to their best interest not to fortify the District Attorney in his assurance that what they say is what they do. A man as obviously spirited and unafraid as Tabor, who has three guns at hand and enough time to ready them after the police knock on his door and who takes that time to decide to give himself over, peaceably and proudly, is someone rather different from Phillips's crude drawing of a thug living by the gun. But these defendants are different from ordinary defendants peculiarly in their scorn for their own best interest; they are incapable of pretense.

Except perhaps pretense to themselves. The Black Panther Party grew, after all, out of an environment where, to be recognized as gallant, it is too often necessary to present oneself as suicidal. Their enemy, more intimate than the policeman, is the Street hustler, for it is the style of the hustler—slickness, evasiveness, absolute self-interest—against whose temptations to the young the Panthers place their own model.

The element of violence in the Panther model is an extraordinarily subtle thing to assay. The most conspicuous creation of what the Panthers think of as the genius of Huey P. Newton was his discovery and elevation of the gun to religious symbol. Now to accept Tabor's description of the chasteness of his domestic life and his apparent freedom from any temptation to pick up his weapon and turn his home into a charnel house is to conceive of how many Panthers there must be to whom the gun is less an implement than a metaphor, to be hung on the wall as the devout of another religion might hang a cross. Confined to those terms, essentially abstract, the gun, one supposes, can be thought of as a symbol of all those qualities—courage, resistance to oppression, manhood (also womanhood and childhood, the Panthers having a deep respect for the dignity of every identity)—which the creed aims to inspire.

But a gun *is* an instrument; it has a function which no conversion into metaphor can ever remove from the mind of its beholder; and, every step it is brought from the abstract toward the concrete, carries us toward uses which, in all prior experience, have been overwhelmingly more for the bad than the good.

There is the same troubling ambiguity in the Panther rhetoric, so familiar for its emphasis on calling policemen "pigs." We may very well assume that Huey Newton thought of this epithet—like the gun—as a symbol and sign to his community and the indifferent America outside that there are young black people who refuse any longer to be afraid. And yet the epithet like the gun can be a very dangerous way to cast out fear; you wonder, indeed, after meeting so many Panthers, how they can say such things and retain spirits so tangibly undisabled by that process. To call a man a "pig" is to say that he is less than human and its main function is as preparation to treating him that way. Joseph Phillips would hardly have been so cruel to Lee Berry if he had not first told himself that he was dealing with a vicious animal undeserving of considerations of humanity. Phillips had to take the first step in order to take the second; but, in general certainly, Panthers do not take the second step. Why then do all of them insist on taking the first?

A wise man greatly sympathetic to the Panthers has said of them, "Panthers are mirror images of cops. Panthers are hung up on masculinity, guns and cops. Cops are hung up on masculinity, guns and Panthers." But the matter does not reduce itself this simply; if it did we should not have the memory of those moments when Panthers have the ability to evoke the sympathy of almost everyone who watches them. Are those not the moments when the Panther shows himself not the mirror but the better of the enemy who holds him, as Bobby Seale was better than Judge Hoffman and Michael Tabor, on that scene at least, was better than Joseph Phillips? An adept, such occasions suggest, can maintain that balance of harshness of rhetoric with humanity of nature which the Panthers inflict on themselves; one can say of the Black Panther Party that, as religion, it deserves the highest compliment to a religion from any outside observer: it does have the power to make worthy people better and unworthy ones no worse.

But no religion begins with converts who entirely understand the metaphor which draws them to it. That is the peril of the symbols of the gun and the epithet. The Panthers were young; they are in all matters candid. We can appreciate how open they were, and how trusting of strangers, from the vulnerability to police informants which has been an element in almost every case brought against them. They could hardly have been more vulnerable to the driftings in and out of irresponsibles. And then there were their conversations—the style of talk they brought with them from the Street, what one Panther called "Afro-American kidding," talk whose main purpose is relief of the self from the reality around.

Once Joseph Phillips asked Michael Tabor if he had ever thought of killing a policeman.

"I could not suppose that there is any Black person who has not at one time or another thought about killing a policeman," Michael Tabor gravely answered.

There is an allegation that these defendants planned to blow up the Bronx Botanical Gardens which sits in the indictment unsupported by any charges of acts suggestive of real intention. Yet it is difficult to believe that a police officer could have the imagination to invent the idea of the Botanical Gardens as a target. It is one of those fantasies of apocalypse—the image of all that glass splintering in the air above the surrounding tenements—that demand an imagination of the sort which comes from the Street and not the station house. Someone somewhere in the Panther ambience must idly have talked about it some afternoon.

These defendants, then, have armed their enemies with excuses even to the point where every casual word of theirs may now be judged as though it were an act of fixed criminal intent. But to suspect that such trivial things contributed to their present troubles is not to suggest that they are trivial persons. They are, to the contrary, entirely worthy to be recognized as enemies of the American system as it is.

What is most impressive is their resource; the dreadful experiences of the past year which ought to have dulled and made them, if not visibly beaten, certainly no better than sullen, seem instead to have made them more open to fraternity, more curious about the promise of the future than their party's rhetoric ever seemed to suggest in the days when they were safer.

One grew to notice, for example, how seldom their interruptions of Judge Murtagh's proceedings were beside the point. They were almost always reactions to something that had just been said in the courtroom. The style of these interventions was less important than their desperation to be heard; you recognized not just the rage at what America is but the surviving
respect for what it might be. They are, then, young persons of complexity which can be
described and not explained in one of Richard Moore's outcries:

"You are denying me my *rights* under the Fourth Amendment of your *racist* Constitution."

The painful, in this case almost heroic, interior quarrel about America these words convey is, in heightened intensity, very like the quarrel in so many of the rest of us these days. Finding it, one feels the company not of the alien but of the native, not of the stranger but of one's old and admired acquaintance, the soldier in the war of this country with itself. He is being tried and in danger of being judged only as his caricature.

"One underappreciated advantage to being a pauper . . ."

9·9·71

One underappreciated advantage to being a pauper is that you have the good luck to belong to the only group of Americans in whose morals your government takes a consuming interest.

The noun "fraud" is seldom uttered in respectable precincts unless the adjective "welfare" is attached to it. In New York, a Republican Governor and a Democratic Controller are currently contending to be loudest to cry up the newest welfare fraud.

The most recent annoyance devised for us by the poor turns out to be receiving a welfare check, swearing it was stolen, getting oneself issued another, and then having both cashed. Forty-four thousand relief checks were thus guided astray last year, and the consequent fraud is estimated at $4 million annually. The State Controller also charges that nearly 5 percent of the persons on relief in New York City are ineligible for assistance because they have assets concealed from the investigators. The poor are notoriously more ingenious and their welfare officials more permissive in New York City than elsewhere, of course; but if we accept this percentage as the national average we can judge that false claims for welfare cost the whole country some $60 million a year.

Now what is striking in these figures is their comparative precisions; but then the defalcations of the poor are the only swindles in America that anyone seems to bother to count. The Federal government did recently report that the defense contractors overcharged it $65 million last year; more by the way than the best estimate of our annual loss to welfare cheats; but then no one thinks of excess profits as a fraud; they are merely an ordinary business precaution.

But when you come to devices that everybody agrees are dishonest and that middle-class persons are licensed to perform, we have no way of telling how much anyone steals. Not long ago, *The Wall Street Journal* reported on the national growth of short-weighting in stores. "The pennies add up fast enough," the *Journal* decided, "that estimates of the total U.S. loss from short-weighting start at one-and-one half billion dollars and rise to as high as 10 billion a year." Now *The Wall Street Journal* is our great model for exactitude in computations; but like us all, it is in this case a victim of our habit of counting only what we think worth counting; and so it can tell us within $1,000 what the poor of New York steal each year by forging welfare checks; but it can't tell us within $4 billion what the merchant steals by shorting-weighting his merchandise.

We ought then altogether to be grateful to the poor for being there for us to investigate; otherwise there might be no one to investigate except us respectable people.

My Last Mugging

December 1971

We are all addicts in various stages of degradation where I live on the Upper West Side, some to heroin, some to small dogs, and some to *The New York Times*. The heroin is cut, the dogs are paranoid, and the *Times* cheats by skimping on the West Coast ball scores. No matter; each of us goes upon the street solely in pursuit of his own particular curse.

I was plodding homeward with my *Times* at an hour no less decent than eleven on an evening in March when two figures, conspicuous through the dark for a condition of nerves frantic even for West 97th Street, came round the corner and converged upon me, one to the left and one to the right.

The one to the right was short and wore a porkpie hat of the kind one used to associate with the first account executive laid off in the agency's economy drive in the first Eisenhower recession. The one to the left was taller, sticklike, indeed, with those whitened cracks in the skin of his face that the winter of cities inflicts upon Negroes and that they call "the ashes"; and he held a knife at what I supposed to be my kidneys.

"Give us all your money," the little one stuttered. "Or we're going to cut you up right now."

"Now, be cool," the tall one said. "And just hand over your money. He means it."

Cops are said to go at criminal suspects in this fashion, in pairs, one short and mean, the other tall and protective. So here, then, were those two familiars of the station house, Jeff ravening on one side of the detainee and Mutt conciliating on the other. As jail seems to be the only institution left that can teach young black men to write, the back room of the precinct house is the last school for the techniques of negotiation. I was being accosted by ruffians who had learned their trade by losing—laboratory animals who knew nothing of the science except what could be studied while being vivisected.

The knife was, to be sure, long enough and broad enough to establish itself as the one commanding presence in the assembly; still, it was a very old knife, with no sign of any recent impulse to clean it; the hand at my kidneys had, then, quite a while ago lost either the vanity that might have shined that knife or the hope that might have sharpened it.

The mind could grasp it only as an abstraction. Courage is the product of rehearsal, as cowardice is of recollection; neither comes on call upon occasions of surprise: Surprised, one merely stands and the head wanders down paths that prove how empty the event is, since they are not even literary, only sociological—a disgraceful knife, a failure of a knife, good only for my neighborhood, a knife a man would be embarrassed to carry in the East Sixties, less a knife, indeed, than an artifact of urban decay. Where I live, we get the criminals and even the weapons of hopelessness we deserve.

"Gentlemen," I began, "I haven't got so much as a dollar. I do have some change and a subway token. But that's all I have. I'm sorry."

I took out my wallet and showed it to them with an anxiety to please that, at the moment, at least, had curiously less to do with the knife than with the recurrent sense of my own inadequacy on social occasions. I felt like a welsher. They had done their job; they had pulled a knife, such as it was, and quite enough for me; and I wasn't doing mine. Jeff was already exhausted from his contrivings of desperate aggression; and poor Mutt was left to manage the affair to its end in disillusion.

"Let's get off the street," he said. "I gotta search you." And they pushed me unzestfully into the entranceway of a building I had never before known to be other than packed with inexplicably cheerful Latins, but empty now; and there, in the bright light that illuminated how much too old all of us were for such a scene, Mutt searched me, as the police must have trained him during his service in their laboratories, all the way to the crotch.

He came up empty and reproachful.

"You look like a workingman," he said. "What you doing out in the street with no money?"

It seemed entirely proper to apologize.

"Gentlemen," I said at last, "I feel like a shit."

"Don't you think we feel like shits?" Mutt answered. "We don't like to do this kind of thing. All we're looking for is a couple of bucks to get a shot of dope."

Where I live, we are rather stiff-necked about permitting someone else to claim the moral advantage. They turned and left the lobby, with Mutt trailing the knife slackly against his trouser leg, the whole night yet before him and without the will to recover from this first mischance.

I felt the sixty cents still in my hand and called after them, "Well, anyway, take the change."

And Mutt came back and took it, and we said good night, and I went home with no sense that I had made it up to them.

For a while afterward, I dined out on this event, and everyone I told it to seemed to find it a great relief from urban tensions. And yet the experience, whose telling seems to work to lessen the paranoia of other persons, has impossibly increased my own. Not just 97th Street but nearly every other in the city has become for me a swarm of horrible shadows. I have no way even of knowing when the fear will come over me; the other day a Negro teenager approached me in a subway station and just stood there. At last he asked for a dime and, sweating, I gave him all the change I had. He had intended nothing; and yet I was his victim; my flesh could not have crawled more shudderingly if he had pulled a gun. I have thought of buying a heavy cane. Yet if I went thus armed, I should suppose that I would bring my weapon down upon the head of whoever accosted me and then beat him passionately, if ineffectually, for mere rage at this city that has taught me that I am old and a coward. For these are scenes from which it is impossible to emerge unashamed. And I am thinking of moving away to some far place where a man can keep his mask and have no need to choose between wearing the face of the victim or the face of the beast.

“Our war with North Vietnam . . .”

1 • 30 • 73

Our war with North Vietnam is a wound upon our history at once so murky and so melancholy that it is impossible even to say precisely when we began it.

There were less than 1,000 Americans in uniform in Indochina when President Eisenhower left office; and there were 16,000 when President Kennedy was killed. But we did not speak of having soldiers in combat until 1965 when President Johnson commenced the bombing of North Vietnam and began that infusion of American troops which was to crest at 536,000 by the time he left office.

The war’s beginning, like its end, is in shadows. But suppose we date it from the moment when the reality became too loud and too terrible to be concealed. That would be in the spring of 1965, which is nearly eight years ago.

At that time our intelligence officers judged that there were no more than 14,000 regular North Vietnamese troops in South Vietnam.

Since then nearly 45,000 American soldiers have been killed, close to 150,000 seriously wounded and perhaps 100,000 fallen into drug addiction. The available estimates put the number of South Vietnamese civilians killed as a by-product of combat at 415,000. How many of these objects of our concern and sacrifice were killed by American soldiers cannot be estimated. But it is a very large figure indeed; for altogether, in seven and a half years, our Air Force dropped 289 pounds of explosives for every living inhabitant of the four countries of Indochina.

And as they bore the bombs, we bore an expense which seems to share out at about $50,000 for every inhabitant of the United States.

When we embarked upon our resistance to aggression, there were, as I have said, perhaps 14,000 North Vietnamese regulars in the South. Now there are at least 145,000 and by our consent they will remain.

So much for where we have been and so much for what we have brought back from there. Never in our history, when we have thought of our dead in war, indeed when we have thought of everyone's dead, has it ever been less possible to hope that these were not useless deaths. Let us remember them all and not least when the next wise man in Government tells us that he knows more than the rest of us about how to secure the honor and the dignity of the United States of America.

"The streakers seem to have disappeared . . ."

3 • 21 • 74

The streakers seem to have disappeared over the horizon almost as rapidly as they flashed upon us. Their fleeting passage as a social phenomenon was less striking for the performance than for its reception, which was a mingling of the laughter of the few and the yawns of the many.

They were indeed so transient that it is hard to believe that they had time to provide material for so much as one PhD thesis on mass observation. The streakers arrived too late for most of us to care—like those nude bars in Southern California which struggle to convince an indifferent public that it is worth two dollars to see two and a half more inches of skin than is free to the eye at the public beach next door.

The erotic revolution in America has reached the destination that seems appointed for most revolutions these days: It is bankrupt, and can offer only the ultimate redeeming social purpose, which is boredom.

The streakers indeed managed to provide no more interesting measure of the state of our culture than the studied inattention to their comings and goings from the appointed guardians of the national morality. But then the guardians of the national morality are distracted these days, since so many of them are friends of persons currently undergoing the future peril or the present affliction of some criminal indictment. Still the silence of the Rev. Billy Graham is considerably more refreshing than the proclamation of any streaker; and when Norman Vincent Peale tells us that he does not feel called upon to give spiritual advice to his friend Mr. Nixon, we have the lively consolation of knowing that this abstention at least bars him a while from preaching to any of the rest of us.

If the streakers had manifested themselves a year ago, we should no doubt have had to endure from Vice President Agnew no end of lamentation about the erosion of national morals their appearance represented. But it is our good fortune that Mr. Agnew has been unfrocked from his calling as Cato the Censor, and is working in decent obscurity on a novel about a Vice President whose only sin seems to be adultery with the Madame Secretary of Health Education and Welfare. And after burglary and bribery, it will seem almost a return to our original illusion of innocence to be able to read about politicians who sternly limit themselves to old fashioned practices like adultery and drunkenness. We have never been quite this conscious of how many frauds there are among our governors but we can be grateful that their exposure debars them from being pious frauds for a while.

Witnesses

6 • 10 • 76

Scoundrel Time is the third of the meditations of Lillian Hellman's memory. Its single theme is her summons by the House Committee on Un-American Activities in 1952, her decision to refuse to yield up the names of Communists she had known, the worse trouble with the Hollywood blacklist that followed that trouble, and the dignity and the shrewdness that carried her through both.

Miss Hellman has developed a style for these discourses very close to the ideal for letters, say, from an aunt who is envied for her experience of the world and enjoyed for her candor and her comic sense whenever they are directed at persons other than yourself—always a comfortable majority of the cases—amusing, affecting, persuasive, entirely charming, if you don't too much mind being hectored now and then.

Her nieces seem somehow luckier than her nephews. Nieces, I suspect, read her letters for that feminine wisdom condemned to be misunderstood as womanly folly: the sensibility that armors itself with a Balmain dress for the ordeal by the Committee on Un-American Activities, the taste that notices the habit awkward social occasions have of being accompanied by bad food, the gaiety that conquers dread with shopping sprees. It is hard for nephews to find that much unforced pleasure in Miss Hellman; they have to be wary of possible disapproval.

I have never quite understood upon what altar Miss Hellman's moral authority was consecrated; but that authority is there, was there even before the apotheosis of her risky yet grand appearance before the Committee on Un-American Activities. To measure how far and for how long a time her writ has run we need only to consider the case of Elia Kazan, who had decided that it was necessary for him, as they used to say in those days, to "come clean" with the Committee on Un-American Activities. Kazan is one of those persons who would have especially profited from the injunction "Never Apologize, Never Explain." As it was, in his ignorance, he spread apologies for his small sins and explanations of his vast redemption all over the advertising pages of *The New York Times*, and lifted them like prayers to heaven to Spyros Skouras, president of Twentieth Century Fox.

That was an acceptance of humiliation for the sake of survival in a confiscatory tax bracket, an impulse for which, if we cannot often find enough excuse, we can at least locate an identifiable source. But then, in the midst of his flagellations, Kazan sought out Miss Hellman, who had not yet appeared before the committee, to explain himself to her. It was an overture to humiliation for humiliation's own sake that does not now lend itself to reasonable understanding. The scene can only be guessed at among the clouds that surround Miss Hellman's reincarnation in the memoir, but we can glimpse in it the Confederate lady who uplifted the soldier in the heat of his youth and waited in the twilight to receive, but in no measure to entertain, the veteran's apology for having joined the board of directors of the carpetbagger's railroad.

Miss Hellman's strength of character is great, but of a kind that is hard to comprehend apart from its candid snobbishness. When she searches for the core of the self that enabled her to resist and left Clifford Odets naked to surrender to the House Committee on Un-American Activities, she can return with no discovery more useful than:

> It is impossible to think that a grown man, intelligent, doesn't have some sense of how he will act under pressure. It's all been decided so long ago, when you are very young, all mixed up with your childhood's definition of pride or dignity.

Many [American intellectuals] found in the sins of Stalin Communism—and there were plenty of sins and plenty that for a long time I mistakenly denied—the excuse to join those who should have been their hereditary enemies. Perhaps that, in part, was the penalty of nineteenth-century immigration. The children of timid immigrants are often remarkable people: energetic, intelligent, hard-working, and often they make it so good that they are determined to keep it at any cost.

Observations of that tenor somehow suggest that for strong spirits like Miss Hellman's, the Sunday family dinner is material for rebellion in childhood, comedy in middle age, and attitudes in final maturity. What is here intimated is some doctrine of predestination by growing up with servants in the kitchen, but it is not easy to think such a notion prepossessing and impossible to find it serviceable as a measurement for moral development. We are left to wonder why Sen. Harry Flood Byrd, whose mother was in every way a Virginia lady, should have arrived at his fullest spiritual bloom ringing changes on the word "nigger" on public platforms, or why John Foster Dulles, grandson of an American secretary of state, should have managed a career whose most striking achievement was the avoidance of any suspicion that the impulse of a gentleman might ever intrude upon his conduct. Let us settle for saying that *Commentary*'s tone was lamentable in the early fifties, when its editor was Eliot Cohen; for what worse epithet must we thereupon reach to describe *Time*, the weekly newsmagazine, in the days when its managing editor was Thomas S. Matthews, son of the Episcopal Bishop of the Diocese of New Jersey?

We move, I think, closer to the truth about those years when Miss Hellman swam against the current and Odets sank beneath it if we think of the fifties as a time not much different from this one and a majority of others when most people acted badly, and public faces passed by as a succession of gray embarrassments infrequently illuminated by displays of dignity like Miss Hellman's. Banality is the only sort of chic that always has its fashion; and we need not be surprised that Miss Hellman, thanks to her superb hour of resistance to banal chic, should now be punished with the comfortable indignity of being enshrined by it.

". . . An intense, moving moral," *Time* says of her story now. "She was brave because her private code would not allow her to be anything else. She dabbled in radical politics and befriended Communists because she thought it was her right as an American to associate with whomever she damn well pleased. . . . *Scoundrel Time* is a memorable portrait of . . . a polished stylist and an invaluable American."

The tone of *Time*'s original report on Miss Hellman's encounter with the House Committee on Un-American Activities had, of course, been faithfully cast into the cadences of what Edmund Wilson once called its "peculiar kind of jeering rancor."

> Her sympathies [had] led her to attend countless Red-inspired rallies and lend her name to various Communist-front crusades . . . as the record shows, a skilled playwright and a great meeting goer.

Caption on Miss Hellman's photograph, *Time*, May 10, 1976:

> PLAYWRIGHT HELLMAN: "An expert at smooth dialogue."

But after all, as Burke said, "We are very uncorrupt and tolerably enlightened judges of the transactions of past ages. . . . Few are the partisans of departed tyrannies." So, when Mr. Nixon was in his terminal throes, we were treated to the spectacle of White House Counsel Dean Burch, who had come first to our notice as manager of Sen. Goldwater's presidential campaign, complaining to the journalists about the "McCarthyite tactics" of the House Judiciary Committee. A year or so ago, *New York* magazine published an interview with Ted Ashley, the talent agent. Its most inspiring passages recited Ashley's brave, lonely, and, so far as his own memory seemed to suggest, successful struggle to defend Philip Loeb, the actor, against the blacklist. It seems to have been of no consequence to the glory of this Iliad that, if not by Ashley's will, certainly with his ultimate compliance, Loeb had been so effectively blacklisted that throughout the year before his suicide he had been able to find no employment above the $87.50 a week Off-Broadway scale. Those who can forget their own history are rewarded by having it forgotten by pretty much everyone else.

When we consider the general practice of using memory so earnestly as an instrument for mendacity, it is a sufficient miracle for Miss Hellman to be so honest a witness; and our admiration for her integrity cannot grow smaller for a final impression that *Scoundrel Time* is not quite true. Honesty and truth are not just the same thing, since the first has to do with character and the second with self-understanding of a cruder kind than hers.

Miss Hellman cannot be blamed for *Time*'s having spoken of her political history as a business of having "dabbled in radical politics." But, even so, the very light brush she brings to her treatment of what must have been a commitment of high self-discipline could well contribute to such a misapprehension. She was, by every evidence, what she most puzzlingly denies she was—one of "those serious, dedicated people"—and she would not have needed to rely so entirely upon herself in her troubles if she hadn't been. It is therefore rather unsettling to come upon musings like:

> the mishmash of those years, beginning before my congressional debut and for years after, took a heavy penalty. My belief in liberalism was mostly gone. . . . There was nothing strange about my problem, it is native to our time; but it is painful for a nature that can no longer accept liberalism not to be able to accept radicalism.

Now except for the lonely period when she could have used their goodwill most, the run of liberals has shown great respect and no little affection for Miss Hellman, and for more substantial reasons than the reverence liberals render to success and the odd pleasure so many of them draw from being scolded. But all the same it would be surprising if Miss Hellman could have been left with many illusions about liberals by the time, long before McCarthyism, when she had completed her apprenticeship with Horace Liveright. By the late forties, the most prominent liberals were busy antagonists of her two most heartfelt causes, Henry Wallace's campaign for president as a Progressive in 1948, and the Cultural and Scientific Conference for World Peace at the Waldorf-Astoria in 1949.

The Waldorf conference was beset with more obloquy than it deserved; but I cannot think that Garry Wills has come quite up to the lofty mark for historical objectivity that he has maintained almost everywhere else when he speaks, in his introduction, of Miss Hellman's having, in her wartime trips to the Soviet Union, "formed friendships there not subject to any government line, so she helped arrange for artists and scholars to meet and discuss what would later (when a new line came in) be called 'detente.'" What had been arranged might less enthusiastically be described as a discussion between Americans who spoke critically of their government and Russians who could hardly have offered theirs any such treatment and safely gone home. It is doubtful that the Waldorf conference provided any historical lesson more significant than that Lillian Hellman got in trouble because she attended it and Dmitri Shostakovich risked worse trouble if he hadn't. But, all the same, there is, I suppose, a case to be made for encounters of this sort, and it seems a loss that Miss Hellman takes note of the affair in terms so cursory as to afford us no reflections upon it at all.*

Miss Hellman does tarry longer with the Wallace campaign, but her pause there is not productive of one of her better effects. Very little about Wallace himself seems to have endured in her memory except for "certain embarrassing scenes" in restaurants arising from his inadequacies as a tipper and "the stingy, discourteous supper" (poached eggs on shredded wheat) that he served her when last they parted. Granted that Miss Hellman's generosity of spirit is not one of her

* Cedric Belfrage's *American Inquisition, 1945–1960* (Bobbs-Merrill, 1973), the best perhaps because it is the most radical account that I know of those days, contains a tidy summary of the Waldorf conference, and makes it sound much more interesting than most of us permitted ourselves to imagine. The remarks of Harlow Shapley, Norman Mailer, and I. F. Stone sound especially notable for critical independence; for the flavor of the Russians we can be satisfied with this: "Shostakovich described Russia's mushroom growth of music activity, *especially in Soviet Asia*, which had neither an orchestra, a chorus nor an opera house thirty years ago."

more remarkable qualities, she is in no way a trivial woman; and it is some trial to the patience to see her reducing what, for someone like her, must have been convictions intensely and even fiercely felt to stuff so trivial as this.

She remembers that she quarreled with the Communists over the conduct of the Progressive Party's campaign because she would not abate her "constant pleas that we turn attention and money away from the presidential campaign and put them into building small chapters around the country in hope of a solid, modest future." Again there is that uneasy sense of diversion to the marginal. Are we really to imagine that Miss Hellman found the influence of the Communist caucus on the Progressive Party more objectionable when it was merely blundering about tactics than when it was upholding its stern principles by persuading the 1948 convention to reject a motion that the party platform include the statement that "it is not our intention to give blanket endorsement to the foreign policy of any nation"? For the Old Left had principles, good ones and bad ones, or for that matter bad good and good bad ones, and they must have held a substantial place in Miss Hellman's consciousness a long while before the day she embodied the simple and pure principle that she served so well in her troubles. It is an annoyance to have her leave so many mists around them.

We do not diminish the final admiration we feel owed to Dashiell Hammett when we wonder what he might have said to Miss Hellman on the night he came home from the meeting of the board of the Civil Rights Congress which voted to refuse its support to the cause of James Kutcher, a paraplegic veteran who had been discharged as a government clerical worker because he belonged to the Trotskyite Socialist Workers party. But then Hammett was a Communist and it was an article of the party faith that Leon Trotsky, having worked for the Emperor of Japan since 1904, had then improved his social standing by taking employment with the Nazis in 1934. Thus any member of the Socialist Workers party could be considered by extension to be no more than an agent of Hitler's ghost. Given that interpretation of history, Paul Robeson spoke from principle when a proposal to assist the Trotskyite Kutcher was raised at a public meeting of the Civil Rights Congress. Robeson drove it from the floor with a declaration to the effect that you don't ask Jews to help a Nazi or Negroes to help the KKK.

Such recollections, of course, by no means tell all or even much about either Robeson or Hammett. But they do suggest that the matter is not entirely simple; and to appreciate its complexity is to recognize that what was imperishable in the hour of Miss Hellman's witness was that she managed to extract and make incarnate its one important and authentic element of simplicity. Hammett had served a prison term the year before for refusing to surrender to the police the names of contributors to the Civil Rights Congress bail fund. Political considerations had hardly entered into his choice at all: He endured his punishment not for the advancement of Marxism-Leninism but because he felt that to keep inviolate the privacy of those who had contributed to a bail fund for Communists had "something to do with keeping my word."

It would be unjust to Miss Hellman's independence of will to suggest that she was brought to her position by the force of Hammett's example. But all the same, if you presumptuously imagine her offering her objections to his course, if only from tenderness, her words hanging there as though unheard, and being left to argue the dilemma through by herself, then you have to suspect that this was one of those experiences that, however otherwise painful, serve to bring its victim to the confrontation of an essential point, which like most good points was a domestic and not a political one.

The enduring eloquence of her statement to the Committee on Un-American Activities belongs not to rhetoric but to conversation:

> I am not willing, now or in the future, to bring bad trouble to people who, in my past association with them, were completely innocent of any talk or any action that was disloyal or subversive. . . . But to hurt innocent people whom I knew many years ago in order to save myself is, to me, inhuman and indecent and dishonorable.

That is not just a fine way of putting the question but the only way, and it seems sufficient to itself. It was enough for Miss Hellman to have done the single great thing of having once and for all defined the issue.

She was by no means the only one who acted well. Arthur Miller acted as well as she—if he could not be said to have performed as superbly—and he took a larger risk of going to prison. If what we call the serious theater otherwise ran short of representatives anxious to enlist as embodiments of its will to resist, comedians like Lionel Stander and Zero Mostel took their places handsomely.

The open Communists absorbed the beatings inflicted upon them by an indifferent official malignity with barely a whimper, not just Robeson and Hammett but scores of others more ordinary. It is ridiculous to give grades in matters like this; but if I had to select just one man who ennobled that age, I think it might be Steve Nelson, Communist party chairman of western Pennsylvania, to the press then only a piece of boilerplate ("Atom Spy Clams Up"), to prosecuting attorneys only a basic natural resource for the process of conspiracy trials.

Standing on his crutches, he acted as his own defense counsel, questioning with some good humor the newest of the prosecution's witnesses ("Tell me, Mr. Stoolpigeon . . ."). It is unlikely that Steve Nelson had ever known many conscious moments when he had not been a Communist, and by then he may no longer have been entirely certain of the wisdom and kindness of Stalin, but he was dead sure that the one inexcusable act was to be a fink. Miss Hellman did not act better than people like those; but what she alone did had its special grandeur: Without mentioning any of them, she drew them about herself and, as none of them had ever been quite able to do, spoke their real reasons for acting as they had.

"I am not willing to bring bad trouble to people. . . ." Rather that I endure my own. That is all that seems finally important about the way she did what she did, and it is a great deal. It would be too much to credit it with any more tangible historical result. The Committee went on just as it had; the blacklist grew if anything more savage and its depredations wider. Miss Hellman's words are memorable not for what they did but for what they said.

It is hard to believe that she ran her course with much risk of going to jail. These doubts have nothing to do with her courage; she would have done her time and been no doubt an excellent con. She might have run serious danger all the same (dignity is always risky) if she had not, quite by accident, come as close as it was ever possible to get to an iron-clad promise of immunity when she retained Joseph L. Rauh as her counsel. She had no way of knowing how seldom an unfriendly witness represented by Joseph L. Rauh ended up convicted of contempt. Rauh's professional skills and high personal honor were the major factors in this record; but it could also be suspected that a less measurable element in his success may have been the general knowledge that Rauh was not inclined to take a client he thought to be a Communist party member, not because of any want of fervor for the rights of such people but rather because he felt that their difference of temperament might make mutual confidence difficult.

Justice Felix Frankfurter's was the crucial vote on a Supreme Court whose rulings on Un-American Activities Committee prosecution were by then gyrating so wildly that there seemed to be no way of explaining them except by Justice Frankfurter's solicitude for the liberties of any American so long as it was reasonably certain that he was not a Communist. If Miss Hellman had been indicted, Rauh's name would have been on the brief for her appeal to the Supreme Court, and Rauh's name by then may well have carried for Justice Frankfurter enough assurance that the appellant was not a Communist to permit him to consider the issues in those abstract realms where freedom debates order. There Justice Frankfurter could often be a libertarian.

But if Miss Hellman had been to any degree calculating in her choice of Rauh, she would hardly have treated his advice as starchily as she did. *Watch on the Rhine*, her anti-Nazi drama, had opened in New York, most tactlessly in the Communist Party's view, a few months before Hitler's tanks announced the demise of his friendship treaty with the Soviets. *The Daily Worker* had criticized Miss Hellman for warmongering and Rauh suggested that this evidence of her independence of the Communist line be submitted to the Un-American Activities Committee as a defense exhibit. (These were days, as Stefan Kanfer has observed, when "the artist was pitiably grateful for bad reviews.") Miss Hellman refused to avail herself of any such umbrella because:

> my use of their attacks on me would amount to my attacking them at a time when they were being persecuted and I would, therefore, be playing the enemy's game. In my thin morality book it is plain not cricket to clear yourself by jumping on people who are themselves in trouble.

We would pay Miss Hellman much less than the due such a sense of honor deserves if we credited it solely to a primal innocence. You feel here the operations of a genuine nobility and no small part of a shrewd instinct about the future, an awareness and such senses have much to do with honor—of how the thing would look in due course. I hardly know Miss Hellman; our only real conversation happened a few days after her testimony. I had read the *New York Times* summary of her statement, and had been moved to express my admiration for it in print, haltingly but with very little competition. Miss Hellman was grateful; but then I was no less grateful to her as I was becoming more and more grateful when members of the Old Left entered my consciousness, reminding me not just of their general humanity but of their personal dignity, and throwing sand into what had for a long time been the mechanical workings of my anti-Communism.

She told me then about her discussion with Elia Kazan, which had preceded his acceptance, and her rejection, of HUAC's demands. She had observed to Kazan at that time, as I remember her account, that they did not, after all, have to make as much money as they had over the years and that, if Hollywood was closed to them, there would still remain the theater and the smaller but by no means uncomfortable living it could afford.

It was her recollection at that time that Kazan had replied that it was all very well for her to say that, because she had spent everything she had ever earned, but that he had savings. And then she told me that her first thought was of how her aunt used to say that you don't go into capital. In her book she remembers a quite different interior response to Kazan's observations—something her grandmother said. Although her memory is clearly the authoritative one, the years have given me too much affection for my own version to give it up; because it seems to me that one of her most important lessons is that there come times when you have to go into capital, and be ready to face up to the loss of a lot, because you are wise enough to sense that the alternative is to lose everything. You will get through, and there will be a time to come when all that will be remembered about you is whether or not you gave the names.

I have to confess, although it is never gracious to say such things, that Miss Hellman's voice in these discourses does not fall upon my ear as coming from someone I should want overmuch as a comrade. She is too vain about judgmental qualities that seem to me by no means her best ones; she is a bit of a bully; and she is inclined to be a hanging judge of the motives of persons whose opinions differ from her own.*

---

* It is a matter of limited moment except to me perhaps, but I cannot contain a desire to express the liveliest resentment of Miss Hellman's statement that James Wechsler "not only was a friendly witness" before the House Un-American Activities Committee "but had high-class pious reasons for what he did." The least offensive thing about this assertion is that it is factually in error. What is far less forgivable is a rancor that Miss Hellman's very eminence and authority ought to instruct her most carefully to ration. Wechsler was never called by the House Un-American Activities Committee: he was subpoenaed by Joe McCarthy after he was made editor of the *New York Post*, and, far from being a friendly witness, he was a manifestly hostile one. ("I may say," he told McCarthy's committee, ". . . that we have repeatedly taken the position that the *New York Post* is as bitterly opposed to Joe Stalin as it is to Joe McCarthy and we believe that a free society can combat both.")

He did decide that the fight against McCarthy would be damaged if he as a conspicuous opponent did not demonstrate his good faith as an anti-Communist by submitting to the committee a list of persons he had known when he was a member of the Young Communist League. I considered his reasons idiotic and told him so; I thought this action lacking, among other things, in proper concern for his personal welfare, because it is seldom possible to explain the giving of names, no matter how high your motive. But if there have been many occasions when I have wondered about Wechsler's good sense, I have never known a time when I felt the smallest doubt about his honor. Perhaps I have a right to say this because, as it happens, I was one of the former Communists that Wechsler named in public while he was wrestling with McCarthy. I also think it a duty of fairness to Miss Hellman to say that my strictures on her disposition are inspired in part by personal feelings in this matter.

But such feelings, even if they were just, would not finally matter when set against that one great moment of hers. It is her summit. We can ask from her nothing more; I do not suppose that, in the only critical sense, we really need to. The most important thing is never to forget that here is someone who knew how to act when there was nothing harder on earth than knowing how to act.

Yes, the Ferry Is Far from Perfect

5 • 18 • 78

There comes to hand, the first of so many fiery red blossoms he will no doubt strew behind him on the path of his recessional, a report from State Controller Arthur Levitt on the deficiencies of the Staten Island Ferry system.

This catalogue of horrors will not be made official until tomorrow; but it can be no dreadful breach of honor to reveal that the controller's agents travelled the ferries through three months of last summer to equip themselves to propel us reeling into shock with the intelligence:

- That ferry boat mates do not tread the bridge on properly purposeful alert for ice floes, sperm whales, monsoons, lascar corsairs and like perils of main;
- That telltale gray is too frequently observed on the dazzling white prescribed for ferry crewmen's ducks;
- And that so lapsed is the fleet from its ancient discipline, ferry boat deckhands often stoop to fraternization with male, and even female, passengers.

These cosmic disclosures will, of course, be published with due solemnity tomorrow, since controllers are sacred objects to journalism, possessed as they are of a primarily ritual function. No matter how trivial their stuff, its tone is unvaryingly portentous.

I myself can never think of the Staten Island ferry without remembering that, by a kind of divine accident, it once provided the most wonderful evening this city has ever given me. I had promised to take my youngest son to see the Bicentennial fireworks at the Statue of Liberty, and, laggard as always, I had led him forth too late for comfort.

I had never more acutely felt the disadvantages of simple citizenship. On scenes like this one promised to be, there is nothing to do except to go to the very center, which is usually empty. My son and I followed that rule, disembarked among the smoking reefers of Bowling Green; and there was no recourse but to go to the ferry shed and trust to chance.

Chance did her duty; the doors opened and we set forth to Staten Island, paused there; and while I was wondering whether to debark and trust to chance on the farther shore, the gates closed and the ferry started back toward Manhattan.

And just at that moment the fireworks began. We proceeded toward the rocket's red glare and then, full in the face of the Statue of Liberty, the captain stopped the ship, and we were there for half an hour while fireballs attacked the night and dissipated a foot from us, and little sailboats slipped silently past, and the voice of Howard Cosell in high polysyllabic frenzy was heard describing it all on a portable radio.

And watching my son's face lit by this wildest of sham battles, I could not quite tell when I was Francis Scott Key at Fort McHenry, when I was David Levinsky approaching Ellis Island and when I was Henry Hudson coming up the channel and crying out, with the recognition of the seasoned sailor he was, "Land ho! The Hudson River."

When it was over, the ferry proceeded to the landing slip; and there the captain appeared on his bridge—a rare manifestation by the controller's account—and we raised to him one great universal cheer.

Leaving, we passed through a crowd of the young who had come too late to make the voyage. A cop was leading them in singing "God Bless America." The glory of that occasion, of course, was not in what this city might be but in what it is. And, if one of the Controller's auditors had happened upon that boat on inspection bent on July 4, 1976, there is no conceiving the severities that tomorrow's report would inflict upon that captain and the single grandest public night of his life and ours. Let him go down on his knees and confess to the auditors; that ferry boat did not, undeniably, arrive on schedule.

We Owe the Mob a Lot

3 • 25 • 78

The police yesterday removed the remains of Leopold Landenhauf from their appointed resting place in the trunk of a car in Parking Lot 8 of Kennedy Airport, that Valhalla of the Honored Society.

The ventilated carcass of some brother or in-law of the Family is now showing up for display somewhere within our city limits every nineteen hours. This is not a depletion rate for a precious natural resource that the healthiest economy can endure.

The astromancers of Mafia Studies, our most venerated branch of the occult, have never estimated the membership of the Honored Society at more than five thousand, which is only enough to last us for eleven years at the present rate of consumption.

The Mafia makes an immense contribution to our economy not because it exploits us but because we exploit it. The only Families to have made a truly handsome score from organized crime in the last decade are the Puzos and the Coppolas. Practice the Mafia's code of silence and you glower your life out in the Cafe Roma and die in any alley; write about the Mafia and you sleep at the Plaza and die of a surfeit of Kron's chocolate.

The history of organized crime is a melancholy chronicle of successive discoveries of avenues of profit that were in due time stolen from it by organized respectability. Nothing illegal stays illegal once it is shown that there is money to be made from it. No sooner had the gangs structured the beer and whisky market, than government repealed Prohibition and cut itself in for a share of the business. Mobsters built Las Vegas and then lost it to a partnership of their accountants and the State of Nevada.

The *mafiosi* have continued to struggle through this losing war with the decent elements, because the decent elements have most cunningly managed to make them think they are winning it. Every member of the Cavalcante Family knows that he's barely making ends meet; but his voracious swallowing of the public prints has left him with the fixed delusion that the Gambino Family dines each night on peacock's tongues.

Every now and then one of these slaves of superstition will have the mystical experience of reality and recognize that the real rewards are not in the Mafia but in the Myth of the Mafia.

It is said, for example, that Albert Anastasia was terminated with extreme prejudice because he was caught selling Mafia memberships for $45,000 apiece. That is the sort of fate any creative spirit must endure when he tries to breathe imagination in moldering enterprises.

Anastasia knew there was no Mafia. He also knew that the land teemed with persons certain there was a Mafia, wandering about buying penny uranium stocks, moving along chain letters, and otherwise daring to be great, a great lowing herd of the gullible slavering for the opportunity to purchase a Mafia franchise.

Then there was Joe Columbo, who took proper accounting of the commercial superiority of high-minded endeavors over low-minded ones and organized the Italian-American Civil Rights League. Given time, he would have shaken more merchants down in the cause of charity than he ever could have done in the pursuit of extortion. Naturally, his colleagues shot him too; if there is one kind of sin the wicked cannot abide it is cynicism. There are legitimate ways of doing business to which the Honored Society will not stoop, and that disabling innocence has made serving the Mafia much less sound a commercial proposition than attacking the Mafia.

Every time another car trunk opens to disgorge the residue of one another of these poor fools, we become more aware of the shocking waste of commodities too useful to the national commerce in myth and delusion not to be given the protections and status reserved for any other endangered species of value.

The Making of the Pope

9 • 11 • 78

The cardinals made their way into St. Peter's for the last mass before their withdrawal into conclave through the entranceway beneath the tomb of Alexander VII, where the bare-boned black arm of Death holds up its swirling blanket of the rosiest, cheeriest jasper. They walked, savoring the presence of gossip, through an aisle of the gossipy—Cardinal Pignadoli of the Secretariat for Non-Christians in smiling communion with himself, Cardinal Benelli of Florence in the smiling community with all the world that defines the man who has arrayed his forces and knows that very shortly he will be, if not king of Rome, the mayor of its palace. Cardinal Gouyon of Rennes, as tall as but by no means so solemn as the husband in a Feydeau farce, kept stopping, plunging to the barriers to shake hands with believer and doubter with absolute impartiality, at once a bottomless fount and a universal object of merriment. Charm is a cardinal virtue.

They went sauntering without gravity across the largest indoor piazza under the eye of God, past the great altar where Bernini indulged his pranks high above with the little angels that seem almost to play toss with the papal tiara. No one, of course, paid the slightest attention to the patriarch of Venice.

The bronze statue of Saint Peter seems to have been appointed as a sort of caution light for solemnity. As the cardinals came to it, every now and then one of them would halt there and kneel for a moment's prayer. They were by all odds praying to Jupiter, whose fourth-century B.C. statue in the Capitoline is this one's very likeness and a compelling argument against the Christian origin of either. You think of Saint Peter as looking altogether more like Cardinal Wyszyński of Warsaw, that least inauthentic of modern heroes, with the step of an old lion and the look of a by no means welcoming innkeeper. No matter: St. Peter's is a mountain over the graveyards of its enemies.

Michelangelo for terror, Bernini for caprice, Raphael for refined reason, Caravaggio for divinely coarse reality, the pagan statues chained to their altars for trophies of victory, the martyrs in their catacombs for memories of defeat—vanity, humility, awe, condescension, simplicity, guile, gaiety, and melancholy, all of it, the whole uncountable mix of incompatibles that makes up the single impenetrable mystery of this church. And below, at its feet, the Romans, who have faith in nothing, except of course, this evening's miracle.

Rome is where the gypsies steal your wallet and the church robs you of every faith in the laws of probability. Only 11 of these 111 cardinals had ever been in a conclave until now. They ran a range whose distance may have extended even beyond the one side of Cardinal Silva of Santiago, who has gotten himself called "an ally of Communist subversion" by the lay votaries of the Pinochet government, and the other side of Cardinal-Deacon Felici of Rome, who is supposed to have pronounced on the reforms projected by the Second Vatican Council with the judgment that Pope John XXIII had simply gone mad.

Beyond their disparities, these cardinals were so tenuously acquainted with one another that the holy office thought to forestall any possible embarrassment at mistaking a face or a name by giving each one a booklet with a photograph and a biography of all his brothers in Christ. There was no evidence of the mutual spite so often unconcealed in the days following the death of Pope Pius XII, twenty years ago, but then everyone knew pretty much everyone else. Nothing advances amiability like unfamiliarity.

Even so, for all their social harmony, the cardinals seemed much too divided in principle to arrive at an easy agreement. Naturally, then, they needed only nine hours to elect as their pope Cardinal Luciani, the patriarch of Venice. It had taken six ballots to elect Cardinal Montini, who everyone knew would be pope. And now it has taken only three ballots to elect Cardinal Luciani, who had been imagined as pope by almost no one.

The result has so confounded the speculative and abashed the informed as to have produced the miracle of a Rome without gossip. The Italian press normally treats the Vatican's affairs with altogether less reverence than our own extends to the White House, and the pleasure it habitually takes in intimations of intrigue once stung Cardinal Felici into describing the journalists attendant upon the Second Vatican Council as "parasites and fungus growths . . . promoting confusion, insubordination, and error." But now all the journalists have been struck dumb and gone to their knees before this prodigy. Even *La Stampa* of Turin, for which only Fiat is holy, has in its stupefaction made *L'Osservatore Romano* sound like the *Protestant Herald.*

Still there are explanations—governed, of course, by the device the church holds up to all who dare pretend to understand her: "You think, and therefore I am not what you think."

Whatever the workings of the Holy Spirit, the operations of the memory of Pope John XXIII are unmistakable: Angelo Roncalli, patriarch of Venice, brothers who were socialists; Albino Luciani, patriarch of Venice, father who was a socialist. Both easy smilers, both kept a pleasant acquaintanceship with other primates whose Romanism was so much less orthodox than their own as to smell like heresy to the traditionalists. The parallels are obvious, but so are the differences. For all his air of the country priest, Roncalli was an intricately sophisticated papal diplomat who had charmed Paris not just with his good humor but with his wit. Question: "Monsignor, do you *really* believe in the miracle at Lourdes?" Answer: "I am sorry, but I never discuss religion at cocktail parties."

There was just the trace of the serpent in Roncalli's smile. The scanty published conjectures that Cardinal Luciani might emerge as the elected were all too often accompanied by adjectives like "gray" and "colorless." When you have seen one humble origin, you have by no means seen them all. Roncalli was from a farm near Bergamo, and Luciani is from a town in the Veneto. The inhabitants of Italian towns tend to separate into the gullers and the gulled, and there are certain suspicions of the gulled in the radiant innocence of the smile of Pope Giovanni Paolo I. If he is Roncalli, it is not without point that Roncalli was twenty hectic years ago, and to be Roncalli now is almost to promise the restoration of the papacy as it was. He was the candidate of the right—for Cardinal Felici, one more chance with a Roncalli who this time might not go crazy—and acceptable to the left for its sentimental recollections of a Roncalli it had cherished. But then the church's rule of never being what it seems is so rigid that victories for the right quite often turn out to be disasters for the right, as the left's anointment of Pius XII turned out to be a disaster for the left.

If those cardinals with ecclesiastical duties outside of Rome had a single sentiment in common, it was their desire that the hand of the Vatican be light upon them. There begin to be signs, uncertain as always, of a certain rhythm of alternating pastoral popes with political popes: Pius XII, political; John XXIII, pastoral; Paul VI, political. Now John Paul I, presumably pastoral. Political popes tend to tighten the government of the church and pastoral ones to loosen it.

Pope John's memory is a particularly blessed one in the Sacred College because he left the cardinals alone and was no less pleased to see the archbishop of Naples holding aloft the liquefied blood of San Gennario in the unpromising expectation of saving the souls of Neapolitans than he was to hear that the bishop of Recife was fomenting unrest among the poor. He combined a French affection for the priest who was interestingly venturesome and an Italian affection for the priest who was properly superstitious.

Political papacies generally come to an end with the Vatican cadre more intrusive and interfering than the bishops enjoy having it be. Even though Pope Paul is tenderly remembered, for his sorrows and for his generosity with the hats, the curia that enforced his decrees when they were rigorous and occasionally overlooked them when they were too gentle for its taste is by no means the object of the church's otherwise universal love. It cannot be an accident that all the candidates thought most likely were curialists and that all were so swiftly discarded for a patriarch whose experience was entirely pastoral.

All the same, the ascension of John Paul I is a triumph of that Italian subtlety of which he himself appears so remarkably innocent. The Italians were enormously outnumbered in this conclave, and it had seemed reasonable to suppose that, if the bishop of Rome would probably be an Italian this time round, he could hardly be on the next. The longer the conclave, the more likely a foreign choice would be.

The Italians addressed this problem with the suppleness born in their natures and developed by their experience. Their motives were in few ways selfish and in none ignoble. They were simply acting on their belief that Rome is the teacher and the provinces are her pupils. To consider, or more precisely to guess at, their performance is to understand that Machiavelli was put on the index not only because *The Prince* is evil but also because its prescriptions are clumsy and crude.

Every day for two weeks before their conclave, the cardinals met in congregation to discuss the general state of the church. Cardinal Felici, who is at the same time a great classicist and a student of Freud, a genial spirit and an autocrat, suspended his vanity as a Latinist and made the welcoming address in Italian, thereby establishing it as the language of the congregations. All the cardinals had studied in Rome and earned themselves a working knowledge of Italian. But they had grown so used to employing it with docility and diffidence toward those older and wiser than they that, as it turned out, the Italians, with less than a quarter of the representation, delivered more than two-thirds of the utterances. The conclave was, of course, a forbidden subject, but the very tone of the congregations had to be a most forceful reminder that Rome is the mother of churches and Italians first among her servants.

What Felici had commenced with style, Cardinal Benelli completed with cunning. At fifty-seven, he was too young to conquer the college's ingrained distrust of twenty-year papacies, and since he had been Pope Paul's chief executive assistant he was additionally burdened with the rancors that function inevitably attracts to its holder. His preconclave role was an infinite run on all the changes of the obscure and the ostentatious. He at once let it be known that he had an active strategy and managed to hide it in realms beyond comprehension. Now he seemed to be promoting Cardinal Felici, then Cardinal Baggio, and from time to time Cardinal Luciani. Luciani's views were old-fashioned enough to content many traditionalists; he was far enough from the curia to satisfy several moderates; and he was open enough to discussion to be more than attractive to a few progressives. That combination of agreeable qualities promised the collection of some votes in his name—perhaps as many as twenty—from all around the board. But no one outside the walls could conceive of his candidacy as having any use except as a bank for holding votes in reserve. He hardly seemed enough of a presence to fit whatever grand design Benelli might have.

In Rome the cardinals are conditioned to do as the Romans do, and the Romans, a people made savage by necessity, are fond of saints so long as they are mild-mannered and forgiving by nature. The day before the conclave, Benelli publicly pointed to the church's duty to extend more power and authority to the diocesan bishops. He could not have emitted a shrewder campaign promise, and by nightfall he had become the maker of a pope and perhaps in due course would become a pope himself. There seems little doubt that he will be Richelieu to Pope John Paul's Louis XIII.

Not the smallest stake in Benelli's search for an acceptable Italian candidate may have been his concern for the weakening of the church's role in the politics of Italy. Curiously, although the church's world dominion has not in centuries seemed broader and more vigorous than now, she is stronger in Latin America, where until now she had always been weak, and weaker in Italy, where she has always been strong. In the past two years, the Italian parliament has enacted an abortion law and Italian voters have returned a thundering no on a church-sponsored resolution to repeal the divorce code. Catholics who otherwise think themselves comfortable in a state of grace serenely vote the Communist ticket, and the Christian Democrats, the official Catholic party, have been reduced to trafficking with the Communists in their anxiety to save the property they have increasingly abused. There has always been the suspicion, even outside the Vatican, that, if church and state were ever separated, the state would collapse. But separating they seem to be by the will of a populace that more and more prefers its convenience to its salvation.

Benelli actively pushed the divorce referendum, which the new pope is said to have thought a risk the church would be wise not to take. Benelli is reputed to be the chief inspiration for the Italian Right to Life Movement, and he insists that Catholics have a duty to vote for a Catholic political party. These are all articles of faith that have been held equally, if less aggressively, by Cardinal Luciani, and Benelli may well have judged that, if Italians could no longer be usefully exhorted, they could well be beguiled for their own good by a pope as persevering in his affability as in his adherence to tradition.

Certainly Rome—even evil old Rome—has never seemed more depleted of faith, whether sacred or secular. Romans are not gloomy of course; as Stendhal said, to be gloomy one must have hope. The Communist party is ashamed of its past and weary of its present. When Ignazio Silone, its grandest apostate, died two weeks ago, the Communist press was plunged into mourning for this "socialist without a party and Christian without a church" who was expelled as a Trotskyist fifty years ago. So much for the religion of the twentieth century. It has no one to canonize except its heretics.

And, as to the faith of the seventeenth and every century before it, St. Peter's was hardly half full for the mass for the election of the pope, even though, just as sound and spectacle, it had to be altogether superior to the nudes at Piper's Theatre Restaurant. Very few of those present were young—and most of those were plainly tourists. There were far more nuns than priests in attendance, and far more women than men. A rebel priest in Florence wrote twenty years ago that, in Italy, religion was becoming the stuff of women, and that seems more and more the case now. They are, of course, women in the awful torment of being condemned to serve and never to command, women who seem desperate for a miracle. Where the faith keeps its amateur passion, it is almost hysterical. And where it is professional, at least at the journeyman level, it seems bored, which is, if anything, considerably worse.

During the cardinal's mass, a priest walked the aisles by the high altar handing out the platens and repeating in a tone mechanical and distinctly put-upon, "Body of Christ, body of Christ, body of Christ," while the women clutched at him in the extremity of their prayer for some hope somewhere, until you almost wanted to grab and shake him with all the consequential perils of hellfire and fairly scream at him to remember that what he had in his charge was, after all, a flame.

The election of the new pope seemed to draw a marked lack of attention in Rome until it produced the delight of a surprise. But then, this was August, when you can ask of her no more than the somber pleasures of a melancholy heart. Rome is never crueler than in August, when its luckier citizens always flee, leaving only unfortunate savages behind them. The prices made it certain that it wasn't the Borgias who drove Martin Luther to heresy but the Roman hotel keepers in a jubilee year. Thievery was a plague: My pocket was picked in St. Mary of the Angels and Martyrs. I reported it to the police, who laughed with that affinity between cops and bandits that can be found only in Balzac and the Roman *questura*. Then I trailed to the American Embassy to find my identity, feeling that no one could be so wanting in vigilance as I, and there I found the largest group of pilgrims the town had drawn to its sacred ceremonies, Americans seeking a replacement for passports stolen on the street. There are only two basic consumer rules for Rome in August: When you look upward at a cupola, always put your hand on your wallet, and, unless you are very rich indeed, never sit down at a trattoria that has a splendid view.

St. Peter's Square was all but empty for the conclave's first day, since everyone sensible knew that it could produce nothing. The black smoke came up at noon to be lustily cheered by the cabdrivers who thought it assured them another day's business. By then the sun had stopped in the sky, as though Joshua had chosen this high moment to make a fool of Galileo and ratify the judgment of the Inquisition. August is vicious to Bernini's Colonnade, bleaching and desiccating and blotching it. The most stupendous work of man I have ever known had been transformed into a waste habitable only by the camels of the desert.

As the day continued its torments, the little clusters of the curious began to collapse into what patches of shade the sun permitted the columns to provide. They seemed not so much curious any longer as drained of the will to move anywhere. By 5:30 p.m. someone kindlier among the gods relented. There was almost a breeze. The light that had been so brutal on the facade of the cathedral grew suddenly soft and darkening and lovely as ever, and an hour or so later a cloud of white smoke began floating from the chimney over the Sistine Chapel.

On the balconies outside the papal apartments, attendants could be seen running. The signal appeared plainly white. But then in a few moments it darkened or at least began to muddy a little, and confusion rose to assert the rule that, with the church, you can never be less sure than when you find yourself most certain. For this conclave, the Vatican had bought chemicals guaranteed to produce unmistakably black or unmistakably white smoke, and yet the thing was unclear still. The church has never been on safer ground than in its distrust of everything modern.

The feeders of the fire went on and on in the search for clarity, and, over the next half hour, there were five emanations of acceptably white smoke. The square had begun to fill. After fifty minutes, the longest wait between the signal and the proclamation in this century, the glass doors of the central loggia opened, and, with great deliberation, the purple papal tapestry was spread over the balcony, and there appeared Cardinal-Deacon Felici to pronounce the old words with the Ciceronian perfection he must always have found wanting in every messenger before him:

"Annuncio vobis gaudium magnum. Habemus papam . . ."

He paused. The church in her supreme moment could not forbear to tease.

He rolled on: "Eminentissimum ac reverendissimum dominum ecclesiae sanctae cardinalem . . ." He paused again. "Albinum."

A thousand heads laboriously prepared for a Sergium, a Sebastium, or any one of four Johannim began scuffling vainly for an Albinum. And Cardinal Felici waited for the shout to die, and then finished: "Lucius." After that, every window on the loggia was thrown open, and the cardinals looked sociably out of them, now and then waving to the crowd. And then Pope John Paul appeared. At that distance he looked surprisingly the way Pope John had, small, smiling, and wonderfully uninhibited with his hands.

He read the blessing to the city and the world in a voice rather high and tremulous for an aria in an opera that had as much of the *jocoso* as the *serioso* in it. The Swiss Guards entered the plaza and performed their drill march in his honor.

"Look at that scene," I said pompously to my neighbor. "Michelangelo saw it. Stendhal saw it. Henry James saw it." That happened, of course, to be even less true than most assertions about the church:

Michelangelo was dead long before St. Peter's had its facade. Stendhal, if he saw the scene at all—and he was a most adroit fabulist—would have seen it at the Quirinale. And as to James, I forget, but he would have needed to have been in Rome in 1878 or 1903, and he does not impress me as having often enough been that lucky. One of the somber joys of the melancholy heart is that one is sometimes more fortunate than one's betters.

And why do you suppose that seventy-five cardinals, in so many profound ways so different from one another in temperament and visions, could come so quickly to agreement in this case? Naturally, of course, in this church of contradictions, divine and profane, so that they would thereafter be free to disagree with one another about everything else.

A Name for a Crime

10 • 15 • 78

Come to our old-world desert
Where everyone goes to pieces
You can pick up tears
For souvenirs
Or genuine diseases
—W. H. AUDEN

Sid Vicious was arraigned for homicide as John Simon Ritchie, the name given at his christening, and an altogether more suitable label for the face of violence in our criminal courts.

No true American savage would lower his dignity to call himself Sid Vicious or Johnny Rotten. Our ruffians grow up and grow worse still calling themselves Frankie, Charlie, Leroy, sometimes even Sonny or Buddy. Over here, Sid Vicious is not a tough guy's name, but an almost jocular incongruity. The Vicious is pretentious; and, in criminal court, Sid is the name of the court attendant.

Sid Vicious and Johnny Rotten failed in the United States, having made the commercial mistake of opening in Memphis and Atlanta, precincts where the audience runs to elements rather more frightening than anything they could contrive.

That rejection for want of being authentic broke their spirit; the Sex Pistols disintegrated; Johnny Rotten went home and Sid Vicious settled or more precisely collapsed into the Hotel Chelsea with Nancy Spungen. He worked occasionally with Johnny Nolan and the Idols; but such as his will had been gone, and it is said that he dragged himself through his counterfeit ferocities only because he and Nancy needed the cash to buy dope.

Now the People say that he stabbed her to death on Thursday morning. At last Sid Vicious seems to have become the real thing.

Come to our well-run desert
Where anguish arrives by cable
And the deadly sins
May be bought in tins
With instructions on the label.

There has always been something curiously immature about British rock, some incapacity to rise to any level more awesome than is reached by the cruelty of children. *The Sorrows of Satan* as written by Beatrice Potter.

And, even now, catatonic on the bench waiting to be called, Sid Vicious seemed more victim than executioner—the face chalky white as though embalmed by a mortician who had apprenticed at a clown school, the hair still vaulting up in the unconquerably disciplined disarray that Elsa Maxwell fashioned for playing witches more comic than menacing.

He managed to stand for most of the time while the lawyers argued over bail, and then, just while Joseph Epstein, his counsel, was saying that he had shown himself trustworthy by reporting Nancy's death to the police and that he would need to be free so that he could work, he sank down and sat with his head in his hands.

Bail was set at $50,000, and Malcolm McLaren, the Sex Pistols' manager, went forth to raise it. McLaren discovered the Pistols and directed their affairs through their puffing up and into their deflation. He had flown here from London to bring what help he could to Sid Vicious in his troubles.

McLaren was asked to describe Sid Vicious and he answered, "Outrageous. A very passionate young man." He seemed to have taken up this burden of sorrows with remarkably good cheer; but then there is always a certain ambivalence about the friend who is also the promoter.

Honest, as his sympathy seemed, McLaren could somehow not be entirely acquitted of the suspicion that somewhere in his interior a small, not undelighted voice was observing that, after all, bad as this is, Sid is at least in being again, maybe more than ever in being, because he can at last be billed as the real thing.

And that voice can by no means be called an unkindly one; where, after all, could McLaren find anyone to go $50,000 bail except an investor capable of imagining a Sid Vicious tour before the trial? Come to our jolly desert, where the sinner's only true friend is his promoter.

"And all the papers will say that this is where punk rock leads," said Lester Bangs, a wise man there present. "Nothing leads to things like this. This was just babies sticking pins in each other. And it went too far."

Offsides for False Modesty

11 • 2 • 78

The fantasies of my sex are among the more institutionalized of our national religions; and yesterday there arrived the climax of the schism between the National Football League, a temple of false piety, and *Playboy*, a shrine of dogged paganism.

The quartet of former NFL cheerleaders, who had been unfrocked for displaying in *Playboy* what their sponsoring teams had been careful only to intimate, lent a tone of modesty and decorum to the Playboy Club hardly congruous with its image.

Lynita Shilling, late of the San Diego Chargerettes, appeared in a granny dress that must have been the most excessive public swaddling by cloth seen on a resident of Orange County since Richard Nixon was photographed prowling the beach at San Clemente, with his brogans laced, his jacket buttoned and his necktie tightened to just the safe side of strangulation. The whole tableau was another reminder that in America sexual imagery is a branch of commerce where care for the essentials of one's virtue is a female monopoly.

"All the biggies in the NFL had this meeting about *us*," Jacqueline Rohrs, ex–Chicago Honey Bear, observed. "You'd think there'd be other things wrong with football they'd worry about. There's people laid up in hospitals and they're reviewing *my* pictures."

But then violence is so primary an item in the NFL's sales catalogue that the cult poster of the Dallas Cowgirls, with those pistol-packing eyes and those vests like white chain mail, seems almost calculated to make any observer unconfident of his kidney feel faintly like a quarterback intruded upon by Harvey Martin.

In untying those halters, *Playboy* at least softened the prior effect of the Cowgirls by inserting the redeeming social value of vulnerability. But then the NFL stocks visions of humanity as conqueror; and *Playboy* stocks visions of humanity as surrenderer, and that conflict may very well be the core of the NFL's grievance at *Playboy*'s violation of its image.

The Baltimore Colts fired Andrea Mann from a job for which they had never paid her with the chill judgment that they did not want her kind around.

"You know they're making us sexier and sexier all the time," Miss Mann reflected.

"We have these suggestive cheers. 'When we're hot, we're hot.' What's that got to do with football? They have us bending over and grabbing ourselves by the bottom and throwing our heads back and waving our bosoms. I was beginning to feel that it was very embarrassing. All right, we're none of us shy, retiring wallflowers. But it was kind of tacky."

Miss Mann is a postal clerk, who expects to go on being one, quite content that her new notoriety had so far drawn her no offers of madder music and stronger wine.

"Our mother raised us to be proud of her bodies," she said. "I do not feel that I should be ashamed of mine."

"I only did this," she said, "because I was such a Colt fan. I've had season tickets since I was much younger. I think it would be much better if we really had been cheerleaders. The people would have had much more fun."

There Miss Mann sat in her white silk blouse and her skirt falling naturally below her knees, the wise and shameless innocent condemned by the obtuse and shamefaced guilty. No nicer young lady had ever been introduced to a stranger whose first notice of her face and form had been in a delineation so revelatory as normally to be justified only by circumstances of the closest sort of friendship. Very few nicer young ladies could indeed have ever been introduced to any stranger.

Still, she had let the team down because she had violated its highest moral code, which stipulates that pretty much any degree of bawdy insinuation is decent, and that only bare candor is offensive.

The Scribblers' Choice

9 • 18 • 80

My betters at analyzing this sort of thing seem widely agreed that these days presidential candidates are made or broken not by the politicians but by the newspapers and the broadcasters. This trend is another illustration of a fundamental law of social change in America, which is that every new development began as an idea conceived by criminals and then brought to fruition by respectable persons.

Las Vegas was invented by the mob and then stolen from it by its accountants. Loan-sharking used to be an underworld monopoly, but now the banks have so encroached upon the field that there are states where a finance company can charge the victim 36 percent interest a year without risk of legal penalty for usury. A state of affairs where Americans are governed by presidents selected by the press is just one more product of this pattern. Organized crime has been governed that way for years; the Boss of Bosses dies, journalism designates his successor, and every good soldier closes ranks behind him as every good American rallies to the new president.

But now comes the case of Frank Tieri to cast the darkest of shadows upon this system of election by journalistic decree. In the fall of 1978, Tieri, a.k.a. "Funzi" and "The Old Man," was certified as Boss of Bosses of Cosa Nostra by a landslide of those press clippings that constitute the ballots in this process. There followed the customary inaugural ceremony, the serving of a grand jury subpoena; and Tieri then undertook the prime duties of his office, which were, as usual, to be indicted and tried as Unholy Roman Emperor of the Honored Society.

Jay Goldberg, his counsel, objected that Tieri lacked the physical and mental capacity to endure a trial, and the medical profession was recruited to assess the health and capacities of this titan among executives. The U.S. Attorney's office designated as its expert Stanley L. Portnow, whose personal eminence and status as the government's own instrument should certainly free him of any suspicion of having taken a mob contract. Dr. Portnow found:

In 1977 Frank Tieri suffered a stroke that had produced organic brain damage enough to impair seriously his ability to reason.

His Intelligence Quotient is now 79.

He was asked how many pennies he would have left if he had three and gave away one. His answer was one. He was asked how much is $4 plus $5. He answered $4. He was asked the meaning of the expression: "Strike while the iron is hot" and he answered: "Press." He was asked to recite the months of the year in order and he replied: "January, February, March, April, May, September, August, June."

There was one sad revelation of the loneliness of grandeur. Frank Tieri could think of nothing he liked to do these days except play cards, but "they don't like to play with me because I keep forgetting."

Frank Tieri had his first heart attack in 1950, developed cancer of the throat in 1956, and has diabetes and arteriosclerosis. He is so wounded a pincushion for surgeons that his first remark to Dr. Portnow was that he hoped he hadn't come there for another operation.

Nonetheless Judge Thomas Griesa has ruled him fit for trial. Judge Griesa is known for his personal crotchets, and I have commended him so often when they accorded with my own that I shall not criticize him for one that seems to me to have produced a result of almost measureless cruelty.

In any case Frank Tieri, if still breathing, will be found at his post doing his duty to the code of Cosa Nostra, whose first command is unswerving service to the myths of journalism and the careers of assistant prosecutors. There is some disquiet in reflecting on the massive authority we journalists have attained in the political process when you discover that we have elected a Boss of Bosses who, a year before conquering that pinnacle, had sunk so far toward imbecility that he probably didn't even know he had won.

IV

WATCHMAN'S ROUNDS

He doesn't use a tape recorder, just the binder notebook, and he works alone, selecting the events he will cover off the AP wire and sometimes spending eight hours on his feet going from one story to the next.

— LEWIS COLE (*MORE*), 1978

Saving a Whale

6 • 11 • 81

A Choice of Days and *On Mencken* make up Knopf's testament to Henry L. Mencken on the hundredth year since his birth. We should, of course, be grateful to have any memorial less degrading than those essays of R. Emmett Tyrrell through which Mencken's ghost now and then flickers like some damned soul in hell. All the same, these garlands, though altogether worthier and more scrupulously worked, seem somehow not quite up to their subject.

But then there are subjects that fairly prohibit adequacy. Whales are the only mammals that the museums have never managed to stuff and mount in their original skins. The great whale in New York's Museum of Natural History is a Styrofoam reproduction; and the museum's orca, despite its more modest proportions, is only a compound of burlap and plaster. These counterfeits are the best the taxidermists can do, because, they have found, something in the very nature of the whale's original skin makes its preservation impractical.

Mencken is a very great whale and can stove all boats that sail too close too soon. The careful sailor begins at a respectful distance and looks for what the creature is not before grappling with what it might be.

The first sight is the spouting, and who cannot be forgiven for coming upon such a spectacle and henceforth and forever deciding that this sportive play in the warm waters is most of what whales are about? Alistair Cooke, who knew him well and read him keenly, settles for defining Mencken as "a humorist in the classic American tradition, about halfway between Mark Twain and Woody Allen."*

Even those of us least satisfied with the notion that his spout is all there is to the whale have to concede that any geyser is a joyous sight indeed. Here, as an instance, is the thirty-six-year-old Mencken on Tchaikovsky's Sixth Symphony:

> In this grand complex of tunes, indeed, Tschaikowsky tells all his troubles—how he was forced into marriage against his will; how he lost three thousand roubles on Russian government bonds; how his pet dog Wolfgang was run over by the Moscow-Petersburg D-Zug and lost an ear; how the concert-master was in liquor at Dresden and spoiled his *Romeo and Juliet*; how ill he was after eating that *gekochter Schellfisch* at Prague; how the wine merchant, Oroshatovich, swindled him with synthetic Burgundy; how he lost his baggage between Leipzig and Berlin, and had to conduct in borrowed cuffs; how the summer boarders at Maidanovo played "Monastery Bells" on their tin-pan pianos; how that *Schuft* of a critic at Köln accused him of borrowing his Capriccio in G sharp minor from Offenbach; how his friend Kashkin won a hundred roubles from him at *yeralash*; how he cut his hand opening a can of asparagus; how melancholy it was to come to fifty-year.

This is, of course, pure sport with no destination except the disposable tissue that is any day's newspaper, and we would not even know this flight existed if it were not for Carl Bode's exemplary efforts at retrieval in *The Young Mencken*. Such stuff goes about as far as Woody Allen has ever contrived to go. But, after the mockeries of all self-seriousness, there comes the note of appreciation of the serious that lifts the man of true sensibility above the one who merely jests for the ostentation of the cap and the bells:

> And yet, for all that maudlin confidence, a great work of art. A work to torture and delight the sentimentalist, but at the same

* Dorsey, John, ed. "Mencken and the English Language," in *On Mencken* (New York: Knopf, 1980), p. 112.

> time a work to interest and edify the musician. In the midst of all its mawkishness it is written superbly.*

The point of Mencken is not just the ear for those elements of the ridiculous that are pretension's close companions but the eye for those elements of genuine feeling that can redeem the worst pretension. He knew that what deserves to be esteemed lives very often with what deserves to be laughed at. It is this ability to render justice and what he would have scoffed to hear called his capacity to love that separate him from so many of those who mistake him for their model.

Cooke's judgment that Mencken's claim upon posterity resides mainly in his place among classic American humorists is, I am afraid, one more example of the trouble we have accepting ungainly, outsized, and troublesome articles of our cultural furniture unless we trim and trivialize them into domestic comforts.

The special service of Bode's anthology is the help it gives us in understanding that Mencken's mind took its mold very early on. Just because he so recognized the difference between himself and the run of his countrymen, the brands preserved in *The Young Mencken* glow especially with anticipations of the mistaken identity his shade now threatens to carry through the eternal snows.

That fate had, after all, been Mark Twain's:

> While he lived he was several times labeled and relabeled, and always inaccurately and vainly. At the start the national guardians of letters sought to dismiss him loftily as a hollow buffoon, a brother to Josh Billings and Petroleum V. Nasby. This enterprise failing, they made him a comic moralist, a sort of chatauquan in motley, a William Jennings Bryan armed with a slapstick. Foiled again, they promoted him to the rank of Thomas Bailey Aldrich and William Dean Howells, and issued an impertinent amnesty for the sins of his youth. Thus he passed from these scenes—ratified at last but somewhat heavily patronized.**

---

* Bode, Carl, ed. *The Young Mencken: The Best of His Work* (New York: Dial, 1973), p. 541.
** Bode, p. 566.

And then, after Mark Twain was buried and his habitual alarms about being a cause of scandal were no longer relevant, those black posthumous works *What Is Man?* and *The Mysterious Stranger* were at last published, and in Mencken's words,

> The parlor entertainer . . . completely disappears; in his place there arises a satirist, with something of Rabelais's vast resourcefulness and dexterity in him, and all of Dean Swift's devastating ferocity. . . . No wonder the pious critic of the New York *Times*, horrified by [*What Is Man's*] doctrine, was forced to take refuge behind the theory that Mark intended it as a joke.

Mencken had barely passed his apprenticeship before he resigned himself to the same destiny of misunderstanding. While still young, he demonstrated a knack for clarifying and compacting the ideas of alien and distant prophets. His first appearances between boards were *vade mecums* to Nietzsche and Shaw; and his formidable learning owed itself in considerable part to the force-feeding such drudgeries extort. He was only twenty-seven when he was at work on *George Bernard Shaw: His Plays*, and gave voice to his doubts that,

> . . . Shaw will ever become a popular dramatist, in the sense that Sardou and Pinero are popular. . . .
>
> One cannot expect a man, however keen his sense of humor, to laugh at the things he considers eminently proper and honorable. Shaw's demand that he do so has greatly restricted the size of the Shaw audience.*

This early insight may best explain why the Mencken manner, to the extent that it survives at all, has its awkward existence in the language of disciples who reserve their scorn for whatever the respectable conceive as improper and dishonorable, and who confine their nonconformity to mock heroic gestures of refusing to crook the knee to anyone who declines to conform. Thus we have R. Emmett Tyrrell, who walks so lamely among

* Bode, pp. 73 and 75.

us as Mencken's bitterest enemy, the enforcer of loyalty oaths, born again in the disguise of Mencken *revivivus.*

Would he be ashamed to have progeny no seemlier than this one? We can by no means be sure that he would. There sits, by no means uncherished, some Aunt Polly at the back of all our minds, and as the years go by, her voice grows ever more compelling. What we rejected we now embrace; suddenly we are ashamed to be a trial and long to be accepted as a comfort.

Mencken was forty when he caught the pathos and arraigned the betrayal of Mark Twain's later years:

> returning to the native mob as its premier clown—monkey-shining at banquets, cavorting in the newspapers, shrinking poltroonishly from his own ideas, obscenely eager to give no offense.*

And yet, if they are free of pathos and innocent of betrayal, what are those yarns that Knopf now abridges and reissues as *A Choice of Days* except the effort simply to please that overcomes all of us in an old age anxious to be amnestied for the sins of our youth?

Both *A Choice of Days* and *On Mencken* are almost all *allegro*, youth as sunrise in Baltimore as Eden. They are delightful, but they are far from the whole symphony. *On Mencken* beguiles us with a full chapter of tributes to the city of Baltimore collated by Huntington Cairns. We are in Cairns' debt for *The American Scene*, the most acute and discriminating of all selections of Mencken's work. But in this case the employment assigned him is the mining and exhalation of roseate memories of Mencken's native place. His Baltimore was certainly charming and easy enough, but there were cruel limits to the tolerance Mencken celebrates.

It was, after all, Baltimore whose citizens grew so abraded by his enthusiasm for the German cause in the First World War that by the autumn of 1916 their *Sun* papers were driven to put him on forced leave. The city he loved was also the city that exiled him from its journalism for three years and the city whose public librarian declined

* Mencken, H. L., *The American Scene: A Reader*, Huntington Cairns, ed. (New York: Knopf, 1965), p. 108.

to stock the novels of Theodore Dreiser while they sat untrammeled on the shelves of Philadelphia, Kansas City and Indianapolis. There was darkness as well as sunshine in this life; and the swimmer swam against the current, gaily to be sure, but all the same strenuously.

His community with Dreiser was the expression of Mencken's nature that comes nearest to an accurate perception of him:

> All the latter-day American novelists of consideration are vastly more facile than Dreiser in their philosophy, as they are in their style. In the fact, perhaps, lies the measure of their difference. What they lack, great and small, is the gesture of pity, the note of awe, the profound sense of wonder—in a phrase, that "soberness of mind" which William Lyon Phelps sees as the hallmark of Conrad and Hardy, and which even the most stupid cannot escape in Dreiser. . . . In the arts, as in the concerns of everyday, the American seeks escape from the insoluble by pretending that it is solved. A comfortable phrase is what he craves beyond all things—and comfortable phrases are surely not to be found in Dreiser's stock.*

One swiftly forgets his intolerable writing, his mirthless, sedulous, repellent manner, in the face of the Athenian tragedy he instills into his seduced and soul-sick servant girls, his barbaric pirates of finances, his conquered and hamstrung supermen, his wives who sit and wait. . . . Such a novel as *Sister Carrie* stands quite outside the brief traffic of the customary stage. . . . . It is not a mere story, not a novel in the customary American meaning of the word; it is at once a psalm of life and a criticism of life—and that criticism loses nothing by the fact that its burden is despair. . . . The thing he seeks to do is to stir, to awaken, to move. One does not arise from such a book as *Sister Carrie* with a smirk of satisfaction; one leaves it infinitely touched.**

Cooke notices a strain of cruelty in Mencken; and it is inescapably there, although you rather wish that he had found a specimen more inarguably gross than the obituary of William Jennings Bryan that

* *The American Scene*, p. 112.
** *The American Scene*, p. 128.

was printed the day after his death and polluted the attendant clouds of incense with the stink bomb of the insistence that the deceased was "a charlatan, a mountebank, a zany without sense of dignity . . . full of an almost pathological hatred of all learning, all beauty, all fine and noble things."*

This style of having at the carcass pays the price of getting itself thought cruel but that cost seems meager when set against its rewards. For the Mencken who was unafraid to violate the proprieties is the Mencken who speaks most eloquently to us still; he dared in that high fashion Whitman marked in Thoreau: "his lawlessness—his dissent—his going down his own absolute road, let hell blaze as it pleases."

But then Mencken's grand advantage over the journalists of his or any later time was not merely that he did not worry about Hell or Heaven. Indifference to and even disbelief in an afterlife of blessings and punishments are more common than unique to man. But, if it is a rare journalist who quakes at the prospect of the Lake of Fire, it is a rarer one still who does not worry about the hot water that can scald anyone who gives cause for scandal.

The conventional obituary escorts the defunct to the bar of heaven with a deference made particularly ceremonious by the fear of being caught jogging the elbow of the Recording Angel. Mencken did not believe that there is such a being as the Recording Angel; and yet the precipitate death of William Jennings Bryan, whom he had watched raving and fuming at the Scopes trial only days before, pressed upon him the awful transience of everyone's life. We could hardly otherwise explain the image he summoned up at the opening of his dispatch to the Baltimore *Evening Sun*:

> Has it been duly marked by historians that William Jennings Bryan's last secular act on this globe of sin was to catch flies? A curious detail, and not without its sardonic overtones. He was the most sedulous fly catcher in American history, and in many ways the most successful. His quarry, of course, was not *Musca domestica* but *Homo neandertalensis*. For forty years he traced

* A revised version of this grand remonstrance, more carefully groomed but in no way tamed can be found in Mencken, H.L. *A Mencken Chrestomathy* (New York: Knopf, 1956), pp. 243–248.

> it with coo and bellow, up and down the backwaters of the Republic. Wherever the flambeaux of Chatauqua smoked and guttered, and the bilge of idealism ran in the veins, and Baptist pastors damned the brooks with the sanctified . . . —there the indefatigable Jennings set up his traps and spread his bait.*

This is an image of the sort that is started by the most vivid intimations of your own mortality and the sharpened perception that all of it could end for you tonight as it had so suddenly for so many men, run over, say, by some rackety Ford on the way back to bed after filing at the Western Union office.

These then might be the last lines you would write on earth, and that thought serves to expel every inhibition about how they might look to the proper-minded. Mencken once remembered or perhaps imagined that he had composed his *envoi* to Bryan on a July night in a Chattanooga hotel room sitting in his undershorts with all the windows open and nothing between him and suffocation except a languorous overhead fan. We can conceive of him standing up when he had finished and putting his shirt back on and saying to himself, "What I have done this night no man alive could have done and I am the king of the cats."

The kingdom runs to fairly tame cats with ribboned necks and clipped claws; and in the times when their king runs raucous on the rooftops, he has very little company; but no matter: Moments of self-coronation like those excuse staying too late at the journalist's trade.

I don't think it can be sensibly argued that Mencken did not stay too late at his trade. Victimage has its uses. Blacklisting deprived Zero Mostel of every chance except that of being a very great artist at the $75 a week Equity minimum; and absolution only liberated him for increasing excesses of clownish vulgarity, irresistible in their way but travesties of his higher self. Mencken was expelled from daily journalism for his heresies in wartime; and when his term of banishment was over, he had made himself the first American editor to publish

---

* *A Mencken Chrestomathy*, p. 243.

Joyce and the first living American critic to earn the admiration of Joseph Conrad.

In exile, he had brought himself to the place from which great leaps are made. And then the *Sun* papers opened themselves up to him again and he went zestfully back to inspecting statesmen, reporting on prize-fights, and exulting in the stable smells of conventions and campaigns. He did this kind of thing better than any other first-rate journalist has done since the death of John Reed; but it is easy work really, and third-rate novelists try it now and then and almost automatically do it better than first-rate journalists, and novelists like Gore Vidal, Norman Mailer, and Truman Capote, being well above the third-rate, do it better than anyone else on earth.

Still Mencken's turn back to the journalism he had outgrown was not so much a surrender as an engagement with a felt duty to a cause. He always boasted that he had no more social conscience than a cat; and yet now he took up the sword and threw away the scabbard, and there ensued a great war with the American consensus of the twenties that could not have been pressed so vehemently unless fructified by the anger of a victim of intolerance who felt himself one with every other victim.

A month before the Armistice, he had written Ellery Sedgwick at the *Atlantic Monthly*:

> Once it is over, I'll be glad to write you, if you dare me, a frank statement of the feelings and sensations of an American of German blood, facing for a year or more the ecstatic Germanophobia of the rest of the population. It has been a curious time and I think it has changed me a lot.*

* Forgue, Guy J., ed., *The Letters of H.L. Mencken* (New York: Knopf, 1961), p. 130. This is a collection full of flaws and of fascinations, a deplorable example of the dangers of loving not wisely but too well. Knopf's adoration for Mencken was of that doting variety that blinds the lover to every danger that the beloved might go about the streets untidily arrayed. I doubt if any artist of Mencken's proportions has ever been edited with a hand as slovenly as this one. One even comes upon a letter identified as addressed to F. Scott Fitzgerald which the most casual reader would at once recognize as written to the child Frances Scott Fitzgerald. And yet, for all the indifference of publisher and editor minimal dictates of grooming, what they so carelessly served forth to us remains sufficiently wonderful.

It had changed him into a radical in unremitting conflict with the spirit of his age. I confess to thinking of him with idolatry; and it is idolatry's worst defect that the idolator molds his idol from the clay of his personal prejudices. The minimal respect we owe any man is to begin by taking him at his word; and Mencken never presented himself as other than a Tory, contemptuous of democracy and scornful of the masses. But, faithful as he tried to be to that vision of himself in the abstract, he was almost invariably false to it in confrontations with the here and now. He had the luck of the disability that afflicts William F. Buckley: His nature was not cold enough to make a good Tory or a good Bolshevik; he was deficient in the high-mindedness the disciplined coldhearted need. He worked as best he could to corral his sentiments and pen them away; and yet some fugitive feeling constantly drew him into places where the complacent do not choose to travel.

He was only too successful at making us think him the bourgeois undiluted. But for all his origins in the overheated, overbundled, overfed cocoon of a German-American middle-class household, he was thrown into a workingman's world while barely out of adolescence. He was established on the old Baltimore *Herald* when he was eighteen and had already learned to look with a detached and eventually ribald eye while sheriffs lurched through hangings they could not execute until they were drunk enough not to notice. He saw men die of rabies in the country's earliest Pasteur clinic and suicides with their mouths distorted by carbolic acid and the cops badgering their distracted mothers. These experiences were a permanent coarsening; but they also bred a lasting tenderness toward the victims of life.

"It seems plain to me," he once wrote Dreiser, "that the most valuable baggage that you carry is your capacity for seeing the world from a proletarian standpoint. It is responsible for all your talent for evoking feeling. Imagine *Sister Carrie* written by a man without that capacity, say Nietzsche. It would have been a mess."*

There is no explaining their affinity unless we understand that Mencken, incompletely and therefore rebelliously, and Dreiser,

---

* Forgue, p. 221.

entirely and therefore resignedly, each saw the world from a proletarian viewpoint.

Even in the thirties, when he was bleakly and even grouchily conservative, Mencken never forgot that society is divided between those who own property and those who work for a living, and he could continue to describe the American Newspaper Guild as a necessary instrument to protect "working newspapermen . . . against the forays of the predatory Babbitts who control only too many of the American newspapers."*

There was a black strain of pessimism beneath the motley he so often affected. As it early convinced him that all gods were illusions, it almost as swiftly persuaded him that all rulers were frauds and most social action a futility. When the New Deal is finished, he wrote Ezra Pound in 1937, "the poor fish who now sweat with hope will still be slaves, doomed to dull and ignominious toil for scoundrels, world without end."

Pound had solicited his interest in Major Douglas' Social Credit Movement a few weeks before, and Mencken had replied:

> You made your great mistake when you abandoned the poetry business, and set up shop as a wizard in general practise. . . . All your native common sense oozed out of you, and you set up a caterwauling for all sorts of brummagem Utopias, at first in the aesthetic region only but later in the regions of aesthetic and political baloney. Thus a competent poet was spoiled to make a tin-horn politician.

It does not seem unfair to suspect certain suggestions of the confessional in the harshness of these words. Mencken had made a choice not unlike Pound's when he congratulated Louis Untermeyer for the promise that

---

* Mencken, H. L., *A Gang of Pecksniffs and Other Comments on Newspaper Publishers*, selected by Theo Lippman Jr. (New Rochelle, NY: Arlington House, 1975), p. 187. Persons innocent of the reality of class can instruct themselves by noticing that these sentiments, prepared for the readers of the Baltimore Evening Sun, went unpublished therein.

> You will escape from literary criticism, too, as I am trying to do. The wider field of ideas in general is too alluring. . . . We live, not in a literary age, but in a fiercely political age.*

He had traded detachment for alienation and, throughout the twenties, he would treat politics as a grinding of victims by their oppressors. The continued imprisonment of Eugene Victor Debs galled him almost as much as the prohibition amendment, which especially galled him as an assault upon private liberties. The political commentaries that Malcolm Moos collected under the rubric *A Carnival of Buncombe* deserve to be read not so much for their gibes at charlatanry as for their social outrage. Consider his 1924 endorsement of the Progressive Party presidential candidacy of Robert M. LaFollette,

> . . . the Wisconsin Red, with his pockets stuffed with Soviet gold. I shall vote for him unhesitatingly, and for a plain reason: he is the best man in the running, *as a man*. . . .
>
> Suppose all Americans were like LaFollette? What a country it would be! No more depressing goose-stepping. No more gorillas in hysterical herds. No more trimming and trembling. Does it matter what his ideas are? Personally I am against four-fifths of them, but what are the odds? They are, at worst, better than the ignominious platitudes of Coolidge. . . .
>
> The older I grow the less I esteem mere ideas. In politics, particularly, they are transient and unimportant. . . . There are only men who have character and men who lack it. LaFollette has it. . . . He is devoid of caution, policy, timidity, baseness—all the immemorial qualities of the politician. He is tremendous when he is right, and he is even more tremendous when he is wrong.

And this on the mind of Calvin Coolidge:

> Every idea that is honorable and of good report in Pullman smokerooms, on the verandas of golf clubs, among university

* The letters to Pound can be found in Forgue, pp. 411 and 413. The letter to Untermeyer is on p. 210.

> presidents at luncheons of the Kiwanis Club and where sweaters and usurer meet—all this rubbish he has welded into a system of politics, nay of statecraft, of jurisprudence, of epistemology, almost of theology, and made himself the prophet of it. He has shoved himself an inch ahead of his lieges. He is one degree hotter for the existing order than they are themselves.*

But the commitment to politics leads down two roads, each with a pit at its end. One is the path of embracing, the other is the path of rejecting; and you finish either embracing or rejecting everything. When the time came to recoil from Franklin Roosevelt as from every other incumbent, Mencken could only recoil on the terms and in the posture of the plutocracy he had always reviled; and sixteen years afterward, when he chose his own favorites among his writings, he included a philippic against the New Deal that reached the apogee of its disgust in the revelation that Harry Hopkins had a staff of nonentities so dim that they were not even listed in *Who's Who in America.***

The matter had shrunk down to no more than the manner. We may suppose that he was surprised to meet that empty hour, for he had long before shown the acuity with which the true critic anticipates his own twilight in the fallings-off of his elders. He had seen that shadow in 1920 in the remarkable tour d'horizon he called "The National Letters" when his eye fell upon "the literature that fills the magazines and burdens the book counters of the department stores":

> One constantly observes the collapse and surrender of writers who started out with aims far above those of the magazine nabob. . . . It is, indeed, a characteristic American phenomenon for a young writer to score a success with novel and meritorious work, and then to yield himself to the best-seller fever, and so disappear down the sewers. . . . The pull is genuinely powerful.

---

* The comments on LaFollette are in Moos, Malcolm, ed., *H. L. Mencken on Politics: A Carnival of Buncombe* (New York: Vintage, 1960), pp. 119–120. The judgment on Coolidge is on pp. 102–103.

** *A Mencken Chrestomathy*, p. 427. We might not imprecisely define the whole of Mencken's thought as rising from the assumption that we live in a country where anyone curious about a truly interesting fellow citizen can look him up in *Who's Who* and seldom find his name there.

> Above lies not only isolation, but also a dogged and malignant sort of opposition. Below, as [Gouverneur] Morris has frankly admitted, there is the place at Aiken, the motor-car, money in the bank, and the dignity of an important man.*

"We all end up as packaged goods," Westbrook Pegler remarked a little while before he died. The dreary road to the wrapping and bundling counter is probably inescapable: there is the hunt for the discovery of what works, then the erosion of curiosity about what else might work, then the disappearance of all curiosity about anything unfamiliar, and at last the prison of the safety of one's own accepted manner. Yeats was a little way off the mark; the peril for the artisan no less than for the artist is not that his circus animals may desert him but that he will let slip past the time when he ought to turn them back to the forest.

I do not suppose it makes too much difference that Mencken lodged too long with his circus animals. The worst result of this capitulation to the habitual was that it distorted his reputation and limited him to followers drawn to the frozen model of his manner instead of the warm example of his intelligence. And yet the manner had been only a device to make a savage indignation less lacerating by transmitting uncomfortable thoughts in the language of an hyperbole so exuberant as almost to turn them into jokes.

But then, if it is one of life's major blessings that, in time, savage indignation ceases to lacerate, it is one of life's minor curses that the cured sufferer so often loses interest thereafter. The loss of interest was the likely reason why, in his last twenty-five years, Mencken produced so much that remained engaging and so little that is still exciting.

His flagging attention to literature may have been the most discernible cost to us. Mencken the critic was the very best Mencken, for, as it was his pose to look at the affairs of the Republic with monarchical disdain, it was his nature to confront the institutions of the kingdom of letters with the passion of a Leveller.

---

* *The American Scene*, p. 70.

His most fervid responses were reserved for young and otherwise half-buried writers whose motive force was, as he said of Dreiser's, "to depict the life of struggling peoples." He forgave their infelicities mostly for the sake of the poetry that infused their mission but partly because he took such delight in the banalities of common speech.

His editorial functions at the *American Mercury* continued after his decampment from aesthetics to politics in the twenties, and they conscripted him to keep an eye on the literary marketplace. That eye retained its keenness whenever it lighted upon whatever came from below or outside the conventional culture. He displayed a quick appreciation for Ring Lardner, Willa Cather, and Ruth Suckow; and Sinclair Lewis dedicated *Elmer Gantry* to him. That last piece of homage was a symbol of what was happening to him; he had begun to harden into a monument. He appears to have disliked Hemingway's work no less than his person; and what scraps of their correspondence we have suggest a larger affection for Fitzgerald's person than for his work. There is no evidence that he even read Faulkner.

Dreiser seems to have spent his life with a peasant's timidity about being detected in semiliteracy, and, in 1937, he wrote to ask Mencken for a list of the more notable works of fiction produced in the last decade.

"I suggest," Mencken replied, "that we have dinner alone and go through the matters you discuss. It seems to me that there is a great deal of quackery in literature, as there is in politics. Most of the geniuses discovered by the Communists are simply imbeciles. But I have considerable confidence in young [James T.] Farrell, despite his political hallucinations."*

Dreiser had never much kept up with the course of letters, and by then we may surmise that Mencken had stopped keeping up with it too. He was coming to rest in that lovable anecdotage whose fragments Knopf now serves forth as its ceremonial wreath. Here is a deservedly admired publishing house; and here was quite the most original American mind ever to be sent forth under its imprint. And the samples of that mind the owners of its copyright have now judged

* Forgue, p. 413.

the most relevant memorials have little more fresh and original to tell us—however marvelously they tell it—than that the kitchen was more fragrant and the carnival livelier when the teller was young.

And about that kind of circumstance Mencken would, I suppose, have only said what he did in the final sentence of his obituary of Theodore Roosevelt, which was, "Oh well, one does what one can."

The Sad Secrets of an Assassin's Mind

10 • 15 • 81

Daniel Schwartz's psychiatric report on Mark Chapman was commissioned by a counsel for the defense aware that his client had no chance with a jury unless it could be persuaded that John Lennon's murder was the act of a man innocent because insane. But Mark Chapman was not to be tried by a jury. Last spring he informed his judge that God had spoken to him in his cell and ordered him to plead guilty. His plea thus disposed of the insanity defense as an option.

Men of the most refined intelligence have spent centuries scouring for ways to make criminal justice more rational; and their search has brought us a system where a criminal can get himself certified as in a state of reason by submitting a hallucination as its evidence.

Schwartz's findings had no further function after that except to be tendered to Criminal Court Justice Dennis Edwards Jr. as an argument for mitigating Chapman's punishment. Schwartz presented his report as a witness at Justice Edwards' presentence hearing on August 24. His testimony is published here, having come and gone with very little notice except by Justice Edwards, who recommended that Chapman undergo further psychiatric treatment during his twenty-years-to-life prison term.

A small party of the many to whom John Lennon's death remains an unhealable wound had come to court; and afterward one of its members said that the appointed punishment was insufficient and that Chapman would more fitly be burned alive after trial by a jury that loved the Beatles. It was strange to hear the point so missed by someone still mourning the death of a man whose whole life suggests he would have been better equipped than almost anyone else to understand, to feel for and, curious as it may sound, respect his murderer.

For Schwartz's Chapman had endured seventeen years with a surface that seemed in all ways inoffensively negligible and with an interior packed to bursting. He had struggled to order the discordant swarms within him until his containing walls broke and were overrun; and, dreadful as were his defeat's results, he had earned some measure of the respect that is due the resister who fights alone and loses.

Schwartz's accounting is a condensed epic of the schizophrenic's always brave and too often hopeless struggle against unknown armies that have invaded and invested him. That is its achievement as work of art; its import as labor of instruction is to bring us closer than we have ever been to the mind of an assassin. Not *The* Assassin but *an* assassin, for, in cases like this one, there is a crucial distinction between *an* and *the*.

The Assassin is a general and therefore imprecise term for the body of strangers who, through nearly twenty years of recurring nightmares, have raised the gun and changed our histories and torn our hearts. But an assassin is a mortal being, and every mortal being differs from every other in the possession of and, in the cruelest circumstance, possession by an interior as unique as his fingerprint.

Schwartz's Chapman was barely ten years old when he commenced to withdraw from a world to which he would return only in disguise. What those who saw him take to be actual was imaginary; all that was real about him was what he imagined. His childhood room became his whole terrestrial globe; and he populated its walls with thousands of tiny people. "I had control over their lives," he told Schwartz. "They'd worship me like a king." He thought of them as his creations as man is God's; and, as God sometimes seems to, he coddled them or destroyed them according to his whim.

He grew older and, as governor of his private universe, acted out the history of political science and advanced from despotism to constitutional monarchy, giving ground to his subjects as the old absolute kings were forced to by the recognition of disorders below them, and tumults around them threatening loss of control.

He set out to prop up this sovereignty whose territory ran only to his self by devising a government of checks and balances with himself as constitutional ruler subject to advice by a cabinet and restraint by a parliament. There was a committee to supervise his budget, another to take care of his health and another—of defense—to hold him back whenever some slight goaded him toward an aggressive response.

With time, as our own presidents have a habit of doing, he withdrew from the ordinary inhabitants of this kingdom of his fancy and confined his contacts with them to state appearances on television. But his dependence upon the elite of his advisers grew continually more intense; sometimes he lay awake through the night while his parliament debated until it could decide his course for him. He was twenty-five before he dissolved his government and was left all alone.

He grew increasingly inclined toward suicide and continually unable to manage it. Somewhere, in his helplessness, Schwartz suggests, he found his surrogate suicide in John Lennon, began to model his life after Lennon's, married a woman of Asiatic provenance, decided to retire from active work as Lennon had, and quit his job and signed himself out on his last day as "John Lennon." Then he reassembled his cabinet and submitted to it the proposal of this assassination. "They didn't want any part of it," he told Schwartz. "They were shocked."

Chapman had argued, Schwartz guesses, that if he killed the John Lennon to whose model he had fitted himself, he would at once have killed this image of himself and had been reborn as a new and true self. His cabinet had heard him out and shrunk from him. Mark Chapman's interior walls, so ingeniously, so painfully, indeed so charmingly constructed, had collapsed and he was deserted. And yet this lost phantom kingdom remains so alive in his imagination that he could tell Schwartz that several still loyal members of his old cabinet had asked him to reconstitute his government but that he dared not, because once they found their king in prison and disgrace, they would be repelled and go away.

Schwartz's portrait is so intimate and so singular that the more persuaded he makes us that at last we know Mark Chapman, the less confident he leaves us that at last we know enough about anyone else.

All general explanations of human conduct seem blown to smoke after the particularity of this one. It ceases to be useful to speculate whether Chapman acted as part of a conspiracy; he is revealed instead as himself the victim of a conspiracy whose origins are beyond any powers of identification we have because the parties to it are immaterial and unknowable. John Lennon died the casualty of a casualty.

Theories of conspiracy keep their inexhaustible powers of temptation because they so appeal to the obstinacy of our belief that no great event can have a source except in somebody's rational purpose. Their parodies of reason are a response to our anxiety to defend the primacy of reason, and Schwartz's overmastering logic is his way of teaching us the magnitude of the illogical.

We are different from Schwartz's Chapman because we do not "feel the presence of Satan's demons." But for him to whom those chimeras have been made real, they are apparitions formidable and monstrous enough to displace every other figure on his landscape; and to be made conscious of their consequence is to be unsettled in every notion that man is only the creature of his environment. The books Chapman read and the songs he heard come, in this sudden illumination, to be seen as elements that, if not entirely irrelevant, are secondary in his psyche.

The Catcher in the Rye has been most frequently put forward as exhibit for the argument that Chapman was the product of infection by the air around him. But Schwartz makes it seem altogether more plausible that what Chapman found in Salinger was not at all a message of revelation but only an echo of the inner voices that had been murmuring and shouting to him all along. He lived in a cave of the self, and he brought back any shards of culture he encountered on his occasional excursions outside only as items of interior decoration. They were, almost always, we have to suspect, hung as mirrors.

Common sense does not permit us to think of Mark Chapman as someone drawn to John Lennon by love and turned against him by hate, because there seems so little likelihood that Chapman had been left with any capacity for loving and hating anything and anyone outside himself. All his friends and all his enemies and his only true family were the tenants of the quarrelsome household of his own divided self. There will always be meaning to John Lennon's life, but there can be no meaning to his death unless it can fix in our attention the loneliness of the schizophrenic and the gallantry of his resistance and the high tragedy of his defeat.

Captain Jolly Hasn't Noticed We're Adrift

1·6·83

It is not for me to know whether Ronald Reagan will ever be elected president again. He is irredeemably no longer president. Speculations as to whether his descent can be arrested have lost their relevance. He is a falling body and the observer on the 32nd floor has nothing to tell us that is to any degree different from the prior bulletin from the observer on the 48th floor.

He owes his inalterable good cheer to his inattention as a captain; otherwise the sound of the rats scurrying over the side could hardly have escaped his notice.

The secretary of health and human services departed last week and the secretary of transportation the week before.

They took opulent appointments in the private sector; and there were the customary explanations that they have children to raise and private stringencies to meet.

The need to make money, of course, comes only to the mind of persons who have abandoned hope that life can hold any higher purpose.

Nobody starts thinking of himself as nothing more than a consumer if any useful work still lies at hand.

Can you conceive of anyone reading a restaurant review or studying a gourmet cookbook if he had been left with any larger portion of existence?

Both new secretaries are women. Their anointment is viewed by the President's assistants as proof that he does not deserve the distrust that women voters have so consistently if mysteriously manifested in the polls.

His enemies say that, when the President designates a woman as secretary of health and human services, he is showing his disdain for both. Neither the benign nor the malignant explanation seems entirely satisfactory.

Margaret Heckler was an admirable congresswoman and is, all in all, better qualified for cabinet office than her predecessor or anyway would be if we could find anything in her previous experience remotely preparing her for the Department of Health and Human Services.

The real point is that the President wouldn't be choosing women if there were men of equal parts who wanted the job.

The truly glittering chances are still reserved for men, even in a modern society, let alone one as antediluvian as this President's.

The American presidency can never sink into a position of such universal disdain that its occupant will have trouble persuading a person of grandiose disposition to be secretary of state or treasury. But the secondary cabinet posts go begging and we may anticipate the universal flight of their current holders, except possibly the secretary of labor, who cannot resign because to do so might be taken as a confession of taint.

Such is the disorder inevitable for a President who imagines that the thing said is inevitably the act performed.

Curiously enough the thing said more often than not contributes to the directly opposite result.

Now he finds that we cannot afford the budget he has projected; he will have to cut back.

And what is the consequence? The arousal of alarms at least disputable, followed by the demand for expenditures beyond our resources, followed by the concession that we cannot do what we had been told we must do.

The impulse to show our will has thus proceeded to a display of our lack.

The President is arraigned for being unfair to the poor.

The truth is that he isn't attentive or competent enough to manage even that dirty job.

He is contemptuous of the Department of Health and Human Services and thinks that most of what it does is a waste of breath and money.

And anyone who agrees with him might be puzzled to discover

that he has permitted the waste of more breath and money than any president before him.

The expenditures of the Department of Health and Human Services have risen 20 percent since his inauguration.

Is he the President of the rich? Whatever his aspirations in that direction, he is a failure even there. The last time the pollsters asked, his confidence rating with business executives was down to 27 percent, the approximate level prevailing among the horny-handed.

The great rivalry between the United States and the Soviet Union seems to be no more than a hectic race to see whether Yuri Andropov is first to destroy communism or Ronald Reagan to wreck capitalism.

Still it would be unjust to deny this President the glory that escaped Lenin: No statesman before him has offered so much promise of accomplishing the withering away of the state.

Mussolini in Concert

4 • 14 • 83

1.

Finche ch'e la morta, ch'e la speranza.
—Lampedusa, Il Gattopardo

So long as there is death, there is hope? That is a sentiment so singular and so rooted to its place of origin that, if you found it upon a shard in the farthest desert, you could guess that someone had tarried there who had spent most of his life in Sicily.

There is no part of Sicily less Sicilian than Ortygia, the last extremity of its southeast corner. It is all the flower and none of the thorn. And yet nowhere else does the odd notion of death as man's last best hope press a stronger claim. For here is the most wonderful city that any of us is ever likely to see and a great piece of its wonder is that it is dying.

Ortygia is the island fortress of the old Greek Syracuse from which the new Syracuse has fled. In its abandonment it cries out to the portion of us all that cherishes its fellow creatures and deplores their aspirations. It achingly and joyously reminds us that the blessings of the modern arrive in the company of two curses: nothing speeds decay like progress and nothing preserves except neglect.

Aeschylus staged *The Persians* in Syracuse. The tyrant Dionysius called Plato here as instructor in the arts of government and repaid him with so valuable a lesson in the nature of governors that only an unceremonious debarkation for Athens saved him from sale into slavery. Pindar was inspired and Cicero edified here. Archimedes glared across these seas and employed their sun and his mirror to set Roman ships afire. Syracuse had broken Athens and sent the Carthaginians limping away; and, this time round, she and Archimedes came close to beating back Rome herself.

The Syracusans were moderate in their moments of aggression and implacable in their hours of resistance. Ortygia has been violated again and again, and always it has outworn its conquerors and restored its own inviolable self. And always, when the Syracusans turned at bay, their last asylum was this little island a hundred feet from their mainland.

Naturally then, the huge and formerly swarming Hotel des Etrangers stands empty, the once arrogant crimson of its facade paled and chastened by the sun. The tourists are no longer a force in occupation; dying, Ortygia has outlived the last of its barbarian invasions. The grandeur of the names in this great history seems rather beside the point now, because Ortygia owes so much of its command over the sensibilities for being a monument to anonymous artisans. By no means the smallest of its charms is the refuge it affords from distraction by certified masterpieces.

Aside from its Greek coins, Syracuse possesses only two works eligible for notice in college surveys of the history of art. They are the *Venus Anadiomene*, which could dangerously ignite the libido of a Capuchin who had lain for a century dead, and the ravaged *Annunciation* of Antonello da Messina. And, with perfect tact, Syracuse has spared the visitor the perturbations of awe by sending both on voyage, the *Venus* to Canada and the Antonello on a ramble about Sicily before being dispatched to America as part of the exhibition of a master whose work, since Sicily is the sport of foreign conquerors and alien tastes, seems far more Flemish than Italianate.

We must then happily make do with the comfortable companionship of masons and stone carvers whose names long ago were mixed into the dust toward which their buildings are exquisitely sinking. Few of them were allowed the pretension of calling themselves architects; Luciano Ali, who designed the superb Benevantano del Bosco palace, is identified merely as "a local master mason." Still he has left a name that has endured for two centuries, and that is a distinction unique for his class and his kind. The workmen who rebuilt Ortygia after the 1693 earthquake are otherwise almost all unknown gods; and yet they have left everywhere behind them the mark of their pride of craft and their recognition of the law that cities live or die according to the opportunities they offer to those who glory in work. Ortygia never erected a palace for some Spanish proprietor without reserving its ground floor for the shops of artisans.

All those artisans are gone now and they have left no descendants, because it has been more than a century since Ortygia has had any function except to enchant the beholder and stifle the inhabitant. The Church of Rome was its last major employer; when the eighteenth century ended, this island that a laggardly wayfarer can walk all the way around in forty minutes held twenty-two parish churches, fifteen monasteries, and eleven convents.

In 1861, the new and anticlerical kingdom of Italy nationalized the monastic properties; and this triumph over superstition was followed by one of those cataclysms for the life spirit that serve to teach even the most radical temperament that it cannot keep touch with reality unless it keeps a few reactionary ideas firmly in place.

The monasteries had been the chief labor market for Ortygia's lay population; and, as they declined, there was less and less use for the old skills, and the old craftsmen left when they could or withered away when they stayed. Ortygia has quarters that have lost three-fifths of their population in the last fifteen years; and, in a while, there will be no one living there except those who would rather live anywhere else if poverty had not stranded them in warrens so tortuous that appellations like *via* for street and *vicolo* for alley are inadequate to describe the extreme limits of their constriction. Ortygia's street plan is singular for needing recourse to the word *rione* to designate passageways that are too narrow for the shoulders of any National Football League linebacker.

To wander past the all-but-empty palaces and to peer through the poor garments hung out to dry in the fifteenth-century courtyards of this bleached, airless but still most seigneurial of slums is to reflect how hateful to the dweller a place so lovable to the visitor must truly be and to understand that the flight to the salmon-colored cement blocks of modern Syracuse across the bridge has been the desertion of poetry in the cause of common sense.

From time to time, over the last hundred years, one or another cloud conqueror has given way to the vision of dragging Ortygia into the modern age, if only to the extent of renaming its streets Via Cavour or Via Nizza or Via Vittorio Veneto or Via Trieste, as though its inhabitants might feel at one with a greater Italy if they walked past signs affirming their community with personages and places so distant from themselves as to seem inscriptions in some foreign tongue.

The Italy of fascism undertook the last of these ventures into salvation by destruction; and its scars survive in the terrible swarth where Benito Mussolini's engineers made hecatombs of palazzi to create an avenue fit for the local branches of Alitalia and UPIM, the department-store chain. It is only one more instance of Ortygia's endless capacity for absorption that this Corso Littorio, the name Mussolini chose to celebrate his newest battleship, is now called Corso Matteoti as a tribute to the socialist parliamentarian murdered by the fascists.

Post-Mussolini Italy has been uniformly subject to the ministrations of governments with a philosophical commitment to leaving bad enough alone; and they have been conscientious about resisting most temptations to rescue Ortygia.

2.

Whatever is new on Ortygia's walls is most often a reminder of death. When a soul departs, those it has left behind signify their sorrows with broadsheets plastered about the streets or, in the cases of more penurious circumstance, notepaper-sized placards on the doors of the bereaved. They run from the humble ("My Dear Husband") to the grand ("The Marchesa Ada Gardella de Castel Lentini, 26 May, in Rome"). Of course: *marchesi* may give up the ghost in quite dreadful ambiences; but they don't die in birthplaces the world has since forgotten.

Occasionally an eminence passes who is more locally familiar, and then the walls flower with memorial testaments: "The Communists of Syracuse remember the intense social and civic involvement of Comrade the Attorney Salvatore Di Giovanni." And right next to that affirmation of a faith that has no need for God, the wife, the sons, and the daughter of this deceased Bolshevik have certified a more intimate grief on a placard bordered with lilies and crowned with the head of Christ in thorns. Sicilians are Italian only for being part of a shared community of divided souls.

One day there was a new sheet on the walls and, for once, it had to do with life, if only, Ortygia being Ortygia, with life whose liveliest claim is upon the historical memory: the next offering of the Syracuse Tourist Agency's cultural program would be a concert by the Romano Mussolini Quintet.

Romano Mussolini is the third and youngest son of fascism's founder. He was, one has to think, more the fruit of policy than of passion, since Mussolini was obsessed with the acceleration of Italy's birthrate and felt it a leader's duty to teach by example.

Romano Mussolini was only thirteen when his father lurched into the Second World War; and, in less than three years, his family was expelled from the Rome that had felt complimented to leave its name at his christening font. His public debut as a jazz pianist returned him to transient notice twenty-five years ago; but it did not seem a career option that held much promise or was worth much attention. He had come old to his apprenticeship and had brought there a taste even more obsolescent than his name; when he began, by all accounts, time had stopped for him where it did for the New Orleans Rhythm Kings, somewhere in 1925 in the exhausted vein of "Tin Roof Blues" and "The Original Dixieland One-Step." Still Syracuse is the attic of the world; and there could not have been conceived a more proper place to find one of history's discards at work on a selection of jazz's.

The visitor was then drawn across the bridge to mainland Syracuse's archaeological park by the same irresistibly unsavory impulse that used to carry the crowds to watch Lola Montez in her cage or Joe Louis at Caesar's Place; and nothing could have been less to be imagined than to have this discreditable pilgrimage end with the discovery of a piece of flesh that is Italy's only inarguable repudiation of every vestige of the fascist spirit.

The stage had been lit for the Mussolini Quintet in the open-air amphitheater whose vegetation has immured and softened most traces of tyrants dead twenty centuries ago. Romano Mussolini would play with his back to the altar of Hieron II, a pile of stones no longer capable of evoking their original function, which is just as well, because Hieron, an otherwise temperate ruler, was accustomed to celebrating his and Syracuse's prosperity with the annual sacrifice to Zeus of upward of 450 oxen there. The conjunction of relics of despots, varyingly benevolent, and 2,200 years apart, could have served to inspire fashionably ironic reflections if Romano Mussolini had not so startlingly turned out to have nothing whatsoever to do with that sort of thing. He was found at the soda wagon beside the gate, drinking a can of the orange pop called Fante. *Fante* is also the Italian word for "infantryman," and there can still be seen in Palermo a fascist construction flourishing Benito Mussolini's slogan: "The *fante* is the bud and victory is the flower."

Romano Mussolini has let his figure go most agreeably, and his countenance is rubicund, humorous, and forever immune to his father's itch for the display of the self as counterfeit of iron. The peaceful and the pleasant sat upon him as comfortably as the old coat over his shoulders. Somewhere back on the road, his mother's genes had expelled his father's; and here was the proof of her victory.

He had, he said, found his path when he was a little boy, and his inspiration had been his brother Vittorio, who is ten years older. "My brother," he remembered, "was one of Italy's first jazz critics. He used to contribute articles to the university reviews. I was only ten when he gave me a big picture of Duke Ellington."

Most of what his visitor had known about Vittorio Mussolini before then had been that he had been a pilot in the Ethiopian war and that, afterward, he had published a reminiscence that included this image:

> One group of cavalrymen gave me the impression of a budding rose unfolding as the bomb fell in their midst and blew them up.

But now it had become possible to wonder whether some fascist hack had not conjured up this atrocious picture and whether Vittorio Mussolini had not just signed without reading it, and turned back to Jelly Roll Morton. The brothers Mussolini were coming to sound like children whose tastes were enough better than their father's as to make them fortunate that he came home too seldom to notice where their minds were tending.

Suddenly there arose the fantasy of some secret life of fascism in its terminal writhings: the Anglo-American fleet lowering upon the southern coast of Sicily, and, in Rome, at the Villa Torlonia, Benito Mussolini upstairs abed under assault by his ulcers and intimations that it might all be coming apart, and downstairs little Romano listening to Count Basie on the American Armed Forces Radio and rejoicing that its signal was growing louder and louder.

"Duke Ellington came to see me in 1950, the first time he got to Rome after the war." There have been better years than 1950 to be a Mussolini in Italy; and his recital of that memory summoned up all his loneliness and the renewed recognition that, in Duke Ellington, America had raised up its only purely perfect gentleman.

Then it was time for Romano Mussolini to go about his business and he set to arranging the microphones. There was no telling him from any other workingman who, having taken his ease, is now about to return to the task he loves. If only for a little while, the spirit of its ancient artisans had come back to the neighborhood of Ortygia. After which, there occurred as the ultimate surprise the revelation that Romano Mussolini is a very good workman indeed. There were barriers to the fullest expression of his best, to be sure; his drummer and his trombonist are both Argentine imports and, to speak as kindly as possible, rather too stuck in the primeval, the one too clumsily intrusive in any vein except the Afro-Cuban, and the other too much the victim of what Henry James once called "the demoralizing influence of lavish opportunity," in this case the open horn.

But there arrived occasions even so when Romano Mussolini worked alone with Julius Farmer, his contrabassist, and only then could there be heard vivid suggestions of high possibility.

Julius Farmer is twenty-eight and was born in New Orleans, a city that Romano Mussolini cites as the founding capital of a vast territory with the same fervor that his father brought to his invocations of imperial Rome. But Farmer does not work in the New Orleans tradition; his line is like Tommy Potter's or Curly Russell's, lean, spare, and thrifty of notes.

When their companions rested from their clutter, bass and piano worked alone with the entire intimacy that is the particular marvel of jazz; and there came a moment on Ellington's "A Train" when Romano Mussolini left Julius Farmer on his own and sat there, his fingers off the keys, looking at the soloist as though this young man had some secret that he himself proposed to go to his grave pursuing, and as though this was one of those nights that bring the belief that someday he will find it.

The Mussolini family's African empire had shrunk down to one young black American, and that one not subject but comrade. Trajan's legions could hardly ever have marched across richer possessions than those these two were sharing then.

Near the close Romano Mussolini confessed himself so happy that he could not resist singing, and he stood up and hoarsely chanted that most dignified statement of emancipation from all forms of false pride: "All right, hokay, you win. Honey honey come back to me."

Between whiles, he explained the music, and told jovial anecdotes about life on the road, and held a contest with a free record as prize for the first scholar to name the composer of "Honeysuckle Rose." By then there was the most honest sweat upon his forehead and the dark blue tails of his sport shirt had worked their way free of his trouser belt and he was talking beguilingly with his hands.

He was the incarnation of all the Italy his father had tried to harden into something fierce and stern; when Benito Mussolini sought an adjective to describe the sort of Italian who most roused his contempt, he settled for "picturesque"; and that is just what his son Romano is and no less serious a man for it.

Afterward his visitor remarked, by no means insincerely, that he had detected echoes of Art Tatum in the style. "*Magari,*" Romano Mussolini replied. *Magari* is an all-purpose Italian word which the dictionaries define as meaning both "maybe" and "even," and then collapse in despair before the whole spectrum of its nuances. In this instance, we may take magari to have meant, "If only . . ." His father's dream was to be Julius Caesar; and his is to approach, in time, the level of a blind, black piano player. We old men are wrong: taste does not necessarily deteriorate from generation to generation.

History has set Benito Mussolini down as an inattentive parent. And that may have been the best gift he could have given his children; how otherwise could he have left behind a son this utterly unfascist? Ortygia turned out, after all, to be the most appropriate of places to come upon Romano Mussolini. They are both splendid examples of the sovereign uses of neglect.

The Ambivalence of J. Robert Oppenheimer

12 • 1 • 83

Thirty-nine years ago come next July, Robert Oppenheimer looked across the New Mexico sands, took the fireball's measure, and knew that he was the usher who had escorted all the creatures of the earth to the tenebrous dawn of the atomic age. Afterward he would remember—or prefer to believe—that his first conscious thought had been Krishna's: "I am become death, the shatterer of worlds."

It is unlikely that he himself could say with any assurance whether here was the cry of the stricken sinner or the exultation of the conqueror. His essence was, as always, in the ambiguities of the divided soul and equivocal presence of someone who had come in triumph to a world that would have been safer if he and everyone else who tried had failed.

But then he would himself have been safer if, at the hour that so precipitately discovered him, he had known enough more about the world than it had about him. He had been wrapped at birth in the soft bunting of a well-to-do German Jewish household on Manhattan's Riverside Drive. He came to consciousness in an ambience secure—indeed, smug—about the refinement of the air it breathed but timid about the rough winds beyond. He began his education at the Ethical Culture School, a place of refuge for families that had cast aside the few rags of superstition still adhering to Reform Judaism and swaddled themselves in the credulities of secular humanism. He passed on to Harvard, where Jewish applicants from New York had no large chance of arriving unless they brought with them the promise of departing summa cum laude. He was graduated with honors more than justifying Harvard's confidence and embarked at once for England and Christ's College, Cambridge, and then to Germany and the University of Göttingen. At Cambridge he met Niels Bohr and Paul Dirac, and at Göttingen he studied with Max Born; the great men of theoretical physics had become familiars to him while they were still strangers to the most cultivated of his countrymen.

He carried his German doctorate back to Harvard; he had already begun to robe himself in folds of mystery; Philip Morse, a Princeton graduate student who met him at a Harvard conference on molecular vibrations, had no more vivid recollection of their first encounter than "I didn't know what he was talking about."

His four months at Harvard and five at the California Institute of Technology made the year 1927 the least purposeful he had ever experienced; and it was a relief for him to accept a Rockefeller Foundation grant and escape for twelve months in the European centers of the new physics that were altogether more congenial to him for being so much more aware.

He returned in the summer of 1929 to an assistant professorship at the University of California in Berkeley, where, as he afterward remembered, "I was the only one who knew what this was all about." But even though, or perhaps because, Berkeley had so long been a desert for theoretical physics, he found it most suitable for cultivating a comfortable, if modest, bloom. Its experimentalists never quite found out what he was talking about; but they learned quickly to trust and more and more to depend on the sound and clear assessments of the practicalities of their projects he drew up from his reservoir of the indecipherable.

But for all their affectionate admiration, they never got over the sense that they were in the company of an abstract being, and they were correct in that judgment. His father's textile properties were essentially undamaged by the Depression; and Robert Oppenheimer often recalled that in those days he so seldom glanced at the newspapers that he did not know the stock market had crashed until a long time after it had. The world's coarse rubbings had never chafed his flesh until Hitler shocked him into a political activism that was the more febrile because belated and that so faithfully followed the customary courses of his divorcement from reality as to make him a fellow traveler of the Communists. Those delusions had already grown wispy when the outbreak of the war drew him into research on the potentials of nuclear fission for weaponry.

It was an area of exploration that gave the new physics an authority it had never known before; and Oppenheimer swiftly displayed such unique attributes as bridge between the abstract and the concrete that he was recognized as essential. His earlier leftward excursion was a source of doubts and trepidations, but they yielded to the overpowering necessity for his special qualities, and he was appointed director of the Los Alamos laboratory.

There he showed gifts of command quite beyond any suggested by either his prior history or the highest expectations of his sponsors. He persuaded a hundred scientists to leave the cozy precincts where they were already satisfactorily engaged in military research and to come with him to a closed military outpost in the desert. In the end he was managing a work force of over three thousand.

Here had been the utmost prodigy of practical achievement; and yet it had been brought about in an isolation sealed off from the run of humanity; there, as always, he had been protected from the routine troubles, discontents, and worries that instruct even while they are cankering ordinary persons, and he was transported to his glittering summit innocent of all the traps that every other man of affairs has grown used to well before he is forty-two years old.

After the war the United States government established an Atomic Energy Commission, and one of its earliest decisions was to approve Robert Oppenheimer as chairman of its General Advisory Committee. One of the commissioners, Lewis Strauss, was also a leading trustee of the Institute for Advanced Study at Princeton. He saw his chance to add to its collection a jewel hardly less precious than Albert Einstein and went down on his knees to persuade Oppenheimer to be director of the institute.

The slow work of Robert Oppenheimer's undoing began in the awe that Strauss brought to their earliest encounters. For it was the awe evoked by a presence whose singular curse was that he was easier to adore than comfortably like. The aura of otherworldly properties is the riskiest of capitals, because the gullible, once disappointed in imagining them divine, are apt to fall into imagining them diabolical. Strauss was one of nature's gullibles, and, having come to worship, he would remain to destroy. There would be others.

As director of Los Alamos' laboratory, he had been all else but the solitary creator of the nuclear weapon; but he had been master of its macabre ceremonies and he could not escape becoming its personification, not just for the public but for a government too quick to assume that since he produced the riddle, he must have brought along its answer. But it did not take long for his country's governors to recognize that Oppenheimer was more riddle than answer.

To their ultimate common despair, he was conscripted as physics tutor to paladins like Under Secretary of State Dean Acheson and Wise-About-Everything John J. McCloy; and he was an automatic choice as scientific member of his country's delegation to the United Nations Conference on International Control of Atomic Energy, the first flight in a search of ever-diminishing expectations.

He complained early in his tenure as chief adviser on international atomic policy that whatever he proposed was uncritically accepted. His wait for relief from that distress was a short one; within a few months his advice was being just as uncritically disregarded.

He first began to sense the limitations of his writ when President Truman asked him, in 1946, to guess when the Russians would develop their own atomic bomb. Oppenheimer replied that he did not know; and Mr. Truman said that he knew the answer and that it was "Never." The misapprehension of Robert Oppenheimer's supernatural qualities had done its worst damage; Mr. Truman could not conceive that the Russians could find the secret because he could not imagine a Soviet Oppenheimer and did not understand that no such ultimately delicate instrument was needed for work rather coarser than he knew.

But even if he had consumed a bit too much of his credit as sage, Oppenheimer's repute as mechanic resided so far beyond doubt that, for the first six years of the AEC's history, it was a matter of course for him to have been the only chairman of its General Advisory Committee.

On November 25, 1947, the young, standing or sitting in the auditorium of the Massachusetts Institute of Technology, listened as if at their devotionals while he recited science's general confession: ". . . in some sort of crude sense, which no vulgarity, no humor, no overstatement can extinguish, the physicists have known sin; and that is a knowledge they cannot lose." Half a week before, the eight other members of the General Advisory Committee had watched with no less admiration for their chairman's dedication as he led them through the preliminaries of what they had agreed upon—"without debate [but] I suppose not without melancholy"—as their prime task: "To provide atomic weapons and many atomic weapons."

His ambiguities were already traveling into the ambivalence that is the first leg of every journey toward exhaustion.

Long afterward, in his troubles he replied to the charge that he had been less than wholehearted in serving his government's desires, if not its truest interests, by saying: "I did my job, the job I was supposed to do." There was in those words a cold tone stripped of every ideal except the rules of function. It was just that pinnacle of spiritual dispossession that Robert Oppenheimer tried his best to reach, and he would fall short only because he traveled encumbered with too many pieces of baggage he could not quite bear to throw away.

He had crashingly entered the great world without bringing along enough familiarity with the ordinary one. Every famous American physicist before him had been a species of grand tinker more conspicuous for the size of his machines than the breadth of his concepts. Oppenheimer represented instead that first generation of theoretical physicists who had voyaged to Europe and brought it home with them.

This susceptibility to abstraction seems the most plausible explanation for his attraction to communism in the years before he fell into practical affairs. Marx's message could never have been as compelling as it was if he had not presumed to call his system "scientific socialism." Oppenheimer would always say that his fear of the Nazis had first brought him close to the Communists; and yet in 1939, when Stalin consummated a treaty of friendship and even a spot of collaboration with Hitler, Oppenheimer's reaction, while by no means uncritical, was somewhat this side of repulsion: Stalin was, after all, a scientific socialist and might know something he didn't.

In July 1945 Edward Teller had solicited Robert Oppenheimer's support for a muster of Los Alamos physicists petitioning Mr. Truman not to drop the bomb on Japan itself.

"He told me in a polite and convincing way," Teller said later, "that he thought it improper for a scientist to use his prestige as a platform for political pronouncements. . . . Our fate was in the hands of the best, the most conscientious men in the nation. And they had information which we did not possess."

Now he had taken upon himself the felt duty of speaking for physics to government and for government to physics. He would be guardian angel over an alliance with too much of the imbalance that obtains when one side is the caterer and the other is the customer and disputes about taste are settled by the palate of the payer.

Oppenheimer maintained this singular legation for five years. He was all but final judge of what could be done and what could not and, consequently, keeper of the gate between the ambitions of others and the official funds that could give them life and force.

He had risen beyond Berkeley and even beyond physics to a grandeur that is at once an affront and a promise, because its object arouses envy and inspires emulation. He had shown the way to an eminence there was no reaching except by a conquest more resounding even than his. He had become a huge shadow between other men and whatever bright particular moon they happened to be baying at.

At Berkeley Oppenheimer had never been more than an honored guest in a house whose master was Ernest Lawrence. Lawrence had earned his Nobel Prize with the great machines he had forced to the outer limits of those laws of physics he insecurely understood and expected someday successfully to defy.

In 1946 Lawrence designed his Materials Testing Accelerator, a piece of hardware too expensively enormous even for his private patrons, his magnificoes. He laid the MTA's conception before the AEC's General Advisory Committee, where he sustained the shock of having it dismissed by Oppenheimer as a vision that, "imaginative" as it was, "cannot do what is expected of it." Lawrence was too powerful for any such summary disposal; he turned, in his wrath, to the Department of Defense and the Joint Congressional Committee on Atomic Energy and so intoxicated them with his promises that the AEC could only give way and buy Lawrence his Materials Testing Accelerator, which swiftly burned itself out.

This demonstration of Oppenheimer's sound judgment increased rather than abated Lawrence's rage at his presumption. For at Berkeley he had taken on the ineffaceable taint of the deserter. He himself had all but ceased to search, whether because he had realized his ambition or because he had shrunk from its consequences. He could be seen as someone who existed only to frustrate the ambitions of others, having lost and perhaps, indeed, deserted the high American confidence that overrides all doubts and compunctions.

Major General Roscoe Wilson was sitting, in January 1951, as the Air Force's representative on an AEC panel on long-range weapon objectives. As always, Oppenheimer was its chairman; and General Wilson went back to headquarters deeply shaken as "a dedicated airman" at having found his country's most authoritative scientific adviser dubious about current prospects for a thermonuclear weapon, pessimistic about any early improvement in devices for detecting atomic explosions, and chilling to notions that anyone present would live long enough to see a nuclear-powered aircraft.

After this cold bath to his dreams, General Wilson felt that he had to "go to the director of [Air Force] intelligence to express my concern over what I felt was a pattern of action not helpful to the national defense."

By the time General Wilson cast his stone at this consecrated object, the odor of incense had already grown faint around it. After September 1949, and the fact of the first successful Soviet nuclear test, Oppenheimer could never again be the symbol, or even personally the sharer, of a national complacency secure in the possession of a weapon beyond any alien's attainment.

Ordinary laymen and officials had taken for granted their country's monopoly of a secret uniquely Robert Oppenheimer's, and they could see no way it could have been lost if it had not been stolen. They kept faith with that misconception well after it had been blown to vapor by executing Julius and Ethel Rosenberg, whose crimes could never have run beyond pilferage too petty to explain the triumph of Soviet research.

Edward Teller knew better than that; he was a theoretical physicist whose attainments and even intuitions were barely less commanding than Oppenheimer's. Teller's contributions at Los Alamos had been smaller than the promise of his talents, because he had spent the war hunting after a thermonuclear weapon quantitatively more dreadful than the bomb delivered upon Hiroshima. His first reaction to the Soviet accomplishment was to recognize in it a public necessity and personal opportunity to renew that pursuit.

He telephoned Oppenheimer to ask what should now be done. "Keep your shirt on, " Oppenheimer advised; and that reply left Teller lastingly certain that the chairman of the General Advisory Committee of the Atomic Energy Commission had dropped out of a race it was his duty to run.

There were doses of moral qualm in the mixture of his objections to what Teller zestfully called the Super, but they were rather smaller than his practical doubts. His remedy for the advantage lost to the Soviets was not to aim for the prodigious but to give more attention to the comparatively modest and to concentrate upon smaller nuclear weapons designed for "getting the atom to work on the battlefield as well as the heartland" and to develop a defense system that might diminish Soviet confidence that the United States could be destroyed.

All five of his colleagues on the General Advisory Committee joined him in recommending a low priority for Teller's quest of the absolute. Oppenheimer later professed himself astonished by a unanimity that his enemies could never afterward explain except as the workings of his malicious animal magnetism.

All but one of the AEC's commissioners seem momentarily to have been given pause by the unity in opinion of their scientific advisers; but that one happened to be Lewis Strauss, a minority of undiscourageable militance, who trundled his alarms to the Secretary of Defense and there raised the battalions that would prevail upon Mr. Truman to decree a crash program for the Super.

Oppenheimer's immediate response to this defeat was the suggestion that he yield his General Advisory Committee chairmanship to someone who would bring the necessary enthusiasm to the Super. Secretary of State Acheson responded to this overture by sending back word, "for heck's sake, not to resign or make any public statements to upset the applecart but accept this decision." Oppenheimer stayed on, puzzled, as he afterward said, that anyone could have even transiently mistaken him for the sort of crank who would seek, let alone "find a way to make a public conflict."

He was able to husband a somber hope drawn from his despairs about the Super's feasibility until June 1951, when Teller arrived at a weapons conference in Princeton with the formula that made the hydrogen bomb workable.

Oppenheimer's certainties had eroded and his will was ebbing; but the old intuitive faculty was swift as ever; and he seems to have divined Teller's breakthrough sooner than anyone else there. "Sweet and lovely and beautiful," he is reported to have observed. There was a sudden reglowing of what embers remained from the fires of his earliest conviction that what could be discovered ought to be discovered, wherever it tended. Once more elegance was for him its own absolution.

He set himself thenceforth to do whatever he could to help Teller. But he had lingered too long in the sin of dubiety to earn gratitude or forgiveness from those he had transiently obstructed. A few months after he had speeded Teller on his road, Oppenheimer's term as GAC chairman expired; and neither he nor his masters had any itch to have it renewed. He was sent off with Mr. Truman's warmest thanks ("You have served your country well").

And then President Truman gave way to President Eisenhower, Lewis Strauss became the Atomic Energy Commission's chairman, and Malice put on the robes of Judgment.

Even though Strauss had not quite been tutored up to his pretensions as an amateur of science, he still deserved to be thought of as a professional of sorts, because he had so often profited as a banker alert to the market potential of the by-products of scientific curiosity. In the years when research funds still depended upon private generosity, he had been Enrico Fermi's patron; and now the federal budget had made him a dispenser of benefices so much more opulent that when he retired as AEC chairman, defense agencies were spending five times as much on scientific research as they had in the Second World War.

Strauss did not carry his empire in his eye. His face, with its rosy hue and the blandness of its spectacles, gave no hint of his resentments; and his manner infrequently deviated from an all-but-universal disbursement of deferences. The Strauss who had been obdurate when alone in the Commission's minority would be tyrannical as commander of its new majority.

Extremes in the worship of anything, even reason, inevitably arrive at superstition. Strauss had made of science a cult; and, all the time he was sure of himself as a child of the Enlightenment, his devotions bore him farther and farther back toward those smoking altars where men adored or shuddered before idols they thought either kind or malign but never indifferent.

For Strauss, science had become confused with magic; and since he saw Oppenheimer as the apotheosis of the scientist, he saw him as a species of wizard who would not withhold his powers for good unless he proposed to employ them for evil.

Oppenheimer had abandoned his resistance to the Super as soon as Mr. Truman had approved it; he had been scrupulous, if not quickly enough enthusiastic, about assisting its achievement; and then, having already laid down his arms, he had with no visible complaint yielded his office and withdrawn from the center of affairs.

The very propriety of such conduct was an especial disturbance to Lewis Strauss, whose own disposition so scorned the concept of majority rule that he never thought a question closed until it had been finally settled in his favor.

Insulating the Atomic Energy Commission from Oppenheimer was no problem at all: he was still on call as a consultant, but Strauss had only to abstain from taking the opportunity to consult him.

But in 1953 Strauss and Air Force Secretary Thomas Finletter learned that Oppenheimer had rebounded to a seat on the Office of Defense Mobilization's Scientific Advisory Committee, which had been moldering unnoticed until President Eisenhower suddenly adopted and lodged it in the National Security Council, the most private chamber in his household. This image of their presumed grand antagonist, his radiance rekindled, bearing his potions and reciting his incantations before the President himself, threw the Strategic Air Command and the AEC into the determination that there was no remedy for Robert Oppenheimer's contagions except to get him stripped of the security clearance that was his license.

He had obeyed the state too conscientiously to afford it an easy excuse to find points where he had strayed. He had, of course, been close to the Communists in the lost time when such sympathies were the private citizen's options; but he had candidly confessed his excursions, and even Lewis Strauss had assessed them as trivialities when the AEC reviewed them before approving Oppenheimer's security clearance six years before.

In the interim, to be sure, his security file had grown to a width of four feet and six inches from its birth late in the thirties, when the FBI recorded him as a new subscriber to the *People's World*, a Communist daily. He himself had contributed little to its engorgement since his enlistment to Los Alamos; and the small scraps of his own giving had all been the consequences of the infrequent times when his official discipline had fleetingly been overcome by private feelings:

1) Late in the thirties he had been informally betrothed to Jean Tatlock, an on-again, off-again member of the Berkeley unit of the Communist party. After their courses diverged, Jean Tatlock had wandered into those forests of depression that would lead her to suicide in 1944. At one point in the months before the end, she sent word to Oppenheimer that she was anxious to see him. He was too occupied to respond to her appeal until June 1943; but he must have been touched in places he had thought forgotten, because he missed the Los Alamos train to sit with her, talking through the night in her father's house.

Oppenheimer did not yet know that he had embarked upon an existence that did not hold many hours of unobserved privacy. His government's agents had watched them enter the Tatlock home and had remained outside it until the next morning when she drove him to the airport.

2) During his affair with the Left, Oppenheimer's nearest and most mutually ill-fortuned masculine friendship had been with Haakon Chevalier, who taught French at Berkeley. Chevalier's romantic and innocent ardor for the Marxist-Leninist simplicities endured after Oppenheimer's disenchantment with them; but their personal affections survived. One evening, while Oppenheimer was mixing their martinis, Chevalier told him that he had been approached by an industrial chemist on the lookout for physicists who might be willing to use the Soviet consulate as conduit for transmitting information to Russian scientists.

Oppenheimer's only recollected comment was, "That would be a terrible thing to do." But later he had thought it no less than his duty to warn the authorities against the intrusive chemist without identifying Chevalier as his go-between.

This effort to serve both his friend and his nation failed so utterly that the government's agents did not relax their pressure until he surrendered Chevalier's name. He had revealed the weakness that those who thought they knew him best would be the last to impute to him; he was a man who could be bullied.

With this revelation, Chevalier's career commenced a steady decline; and now and then, from promptings livelier in his conscience than his affections, we may suppose, Oppenheimer would make a feeble stab at clearing his name.

3) Communism had attracted—or as the fifties would prefer to say, infected—several of his Berkeley graduate students. In 1949 the House Un-American Activities Committee called him to an inquiry on two or three of them. By now Oppenheimer was thoroughly infused with the developing spirit of his age and in that key he poured out his direct suspicions of Bernard Peters, who had come to California as an exile from Nazi Germany and had gone on to teach physics at the University of Rochester.

Oppenheimer told the Committee that Peters had brought with him to California an abounding fraternal affection for the German Communists, beside whom he had fought Nazi gangs in the Berlin streets before being imprisoned in Dachau, from which he had escaped by guile. To Oppenheimer any such history betrayed a character "not pointing to temperance," an assessment most curiously founded upon little more evidence than the indications of light-mindedness that Peters had shown when he had been so wanting in respect for Hitler's system of justice as to commit the insolence of levanting from one of its concentration camps.

The Committee had listened to Oppenheimer in an executive session and he had been sent away with a warm testimonial from Congressman Richard Nixon for this among so many even larger services to his country. He had felt secure against anyone outside the hearing room ever knowing what he had said about Peters; but he was about to learn how much more careless the government was with his secrets than he could ever be with its.

The Committee's staff provided a Rochester journalist with snippets of Oppenheimer's strictures on Peters; and their publication left the accused jobless and the accuser beset with protests from other physicists. The harm done Peters only too probably distressed him less than the damage he had inflicted upon himself with portions of his old fraternity. He sought to repair both with a letter to a Rochester newspaper, taking note of Peters' denial of affiliation with any Communist party anywhere and hoping that no word of his own would be taken as impugning "the honor and integrity [of] a brilliant student [and] a man of strong moral principles. . . ." That disclaimer seems to have been little meant and was even less effective; after a futile canvass for some haven in an American academy, Peters went off to teach in India.

An unhopeful attempt to comfort a woman the world thought a Communist and he once thought he loved, a failed essay at shielding a friend who may or may not have made a pass at espionage, and a halfhearted try at calling the dogs off someone against whom he himself had raised the scent—those three uneasy passages were the only departures from prescribed discretion that could be found against him by prosecutors whose obsessive curiosity was more than up to discovering any others.

But no more than this was more than enough. His judges needed those dry straws because they dared not engage the whole, awful bale. Oppenheimer's damning offense was the sin of moral qualm; he had contemplated the shadows of the thermonuclear age and shrunk back, however briefly, at a tidal point in what might or might not be man's march toward his own extinction.

This was inarguably a high crime, but it was one for which the spirit of his time forbade any man's condemnation. The Enlightenment is to be distinguished from the Age of Superstition not because it is invariably so much nicer in its treatment of heretics but because it would never burn one without being careful to condemn him for any and all sins except heresy.

Jean Tatlock, Haakon Chevalier, and Bernard Peters were broken fragments from long ago; but their excavation was essential to proceedings whose verdict could not be satisfactory unless it could contrive to define Robert Oppenheimer's departed past as his present. These minor trespasses adumbrated the major crime; his dealings in each case were signs of a piece of Robert Oppenheimer that some might think the redeeming piece: not even his upmost self-rigors could uniformly subsume the private into the public self. The same unruly heart had given itself away in the gesture to Jean Tatlock and the recoil from the specter of the Super.

Oppenheimer was tried before a three-member Personnel Security Board chosen by Lewis Strauss, a prosecutor uniquely blessed with the right to select his jury. The hearings lasted over three weeks and consumed some 990 pages of transcript. Large portions of them were engaged with inconclusive burrowings into the history of the hydrogen decision. Six of the eight prosecution witnesses gave evidence whose main import fell upon the bad advice they felt the accused had given to his masters.

Two of his three trial judges found Oppenheimer guilty. Their names are dust now but they were paladins in their day; and both were obedient to commands of a time never more zealous, with genuflections before the temple of liberty of thought in general, than when it was punishing somebody or other it suspected of liberty of thought in the particular.

Thus, they so wanted it understood that Oppenheimer's hesitations when faced with the Super were no crucial element in their judgment that they felt themselves impelled "to record [the board's] profound and positive view that no man should be tried for his opinions." What they could not forgive was Jean Tatlock, Haakon Chevalier, and Bernard Peters; a man could be tried for his ghosts.

Their findings were sent upward to the Atomic Energy Commission, where honest venom resided. Lewis Strauss himself undertook the composition of the AEC majority opinion that ruled Robert Oppenheimer unfit for future service.

"The work of Military Intelligence, the Federal Bureau of Investigation and the Atomic Energy Commission—all at one time or another have felt the effect of his falsehoods and misrepresentations."

After these savage rites there followed the customary national drill of accommodation. Oppenheimer was allowed to wither with every material comfort. He was still director of the Institute for Advanced Study, and Strauss was still a trustee, and each kept his place.

The motion to retain Oppenheimer was, in fact, tendered to the institute's board by the same man who had, only three months before, officially found him to have "lived far below acceptable standards of reliability and trustworthiness." If Strauss' principles had been the equal of his rancors, he might better have given the board the option of finding either a new director or a new trustee; but he had sounded the temper of his fellow trustees, and he preferred to keep one of his honors at whatever expense to his honor and did not press his vengeance beyond the limits of his convenience.

Whatever outrage any of the physicists felt never extended to troubling anyone above and beyond their own specialized community, and soon stopped troubling even them. Edward Teller was snubbed at the first physics conference he attended after the revelation that he had been a witness for the prosecution at Oppenheimer's trial. But there was no change in the deference of the physicists when they encountered the formidable Strauss; the unassailable immunity is reserved for the man who pays.

Enrico Fermi and I. I. Rabi had joined Oppenheimer in the General Advisory Committee's early remonstrance against the Super; and yet Strauss went on showering them with his blessings and they went on rejoicing in them. Perhaps the distinction between democratic and totalitarian societies is in economy of victimization: totalitarians suppress wholesale and democrats, when a like fit is upon them, manage a decent retail measure of the same effect by pillorying a representative specimen of a class and depending upon his example to cow the rest of its members. It could now be understood that Robert Oppenheimer was the archetype of the physicist not least because he was someone who could be bullied.

In the summer of 1945 he had done what he could to convince a doubting Teller that this country's governors were "the best and most conscientious men . . . who had information that the rest of us did not possess."

He had believed those words, against increasingly intimate access to contrary evidence, all the while his glory blazed; and even now, when it had been extinguished, he seemed somehow to believe them still. Government, not Krishna, and not even science, had turned out to be God for him; as there could be no disrupting a government's decision to immolate Hiroshima, there could be no real disputing its decision to immolate him.

When the curious approached with questions about himself and his life, he would often recommend the closest attention to the transcript of the Hearings of the Atomic Energy Commission in the Matter of J. Robert Oppenheimer. This record of his degradation seemed almost to have become for him the authorized biography; but then, it bore the authority always most requisite for him: it was a government document.

One day, shortly after his disgrace, he sat with a visitor painfully better acquainted with his history than his person.

"What bothers me." Robert Oppenheimer said, "is the complicity."

But where, his visitor wondered, did the complicity lie?

Was it in making the atomic or resisting the hydrogen bomb, in denouncing Bernard Peters or defending Bernard Peters, in leaving Jean Tatlock or returning to her for a few skimpy hours in the night, in hurting Haakon Chevalier or trying to help him, in serving his government too unquestioningly or not questioningly enough—in all the mess we make of life and life makes of us, just where do we locate and house the complicity?

"In all of it," Robert Oppenheimer answered.

The point of him? Who can feel safe in saying?

But that is a surmise too grand for the almost domestic thoughts that start when we look at his eyes in the old photographs and confront some inexplicable nobility, of stuff so adamant that it can be passed through every variety of the ignoble, do the worst and have the worst done to itself, and somehow shine through all its trash and its trashing.

His death was discreet and his memorial service impeccable. The Juilliard played the Beethoven C-sharp Minor Quartet at the funeral, up through but not beyond the adagio movement. We ought to assume that his was the choice of the C-sharp Minor and that his was the decision to cut it short. Personages of consequence would come to his funeral and bring with them a few troubles of the conscience; and it had never been his way to make uncomfortable the bottoms of his betters.

But all the same, dying as he had living, he had tried to find some means of expressing at once his sense of his own culture and the perfection of his manners.

The C-sharp Minor had been the emblem that Oppenheimer and the aspiring theoretical physicists at his feet in Berkeley had held up to proclaim the difference between their own refinement and the crudities of those stranger cousins, the experimentalists.

Now his votaries were scattered, a few by the main force of public contumely, one chased to India, another to Brazil, and he himself dead, each in his exile.

Young and obscure though they were then, they would have been much too pure to distract themselves from their reveries over the C-sharp Minor to read the program notes and discover that Beethoven had instructed his publisher that "it must be dedicated to Lieutenant General Field Marshal Von Stutterheim." All the while, the portrait of the warrior had hung upon the walls of the little rooms where they dreamed, incarnating the future that would be the unpitying judge of each and all.

Mrs. Velasquez and the Politicians

2 • 2 • 84

The absence of a proper sense of duty to self and society in the impoverished classes is a matter of such continual complaint from our governors that by their own logic they should have been heartened to come upon Zoraida Velasquez.

Mrs. Velasquez is a divorced woman responsible for carrying three children through their formative years in the South Bronx. She works in a plastics factory for gross wages of $636 a month. Our president's exactions for the public revenue are almost as merciful to the working poor as they are to the corporations, and Zoraida Velasquez's wages are taxed only $67—a bare 11 percent—a month. After paying for transportation to work, indulging in her lunch, and paying for childcare, she has $334 a month to dispose of as she pleases.

If Zoraida Velasquez would only sink into total welfare dependence, the city Department of Social Services would send her a monthly check for $424. Until the summer of 1982, Social Services was rendering to her the proper justice of a $90-a-month check for the difference. That supplement had been larger before her oldest daughter passed her eighteenth birthday and ceased to be eligible for Aid to Dependent Children. This newly fledged adult, of course, would need only to leave home to qualify for welfare herself. But her mother pinched her budget and kept the family together for the sake of the better future community college offered her daughter.

Instead of the reward deserved by the evident splendor of her character, Zoraida Velasquez earned only punishment. In July of 1982, she was informed that, under the new regulations of the state Department of Social Services, her family was no longer eligible for its $90 monthly welfare supplement.

She appealed for an administrative trial, and in November, a welfare hearing officer prematurely celebrated Christmas by ruling the Velasquezes henceforth ineligible because the Reagan budget forbade the use of federal funds to assist families whose gross income was more than 150 percent of the basic welfare budget. Mrs. Velasquez's gross income happened to be 50 percent higher than welfare provides, but the cash actually available for the support of self and children was $90 lower.

Most of us, even his detractors, are at one with the president when it comes to scouring for scapegoats whenever we are pressed to explain some social evil. Official liberalism comforts itself in that key by blaming Reaganomics for inequities of the sort visited upon Mrs. Velasquez. And yet Reaganomics is much too narrow a word for describing an all-but-universal public policy. The notion that the reality of the Velasquez situation could be defined according to the illusion of this woman's gross wages was approved by a majority of the Democrats in the Senate. And once it became law, the social instruments of a Democratic governor and a Democratic mayor of New York hastened with enthusiasm to put it into effect.

Mrs. Velasquez has never been one to give up. She turned to Bronx Legal Services, one of nineteen litigating offices for New York's poor, funded since 1966 by the Office of Economic Opportunity and beset, as never before, by a Reagan administration whose distaste for this sort of thing exceeds the hostility of social service administrators of every persuasion only in the vehemence of its aggressions.

Congressmen have come to cherish the federally subsidized poverty-law offices as places useful for the deposit and quite often the satisfaction of constituent grievances; and legislators have so far stoutly preferred their own convenience to relieving mayors, governors, and even presidents from the resultant inconvenience. And so the federal poverty-law agencies still endure, impartially disliked by executive officials at every level: when Bronx Legal Services undertook Mrs. Velasquez's cause, it came to court unsurprisingly opposed by an enlightened state attorney general and city corporation counsel whose affirmations of the concern of the mayor and the governor to withhold the protection of their wings from all except the truly needy sounded remarkably like the president's own.

Early in December, New York State Supreme Court Justice Allen Murray Myers ruled that Mrs. Velasquez had been unjustly treated. The city and state could not be permitted to argue that the refusal of federal funds for cases like hers excused them from the responsibility to the needy mandated by the New York State constitution. They must use their own money to make up the gap in her budget.

Pittance though it has won, the Velasquez family could look forward to a better Christmas than last year's. But let us leave off condemning Edwin Meese as a lamentable aberration in the official conscience. Ebenezer Scrooge is counselor and inspiration to both parties.

"If I Leave You, Baby, Count the Days I'm Gone"

4 • 29 • 84

Mourning is probably the only weakness that cannot be indulged to excess, and WKCR, the Columbia University radio station, did a considerable kindness to those of us to whom his memory is imperishable when it spent thirty-six hours of this weekend on no one's discography except Bill Basie's.

I do not suppose it possible to explain to anyone of fewer years than my own what it was like to be young when the Basie band first came east close to fifty years ago. It had started in Kansas City, a faraway place in those days. His records with Benny Moten had made us moderately familiar with Basie, and the small collection that Vocalion had issued as the Jones-Smith Seven had brought us closer still, but all the same we could not have conceived the impact of the actuality.

It must have been 1937 or so when Basie, whose eastward foray was not yet the triumph it would become, brought his full orchestra to the Albert Auditorium, Baltimore's black dance hall.

The first shock was their size. We had grown reverently accustomed to the members of the Duke Ellington Orchestra, who had a smallness of bone consonant with their elegance. But these Southwesterners looked like a waterfront shapeup. No one who came upon Lester Young, the saxophonist, after life was well along in its withering, could imagine how big he seemed when he first came east.

And these roustabouts worked in the appropriately rough key. Better ears than my own recognized at once that they played out of tune, and I am grateful for having been tone-deaf and quicker to appreciate than a more acute sensibility could have been.

Even then, Bill Basie had his intervals of delicacy. Most of them came when the bulk of the band was resting. The Albert had a keener sense of duty to its customers than to its workmen; anyone booked there was obligated never to stop the music except for the briefest pause to catch the breath.

But now and then, the band's melody components would be granted a few minutes of freedom from their joyous toils, and the rhythm section would remain to work by itself. I should not be surprised to be told that it was on these occasions of demi-intermission that Basie refined that style so economical that he only played half the notes and left the others to be suggested in his silences. He too was taking as much ease as he could permit himself.

It was at one such interval during that first sight that Bill Basie forever disposed of any further temptation of mine for dope. Someone handed me and I lit the first reefer that had ever touched my lips. The rhythm section was working by itself on "Oh, Red" as I recall. At one point, Basie took his hands off the keys he had been barely touching and Jo Jones, his drummer, very quietly commenced weaving his sticks in with the bass.

The Albert was already a very old precinct, and by some device of his own, Jo Jones set the whole creaking structure to rock from side to side, east to west, and south to north just with those two thin pieces of wood, and there was the sense that if he were incautious enough to indulge a single crash of the cymbals, the whole structure would come tumbling down around us.

It was at just that moment that I took my first puff of the reefer and knew at once that the alteration that Jo Jones and Walter Paige were performing on my interior had nothing to do with the substance I would later hear spoken of as the Good Brother. Here, strangely gentled, was the force of nature and no man-contrived substitute could ever be more than a distraction from it.

And so I laid aside the gage, the muggle, the Mary Jane then and there, because, in the half-consciousness of adolescence, I had learned that nothing must stand between me and the real thing ever again. As long as I live, Jo Jones and Bill Basie will be for me quite enough of all ye know and all ye ever need to know.

The Basie band smoothed over and even shaped itself most affectingly to the ballad. But for me, its great hours would always be those when it roughened itself again and played the blues. The blues, when all is said and done, are what you finally settle for. There is no language like its: "She's yours, she's mine / she's somebody else's too"; "If I leave you, baby, / count the days I'm gone.' In the best of languages you feel the tune from the meter of the words, and there has never been a language like the blues.

I think of them still: When Jimmy Rushing sang the blues, and Bill Basie lingered quietly and sparsely and then the whole band came home like some great locomotive, you could never afterwards forget what men can do if they are only together. Bill Basie gave us just that great a celebration of life. Death is never enough to erase a ceremony of that high order.

Example of Police Restraint Ends in Coma—and Death

6 • 26 • 84

Near three o'clock in the morning of last September 15, Michael J. Stewart, twenty-five, is alleged to have been caught in the act of inscribing "Ras," a Jamaican incantation, with a magic marker on a wall in Manhattan's Fourteenth Street IRT station.

It is the view of Manhattan District Attorney Robert M. Morgenthau that one transit policeman arrested Stewart, and two others assisted in subduing him, after which the trio carried him to the nearest Transit Authority office where at least eight other officers either watched or participated in further endeavors to pacify him.

Within a half hour after his arrest, Michael Stewart already was so permanent an exhibit of police restraint that he had entered the coma in which he lingered for thirteen days before dying.

Early this month Morgenthau announced that the three original arresting officers had been indicted for contributing to Michael Stewart's death either by direct action of their own or by indifference to the direct action of other policemen.

The heaviest count against these defendants is manslaughter in the second degree, and it is founded on the offense of violating "a legal duty to protect and safeguard Michael J. Stewart's health and life while he was in their care, custody and control."

It appears obvious that Morgenthau's grand jury contemplated what seems to have been in essence a lynching, despaired of finding a witness who could testify to the crime of homicide and had to resort instead to an indictment that, at bottom, does no more than impute the crime of a policeman's failure of responsibility to the prisoner in his charge.

That is a resolution hardly satisfactory for the Stewart family, but it does advance a high standard of public duty that you rather wish would be extended to the official agencies whose conduct has so long obstructed the ghost of Michael Stewart on its way to even the small measure of justice that it may be getting now.

The earliest news reports of the Stewart case were, as always, hopelessly dependent on the version of the transit police. They described a cocaine-crazed suspect who had sunk into "what is believed to be a drug-induced coma" while his solicitous bearers were conveying him to a hospital. The Transit Authority's spokesman said that while its policemen had indeed restrained Stewart—with gauze, naturally—the hospital had "reported no sign of head injuries."

Every one of these assertions has turned out to be false. No cocaine was found. The Bellevue nurses reported that there were more than sixty bruises on Stewart's moribund body and that it arrived shackled with four pairs of handcuffs.

Two days after the death, Dr. Elliott Gross, the county medical examiner, flatly proclaimed that the autopsy showed no evidence of "physical injury resulting in contributing to death." Stewart's parents intervened with their own pathologist and, six weeks later, Gross, with no visible blush, amended his findings to report the discovery of possibly fatal spinal traumas.

Given that history, it is hardly conceivable that Michael Stewart would not be forgotten by now if it had not been for the persistence of his mother and father and for Gabriel Pressman's admirably untiring hue and cry on the local NBC-TV news station. The three defendants came to court last week to have their case laid over until the end of July; it could not fairly be said whether they smiled so broadly because they were embarrassed or self-assured.

There were a few hisses, and a white demonstrator was held in contempt for crying out that there is no justice for black people. Mattie Stewart, the victim's mother, watched that display with manifest disapproval. She does not, to be sure, overmuch trust these proceedings; her prior experience hardly suggests that she should. But it took immense dignity and quiet and unrelenting effort to bring her even this far toward her son's vindication, and she proposed to carry that dignity to the very end.

Pride and Prejudice

12 • 5 • 84

All those who may still adhere to the half-forgotten if not quite abandoned cause of fair housing will have to wait a week before they learn whether Richard Nixon will have a place to lay his head.

It is no easy business to be your country's most conspicuous and enduring symbol of martyrdom to prejudice, which may explain why our lost president is always seeking new quarters. Misfortunes like his engrave the sense that anywhere else might be better than where you are.

Last year, Nixon approached the 61 East 72nd Street Corporation with the requisite $1.8 million purchase price for an apartment. When we speak of this building as an East Side co-op, we identify it as representative of our most powerful evidence for the conservative doctrine that there are few worse tyrannies than unrestrained rule by a democratic majority.

The warmth of his initial reception was tempered by requirements for admission not altogether consonant with a former president's dignity. The building's negotiators stipulated that his Secret Service attendants "be at all times dressed in business suits, i.e., coat and tie, or coat, vest and tie, and at no time loll about the couch or chairs in an ungentlemanly manner." Any police officer assigned to post by the city would be forbidden the premises unless he confined himself to the small office beside the vestibule.

This great historical figure, who had upheld his country's interests through protracted bargaining sessions with the loftiest of its allies and antagonists, seems to have surrendered his own prerogatives, let alone those of the secretary of the treasury and the police commissioner, without a moment's hesitation. He dared to bargain with Brezhnev and Mao, but he knew better than to try to bargain with an East Side co-op.

And even then, having fairly scuttled over the last mile, he could not yet find peace. Jacob M. Kaplan, an owner-tenant, wrote his fellow directors to express alarm at the "unsubstantiated rumor" that Richard Nixon might be their neighbor. Kaplan is over ninety and rich from the pressings of Welch's grapes. He is also a fervent and pitiless liberal Democrat. He enclosed the Columbia Encyclopedia's summary of the applicant's career: "Indications of pervasive corruption."

"We would be forced to ride with Nixon and his entourage in the elevator; curious crowds might gather in front of the building in order to get a glimpse of him," Kaplan protested.

"The substantial and potentially catastrophic consequences" he foresaw included a potential decline in the dollar worth of any apartment at 760 Park Avenue. The threat to real estate values has, of course, always been a staple of the resistance to persons of color aspiring to move in.

Kaplan went to court to enjoin the sale and relented only when the directors agreed to meet and discuss it. They met yesterday while the journalists waited outside. Seven-sixty Park Avenue's canopy leaks; the gilt leaves that form its entrance grate have not lately been polished; and when the superintendent appeared now and then to berate those tormented by the rain, it could be noticed that he was not wearing a coat and tie and that his manner was all else but gentlemanly.

But such is the way with fair-housing controversies: The object of prejudice is always neater and better behaved than those who bar his way. In due course, word came that the directors had approved Nixon with one dissent. Now, he must face the judgment of all the other tenants, including one woman who says she won't vote for him because she doesn't like him.

Who else in America except the tenant of an East Side co-op has a license to lock somebody out for no better reason than his fancied unlikability? Oh well, perhaps Nixon suffers for the best. If this nonsense continues much longer, the new Civil Rights Commission might at last find a case of discrimination worth its attention.

Splendors and Miseries on Gramercy Park

January 1985

The Hotel Gramercy commenced to stake its claim upon the tenderness of my memories under circumstances far from promising. When I found myself the sport of solitude and penury, I at once gave way to the nostalgia for the Hotel Chelsea that suffuses all New Yorkers who never happened to have lived there. The Chelsea's facade is plated with bronze tablets attesting to the prior residence of several of my betters and to the untimely end a majority of them seem to have found there.

Any spiritual reserves left unchilled by these intimations of mortality were turned to ice by a lobby where two men in cowboy hats and shirts with rhinestone trim lay about like stoned statues from some museum of the sixties.

"One can always descend the social ladder," we are told by Henry Adams, whose education in such stumblings must have been inferior to my own if it had not taught him that the fatal steps along the downward path commence when the traveler forgets his duty to decorum.

And so I fled eastward across the unknown ways of 24th Street until I came at last to the neon sign that proclaims the Hotel Gramercy to a Lexington Avenue indifferent to its treasures. I sank there for the night certain that I should improve my locale the next day and there I remained for three years, from inertia at the outset and then, as the weeks went on, from the recognition that ours is an age when we cannot often anticipate a chance to let the noun "gentility" pass our lips unmodified by the adjective "shabby."

The variety of the genteel that abides in the Gramercy is exclusively of the sort we mean when we speak of the social graces. Its age is indeterminate but must be immense. I returned there briefly after one bump on the road toward some approximation of solvency and awoke well into an otherwise sunlit Sunday morning to Old Night with nothing visible outside my window except a brick wall not a foot from my nose.

No architect would face a window on an expanse of masonry; this intruder could only have begun its jostlings after the Gramercy was *in situ*; and yet there was a wall that looked as ancient as if it were Aurelian. Still antiquity asserts itself more by its ghosts than by any calendar; one's very mattress at the Gramercy summons up all the hallboys who used to press their trousers under it before setting forth to venture their social pretensions at the bar of the old Waldorf.

The darkness mandated by the wall was a comedown for me; I had served my prior term at the Gramercy in the best-appointed ambient at its disposal, let alone mine, with its own bathroom and even a closet, and a clear view of the clock on the Metropolitan Life building as surety against some terminal hour when I would have to pawn my watch; and I passed thirteen weeks there before qualifying for the permanent status that transformed the $10 daily into a $48 weekly rate. By then I was already used to thinking of my hotel as the Gram and my small corner of it as the Père Goriot Suite.

I could not in perfect fairness recommend the Gram to anyone whose necessities forced him into my wake without conceding that its struggle against decay is now so desperate that every resident must be a soldier under environmental siege. There is, not to put too fine a point on the terms of discussion, the matter of cockroaches, who constitute, after all, so ubiquitous a presence in New York City that even the United Nations Building is reported open to their free play. The roaches at the Gram are larger than any others in my experience; but their long neglect by the exterminators has left them so torpidly unaware of even the feebler weapons and punier wiles of the adversary relationship that anyone who equips himself with one of the tiny boxes endorsed by Muhammad Ali can trust them to troop in with so complete an indifference to the corpses of their predecessors that, within a day, his room will be as pest-free as a Chase Manhattan vault. It is also sensible–if possibly licentious–for the studious to carry in a supply of light bulbs; the Gram does not aspire to illumination beyond the range of forty watts.

These admonitions to self-help are put forth not as warnings but as precautions. The worm of time has gnawed too long to leave the Gram much margin for the physical amenities; its charms are all reserved for an unwearying solicitude for the social sensibilities. It travels toward its inescapable extinction without ever departing from the fundamental assumption that no one can sleep under its roof, however uncomfortably, who is not a gentleman or a lady.

I should not think that Mrs. Harry Helmsley needs to lie awake over worries like that, for it is only the hotel-keeper at the ragged edge who has to be unwearily attentive to the importance of a rent roll confined to the unoffending.

The Gramercy is an artifact of that lost time when the near-indigent New Yorker could take for granted his convenient access to a premise where he could lay down his head in peace. Reformers used to cry out against the accommodations such precincts provided; but now when the city's streets are more and more cluttered with the homeless, those vanishing rookery are surprisingly warm in recollection because, as one observer recently put it, nothing is worse than bad housing except not enough bad housing.

Bad housing though it inarguably may be, the Gram shines all the same as a refuge for the decent poor, because it has stood firm against all temptation to throw them into discard by selling itself for conversion into one of those warrens the realtors call "luxury condominiums" or to debase them by opening its doors to the mad, the bad, and the dangerous to know. Circumspection, good manners, and accident explain its endurance as they do pretty much any instance of protracted defiance of life's exigencies.

Bernard Berenson needed no subtler and could afford a slower eye than a clerk at the Gram has to bring to his first gaze upon an applicant for lodging. A "Sorry, No Rooms" sign has been a permanent fixture on the registration desk since it was inked in some forgotten time; but it functions less often to describe the true state of affairs than as a measure of courtesy to anyone falling below the standard zealously held up by Abraham Okun, the Gram's proprietor, and Joseph Barrett, its day manager.

"I've had my quarrels with Abe," Joe Barrett said once, "but he has scruples. He's not out for every dime he can get regardless."

Early in my tenure, a covey of New York prostitutes alighted at the corner of 24th Street and Lexington Avenue and roosted there on the scantiest rations of crumbs for a year or so. They came like swallows and like swallows went; and, all the while before they flew away, the Gram barred them from its halls except for those emergent minutes when they were driven to cover by some raiding party from the morals squad and in simple mercy were allowed sanctuary in the lobby's outermost fringe.

Still the occasion of sin can now and then slip past the sharpest of scrutiny and one evening a window washer gained admittance, probably because he took the precaution of hiding his pail and squeegee under his coat. Window washers are by no means unjustifiably catalogued as a suspect caste; they are assumed to work off the books and their subsequent immunity from the Internal Revenue code too often inflates their assurance of exemption from any other. This particular representative of their clan turned out to be more than usually high-flown with insolence and with wine and I came home late one evening to find him insecurely pinned by the three policemen after he had protested his eviction by kicking the glass out of the Gram's entry door. A cluster of the more settled residents had gathered at the scene of combat; and when one of them complained against this rude incursion upon his rest, a cop reminded him that anyone who lived in a place like this had best get used to an occasional breach of the peace.

"A place like this?" he replied. "This is the safest place in the city."

And so it was. I never witnessed any closer approach to a public offense throughout my stay at the Gram; and that one hardly bruised my sensibilities beyond some disappointment that the sentencing judge, if such there be in New York, had not thought to order the miscreant to atone by washing our windows.

The Gram's history is not, of course, entirely untainted by crimes and follies; but here as in everything else the brush of the painter is soft, delicate, and tending to the comic style.

"About five or six years ago, this kid came to us," Joe Barrett remembers. "Very quiet and well-mannered. He always carried the *Times*. He ran a little behind on his bill, as they sometimes do, and one morning he stopped by the desk to tell me that he knew he was owing but not to worry because he was going down to the bank.

"The next thing we heard was that he was holding three people hostage at the bank and asking for $70 million in gold bullion and an escort to the airport. He finally settled for a six-pack of beer.

"Then there was the time when Harry Wilkerson was night clerk and two guys came in and showed him this phony badge and said they had a tip that an armed robber was heading this way and there might be some rough stuff and Harry ought to clear out until they had collared him. So Harry went up to his room and sat there twenty minutes or so and didn't hear any noise so he thought he'd better go down and check. They'd cleaned out our cash register for what that was worth."

But such incidents are so infrequent, not to say bizarre, that this must be unique on the island of Manhattan as a hotel where the register can close his eyes without fear of rough arousal if he leaves his door wide open on a summer's night to allow for the absence of air conditioning mandated by the otherwise rewarding accident of its obsolescence.

For the Gram has never managed the conversion from direct to alternating current and is thus inhospitable to every development in the line of electrical appliances since the passing of Thomas Alva Edison.

"That's why we're so quiet," Joe Barrett says. "The kids can't use their stereos and we're safe from fires because we can't have hot plates and heaters."

The Gram's rooms are also unencumbered by telephones; a while ago, Okun and Barrett contemplated their installation and, as always, recoiled from progress and ruination it generally brings.

"What would it be like," Barrett asked, "to have some drunk yelling all night on the telephone?"

And so, to this day, when there is a call for a resident at the Gram, the clerk goes off to knock at the callee's door and inform him, with an agreeability undiminished by the climb, that he is wanted by the outside world; and, in the majority of cases where he does not want back, he has as good an option to evade pursuit as the shield of two secretaries could ever maintain for an executive of the Music Corporation of America.

One of the happier accidents of the Gram's old age is its name, which provides any resident who would prefer not to have the straitness of his gate noised about with the protective coloration of confusion with the Gramercy Park, a younger hotel with no small cachet.

"I get a lot of my fun," Joe Barrett says, "from all the people who mix up the humble Gramercy with the elegant Gramercy Park. Every Sunday somebody calls up to ask what time we serve brunch and last year I got a call from Japan trying to reserve our banquet room for October tenth."

I have moved on since to lodge with leases all else but secure on social rungs above the Gramercy's if not invariably up to the Gramercy Park's. Still I pass by the old place occasionally and wave to some remembered former sharer in my occupancy standing outside with no particular place to go but holding fast to his dignity and his distance from the bums standing on the corner of Third Avenue. There is a special comfort in knowing that he and the Gram are alive still.

The bricks that must once have been a flame of red have mellowed now to an aching evocation of Vermeer's wall at Delft; and the discreet wooden capital letters nailed up long ago to identify this haven for the hostelers and drovers of the 1890s are weathering toward fragmentation. The *H* is intact; but the *o* and the *t* are gone; and the *r*'s in Gramercy are cracked and sagging. But the *G* remains as elegant as ever and even lovelier for its patina. When the wrecking ball has done its office and the Gram's portion of the respectable poor is dispersed to worse, I suppose that, if I am not a ghost too, I shall come upon that *G* in some Madison Avenue shop and pay more for this scrap of departed memory than I ever had to for the real thing.

Parade's End

6 • 13 • 85

Nothing in the minutes before New York at last lit up its Vietnam memorial last month can ever entrap the memory so lastingly and so painfully as the company of soldiers a decade or more demobilized still wearing their jungle fatigues. Their dress was a badge of how different from the rest of us they remain—they insist on looking as though still on the way back from some long patrol carrying their wounded.

Some of them interrupted the pieties from the loudspeaker with hoarse cries defying interpretation. It could not be said whether they were calling out to one another in a language incomprehensible to anyone except themselves or merely raging at all the comfortable strangers who could never know what they know.

There fell upon the spirit the melancholy conviction that to raise up Vietnam memorials is our bounden duty but that whenever we turn the searchlight on one, we illuminate a scar. These unhealed survivors have become the image of the Vietnam veteran for a popular imagination habituated to identifying the type from presumed exemplars by no means typical.

Most of those who served in Vietnam came back to swallow their bad luck and set themselves to the denial of reality that is the prime responsibility for endurance of civilizations as advanced as ours. Denying reality is so much the requisite formula for making one's way that one ought to cherish these members of the unappeased as much for their refusal to forget what they had to pay as for the payment itself.

The Senate Republicans have lately been struggling with the embarrassment of successive displays of their president's taste in disposing of offices of trust. One adviser to the secretary of education had to bow out when it was discovered that she had once blamed the handicapped for their own troubles, because "a person's external circumstances do fit his level of inner spiritual development."

The new chairman of the Copyright Royalty Tribunal had already been confirmed before she turned out to have been listed as coauthor of a work declaring that most black Americans "insist on preserving their jungle freedoms, their women, their avoidance of personal responsibility."

Aside from their malignity, these statements shock the sensibilities most for their ignorance. No one who ever watched the heroic struggles of a handicapped child could think him deficient in "inner spiritual development," and no one remotely familiar with the run of the black community would describe it in terms applicable to no element in our society except possibly the Pentagon. And yet their authors were rewarded with a rise in the world that has made refusal to face the facts of life the great test for getting ahead in it. The bawls that occasionally intruded upon the present ceremony, trial though they were to its sponsors, had at last asserted a reality rebelling against silence.

The mayor lit the memorial, and a visitor moved among the letters to home incised in its glass walls with those uneasy ghosts in their jungle fatigues all around him. The letters echoed other soldiers in other wars, fed up, fagged out, and far from home. There were a few notes evoking remembered comradeship: Charles Dawson, a First Cavalry medic, telling Richard Carlson's mother how her son had died because, when wounded himself, he persisted in drawing fire while he bound up others of the fallen. "I often wonder," Corporal Dawson concluded, "if what we are fighting for is worth one human life."

In Richard Carlson's case, the cause may very well have been worth a life, but the wall was otherwise stingy with consolations. The uneasy ghosts examined the wall more fixedly than they looked at the fireworks, and so did their fellow visitor, who is generally an addict of these cascades in the skies. Fireworks are for celebrations; and try though we may to salute it, the Vietnam War is only for mourning.

The Landlord State

9•5•85

The world only contains a minority of humans fortunate enough to be free from one or another form of despotism, and the citizens of Manhattan have no such luck. And naturally, since Manhattan is unique, the instruments of her oppression are different from most others.

The commonest form of despotism is the police state; Manhattan is a landlord state.

The ownership and management of real estate is the island's closest approximation of absolute power. Except for rare instances of the fanatically resistant spirit, tenants have ceased to expect equity from their landlords and pray only for mercy.

Absolute power, being a species of disease, progresses in stages. Landlords are human and, like most of us, they become what they are treated as being. They used to be treated with the mere respect that everyone deserves. Then the housing shortage began, and deference took over.

Now the housing shortage is a famine, and abjection is the appointed bearing for engagement with the Manhattan landlord. The more its subjects bend the knee to absolute power, the more overweening the pride of its possessor and the more iron his whim.

You cannot decently compare even the worst landlord with Joseph Stalin, and yet there are parallels in the advance of this particular illness toward its terminal stages.

As long as his partisans stooped no lower than deference, he limited his zest for vengeance to expelling his opponents from office and party. But then he inhaled the heady incense of abjection and very soon began ordering people to the labor camp or the execution wall as his fancy suggested.

At a certain point in the development of the absolutist disposition, the economic interpretation of history, however valuable otherwise, stops being relevant. Stalin did not do these things from any notion of proletarian welfare, but just for the sake of showing himself so powerful that he could do whatever he pleased.

Our court dockets begin to suggest that the disease of absolute power, in instances still extreme to be sure, is working its ravages on Manhattan's landlords until the economic goals of greed commence to give way to the sensuality that resides in showing that you are the boss.

A month or so ago, a few of us were drawn to the summons part of Criminal Court by a report that Robert H. Shapiro, gentrifier of the Lower East Side, had sworn out a harassment summons against his own mother. Susan Robbins, Mr. Shapiro's mother, had visited his office to tax him with what she took to be unfilial behavior, and he had gone to the cops.

Harassment happens to be a criminal violation, however minor, and to charge it against your own mother is curious conduct for a gentrifier. Mr. Shapiro was treated with the deference Manhattan's courts reserve for its landlords, and his mother felt compelled to agree to desist for her importunities.

I talked to both parties and found Mrs. Robbins quite charming and her son all else but. He seemed in no way embarrassed by an action that was, to say the least, singular, and he showed every assurance of rectitude about conduct that might make the rest of us blush.

Then there is the further example of David Walentas, the sovereign lord of 180 W. 58th Street.

Six years ago, Mr. Walentas began an effort to chase away James Green, a $600-a-month rent-stabilized tenant. Mr. Green endured a series of pettifogging litigations and won them all until both he and Mr. Walentas grew exhausted enough to agree that Mr. Green would sell his rights for $78,000.

Mr. Walentas delivered $76,000 and held back $2,000 on the claim that Mr. Green had failed in his commitment to leave the apartment "bone clean." Mr. Green could only sue for his $2,000, and last week

Supreme Court Justice Beverly Cohen sustained his right to have the matter tried.

The disputed sum is less than 3 percent of the whole agreed upon, and Mr. Walentas will spend more than that fighting Mr. Green in court.

Not greed but only a compulsion to show oneself the master of all who stand in your way explains such a posture.

But then effronteries of this order may be Manhattan's own fault: Yield enough prerogatives to a man, and that is the sort of man you produce.

Report from Nicaragua

6 • 27 • 86

Esteli—Back in Managua, Carlos Humbes' visitor had scoured for whatever light might help him divine what an indefinite subsistence in independent inanition must be like for the general secretary of CTN, the wind-tossed umbrella of the Catholic trade unions.

At length the visitor could find no better question than:

"From where you sit are things better or worse or just the same as they were before the revolution?"

"Better" would be the inconceivable from this quarter. "Worse" would be only the expected from a labor leader unevenly competing with rivals whose nurse and keeper is the Sandinista government. No possible answer could surprise except "the same."

"El mismo," Carlos Humbes replied.

"El mismo." The same. The same cruel futility of things.

The visitor is contemplating the shoe factory the revolution has brought to Esteli. Its air is pervaded with the tune of hammer plinking upon nail that fell silent long ago wherever there exist methods of production that can reasonably be called processes of manufacture.

Here hunch twenty figures from centuries gone, cobblers with no machines but their fingers. Each would have worked alone in his cottage before the Industrial Revolution; the only perceptible difference is that now he has been collected in a shed with nineteen other handicraftsmen, each cutting, shaping, and fitting his own materials.

The establishment's best artisan is introduced. He is stitching the side trim on a boot. A young boy sits beside him threading a needle. It is an image from seventeenth-century genre painting, the apprentice learning his trade by observing his master, and the inference is inescapable that, now as then, the apprentice's mother is paying a small fee for the lesson.

The master displays his latest completed work with eminently justifiable pride. It will retail for roughly fifteen dollars and half of that will be his pay for ten 10-hour days of loving care. We have come upon one of Nicaraguan labor's aristocrats, and he fairly glows with the satisfaction of bringing home four dollars every day. Are we to suppose upon such scenes that we have penetrated a core sector of the fearful machine that pours forth the jackboots for what our own President seems seriously to conceive as the imminent trampling of Latin America?

At the cigar factory, a crew of workers, mostly women, puts the tobacco leaves through their preparatory stage by breaking off their stems and stacking them on tables. Things are done here just as they must have been when Samuel Gompers wrapped cigars in Tampa in 1865 before breaking his chains to bemuse the toilers and himself as the first president of the American Federation of Labor.

The revolution's "Outstanding Child Worker," a transient television celebrity, is a member of this work force. She is twelve years old, an intact artifact from the beginnings of capitalism. Nicaragua's methods of production are still so primitive that its Ministry of Labor can find no way to increase output except to encourage all hands to work harder with pay incentives.

She who sorts and stacks seventy pounds of tobacco has achieved the day's norm where her incentive pay begins. At the end of any month where she has averaged 30 percent above the norm, she will have earned twenty-eight thousand cordobas while an equally motivated sister will take home thirty-eight thousand cordobas thanks to the higher level of skill required to wrap the cigars and bundle them.

For the great majority of Nicaraguans who have no access to the black market, a thousand cordobas is worth but a shade more than one American dollar.

The visitor travels on to the garment factory named after Luisa Ajuda Espinoza, a revolutionary martyr, and there he beholds a sight he has all but lost hope of seeing in a Nicaraguan industrial premise—a working spread of mechanized devices.

They are sewing machines, gifts of the unions affiliated with the Belgian Socialist Party.

Nicaragua's sympathizers blame most of her difficulties on the Reagan administration's economic boycott, but, in point of fact, she is the beneficiary of an extraordinary volume of foreign aid not merely from the Communist bloc, but from those Western democratic nations whose kindliness is stimulated by their pleasure in the discreet thumbing of noses at the White House. But it is not often enough aid of the sort that is useful.

For all the pride and even the vainglory of her comandantes, Nicaragua is a beggar nation and cannot be a chooser. She must take what she can get, whether from charity or from barter. Most of the paltry stock in the supermarket at Esteli is of foreign import and so all else but appropriate that customers from a town that could hardly have many more than one hundred flush toilets can find a whole shelf stuffed high with toilet plungers delivered by Bulgaria in exchange possibly for Nicaraguan cigars.

When the Belgians donated these sewing machines, they conferred a treasure upon the Luisa Ajuda Espinoza Cooperative; and its rewards manifest themselves in the schedule on the wall that establishes a forty dollar a month raise for a worker who doubles the norm that expects her to attach fifty-six collars a day. There aren't many trades of moderate skill where the employer can pay even that comparatively decent a wage unless he has functioning machinery.

Still, a few young girls activate the needle even here; and the visitor observes, as delicately as he can, that child labor is no entirely appetizing example of revolutionary social advance. The forelady replies that it is only a temporary recourse in the exigencies of the war that has conscripted the men who would otherwise be working for the national defense. Hers is an answer that serves better to excuse than explain.

Men do not operate sewing machines; it is women's work the world 'round. There are indeed necessities that force a female child into a garment shop, but they are her family's and not her nation's necessities, and they are not temporary: Luisa Ajuda Espinoza's nineteen dollar monthly minimum wage will for a long time mean for these children the difference between an exigent existence and a one nearly unbearable.

Nicaragua's revolutionary leaders demonstrate an inarguable quotient of incompetence, but it increases their difficulties only because their situation allows them not one inch of the wide margin for mistakes available to developed industrial societies. If they were masters of planning, they would have too little with which to plan; the only material that is not in short supply in Nicaragua is the stuff of dreams.

The citizens of Cordoga have been assembled to celebrate the anniversary of one of the earliest Sandinista victories there. Cordoga is perhaps four hundred yards and not less than a hundred years from that lonely symbol of capitalist development, the Pan American Highway.

Nothing seems new there except the Wall of Revolutionary Martyrs and the cellophane banners of the Sandinista National Liberation Front. A troupe from the Nicaraguan National Ballet offers a program of dances from progressive portions of the earth, including a snatch of *The Red Detachment of Women*, the ballet to which his People's Chinese hosts subjected President Richard Nixon, and it appears to baffle this audience as much as it had him. The occasion is nonetheless unexpectedly pleasant, and not least because of the brevity, the quiet tones, and the notes even of apology for past inadequacies in the keynote address of Jose Francisco Mendietta, secretary of the Sandinista Party for the Zone of Esteli.

It is fifty years since the murder of Augusto Sandino, and yet if he had ridden into Cordoga this day, he would have found not one change to surprise him except the martyr's wall and the pictures of himself plastered on so many of the others. A whole forty-three of those years belonged to the Somozas and only seven belong to the revolution, and none of them have brought a detectable difference in the life of Cordoga.

If RICO Wins, We Lose

3 • 8 • 87

John Gotti and the House Committee of the Bergen Hunt and Fish Club were consigned Friday to a jury whose mercies will, if precedent obtains, be otherwise than tender. Assistant U.S. Attorney Diane Giacalone closed for the prosecution with a catalogue of the infamies of Gotti and friends that came to its climax with:

"They corrupt young people to fill their ranks." The eye searched the row of the defendants for one trace of a lost cherub, and it was an unfruitful inspection. These could hardly be the faces Diane Giacalone had in mind when she evoked the image of solitary lambs prey to the prowling wolf.

Might she then have been speaking of the once virgin souls drawn to sin with John Gotti and now snatched from the burning and redeemed as government witnesses against him? Had we been asked to elevate our hearts ruminating upon James Cardinali, whose pre-salvation felonies run from murder to the pistol-whipping of a priest, or upon Salvatore Polisi, whose versatilities extended from selling heroin to kidnapping and all the way up the social scale to stealing financial documents?

It was hard to imagine Mephistopheles, let alone John Gotti, needing to bring more than a shoelace to bargain for the souls of such as these. Yet now Diane Giacalone was telling us that John Gotti should go to prison for forty years for all kinds of transgressions, and not least among them the seduction of the innocent. There had come the hour of collapse for all resistance to the outrageous hope that John Gotti will win his case and Diane Giacalone lose hers.

That hope is a triumph not merely over my decorum but my strongest sympathies. I don't remember ever encountering a gangster with less sense of the tone requisite for discourse among gentlemen than John Gotti, and I have not met many fellow creatures, let alone prosecutors, with as many saving graces as Diane Giacalone. I do not like him much and I altogether like her; but that is not the point. The time has simply come and more than come for the government to lose a RICO case.

The Racketeer-Influenced and Corrupt Organizations statute is founded upon the doctrine that a felon deserves more draconian punishment for enlistment in a continuing criminal conspiracy than he could earn by conviction for any two crimes in its service.

RICO's progress has been one more chapter in a history cluttered with secular dogmas unobjectionable in theory and all else but in practice. Little can be put past our Congress, but it could scarcely have conceived results like these:

(1) Ralph Scopo was president of the district council of the concrete workers union. He was a labor racketeer and unremarkably skilled at that booming trade. He shook down concrete contractors for a percentage of their awards, and busy though he was with his exactions, they were even busier and more adroit at cheating him of his full due. Labor racketeers are regular fodder for the federal dock and are routinely borne off for sentences of two to five years.

Ralph Scopo's crime was on all fours with theirs and yet he was sentenced to one hundred years. He acquired this unique if uncomfortable distinction because his jury found that he was a soldier in the Colombo crime family, had thus indulged his shakedowns as an agent of a criminal conspiracy and thereby qualified himself for a penalty fifty times higher than he would have suffered if he had been an honorable extortioner working for himself and a few fellow business agents.

(2) It is an article of faith for civics classes that no man can be tried twice for the same crime. We can thank RICO for liberating us from that prejudice. Let us take the instance of Carmine Persico, while setting aside the suspicion that he has so bloodied the books of the Recording Angel that all Lent on the ashes in his sackcloth could scarcely cleanse a page.

First, Persico was tried as boss of the Colombo family and sentenced to twenty-seven years for supervising Scopo's misdeeds. He was then tried as a member of the Mafia Commission; the evidence against Scopo was brought forth once more and served to convict Persico anew, and he got one hundred years more.

Scopo and Persico are only small scraps in the litany of RICO's excesses, every one of which has so far been upheld by the appellate courts.

On Friday, Judge Eugene Nickerson instructed the jury in the RICO law, and the binding precedents could hardly seem other than bizarre to an intelligence as keen and sensitive as his.

John Gotti could be convicted and sent away for forty years or more if the jury found that he had conspired to commit a 1975 homicide for which he had already served a prison term and if he had run a horse parlor in violation of the laws of New York State. RICO arithmetic is the science that takes one felony already adjudicated, adds one misdemeanor and sums up the total as a multiplication of felonies.

It has been said that, if such things can be done to the Mafia, they can be done to us all. We would better say that they ought not to be done to anyone. If Gotti gets acquitted, a good woman will mourn and a bad man exult and, distress the finer sensibilities as any such scene must, it would be worth enduring for the sake of equal justice under law.

Verdict on a City

6 • 17 • 87

The trial of Bernhard Goetz is over and the City of New York has been found guilty. The shame of this judgment is all our own and none of it belongs to these jurors. They heard the case for seven weeks and sought its meaning through upwards of twenty-seven hours of deliberation, and their collective conscience has now impelled them to define the issue in Goetz's own terms and all but announce that law and justice have ceased to breathe as realities in this city.

There is about this verdict something of the terrible finality of an autopsy report. These twelve painstaking people have decided that Goetz did what he had to do, and they could not have agreed essentially to acquit him if they had not agreed to condemn the civilization they had so dutifully represented.

Acting State Supreme Court Justice Stephen Crane's courtroom was strangely quiet while foreman James Hurley ran through his successions of "Not Guilty" yesterday. There were no signs or sounds of joy, not even and in fact conspicuously not at all from Goetz himself, and the only rustling was an occasional gasp of surprise when some charge in the indictment that had seemed weighted with peril for Goetz slipped harmlessly by.

Assistant District Attorney Gregory Waples could not be counted among the surprised. One fellow prosecutor reported yesterday that Waples had returned from his final summation last week to say that two or three of the jurors had looked at him with a disbelief barely short of mockery at points in the four hours he had used up his formidable skills on a cause he could feel slip a little further away with each passing minute.

"I've never seen that in a jury before," Waples said. "Three of them almost laughing and the rest stone-faced."

He had been preaching a faith in a church emptied of the faithful and upholding the ideal of order for judges driven by the disorders in the streets to think it just a myth.

It is unlikely that these jurors mistook Goetz for a hero; seven weeks in his presence could not have encouraged that image. He himself had been the first to speak of himself as a pathetic figure, and even this day of his gloomy triumph can hardly inspire him to revise that self-assessment.

But then all the actors in this dreadful story are pathetic creatures. Each of them incarnates what can become of people when they are treated as mere trash day after day. All Goetz did was rise up in the wrath, holy, unholy, or a bit of both, of his grievance at being treated like trash. And so he shot. And the four young men he shot had been trashed by society, and all they had learned to do was to trash society.

And Darrell Cabey will never walk again and will spend such life as he has sliding in and out of his consciousness of reality. To think of him is to be grateful to this jury. When it acquitted Goetz, it pronounced all of us accomplice to his acts; we had done what we could to disable Darrell Cabey, and Goetz finished the job. He is only the pitiable instrument of a destiny appointed by our own pitiless indifference to the fate of the young and the peace of the city.

Gregory Waples observed yesterday that he is assigned next to prosecuting two off-duty transit cops who got into a quarrel with four dope dealers and are accused of shooting one of them in the leg and running away. And so once more Waples will have to argue the dignity of law and order before jurymen imbued with the daily consciousness of its degradation.

All the same even a dope dealer has his rights, and so did Darrell Cabey, who was barely more than a child however close to ruin he may already have been. Turn your back on the worst and you will in time turn your back on everyone. We just about have. For what else has the Goetz jury said to us except that the time is ripe and rotten ripe to square our shoulders, look straight at the huge rock that lies at the bottom of the hill and all together try to push it up the slippery slope back to the top. This is not a morning that offers much hope we will.

Bessie Smith: Poet

7 • 5 • 87

"Woke up this morning when chickens was crowing for day."
—"Young Woman's Blues"

Woke up yesterday morning where there is not a chicken to crow for day and remembered that on September 27 next Bessie Smith will have been dead for fifty years.

She was killed a few miles from Clarksdale, Mississippi. The gods could not have selected a more appropriate place to close her epic, because Clarksdale is not very far from the railroad tracks where the Southern used to cross the Yellow Dog and where Miss Susie Johnson's Jockey Lee had gone.

September is a while away. But what fitter day for filing an advance notice of this special occasion could there be than July 4, which is sacred to the falling-short but undiscourageable pursuit of happiness that is most of what the works of Bessie Smith are about. Most but, as usual with great subjects, by no means all.

The rising sun ain't gonna set in the East no more.
—"Hard Time Blues"

To distill a complexity into the sparest of direct statements and still preserve intact its paradox was among the subtler of Bessie's arts. We have no way to know the source of most of her lyrics; she must have picked up a good many in the carnivals and others were written for her by hands more practiced. But a lot of these words have to be her very own and they bring us the sense of being in the company of the last of the Anglo-Saxon poets. There are, as an instance, those lines in "Lost Your Head Blues" that have been authenticated as pure improvisation: "Once ain't for always and two ain't but twice." I have puzzled over them off and on through my conscious life and am yet to be sure precisely what they mean. All that I know with certainty is that they are entirely beautiful.

> *If I ever get my hands on a dollar again,*
> *I'm gonna hold on to it till the eagle grin.*
> —"Nobody Knows You When You're Down and Out"

Or "My heart's on fire but my love is icy cold." No generation is long enough to produce more than one writer who can bring off this cadence so perfect that, when you think you remember it and look it up, you find that you were wrong because you had allowed some bit of dross—say an adverb—from your own literary baggage to intrude and spoil the rhythm and taint the purity of the original. Those of us who learned to write from the blues are to be envied, and those of us who have since forgotten the lesson are to be pitied.

> *Thirty days in jail and I got to stay there so long.*
> —"Jailhouse Blues"

"Jailhouse Blues" was her first record and the first of hers I ever owned, which is to say that it was the one I have played most and thus the one I have loved most, because the record of Bessie's you have heard most often ends up the deepest in your heart.

I also saw and heard her once at the old Howard Theater in Baltimore in 1933 and was too overwhelmed for any coherent recollection. Witnesses to the apparitions of creatures from another world are seldom useful for details. I have only two memories. One is the shock of the recognition of how faintly even her records conveyed the immensity of her actual presence.

The other involves one of my companions, who was far from having conquered his baby fat and was indeed huge enough to be the most conspicuous figure in the house except of course Bessie herself. At one point she descended from higher things to "One-Hour Woman," one of the requisite dirty songs her grandeur somehow always kept from being quite disgusting, and then she noticed Freddy and, like giantess calling out to giant, she began singing that she had found in him her one-hour man.

He turned turkey red and fled the theater. Long afterward I ran into him and wondered as tactfully as I could if he remembered the afternoon we had gone to hear Bessie. He replied that he had and that, even though dozens of women had since bruised his heart, it was the supreme regret of his life that he had not held his ground and heard the whole set.

"Is it true," he asked, "that she sang 'Muddy Water?'" I answered that she had and his sigh had resonances of sorrow and loss not unworthy of her own. We would still have no more used for her any name except the bare and stately "Bessie" than we would have spoken of Juno as Mrs. Jupiter. Goddesses do not have last names.

Awhile back I fell into one of those tiresome discussions where the other party says you take Julius Erving and I'll take Larry Bird and you take Sarah Vaughan and I'll take Ella Fitzgerald. There was no disposing of such nonsense except to observe that the years have taught me to be grateful for having them all, but I had to say that Sarah Vaughan is the greatest jazz singer I have ever heard. "What about Bessie Smith?" a bystander inquired. I could only answer that I had concluded that there could never have been a Bessie Smith; the molds where they stamp out human beings are just too small for stuff of those proportions.

Strange Landscape at Passion's Height

11 • 15 • 87

The trial of Stella Valenza on charges of hiring three mechanics to rid her of her husband, Felice, is stuff to lift the hearts of those of us who had despaired of ever finding a domestic hearth where the fires of mutual passion still burn hotter than when they first took flame.

Felice and Stella Valenza were married six years ago and are plainly crazier about each other than ever.

He was a witness for the prosecution in Queens Criminal Court Friday and singularly unequipped for the job. It has been well and frequently said that the husband is the last to know. By common account, his wife was so compulsive a shopper for contract killers in the spring of 1986 that all Bayside seems to have resounded with her inquiries.

And yet, when Felice Valenza was fallen upon by unknown parties with baseball bats a year ago last May, he carried his wounds home from the hospital still convinced that he had been had at by hyper-competitive brothers in the fraternity of landscape contractors.

In June, when Stella had barely begun to apply her tender mercies to his convalescence, he tried the air of his front yard and was shot six times by a .25. Even then, he does not appear to have suspected that the heart of these uncomfortable mysteries might lodge in the inflamed bosom of his wife.

But then husbands are notoriously inattentive to the nuances and forgetful about the routine occurrences of the family round and, when Bert Koehler, Stella's counsel, asked if Felice had ever put a pistol to her head and demanded that she serve the cravings of his flesh on short order, he replied, "I don't remember."

There is much that is admirable about any sentiment that has kept its warmth long past the time when it cools for souls more conventional than these, but he who is possessed by this fixed a passion runs the risk of taking any excess in its display as an exercise too normal to be worth the bother of recollection.

And Stella's obsession was a match for Felice's. We have all known and enjoyed the company of those women who cannot spend five minutes of conversation without pulling some reference, generally fond, to their husbands out of the blue sky.

But, if we are to credit the witnesses against her, Stella was incapable of talking about anything else. It is the prosecution's theory that she schemed to have Felice killed because she wanted to collect on his $93,000 of insurance.

No notion so crass can do justice to the apparent selflessness of her commitment. A woman gave witness Friday to the afternoon in April when she and a friend had been driving with Stella to the Valenza home to look at an apartment for the friend. Stella's companions asked about the cost of the rent and the size of the security deposit, and the witness recalled that their hostess had replied that ". . . we shouldn't have to worry about security and rent because she was gonna get her husband taken care of."

So, if Stella Valenza so spoke, would have spoken the woman who had her mind on higher goals than greed pursues.

Her milieu and Felice's was the society of Queens landscape gardening and, unlikely ground for the hiring halls of qualified assassins though these bosky circles might be, Stella seems to have confined her market research to them.

Paul Turchen remembered that one afternoon he and his partner were installing a shrub and Stella Valenza stopped her car and said she needed to find a killer for Felice. He suggested that she might more fitly take her problems to a priest. Even after that sound demurrer, the force of her insistence drew him to a meeting at Garden World, where among the earth pots and leafy branches, she offered to give him $500 and her car to do the office.

He felt that "she was getting a little offhand" and declined the tender. In June, their cars passed again and she stopped to say that she must hurry because "I have to meet the guys who are going to kill my husband and pay them more money."

They parted, and Paul Turchen drove off and thereafter kept his silence about this revelation, as he thought, he explained, any "young gentleman ought." Stella Valenza had already found richer soil in his brother Peter.

Peter Turchen testified that he and Stella had met at Francis Lewis High School, the academy where both had flourished from the seeds of cultivation. She asked if he knew anyone who might kill her husband and he replied that he might. In a day or so, he put the question to a friend and got the answer, "Sure."

At intervals in his witness, Peter Turchen would smile rather charmingly, and it could be seen how cool he was and how casual was the memory for this vessel, as empty as Stella may have been overfilled. Peter Turchen had a poor eye for head hunting; his recruits tried the bat and tried the bullets and botched the job with both. If Stella Valenza was as bent on the final consummation of her bond with Felice as her prosecutors contend, she would have done surer and better if she made the work her own. Such things ought not to be done but, if they are, they are best left to those who really care.

V

LATE STYLE

Though Kempton's hair long ago turned white, he still has the sleek and elegant bearing that his friends remember from decades ago. He is not quite six feet tall, and if he eats at all he does not show it. He is the last gentleman, an amalgam of courtesy, formality, and kindness which is so rare that it strikes some as eccentricity.

—DAVID REMNICK, *The New Yorker*, 1993

Turning Seventy, Just by Chance

12 • 17 • 87

I woke up yesterday morning and found myself seventy years old. It is a matter of scant moment; my rounds will go pleasurably on as they always have, world without end, until my masters trade me in at the antiques show for some dubious bit of art deco. Still, the recollections press an unexpectedly insistent claim:

I have stood twice in St. Peter's Square and heard the oldest cardinal raise the glad cry, "Habemus Papam," once for Angelum Roncallus and once for Johannes Lucianus, and not Henry James, nor Stendhal nor, for that matter, Michelangelo could ever have said the same.

I have had breakfast with Frank Costello, who commended me for the alacrities of my appetite and said that he owed his long life to three axioms. The first was "Always eat a large breakfast." The second was "Never try to cheat on your taxes." He forbore to mention the third, an abjuration perhaps to avoid sitting with one's back to a window.

I have sat a little after twilight in the Dexter Memorial Baptist Church in Montgomery, Alabama, with the congregation singing low and stirring to joy at the entrance of a young man who wore a hat so broad-brimmed that I took him for a sideman in the house band and who turned out, of course, to be Martin Luther King.

I have seen Robert Kennedy with his children and John Kennedy with the nuns whose fidelity to their eternal wedlock to Christ he strained as no other mortal man could. I have been lied to by Joe McCarthy and heard Roy Cohn lie to himself and watched a narcotics hit man weep when the jury pronounced Nicky Barnes guilty. Dwight D. Eisenhower once bawled me out by the numbers, and Richard Nixon once did the unmerited kindness of thanking me for being so old and valued an adviser.

But, if I have feasted with a panther or two, I can remember supping with only one god, and that one had been left without an undeflected worshiper except myself. It was Westbrook Pegler, and he observed at lunch that he had been misunderstood by those who imagined that he had been driven crazy by Mrs. Roosevelt. That, he said, was not the case at all.

"It began," Peg explained, "when I quit sports and went cosmic. It finished when I began writing on Monday to be printed on Friday."

That gospel has been so rooted in my heart ever since that I write every day for the next and walk wide of the cosmic and settle most happily for the local, a precinct less modest than I make it sound, since my local happens to be the only city under the eye of God where the librettist for *Don Giovanni* could find his closest friend in the author of *The Night Before Christmas*.

I talked with Louis Armstrong one night in Basin Street and mentioned his record of "When You're Smilin'," which I had early loved and too soon lost.

"I was working in the house band at the Paramount when I was young," Armstrong said. "And the lead trumpet stood up and played that song, and I just copied what he did note for note. I never found out his name but there was kicks in him. There's kicks everywhere."

And then he went back to the stand and played "When You're Smilin'," still thinking it remembered note-for-note even while he was quite transcending it, and he had made immortal a figure never vivid and faded long ago.

There are, in truth, kicks everywhere, and I have had all these and never one at my own expense. Most of life's epiphanies arise from its accidents, and it is never so much fun as when it conscripts us as prisoners to the luck of the day. Colette says in "The Vagabond," that bible for all us migratory laborers, that "If Chance ever got Herself called God, I should have been a very good Catholic indeed." And so, too, should I.

Hostage to History

6 • 19 • 88

The visitor who carries to Moscow even a scant familiarity with the lights and shadows of its revolution's history is soon surprised to discover how much more he knows than the run of even aware Muscovites have been allowed to.

One visitor's final conversation was with Alexei Adzhubei, the journalist whose vast sophistication was deepened by the intimacy of his years as Nikita Khrushchev's son-in-law.

Their talk turned to the old days and the comments of his guest indicated a knowledge of detail that, skimpy as it was, must have struck Adzhubei as uncommonly informed and he asked, "Are you a Sovietologist?"

That question had been asked before, and the visitor answered as he had learned to a while ago:

"To me, the only Sovietologist who is always up to date is Anton Chekhov."

Adzhubei laughed, and there passed across his face the knowing smile of someone to whom that thought had already occurred and not infrequently. Only the day before, there had been an exchange of similar cast with Sergo Mikoyan and, when it was over, Mikoyan had lit with just that knowing smile.

None of us could be so bold as to advance a particular Chekhov story as the greatest of all but "My Life" would be a splendid candidate. At one juncture, its hero marries a young woman of wealth, who is transiently possessed by an itch to go back to the land. They go off to convert her estate into a working farm and spend a horrid few months until, disgusted by the crafts and coarsenesses of the peasants, she abandons all lofty notions and flees to London to study singing.

From there, she writes to ask for a divorce and to report that she has bought herself a ring engraved in Hebrew, "All things pass away," and that it would be her talisman against future infatuations. And he reflects:

"If I wanted to order a ring for myself, the inscription I should choose would be, 'Nothing passes away.'"

And nothing seems ever to pass away in Moscow. Russian history asserts itself there as all but immutable and immovable, and so it asserted itself for Chekhov in 1900. The on-again, off-again harryings of Andrei Sakharov and Boris Pasternak would have been for him the oldest of tales.

He could have recalled the year when Maxim Gorky, the novelist, was voted into the Russian Academy of Sciences and had his election nullified when it was remembered that he had been arrested for violating Article 10.35 of the czarist penal code, which made it a crime to agitate against the state. Article 10.35 or its equivalent endures as Soviet law today.

Gorky's treatment provoked Chekhov into writing the chairman of the Academy of Sciences "to beg you most humbly to be relieved of the title of honorary academician." He was almost alone in his protest and his resignation, and so were the all too few academicians who stood with Sakharov and Pasternak.

The czars will never be back but, after seventy years, their style of command has yet to pass away, perhaps because tradition is so stubborn in Russia that the techniques of journalism, wondrous as they are, come to appear so inadequate for dealing with her development year by year, let alone day by day. Journalism's engagement is with what is happening, and here so little happens that a good deal of what is taken for important may be insignificant and what looks insignificant may be quite important indeed.

The other day, as an instance, the Soviet Supreme Court announced the acquittal of four distinguished Bolsheviks the Soviets had executed as traitors fifty years ago. Legal scholars will be put to some pains to discover what available evidence of their innocence is any stronger than the stuff that served to prove their guilt, and addicts of irony may be enlivened to take note that the ashes of Andrei Vishinsky, the prosecutor who staged that frame-up, are still interred in the Kremlin wall.

All the same, this gesture, empty as it looks, is not without implications of some consequence. One prime article of the Stalinist creed was that men did not disagree because they were mistaken but because they were evil; for the czars and far more spitefully for the Soviets, to dissent has until now been to betray. Given that history, the formal concession that the defendants in the Moscow trials may have been foolish but were not treasonable can be looked upon as no small advance in the direction of enlightenment.

But it has taken terribly long and been arrived at through incalculable torments of interior quarrel. Long ago, Karl Marx said that the philosophers had described the world and that it was up to man to change it. Now the Soviets are finding out that many things have changed the world—one of them the failure of their revolution to change itself or Russia—and that it is up to man to describe it. For the workers to arise and break the chains of capitalist oppression was unexpectedly easy work in 1917 but those chains were gossamer compared to the cast-iron shackles of a Russian tradition that has so far outworn every idea of the new.

The Beggar of Gracie Mansion

8 • 11 • 88

Edward I. Koch was asked yesterday if he has any idea why his city is filling up with beggars. "I don't know why," he replied. "I guess it's because we're easy marks."

A while ago, I took a vow to abstain from future reference to this man's name. The multiplicity of his offenses had brought me to the borders of personal malice. Annoyance and even anger can claim to speak only so long as they arise from hope for something better.

But I have abandoned all hope for anything better from Koch, and to despair of another man is to approach the bearing of malice and henceforth to feel abjured to silence about him. Koch is conspicuous for his steadfast disobedience to that rule; I have been faithful to it until now; but, at this hour, I can bear no more.

For now he is out to infect us all with his own spite and meanness of spirit. New Yorkers can degrade themselves in many ways and not fall beyond salvation, but the closer they get to being like Edward I. Koch, the nearer they will come to the death of the heart.

It will never be my habit to pass a beggar without giving him or her my mite. I don't do it to feel better about myself, but to keep from feeling worse than I already do.

There are few more shame-making pursuits than beggary, and most of those reduced to it are so sealed away in their abjection that they don't see and remember the faces of those who pause to fee them or those who pass them by. Who among us can count the times when we have given a beggar our small bit and then come upon him a few minutes later and had him lift up his cup, all unconscious that we had ever met before?

New York is a city of beggars, separated into the two classes of those who are capable of shame and those who aren't; the Koch who scorns abject beggars smears his mouth with shoe polish in his dealings with arrogant ones.

On the very day when he declared his war on panhandlers to New York *Newsday*'s Sharman Stein, he made public a letter imploring George Steinbrenner to allow the state and city to make a gift of $90 million to build a new garage, a restaurant and twenty-four skyboxes for corporate squatters in Yankee Stadium.

All the thanks Koch wanted for this bounty was Steinbrenner's promise not to leave town for fifty years, an act of grace and favor that might seem worth something less than $90 million to the swelling numbers of our citizens who would be content to live with ten thousand fewer stately beggars if they could look forward to not having to live with George Steinbrenner.

Koch is himself a singularly all-purpose beggar. He does it on the hog and he does it on the cheap. You can get him with a cup of coffee. Just let him in your house and he will sing your song for his supper. Daniel Ortega got him with a tortilla, and we may suppose that it took no more than a scone for that limey to get him in Belfast.

"For the most part in my judgment," Koch said yesterday, "the money you give to the beggars goes for booze and drugs." When you give to a beggar, you are, in your inadequate fashion, recognizing the humanity that he has been driven almost to forget is the Lord's precious gift, and you are affirming his right to your trust. We may occasionally misplace our trust in beggars, but we threw it away when we elected Koch and condemned ourselves to day after day of malignant nonsense.

"In most cases, they are demented," Koch told Sharman Stein. He was talking about people who, in many if not in most cases, live in the streets and sleep in doorways or on subway grates in the winter. Theirs is a condition that can account for some displacement of the logical processes. We have housed Koch in enviable comfort for eleven years now, and his eccentricities grow ever more excessive, his assaults upon the helpless ever more ravening and the spectacle of his fits ever less endurable. So what's his excuse?

Undertaking Roy Cohn

Autumn 1988

No man's biographer can be so near a companion of his intimacies as the particular worm the gods choose for his devouring. There is no reason then for surprise that in *Citizen Cohn* Nicholas von Hoffman has come upon the epitome of Roy Cohn's existence in the recollections of one of the less baleful of the lights of love who hurried him to the grave with a posterior orifice you could throw a baseball through:

> So many people stole so many things from him . . . I didn't steal anything. I stole only one thing from Roy and that was his Gucci razor. This was solid silver. That's the only thing I stole.

Hardly the colors of memory that endow their object with the grandeur that von Hoffman suggests Cohn might have had and that Sidney Zion in his *Autobiography of Roy Cohn* insists he did have.

Chroniclers of Roy Cohn deserve neither to be envied their enterprise nor blamed for their failure to illuminate large tracts of a life whose ambiguities and obscurities seem almost as resistant to the strenuosities of von Hoffman's efforts as to the languors of Zion's.

Von Hoffman never met Cohn; his is the tale as others tell it. Zion knew Cohn foolishly, which is to say none too well; his is the tale as Cohn told it. Von Hoffman has the advantage of suspecting as Zion does not, how much of Cohn's fabric was the warp of the lies to self; but he has too disciplinedly refrained from noticing how much of its woof might have been woven from the lies others told themselves. For Cohn studies are transacted in shadowed countinghouses on dingy streets, where the teller deals across his greasy counter a coin all but unvaryingly freighted with lead.

It is of small use to complain about the little Zion and von Hoffman can show for their dig at Cohn's interior. I myself made a few stabs in that direction across the years with such meager results as to settle me in the judgment that his interior was a void from which he could draw no breath of a notion of who he was and consequently must lodge all his hope of ever finding out on the air around him and the permeations of the winds, benign or malignant, of what other people thought he was and what he appears obediently to have become.

When he was twenty-four years old and came earliest and so clamorously to our attention, his admirers called him a great lawyer and his detractors said he was homosexual. I cannot yet set him down as either at the time; all the same, he would develop into a splendid advocate, however too untidy to render steady satisfaction to his clients, and he turned out a frenziedly purposeful pederast. The prejudices of friend and enemy alike have proved themselves sounder instruments for assessing him than the sober detachment I had struggled to maintain. I have no excuse for this miscalculation beyond the surmise that the dominant chord in Cohn's being was his susceptibility to every whisper in the surrounding atmosphere, and that, since he was therefore a stranger to himself, he could only adopt whatever shape other strangers conjured up as his.

I would be a severer critic of the persistence of Zion's and von Hoffman's reliance upon reminiscences I cannot quite trust if I could be more secure about trusting my own. To remember Roy Cohn is for me the same delicate exercise in separating truth from falsehood that talking to him used to be. I knew him moderately well, which was about as far as it was safe or rewarding to go; what confounds my recollection is my extended perseverance in propagating fantasies that I knew him better still. For, absent some willed pretense to an intimacy that would be slight cause for vanity had it been substantial, how am I to explain the long familiarity of my tongue with fables like these:

(1) That he and I sat together in my room at Washington's old Willard Hotel and watched the Edward R. Murrow broadcast that signaled more dramatically than it speeded the ruin of Sen. Joe McCarthy.
(2) That he once threatened to visit one of his subpoenas upon me and was repelled by the sword of my defiance and scorn.

(1) Not so. We were not together at the Willard on that evening or any other, and I did not observe such progress as Murrow might have been making toward disturbances to a self-assurance that seldom sat comfortably on Roy Cohn anyway. But I had telephoned him earlier; and, since where reporters were the case, all was fish that came to his net, he called me back and the Murrow broadcast came up.

Cohn dismissed this aggression as a trifle. I replied that, to the contrary, I had felt it as the tolling of a bell of horrid portent for himself and his principal. Murrow might, I suggested, be one of those men blessed with the qualities of honor and courage that the high gods so esteem as to provide him with a guardian angel to protect him from employing them too hastily. Any spirit pressed by its nobility to stand up to risk is, in some curious way, insured against damaging consequences. If McCarthy had not passed his apogee and gone tumbling toward earth like a child's rocket, Murrow would not have mounted an assault that Washington took and that he, in his modest way, must have felt to be recklessly brave. We were coming to the end of the affair; McCarthy was ceasing to be a figure any longer controversial, and the act of challenging him, however sincerely conceived as bold to the point of being rash, had become the mere job of giving a hand to the waste-disposal crew.

Cohn replied that, whether I was right or wrong, McCarthy's fate was no worry for him, because he was a princeling of the Bronx Democratic organization and could rely on the Democrats on the Senate Committee on Investigations to exempt him from any punishments they thought condign for its chairman. There rose in my mind the gelid image of John McClellan, the committee's senior Democrat, ravaged by the ghosts of his dead children and too finally sacked and pillaged of all illusion about the mercies of God to be a soundly caulked vessel for mercies to his fellow man. Cohn could not have counted upon a refuge less welcoming in time of trouble. I had discovered his quite appalling innocence and would have no future reason to doubt that it lodged in his very marrow.

(2) Not altogether so. Cohn did once suggest that he might summon me to crave pardon for my dead past in the Young Communist League; but subsequent fancy has ornamented my response with flourishes as spurious as they are fustian. My answer was that I should be distinctly more confident of heavenly reward if I could recite the Nicene Creed with as little assistance from the prompting box as I would need to run through the liturgy for which he proposed to solicit the bending of my knees.

I had, I assured him, the requisite stock of hyperbole when it came to descriptions of Dark Nights of the Soul and could almost effortlessly fish my memory for the names of those who had shivered through them at my side. I would nonetheless have to decline his invitation and definitely not because it would be ignoble to embarrass, not to say traduce, old acquaintances whose original trespasses were trivial and whose lives had been blameless thereafter. Those were grounds I owed to honor; but they were a shade too high for me to be dead certain of holding to them. Life had taught me, I felt compelled to report, that anyone who stakes all his faith on high-minded reasons to keep him from doing some low-minded thing has only to exercise his wits a little while to locate an equally high-minded reason to do it. I preferred merely to say that such rhetorical flourishes as I might bring to the naming of names would be barely noticed the day afterward and quite forgotten within a week; and all that would be remembered was that I had named the names, and that my commercial future was gray enough already without being dyed blacker with a taint of those proportions.

Cohn dropped the subject as idly as he must have raised it. I should, of course, be happier if the strings of recall could be tuned to pitches more full-throated than these.

But then every age gets the monsters it deserves, and Roy Cohn was about as far as the 1950s could go with the manufacture and distribution of specimens of the fearsome; and, botched counterfeit that he probably was and sodden as his time and mine inarguably was, it would take a highly combustible tongue to kindle to flame when brought beard to beard with a Grand Inquisitor who, even in those days, was commencing to look like some priapic statue incautiously bought at the flea market and left out too long in the garden rains.

In any case, the aforesaid recollections, once stripped of post hoc absurdities, are not inappropriate to our lugubrious pawings after human community, which on my side ran almost exclusively to lectures on the ways of the world. I could not have chosen an endeavor more hopeless. Cohn lived and died in a condition of peculiar innocence, one as disabling to those who cannot credit others with decent motives as it is to those unable to imagine that others may have indecent ones. It may be all very well to have enlisted with the infernal powers so long as you are aware of and keep a close eye out for the snares and deceits of the well-behaved; to do otherwise will serve you no more conveniently than his virtues did Prince Myshkin.

This innocence too pure to be diluted by the lessons of experience must have directed Cohn's choice of an authorized biographer no better equipped than himself to appreciate the power of conventional morality in human affairs. Sidney Zion's appetite for roguery is the glutton's and not the gourmet's; he is too greedy a gobbler of the unappetizing to notice that it can be also the undernourishing. Rascals are endurable and may, now and then, be enjoyable to the degree of their charm, but without charm they are even worse company than respectable people.

And Roy Cohn had an essence as charmless as any I have ever communed with; and, as Disraeli put it in another connection, I have read Stalin on Trotsky and Trotsky on Stalin and have known Francis Cardinal Spellman, who was so warm a friend of Cohn's that von Hoffman can hint that between them vibrated the intimations, if not the consummations, of the flesh; my own preference is for believing that what drew them close was a shared deprivation of the normal faculties for appealing to one's fellow man, and that they had the enforced fraternity of sailors starving together on an ice floe.

Von Hoffman tenders an unexpectedly substantial sheaf of testaments to the pleasures of Cohn's companionship; but their citations are too barren of examples of the feast of his reason and flow of his soul to persuade us that the fascinations of his presence had nearly as much to do with his persona as with his specious repute as mover and shaker. For the real voice, we must turn to Zion's transcriptions; and it is a stream of spite and malice unrelieved by any trace of philosophy or wit. Cohn could frequently manifest a febrile anxiety to please that now and then surprised strangers into the suspicion that he might not be by any means as bad as they assumed he would be; but that is so minimal an accomplishment that rascals even worse than he have brought it off with less exertion.

Von Hoffman appears to have started forth with the conviction that Cohn was a personage of the size appropriate for a conscientious biographer's ambitions; and he tries harder than is entirely plausible to inflate Cohn's stature among the architects of the institutions designed to enforce domestic security and enshrine official paranoia. Their trenches had been thoroughly dug before Cohn took up his post in them, and their revetments could hardly have been made more formidable with the fleeting attentions of someone as disqualified for steady work by a natural disposition as ill-ordered as his was.

Von Hoffman's good sense triumphs soon enough over his early delusions that Cohn's was a figure of significant historical import; and the farther he travels, the more the subject loses the attributes that preserve authentic claims to be taken seriously, until we are left with the pitiful rag that one of the more noisome of his studs refers to as "the poor old thing," an appellation that no one would think to apply to, say, Richard Nixon, or anybody else who ever counted for much.

But Zion clings to the standard that absurdly proclaims Cohn's cosmic consequence with the steadfast will of the chronicler as fixed as the chroniclee in the creed that man's fate is the ordained result of the shifts, the sleights, and the schemes of cabals that deserve our admiration for their sovereign immunity to scruple, and that Roy Cohn lived his life at their very center. That proposition is by no means self-evident; and, as soon as Zion leaves off advancing affirmations of Cohn's skills at furthering the careers of long-since-obliterated unworthies and moves on to persuade us of the importance of his good will to unworthies still in being, we are powerless to resist the inference that the game has been given away.

Cohn informs us, as an instance, that Vice President Bush had been "romancing" Cohn for no end of time. But then of an evening, while Cohn's plane waited to fly off to a White House dinner, word came that all schedules were suspended until the Vice President had been cleared for takeoff. Cohn sat and fumed; and when he arrived at the White House, as timely as he needed to be and higher in dudgeon than any man of reason would think he ought to be, he rushed to tell Mrs. Reagan of this effrontery. It was always thus with Roy Cohn; you would be peaceably tending to your own business, and up he would come with some piece of shit or other.

Mrs. Reagan suggested that he write the Vice President and tell him off. Cohn proceeded to this patriotic duty with passionate intensity and back came a letter from a vice-presidential assistant conveying the sense in tones undisguisedly snotty that if Mr. Bush could be found, he would beyond question be desolated to learn that Mr. Cohn "felt" ill-used. The vice presidency is an office whose occupant is so conditioned to abjection and apology that we could not have imagined until now that the eye of God could fall upon a citizen of the United States whose wounded sensibilities would strike George Bush as of a moment so small that their appeasement could be fobbed off with the disdain of a mere assistant.

We bear with Zion through page after page of assertions of how much Cohn mattered and then, all unconscious, he drops this crashing revelation that Cohn mattered not the slightest to George Bush, whose office commands him to treat everything as though it mattered; and nothing remains for us to do except to say: "Okay, you two, that does it; come off it, both of you."

But then, even if we elevated the trappings of the authority that von Hoffman once believed and Zion is still convinced were Cohn's to dispense for more than the pasty gauds they were, we have grounds to doubt that they would have been what he wanted at all.

The clue to his truest aspiration can, I suspect, be found in the fevers of his exercises on behalf of Private G. David Schine. Schine had been an unpaid consultant for the McCarthy–Cohn committee until he was conscripted into the army. No sooner had he been encumbered with that indignity than Cohn rose up to extort kindnesses for him quite beyond the army's prescribed allotment of such rations to recruits; and the unbridled vehemence of those exertions brought McCarthy to ruin and Cohn too close to it.

Most of the whispers about Cohn's homosexual bent had their origins in the Schine affair; his enemies then and there decided that no man could care this much about another man's ease unless he cared unnaturally overmuch about his body. Schine did indeed have the cast of countenance that too often identifies the Lily White Boy; but that was not, I think, as much the real charm for Cohn and McCarthy as his status as heir presumptive of the cluster of hotels that held out to McCarthy a continental sweep for the freeloading impulses that were the one point of concentration for his otherwise unfocused vision and that opened up to Cohn the promise of a richly endowing client for the great law firm whose star he pursued until he died with it further from his grasp than it had been when he set forth to capture it.

Cohn entered the private practice of law under circumstances unsuggestive of the auspicious. He had almost been flayed from Washington and had come home trailing clouds of sulfurous excesses, maladroit chicaneries, and obsessions with the self that had made him as bad a servant as even a master so slovenly as McCarthy could have been careless enough to employ. He was widely accounted mad, bad, and dangerous to know; and yet this bundle of vices that in justice ought to be a certificate of the bearer's bankruptcy would turn out to be Roy Cohn's only inexhaustible capital.

He could flourish his disgraces as emblems of the kidney that had earned them; he could be relied upon, if for too little else, never to take up the sword without throwing away the scabbard; and every prior demonstration of his pitilessness of purpose constituted just the sort of history that commends itself to the wife or husband whose good temper has too long been tried, or the enterpriser whose conscience has known no trial at all.

When he began, his most noticeable clients were enraged spouses and ex-bootleggers like the Stork Club's Sherman Billingsley and Las Vegas' Moe Dalitz. But the prior behavior of the old bootleggers had been unseemly and the present behavior of the spouses, if anything, worse; and they were not the clientele to suit Roy Cohn's image of the corporation lawyer he really wanted to be.

What else but the desperation of his chase after this childhood dream could explain the history of the firm that never bore Cohn's name but carried to its doom no banner but "Saxe Bacon" with the penultimate addition of "Bolan"? Saxe was long dead and Bacon nearly as long retired; Roy Cohn had bought their shingle and it was worth its price for a ring like the "Cravath, Swaines" and the "Dewey Ballantines" of the great downtown law firms.

His lurches into those uniformly aborted forays as a corporate raider in the sixties could only have had their source in impulses aroused not by greed but by the yearnings of a too-tardy adolescence for retainers that had the authenticity reserved for the large and the respectable.

That was the dream that spurred him to hurl himself against corporate walls that bristled with defenders whose cunning was larger than his; and we have no way to measure the weight of resultant losses that may have been too heavy for him ever to be rid of their encumbrance.

And then he was indicted and tried three times in the federal courts and always on the testimony of fellow passengers in the shipwreck who had turned government witness and earned full absolution by swearing that he had been prime author of their failed conspiracies. He had become an insurance policy for any captain on adventure bent who had only to sign Roy Cohn on to the manifest and sail content with the knowledge that, if the ship should wreck, any prosecutor would delight in granting him immunity for swearing that it was all Cohn's doing. And oddly enough, the Cohn who so often took offense, and not improperly so, at any slight from a good citizen would take none at all from the basest betrayal by a bad one; and he once trotted docilely up the aisle as best man to a groom who could well have been in jail if he had not done his duty to common sense by testifying against Cohn a bare few weeks earlier.

It is impossible not to suspect that all these sweats and bleedings left him broke beyond recovery; and, labor though Zion may to apply the colors of derring-do to his wars with the Internal Revenue Service, there is no way to obscure those strokes that too tellingly delineate the scurryings of the fugitive irretrievably penurious.

Having been defeated in all his hopes for eminence, Cohn could only fall back on notoriety and return to being mercenary soldier for gangsters habitually disreputable or wives made transiently so by the ravenings of their thirst for vengeance. He still possessed the coin of his reputation for prodigies with extremes of the implacable and the perfidious; and the confidence that he would be ready on command was as near as uneasy spirits could get to the self-assurance that could otherwise be theirs only with the acquisition of a Mafia hit man. But, as time went on and his juices clogged, he grew increasingly languid as a servitor for the maliciously inclined; and many a recreant husband who had run shuddering to his lawyer with a letter signed by Roy Cohn would go away comforted with the information that Cohn seldom did much more these days except get off one such loud salvo and fire no longer. He had become, as von Hoffman makes plain, a careless and inattentive practitioner; and I cannot remember a scintilla of his old address at the last except once when I happened upon him on an afternoon when he was pressing the defense of some obscure hoodlum with every ounce of the acumen and penetration that used to be his when he cared; and I could only decide that he had grown so intimate with gangsters that they had come to think of him as one of their own and thus eligible for terminal measures of reproof if he should let any of them down.

Still, in those shadows, there was always Zion credulously swallowing Cohn's every pretension to glory; their talk would come to a dirty trick that had blighted some politician's career, and Cohn would say, of course, that had been his doing. It was a safe enough bit of brag; no one who has done a dirty trick is excessively anxious to proclaim it; and Cohn was free to steal the credit and bemuse Zion with some fresh mark of his power, black and spurious a mark though it might be.

There has, however, been talk of one infamy that may have been the genuine work of Cohn's hand and that he never mentioned to Zion and that none of von Hoffman's informants seem to have mentioned to him. And it could well be more than talk because it was told me by a man who was close to McCarthy and privy to Cohn in his Washington days and whose wisdom, talent, and knowledge of the way the world goes has since earned him a respect amounting to veneration from better judges than either of them. His tale ran thus:

> By 1957, Joe had stopped drinking and decided not to run for the Senate again. All he said he wanted was one hundred thousand dollars to buy "a spread somewhere out in the West for me and Jeanie." That was when Roy Cohn showed up with a guy who was hustling penny uranium stocks. They offered Joe a piece and he scoured up thirty thousand dollars and they went back to New York and sold batches of the stuff on Joe's name. Within two weeks Joe was worth a hundred and fifty thousand dollars on paper, and he went to the Wisconsin woods to hunt. While he was gone, Cohn and the other hustler dumped the stock and Joe came home to find that he had been wiped out. He called Cohn in haste and alarm and Cohn wouldn't take the call.
>
> And Joe went back to drinking and it didn't take long to kill him.

That was all there was to the story; and when it was done I asked, "Do you mean to suggest that Roy Cohn blamed Joe McCarthy for ruining his career?"

"Of course," my friend replied.

The poor son of a bitch.

Bike Theft as a Point of Departure

10 • 2 • 88

The Theft of My Bicycle, a triennial street festival, came round again Thursday, and I observed its recurrence, as my civic and spiritual duties ordain, with a quiet interval of meditation upon developments in the war on crime since last I was called upon to celebrate my return to casualty status.

I had locked my bike to a traffic sign shadowed by the towers of law enforcement at a point equidistant from U.S. Attorney Rudolph Giuliani, Police Commissioner Benjamin Ward and District Attorney Robert Morgenthau. My blunder, not uncommon among military tacticians, had been to neglect to study the actual terrain and instead pursue the abstract ideal of the perfectly placed defense position.

I should, of course, have dug in right next to Criminal Court. Persons transiently inconvenienced by a summons to trial never steal while waiting their turn. The tenure of a felon's susceptibility to moral scruple commences with his arrest and lasts until he is granted his plea and generally released on the promise of good behavior that he will breach at the first clear chance.

In the interim, he reveres the distinction between mine and thine so fervently that it is my conviction that you could leave the Hope diamond on the floor of the Criminal Court building for twenty minutes and find it still there when you came back.

My error had been in locking my bike too close to Civil Court, which is a nest of unindicted coconspirators so bent upon larceny that they can't be trusted not to steal a shoelace.

I do not mean, of course, to suggest that I ever gave way to the wisp of the suspicion that I might have been robbed by a divorce lawyer keeping his hand in during the recess. As it was, I had no sooner confronted a pavement empty of every trace of my property except its broken lock than a parking lot attendant told me that he had shouted his reproaches at a passerby who was assaulting and swiftly breaching my defenses and who had then walked my bike away and around the corner.

My informant had earned all the admiration owed to anyone who had realized what has so long been my own unattainable dream, which is to be a feeble vigilante and a solid witness, and I thanked him and turned to inspect the scene of the crime. Its perpetrator had employed an instrument no more intricate than a pipe to break the shaft of the very Kryptonite lock whose invulnerability was once such an article of faith that its manufacturers used to guarantee $200 to the purchaser if a thief ever succeeded in breaching it.

The writ of that warranty has since been withdrawn from any Kryptonite put at large in New York, a sound commercial judgment and a mark of respect for the crafts and devices unique in this city's criminal element, which steadily contrives technical advances that keep the offense well ahead of the defense. When last my bike was stolen, it took a master workman to penetrate its lock's chamber, and now, mere apprentices have found a way to crack the shaft with a pipe.

I will buy another bike with no hope to escape the inevitable afternoon of my next bereavement, and this time I shall not inform the police. Cops are in the main likable, and their dreary lives entitle them to every chance for gratification, but I cannot further endure the unholy glee with which they greet the news that another bike has been stolen and may, with luck, be on its way to New Mexico or at least out of midtown traffic.

Police officers have the not-entirely-unreasonable view that cyclists are public nuisances. They cannot be contained and, when the mayor tries to forbid them to clutter an already overcluttered Madison Avenue, they sue him and he ends up bound and hog-tied in the Appellate Division. The cops are helpless to enforce the traffic code as it is, and they have no available assistance in their struggle with bicycle clot except the proliferation of bicycle theft.

I should suppose that the desk sergeant would be less exhilarated to have me report that my bicycle had been carried off than he would be to hear that the precinct crack lord had been shot, but the news would obscenely cheer him all the same.

Law enforcement is by now so straitened that it must reserve its resources for the better class of citizens. A felon can live pretty comfortably so long as he confines his depravities to his own social station and does not get caught doing violence to anyone conspicuously more propertied than himself. It looks as if Jean Harris will stay in prison until the end of term because, impeccably bred woman though she is, she lapsed into killing a successful doctor, deserving of the offense though some of us may suspect he was.

But what disreputable people do to other disreputable people is good riddance for police work. The bicycle rider may be otherwise sedately middle-class but, once he is in the saddle, he and the bicycle thief are fellow pariahs. So, back to the war against crime and its inescapable hour of defeat I go, sure to be a loser and with no weapon left to trust and no consolations more heart-soothing than those that reside in philosophical resignation.

On Clemency for Jean Harris

10 • 13 • 88

The only question the governor of New York ought by now to ask himself about Jean Harris is not whether he should grant her clemency but why he already hasn't. She has spent seven and a half years in prison since she was sentenced to fifteen years to life for the murder of Dr. Herman Tarnower, whose treatment of her hardly qualified him for the bullet but might, chivalry may be forgiven for hoping, cost him protractions in purgatory to earn Heaven's pardon.

Former State Supreme Court Justice Russell Leggett, who presided over Jean Harris' trial in 1981, has written the governor to cry mercy for her now. Tarnower had dealt her a copious diet of tranquilizers, possibly to ease her afflictions but probably to reduce her nuisance quotient.

It is Leggett's view that her consequent addiction had disabled her judgment on the night she shot Tarnower and throughout the trial that followed because she had been deprived of the sense to recognize that her best defense was the claim of "extreme emotional disturbance."

The heart is always solaced to find a man readier to help Jean Harris in her troubles than Herman Tarnower seems to have been, but her judge may have missed the point of her when he put so much blame on the tranquilizers.

Our woes and weaknesses grow in ourselves; the drugs come later. Jean Harris' truly disabling addiction was to a man who may have had his values for society but was uniquely worthless for her. There is every excuse for the anger she must have felt after the thirteen years of callousness she endured in his company before finding worse in the penitentiary.

Whenever she tried to explain herself, the conviction grew that, of course, she did not mean to kill Tarnower but that she was furious at him and, by the third shot, may transiently and soon ashamedly been enjoying herself.

To have pleaded extreme emotional disturbance would have won her more kindness than she got from her jury, but it meant also to confess a rage so overpowering that she could no longer contain it. Hers was the sort of character that counts no sin blacker than losing self-control and that is capable of dreadful deed when it finally does. She could not admit that she had been a foolish woman and, having cast off the folly of too little pride, she picked up the folly of too much.

And yet, since we are none of us of a piece, she is also a very wise and strong woman or she could not have come through what she has suffered as intact as her prison memoirs suggest she is. There will be those who tell the governor that since she has descended from a higher social station than the run of her fellow prisoners, any conspicuous kindness to her could be taken as evidence of class bias.

It has been my experience that persons so pure in principle as to object to giving justice to someone because someone equally deserving can't have it don't care overmuch about either and are serenely content to talk about flesh and blood as they would about cardboard.

Snobbishness is no less offensive when it is inverted than when right side up, and Jean Harris' freedom from either is one of the more admirable features of her prison writings.

It is a rare convict who cannot persuade himself that he is the only innocent party on the premises, but she is never so touching as when she tells us about the women who killed the husbands who beat them or who were married to drug dealers who never told them their business until the husband was arrested and the wife was on her way to prison as his accomplice.

For she is better aware than those who scorn her that, if she gets clemency, she will leave behind women who are nearer innocence than even she may think herself. For God's sake, governor, cease to palter and let the woman go, and when you do, call her into your office and ask her about these others she has met who are just as deserving of your mercy as she is.

My File Is Haunted by Hoover

5 • 14 • 89

The Federal Bureau of Investigation has done the courtesy of sending along the file it assembled upon my activities across the fifteen years that ended in the spring of 1973, when it lost interest in future acquaintanceship.

I had until now been disinclined to avail myself of the Freedom of Information Act. Degrees of failure to be taken seriously had been among the pleasanter oppressions of my existence too long for me not to assume that my FBI dossier would either turn up empty or perfumed with references to my gentle and unoffending disposition that would be no less painfully remindful of my want of substance.

But then Natalie Robins set out to compile a documentary history of J. Edgar Hoover's term as recording angel, and asked me to apply for my file as possible fish for her net. Here it comes at last, and I bequeath such riches as careful exegesis may yield to Miss Robins and heirs.

Still, there has been no resisting the personal privilege of a cursory glance.

This sheaf bulks to 401 pages, a token of the subject's consequence that would be more impressive if 210 of them were not given over to a reprint of a report on the activities of the Fulbright International Educational Exchange Program for the year 1957, in which my name nowhere appears.

I held, to say truth, a Fulbright fellowship in Italy in 1958, an overevaluation of my parts as scholar that shocked the FBI when it learned about it four months after I had settled into imperiling the Parioli. When news of this emolument reached Assistant FBI Director

Clyde Tolson, he scribbled below the message, "It would be interesting to know the members of the commission" that allots these awards. Next to that rumination there is a "Yes" and the solitary majesty of those *H*'s that signaled another of Hoover's Red Alerts.

A warning was dispatched to a Mr. Belmont, presumably one of the Fulbright Act's administrators. What survives of this catalog of my political eccentricities seems entirely accurate, although I cannot vouch for what may hide behind the inkblots that cover passages that the FBI still thinks is stuff too hot for the stranger's eye.

Nothing happened. I finished my Fulbright term and came home. But then, nothing ever did happen.

In 1962, when I went to Washington to work for *The New Republic*, Assistant Director C. D. De Loach advised that, "I will see to it that some of our good friends connected with these newspapers are discreetly advised of Kempton's background." Again the *H* and a "yes, do so." And again, nothing happened, and I lived peaceably until I departed to take up with the *New York World-Telegram and Sun*.

Back rose C. D. De Loach, stirred, as was generally the case, by a profanation of the director's shrine: "Kempton, of course, never misses a chance to attack the bureau and the director, and apparently he has hit a new low of vilification in his most recent effort. I have advised (blank) of Kempton's background."

Again the *H* and the scrawl: "When a newspaper hires a snake like Kempton they can expect the worse *[sic]*," which was true to the key of repulsion for those who vilify that had been struck in a prior "I am surprised that Scripps-Howard are taking on this rat."

And again, nothing happened. My career's vicissitudes have all been of my own doing, and my malice toward Hoover, which was always small, and his malice toward me, which seems to have been outsized, were alike inconsequential for help or harm.

Many of these pages detail activities of mine that inarguably fit Hoover's definition of the subversive and can find no quarrel from me. I maintained a fellowship with Communists in trouble in the fifties that shames me not at all and is by no means unfondly recalled even yet.

In December of 1962, FBI National asked FBI Newark for an update on myself, and I am as surprised as Hoover must have been and certainly more gratified to find a reply expressing doubt that any "active investigation is desirable at this time" because "his affiliation with the [Young Communist League] appears to have terminated in his youth" although "he would appear to have a passion for civil liberties."

That was, if anything, too lofty a compliment to the nobility of my soul, but it has warmed my bones after a fairly chilling trip. I was one of those the director tried in his spite to harm and who were too close to the margin of respectability for him to reach. He could hurt only the weak and the helpless, and those were his only authentic victims and, since I wasn't one, they matter and I don't.

And in any case, he probably didn't much care whether I indulged fraternal feelings toward Communists; what set his juices to boil was my want of any for him.

His nights were haunted by the suspicion that somewhere there might be someone who didn't revere him. There aren't many of us cursed with that degree of sensitivity, but I should suppose there are fewer still who are comforted by the discovery that anybody hates us as much as he seems to have hated me, which is why I was wise to wait so long to ask and am rather sorry now that I did.

The Proof that Trump Is a Self-Made Man

6 • 4 • 89

The Rev. Fred L. Shuttlesworth was the heroically exuberant chairman of the Alabama Christian Movement and leader of Birmingham's semi-citizens of color whose uprisings swept to their crest in 1963.

Charles Morgan was the Birmingham lawyer who carried the briefs in civil rights cases in those years when the others of his white colleagues were so hostile or fearful that five firms in a row declined *The New York Times*' offer of a fee handsome beyond dreams of avarice to defend it in a libel suit.

Richard Arrington can thank the lonely struggles of Fred Shuttlesworth and Charles Morgan for the huge change in Birmingham that made him its first black mayor.

The New York City Civil Rights Coalition had invited all three to come here Friday in a hope by no means untinged with irony that their recollections of the flame they had lit and still keep burning might ignite the sodden, not to say toxic, spirit of the cultural capital of the enlightened North.

It was one of those occasions, too frequent these days, when the melancholy of what is overbears every exhilaration of the memories of what used to be.

All hope had begun to slip away that anything, even Birmingham, was left to teach us how to feel again, and then, almost as an aside, Charles Morgan spoke two sentences and the heart took fire with the rage that asserts itself as holy.

"What is happening to us," Charles Morgan asked, "when you have a full-page ad that literally and in a few words comes out for hating? That criticized people for not hating?"

What Donald Trump had been bold to say was: "Mayor Koch has stated that hate and rancor should be removed from our hearts. I don't think so. I want to hate . . ."

My first and until Friday my final response to that pronouncement had been to think, "Oh, well, that's Donald Trump, cheapness packaged at no end of expense."

Until now, it had seemed that the once great blessing of life's multiple erosions is that they wear away anger. But now Chuck Morgan has taught me that, once we can no longer be angry, we are dead in the soul and all we do is but a terminal wriggle.

It is true that the streets are full of persons who are angry at Donald Trump. But theirs is, in too many cases, only the spite of the envious and unworthy not just of them but of its object. As to hate Donald Trump is to be like him, so to envy him is to suggest that you wish you were Donald Trump, a lapse from personal dignity entirely at variance with the properties that qualify anger as honorable.

The last time I saw and heard Donald Trump's boots licked in public, the tongue on the job belonged to Donald King, promoter and debaser of boxing, who first came to official notice as a common felon and has since, by brass and stealth, risen to the eminence of an uncommon rascal. King was the panegyrist perfectly fitted for Trump's desserts, and the competition should have closed with his enrollment. Instead, it teems with his betters and, of course, Trump's.

The man demeans anything he touches, which is any place where he can leave his name permanently engraved and any cause whose sponsors are shameless enough to sell him the privilege. Rudolph Giuliani made him chairman of his inaugural mayoral campaign dinner, a trophy that every other candidate devoutly wishes was his own. He was guest of honor at the unveiling of the city's memorial to the veterans of the Vietnam War. Trump was twenty years old in 1966 and disciplinedly abstained from tendering himself for or getting caught in service.

Decency would have suggested to any society with a taste for the suitable that there are properer ways to do honor to men who toiled and suffered than by begging money from Donald Trump in exchange for a license to appropriate a stage that fairly belonged only to those who had earned it with their bodies.

But then the Episcopal Diocese of New York has appointed him chairman of the finance committee for completing the Cathedral of St. John the Divine. We may suppose that he bought that office too. The cathedral is a noble stab at invoking the thirteenth century, but the smell of simony hardly serves to capture its essence of authenticity. Scoundrels have helped raise many a church, but I can't think of any who were proud to exalt hatred.

To boast of hating used to be an embarrassment for the worst of people. I knew the Birmingham police commissioner who jailed Fred Shuttlesworth, again and again. He was always a mean man and now and then a vicious one, but he went to his grave denying that he had ever hated anyone. Time was when people who sent hate letters had the shame to keep themselves anonymous.

But Donald Trump dresses his hatred up as though it were a peacock's feathers. In any polity entitled to think itself civilized, persons with due regard for their breeding would rise up and leave the room politely but definitely whenever the Donald Trumps entered it. Instead, this perfectly matched pair of the vulgar is fawned upon wherever it condescends to lower the company. We are assured that God does not make trash, which thought disposes of the impression that Donald Trump is not altogether a self-made man.

Death, Life in Painting, Exhibition

11 • 17 • 89

"No one listens to me."
—MARK MORRISOE, thirty, a few days before he died of AIDS

Mark Morrisoe haunts the bleak walls where Artists Space has hung "Witnesses: Against Our Vanishing," a show whose inspiration comes from AIDS and whose tonic chord is pain and grief. His image is before us through every stage of the bare four years between his living and embracing and wasting and dying.

That image is a victory won by him and by the exhibit it dominates, because no one who lingers for more than a minute with those eyes and the bones encroaching upon them can ever again quite hope to meet an hour that brings the ease and quiet of Mark Morrisoe's vanishing from the mind. His face recurs over and over, and its every new manifestation is one more blow of a sledgehammer upon the armorplate of our insensitivity.

The largest piece in the show is a portrait Steve Tashjian painted of Mark Morrisoe in 1985, which may well have been before either knew what waited too soon ahead. But the omen is there: The black scars that serve for eyes and mouth are adumbrations of the cadaver on its way. Disaster has forced Tashjian back to the representational and the strokes and pigments of the campi santi of the Middle Ages, when every child knew what delicacy has forbidden us to tell our own children and ourselves, which is that in the midst of life we are in death. But these artists know that now, and the knowledge had stripped their work of every pretension to please or charm. They have been pitched out of fashion and they have restored for us the face of martyrdom.

Some martyrs may fit our tastes better than others, but there has seldom been one of them whose fate was not assessed as his own fault by judges representative of what qualified as the sound opinion of the time. Even those of us assured that Saint Sebastian died for the truth of the Revelation would have trouble deciding that the Roman arrows would have made him that much less a martyr if he had strayed into Mithraism.

And we cannot stand before Steve Tashjian's canvas without feeling Mark Morrisoe's martyrdom. When we who are old depart, we may at best hope to be missed a little, but we can no longer ask for the tears that burn on the cheek. The deaths that tear the heart belong to the young who die before their time and here they are at Artists Space, and one visitor, more than content with thoughts of higher things than Sen. Jesse Helms, suddenly remembered him amid all these first ravaged and then lost faces with the shock of recognizing that it is upon such as they he makes his wars.

"Witnesses: Against our Vanishing" has drawn its most clamorous public attention because the National Endowment for the Arts at first withdrew a $10,000 subsidy after its chairman took alarm at a catalog contributor's statement that to satisfy his rage as an AIDS patient, he sometimes resorted to fantasies of throwing gasoline on Sen. Helms and setting him afire.

Poor catharsis for tragedy though that may be, the federal budget is already put to considerable expense for supporting Jesse Helms' revilements of private citizens and ought not begrudge $10,000 to a private citizen for reviling him back.

This quarrel is in any case a petty distraction from the true force of a show as to which the NEA's chairman, after various ditherings, settled at last upon complaints of "a lack of artistic merit." "Witnesses" has its portions that strike the eye as unartful, but they bring us into the presence of that supremest of art's expressions, the reminder that in life we are in the midst of death and, what is grander still, that in death we are in the midst of life. But now, this knowledge has stripped the work of all pretension to please and restored for us the face of martyrdom.

In the Oddly Delightful Company of Guerrillas

12 • 3 • 89

The fortunes of war run to infinite varieties of the unexpected, not to say the treacherous; but no happy accident could have seemed less probable than a chance to observe the domestic manners of the FMLN guerrillas taking their transient ease in the suburbs of Soyapango.

The unlikelihood of an encounter this odd may excuse this tourist's protracted failure to recognize it when it came. One had made one's entry into the Colonia Santa Barbara Friday alongside a strand of rubbered wire that looked too much like stuff of the sort employed for detonating land mines.

The puzzlements of this object were compounded when the eye traveled its length to end at a half-open iron gate where a soldier sat in a uniform that had about it an air of the random entirely at variance with the neat if scarcely spruce appearance of government troopers whose clothing always looks as if it had been washed last night and is still unsoiled by the ungainly sprawls toward the sanctuary of the dirt that are the inevitable exigencies of combat. Here were garments not issued but picked up and assembled along the road.

"Of course," one too quickly decided, "this is the militia enlisted by the Republic from the loyalists among its citizens."

They were moving about the pathways in rags and tags of martial costume in numbers enough to uplift the hearts of any U.S. military adviser as misapprehending as oneself.

Mark Uhlig of *The New York Times* had most attentively served as guide and oiler away of the rust from one's too-long-unattended body of experience with the clatters and clutters of war. One has frequently admired and seldom deplored the qualities of the men and women of the *Times*, but not even from one of them could there have been imagined a display as exemplary as Uhlig's of the virtues summed up by the catcher in "Bull Durham" when he observed that you play this game with fear and arrogance. We took a bend in the road behind Uhlig's white flag and then he began a conversation with a young man in a baseball fan's cap with the device "El Salvador, C.A." and another, bulkier man with a bit of red ribbon around his wrist. The younger introduced himself as Vladimir and the slightly elder as Daniel, and if Vladimir's Spanish tongue was incomprehensible to the tourist's ear, his tone was unmistakably that of political discourse and of Radio Venceremos. One had met the enemy in a guise so compellingly Garibaldian that, if just for a moment, one yielded him one's heart. There aren't all that many human creatures more attractive than some revolutionaries can be, at least until they win.

Grenades were crumpling and scattered gunshots crackling from distances by no means comfortably far. One flinched automatically after each; and yet Vladimir and Daniel continued their expositions without trace of tremor, and with a bearing that seemed to assume itself safer in loudly ominous clamors of the fields of war than many Salvadorans feel in church these Sundays.

We had come at last into the company of combat soldiers. Courtesy compelled one to bear with homilies of the political tenor; but it was a relief to arrive at the intimacies of reminiscence of three weeks fighting.

"There has been a mess of combat around LoCinco," said Vladimir, "but the rest has been routine. We are not always fighting. We have our moments of peace. This is one."

This moment of peace has grown even more disturbingly noisy and the temptation larger to do as Ted Koppel does and say, "Gentlemen, I'm afraid our time is up." Even so, the fascinations of this particular absurdity still hold one enchained; and Uhlig asked Daniel why the FMLN forces have profaned the quarters of the rich in Escalon.

"We want the rich to understand as the poor do what it is to really feel the war," he replied. "Peace for the rich has ended and the war for the poor has begun."

He was asked which elements at the government's disposal were the opponents' most troublesome. He replied that the Elite—"so-called"—Brigades were the best trained, but they all have a low combat morale.

"Morale is the essential all troops must have, and that is what they have shattered. We are willing to offer our lives. Of course some bullets will hit us. That is what war is about."

The intermittent rumbles were turning toward thunder; still one tarried to visit with three women warriors, two of them only girls ready with their smiles and one with the look of an NYPD female sergeant, circa 1958. Inside the otherwise barren room of their fleeting sojourn, there was a sofa and a game board with a small screen dividing and concealing one player's pegs from the others. It was that game where the child arrays his pegs one by one in hopes of matching the space where his opponent has concealed his battleship so exactly as to win the battle by sinking the enemy's navy. The warrior girls had passed part of the rest period playing the game called "Tactics."

At last the moment for parting too insistently pressed; and back down the exit trail our party went between intervals of pause when mortality's intimations broke forth too intrusively and one waited them out in the comfort of walls of brick and corners of concrete. Two hundred yards farther on, a detail of thirty or so Treasury Police slumped at the ready, each formidable as to weaponry and morose as to countenance.

It is a singularity of official El Salvador's military formations that nobody visible seems charged with command responsibilities. Perhaps nobody is; and the radioman just calls the rear for helicopter and rockets; and the rear eventually calls back with orders to move. The prospect of waiting a long while for instructions directly to engage may well be the only source of contentment available to troops like these. It hardly lay in the lips of one who had so recently been gimping about on decreasingly serviceable ankles waving his white flag with passionate timidity to impute cowardice to anyone else; but all the same the sight of this prebattle assemblage scarcely suggested the demeanor of soldiers set for fighting or enough used to it to have learned the trade from the combatant's best instructor, the enemy combatant. It would be two hours after one had quit the oddly delightful company of the guerrillas that the battle to disturb their peace began.

After such spectacles, the tourist could only seek advice and counsel from a NATO diplomat sympathetic with our own embassy's cause but detached from its imbecile optimism.

"What worries me," he observed, "is that the FMLN has the discipline and controls the battle order and knows now that they can sustain contact with this army and may be starting to understand that they have a chance to break it." One had seen nothing all day that inclined him to dispute that assessment.

Unsentimental Education

9 • 13 • 91

We may suppose that failure was the first thing Luis Soto learned in school. Maybe he withdrew into himself, maybe he struck out at others. It scarcely matters whether he was too distracted or too distracting for the classroom norm. We have said enough when we identify him as one of those children who are marked and mocked as "retards" as soon as their schoolmates mature enough to know the language of cruelty.

The Board of Education has no remedy for inconveniences like Luis Soto except in the facilities for emotionally disturbed or learning-disabled students it clusters, higgledy-piggledy, in its special education programs.

He was consigned to the Manhattan School of Career Development; and last November, he found out just how special his special education could be. Robert Eichler, Career Development's dean, came to Luis Soto's classroom, collected him and nine other boys, and told them to come with him.

Luis Soto's counsel has sworn by affidavit that the dean who thus conscripted these wards of his keeping did not tell them where or why they were going.

A police lieutenant from the nearest precinct had asked to borrow ten boys to flesh out the lineup around a youthful Hispanic robbery suspect. We have every right to expect a dean of special education to remember that his charges happen to be children peculiarly vulnerable to feeling in the wrong. Instead, this one herded them together, watched them arrayed on the precinct stage holding numbered cards on their chests, and staring, as commanded, at the blank wall behind which the victim sought to pick out the putative offender.

Luis Soto and comrades under draft had no way to tell whether they were not themselves under arrest; and its managers stopped the process only when one of its exhibits began to cry. Luis Soto remembers only one apology and it was tendered, unsurprisingly, not by his own teacher but by a cop.

Luis Soto was paid ten dollars for his yet-to-be-forgotten pains. He came home haunted by the sense that, without knowing why, he had put himself in too much trouble to tell his mother. He finally dared to tell an older sister. She told their mother, whose response, rarely familiar in her son's experience with the world, was to visit the blame on the school instead of him.

Carmen Rodriguez is bound to a wheelchair and untrained in English. But, all the same, she is of the stuff that lodges in heroic natures. Dean Eichler's parade distressed and humiliated nine other families; but only Carmen Rodriguez has pressed her protest until it has finally brought her to sue the Board of Education for damages. But then it must take the strongest sort of parents to live through their child's protracted treatment as worthless and still believe that they themselves are worth enough to be much use in braving the world for him.

By March, Luis Soto was still damaged and afraid to go back to Manhattan Career Development. Over the summer, the Board of Education at last yielded to his mother's pressure and transferred Luis and his sister to Bronx Career Development.

Those two arrived there when the schools opened this week, and they shrank almost immediately homeward. "Those kids," Luis Soto's sister said yesterday, "looked just too rough."

These children had been sent alone, in their shaky state, to bear the shocks of a strange new school with no adult company to ease their passage. But then special education probably doesn't offer escort services gentler than those drovers give to herds.

Stephen Greenberg, the plaintiff family's lawyer, introduced its members to the press yesterday and thought it unsafe to allow more than one question to Luis Soto. It was "How do you feel?" He answered that he was scared and stopped and bowed his head in the withdrawal that wishes the floor would open and hide the person.

He had failed again. He won't always. His parents are in his corner, bearing him up, and fighting to keep his chances alive for the time when he is up to using them.

Oh, for Brawls of Yesteryear

4 • 12 • 92

My next national convention will be the twenty-first of those occasions when I have intruded my fleshly and decreasingly spirited presence upon the company of Democrats, Republicans—and once even Progressives—at their quadrennial abandonments of reason.

Sixty years ago the miracle of bringing the conventions alive for untraveled Americans was work for the radio alone, and it did that office more than handsomely, by reducing commentary to a minimum and leaving the tale to be told by the delegates in a jumble of regional accents and regional prejudices conjuring up the image of a vast continent of exotic provinces, each with its own language.

It was the radio that bound me in a thralldom to the convention process that has only lately commenced to slacken. I was listening to the first ballot of the 1932 Democratic convention that nominated Franklin D. Roosevelt. Tammany Hall, which hated Roosevelt, had demanded a poll of the New York delegation. The convention chairman complied, and when the roll of name after name arrived at James J. Walker, the answer came back bold as brass: "Alfred E. Smith."

Franklin D. Roosevelt was governor of New York State and Jimmy Walker was mayor of New York City. The powers of the governor included removing any mayor who had too far disgraced his office; and the Walker administration's scandals had already provided excuses more than sufficient. But, with his head in Roosevelt's hands, Jimmy Walker had coolly bared his neck and given the knife license to do as it pleased. Roosevelt was more than pleased to expel Walker from City Hall within the month.

I was, of course, too young to know the what and why of this moment; but somehow I could sense its gallantry from the silence of the hall and the chairman's respectful pause before returning to his call of the roll. He and I and all who listened had heard the defiant voice of one more of those lost causes that have ever since been my incurable addiction.

The first stages of love are unfortunately too often the sweetest. For they're the ones when we feel the drama without quite understanding it. That may be why my own romance with political conventions has lost so much of its bloom: the better I learned to understand their dramas, the less intensely I felt them. But then they've pretty well withdrawn permission for dramas anyway.

My earliest steps on a convention floor were with the Democrats in 1936. Luck had blessed me with a job carrying telegraph copy for Western Union.

I would stand in the press rows where Henry Mencken sat weaving gold from the straw of the podium discourse while journalists at leisure craned over his shoulder to watch his next marvel clatter forth. No graven image could be more serenely unconscious of its devotees than Mencken was; he would type on, finish a page, hold it up on an uplifted arm to be seen and seized by one of us Western Union boys and, having never turned around, go back to typing.

I came back from this first brush with two useful lessons. Mencken had taught me by example that the best way to do the job was to sit down with my typewriter just before the gavel and then record the event just as it unfolded, trusting that enough surprises and amusements would bob up to keep the account lively.

I had also found out that a Western Union messenger was free to pass unquestioned wherever he chose. For years I kept the pin that simply said "Western Union," with no further need for credentials, and managed to squirrel my way into no end of secret conclaves full of portent if barren of revelations. Neither lesson is serviceable by now. Western Union has folded its tents; and the convention managers have exercised themselves so strenuously to curtail their proceedings and to suppress the risks of amusement and surprise that the stuff a running account needs for vigor has all but drained away.

There is no crueler way to assess what conventions have become than to remember what they used to be and notice how carefully their managers have labored to eliminate every one of the unexpected, the untidy and the disorderly elements whose mixture made for a brew unique for its tang, flavor and purgatively bitter aftertaste.

We shall never feel again the wicked exhilarations of the sight of the hatred of brother for brother and sister for sister showing the naked face that cares not what visiting strangers might think. There will always be conventions where one set of delegates detests the other; but, since the result is almost invariably known in advance these days, enmity can only manifest itself with the sodden air of depression.

Oh, for the brawls of yesteryear. The Democrats maintained a steadier key of low-level fratricide than the Republicans who, being a church, generally preferred close harmony. But, just because they were a church, the Republicans would now and then lurch into some doctrinal quarrel, and rise to savageries of spleen that would turn the hair of a hockey fan.

I had not thought again to hear the sound of a spite so pure as the one rolled down upon Tom Dewey in the roar of the Ohio delegation to the 1952 Republican convention when it recognized that the Eastern bankers had snatched away the Midwest's chance to crown a President Robert A. Taft. But then I saw Nelson Rockefeller take the microphone at the 1964 GOP convention and be met with the ravening fury of Goldwater delegates envenomed by victory as they had never before been in defeat.

One of the charms of what conventions used to be was their curious habit of passing out a battered trophy to the winner and then heaping all the laurels on the defeated. The most delightful of their vagaries was an insistence upon upstaging the nominee. John F. Kennedy was upstaged at the 1960 Democratic convention by Sen. Eugene McCarthy's futilely magnificent appeal to stand by Adlai E. Stevenson and not abandon the man who had made them all proud to be Democrats. Ronald Reagan contrived with superb delicacy to upstage Gerald Ford barely a minute after he had been renominated for president. Ted Kennedy quite coarsely upstaged Jimmy Carter in 1980; and even Barry Goldwater, who had neither the inclination nor much of the knack for upstaging, brought it off with Richard Nixon in 1960. The best part of what addicted me to conventions was their generosity in giving the best exit lines to the lost cause.

But now every peril of uninvited apparitions of the spontaneous or improvisatory sort has been suppressed. The artlessness of the political convention has given way to the arts of choreographers whose taste forbids any display that might be embarrassing and could in the process remind the beholder of the lives and feelings of the real humanity that can be sometimes inspiring and sometimes deplorable.

The delegates no longer slurp about in their ridiculous hats and with the wound of their hangovers festering for all to see. They sit rigid instead as though they are a congregation. The journalists who used to ring the platform close enough to be rained with the speaker's spittle are perched in tiers behind it like the audience for Phil Donahue with the singular difference that they have become television's only nonparticipatory audience.

The whole design of these cosmetic revisions was to fit the political conventions to the standards that television was assumed to demand. This vision was by no means ignoble and might have done no harm if its architects had not forgotten that television has no more compelling demand than for the product to be entertaining. The ironic consequence of all these endeavors has been that the conventions are now neat, well-tailored and disciplinedly staged and so implacably tedious that the networks disdain to give them houseroom for more than a few begrudged and diminishing hours a night.

There are no fights anymore, no life-enhancing accidents and seldom a barbaric yawp. Oh well. We go listlessly on to them as we might to an alumni reunion where there isn't much to do except inspect the latest wither on a classmate's cheeks and agree that the old school was a lot more fun when we were young.

Let Me Be Wrong About Clinton

5 • 27 • 93

The wider the suspicion spreads that as a president William J. Clinton will not do, the deeper my heart is stabbed with another reminder that of all the sad words that ebb and flow, the saddest are these: "I told you so."

For I am of the unhappy few who were against Bill Clinton before New Hampshire. All of him—the blitherings of his insincerities, the mouth that refused to close even when he shut up, the dubieties of his promises, the fraudulence of his hugs, even his grin—fell upon me all together with a force like an indecent assault's. Back then I was alone, alienated and mean of spirit; and now my spites clamor from the tongues of the throng.

And where's the joy? Experience has taught me that finding out that I have been right is unvaryingly a stimulus to thoughts so bitter as to push me to prayers that I may turn out to have been wrong after all. Oh Lord, make thy servant William to succor the poor and redeem the rich, and not incidentally, show me up for the fool I would rather have been.

My memory crowds with public faces who have known while seldom bothering to feel my scorn; and the pleasure of recall abides exclusively in the times when I was wrong about them.

When I was rather young to be a judge, I was sent to cover Dwight D. Eisenhower's first presidential campaign. The days are long gone when I thought it useful to weigh my own intelligence against any candidate's; but I was full of cheek then and leaped to assess Eisenhower as hopelessly dumb. Sound him on labor problems and he would almost bring off the prodigy of mispronouncing the word "injunction."

I needed at least a decade to appreciate the cunning beneath this mask of ignorance and to recognize the sovereign prudence and the cold command that made Dwight Eisenhower the last American to arrive at the White House entirely equipped to be the sort of president who does his country the least damage.

In 1956 my errant eye was conscripted to take the measure of William J. Brennan, Eisenhower's newest appointment to the Supreme Court of the United States. Brennan was a New Jersey state judge, not much remarked beyond the Hudson and with a record of few significant public utterances except for a Law Day address from which some distaste for Sen. Joe McCarthy could be inferred.

McCarthy was by that time sunk in his disgraces; but he still retained some of his nose for suspects; and he demanded the personal privilege of cross-examining Brennan before the Senate Judiciary Committee. It would have been the cruelest sort of sport if its victim hadn't looked too soggy for sympathy. Sen. McCarthy would press him to say who he meant when he warned of dark shadows sweeping the land, and Brennan would limply reply that the last such image he would have thought to conjure up was Sen. McCarthy's.

Examples of craven behavior were already familiars of my vocational duty; and Brennan's struck me as dank beyond comparison with any others. Plagiarism was my vice then as now and, to sum up his posture, I borrowed without credit President Theodore Roosevelt's petulant remark that he could carve a better judge than Oliver Wendell Holmes out of a banana. Roosevelt may or may not have been pleased to have been wrong about Justice Holmes; but I myself was delighted to be proved wrong by Justice Brennan. He went on so to shine his light upon the Court that even his enemies could not blame without also praising him.

There are no sweeter discourses than those that run back on the men and women we have dismissed too quickly. To have been harsh and correct can scourge the memory; and to have been severe and incorrect is a balm. We see God's hand whenever some human soul we had thought valueless rises up before our eyes in the fullness of his worth. Please, dear Lord, make Bill Clinton the man to show me up once more.

A Raisin in the Sun

3 • 24 • 94

Havana

Thirty-five years and six weeks are gone since the day Fidel Castro came in glory to the great stage of history, and no one is left among the actors he met there except Jordan's King Hussein and North Korea's Kim Il Sung, minor-league players then and now.

Castro burst from the wings surrounded by the guerrilla conquerors he called his *barbudos*, his men in beards. The beard was so sacred among the revolution's symbols then that gossip had it that his brother and putative heir Raúl had to his ineffaceable shame failed in every effort to raise one and been forced to settle for a pigtail.

It seems odd and is perhaps portentous how rarely the visitor sees a beard in Cuba these days. Only Fidel Castro defiantly flourishes this boldest of his revolutionary banners and his beard has grown gray and long enough for the nesting of an owl. Castro must soon be, if he is not already, the last of the barbudos. He has outlasted most of his enemies with the unvarying exception of incumbent presidents of the United States. At sixty-seven, he has so far survived, however exiguously, the extinction of his friends, the Communists of Eastern Europe.

But he can go no more a-roving as he once did, with troops in Angola, engineers in Nicaragua, military engineers in Grenada. His world has shrunk down to his island, his votaries to his enduring and not quite unadoring people and his treasury down to a beggar's. The central power is still his closely held own; but he is less and less able to exercise it as a force in advancing his country's development or, what is more to the present point, arresting its protracted decay.

"When you cannot pay, you can no longer command," one Cuban observed the other day in a voice at once aware of Castro's faults and still persuaded that "if we lost this symbol," all that followed would be chaos.

"Dignity" is a word that recurs over and over in the voices of those Cubans for whom it has become the last romantic vision after all the follies of romance have withered. González knows the price of dignity. "I had a bad life in the sixties and seventies," he remembers. "I went ten years without being allowed to publish a paragraph and now all my enemies who silenced me have chosen exile and now they are no longer known in Cuba."

He soldiered away in those bad years as a publishing-house editor chafing for time to write for himself. At last a friend in the ministry of culture offered him a chance to escape to Barcelona as a cultural attaché. "I answered that I cannot write outside my own country. I wanted to change my job but I didn't want to change my country. I am not in Cuba because I am a political man. I am in Cuba because I am a Cuban—a little animal of the tropics."

"Whenever a Cuban intellectual leaves," González reflects, "he puts before us the temptation of being a traitor. We paid a big price for ideology. We are now the son who threw away his fortune. We are back to the reality of being a very poor country."

As custodian of Cuba's film archive, González is occasionally invited to visit other Latin American nations. "These are the only countries we can compare ourselves to. Your America is too rich to measure us with. The Latin American countries are poor without dignity. The only thing we have to show the world is that dignity, the rest is wind." And if there is a feeling that can be taken as near universal in Cuba, it is an exhaustion with politics and propaganda so total that visitors to the recent book fair scarcely glanced at the stalls of official publications and then lined up in a row fifty yards long for a chance to buy three privately issued books on Santería, the Afro-Cuban religion more and more venerated for its quasi-Catholic doctrines and its comparatively benign magical properties.

Otherwise, as González puts it, "we are choked with the crisis and when a human being is choking it is very difficult to ask him to stand up." From Castro down through the Young Communist Leaguers who tend the ashes of his flame, there seems to be no answer to the crisis except to exhort ordinary Cubans to work harder than ever and, to take an example, mold fifteen cigars an hour instead of the ten that is their present quota. There is small chance that further escalations of rhetoric can rouse a people repetitively summoned to heroic struggle and now monotonously, although not quite unhealthily, fed off ration cards entitling them to beans and rice and to two pounds of fish every fifteen days, and with luck a bar of soap every six months. Even Fidel Castro seems tired of his larynx and untrusting of its residuary powers. He's seldom sighted in the countryside; and there are days when officials who ought to know appear honestly baffled as to where he might be.

Cubans remain incorrigibly pleasant but subdued to degrees unthinkable thirty years ago. On a recent Saturday citizens of Pinar del Río gathered to watch their baseball team play Havana's Metropolitans. The ballpark's fences were lined with slogans exalting the massive participation in sports as the fundamental cause of success and proclaiming this as "the hour to shout revolution." And yet there were fewer shouts for anything than we are used to hearing in stadiums if only from the vendors whose cries ring no more in Cuba, there being all but nothing available to vend. The joys in Cuba seldom rise above the somber ones of the melancholy heart.

All the same even the openly disillusioned here would not think to suggest the Miami exiles as a plausible alternative. Castro may be harder and harder to see; but Jorge Mas Canosa's Cuban- American National Foundation can hardly be said to exist. Castro's face is visible on just the single one of the multitude of billboards otherwise dominated by the martyred Che Guevara's. The Catholic tradition reserves the worship of saints for the dead. To sense that Castroism is in peril of dying is not to surmise that Fidel Castro does not remain a symbol vividly alive. His aura shines above all his errors. He remains, as Clarendon said of Oliver Cromwell, the man who cannot be blamed without also being praised or praised without also being blamed. What is Fidel if not at once the cross that, bone-tired, the Cubans carry and the savior in whose name they carry it?

Even with too few days of contending with the puzzle of such a people, there keep coming back the lines that Langston Hughes began with the question, "What happens to a dream deferred?" and went on to the further question, "Does it dry up like a raisin in the sun?" The Cuba that waits while nothing seems to happen looks more and more like a raisin in the sun.

Brave Instincts, Affirming Dignity

12 • 1 • 94

On the night before last when he had been robbed and shot, the first human creature Tupac Shakur felt the need to cry out for in his pain was not a friend but his mother. The young may wander the world round; but, when the terrors of the night ask too much of them, they always turn to their mothers.

The burden of Tupac Shakur's sins cannot be dismissed as a light package to carry; but neither can the weight of the fame and the commodity value that you have won all by yourself before you were given time to grow up. Only part of you is the roaring and now and then clawing lion; the rest is still the little boy.

He was on the operating table in Bellevue Hospital yesterday afternoon; and downtown a deliberating Manhattan jury listened to rereadings of bits of the law and the evidence in his trial on charges that he and friends rabbled a young woman in the Parker-Meridien Hotel in November of 1993.

In one and the same hours, Tupac Shakur was being cared for as victim of a violent felony and being judged as suspect perpetrator of another. That coincidence was curious enough and yet not half so odd as the extraordinary resemblance between the crime committed upon Shakur and the crime imputed to him.

Three men had sat in the lobby below a Seventh Avenue recording studio waiting when Shakur and three friends arrived. The order to lie down was delivered; and Shakur's friends bent to the drill with due docility. The affair would have proceeded with professional discipline if Shakur had not breached custom for such transactions by rising up in expletive-undiluted outrage. He was stripped of his jewelry and shot three times.

We may presume that he mounted his stand alone while his friends kept their heads down. It is ever the star's fate to go about not with friends but with hangers-on who cling to him up to the point where it is more politic to abandon him. You cannot be a star unless you are brave, or a hanger-on unless you're not. Shakur's posture on this occasion was admirable and so is life's usefulness for assisting our progress toward adulthood. Painful as the lesson is, there are worse ways to advance the gangster rapper toward self-improvement than afflicting him with the knowledge of how it feels to be a gangster's target.

But the courage of his defiance aside, where are we to find the true glory of Shakur's refusal to permit three armed and rapacious strangers to treat him as though he were no more than a thing? What he was affirming was the fact of his own dignity; and he would not be waiting out his jury now if it had not been for one young woman's insistence upon asserting hers. Some degrees of virtue and propriety may be wanting in both these parties; but they appear to possess in common a redeeming sense of dignity.

On the afternoon before his assault, Tupac Shakur stood in a criminal court corridor and favored the attendant journalists with his version of his trouble. One of the observations reported, among others less appetizing, was that he might not be on trial now if he had been gentleman enough to walk the complainant down to the street and offer his limousine for her trip homeward.

He had caught the whole point. Just that small kindness might well have been sufficient to accord her the recognition owed her dignity. But recognitions of that sort must be felt before they can be tendered; Shakur's had arrived late and might not have arrived at all if his circumstances had not come to this critical juncture. All the same, from whence except in hindsight can we be blessed with even a hint of the intrusions of repentance?

Tupac Shakur triumphed too fast and grew up too slow. His future is for his jury to appoint. I must confess to a fugitive and irrational wish that he might find some small mercies there. It may not be entirely unreasonable to hold on to some hopes for a sinner whose first thought in a bad moment is to call up his mother.

The Reporter's One Commanding Duty

11 • 9 • 95

I have reflected long upon what I might add to the dosages of enlightenment you've ingested in the years since the first Lovejoy lecture. And I have, I'm afraid, come up rather short in these rummagings, because I cannot think of much to say beyond what most of you already know and that those who don't may have to put up with several surprises in the way of disappointment before they find it out for themselves.

I can't even pretend to the wisdom of the years, since I don't seem capable of growing up sufficiently to acquire enough of it and, even in my wither, I'm embarrassed to have to confess that, if I scoured my head for evidence of better seasoning by age, I would find it instead still poorly stocked with the sober reason of the grizzled and bulging with the romantic illusions of the beardless. I remain one of those who have learned that windmills are not giants and monsters and who, all the same, cannot see Rosinante saddled up without itching for another ride.

It has been said somewhere that the one essential sentence in Holy Scripture is "Thy Will Be Done" and that all else is commentary. Our trade remains for me the story you cover, the bumps you take, the people you meet and the struggle to make sense of it all in the only way we can ever hope to make sense, which is by seeing, touching and smelling. All else is commentary.

I have lately noticed not in myself but in my bosses a tendency to think me too old to go around as I used to, and I find myself sliding further and further away from being a reporter and toward becoming a commentator and commencing to rely upon what's in my head, an underpopulated premise not enough different from

Rush Limbaugh's as a resource for public enlightenment and for the stimulations of the self. All my life, when called upon to identify myself to the Internal Revenue Service, the last judgment, I have preferred to enter not journalist, not columnist, not commentator, certainly not author, but simply as "newspaper reporter." And even now, when my entitlement to make that quiet affirmation seems to diminish year by year, a newspaper reporter is as fervently all I want to be as it ever was.

And so I am worse equipped than many of my predecessors in your Pantheon to talk to much purpose about the responsibility of the media for earning the trust of the public. Some of my predecessors were publishers, who are particularly addicted to waxing on the subject of journalism's duty to truth and beauty, although I have lately had reason to wish that my own publisher had extended its admirable alertness to its responsibilities to the future welfare of its own reporters, who are, when all is said and done, the most precious substance in a publisher's care.

It may or may not be parochial of me to say that I am by no means certain that we reporters ought to worry all that much about the dangers of lying to the public. The public is, after all, an abstraction. We would far more serviceably take care not to lie to or about the people we are covering. For after all, if they can trust us, if not to be fair by their lights at least not to lie to them. We may not be correct about them—who can be assured of being correct about anyone else?—but we will not be false to them. When we go among humans, we are unable to deal with them as abstract presences; their very faces command us to be honorable, and once you learn not to lie to a face, you're pretty secure from the peril of lying to the generality of the faceless.

I have lately been commissioned to review the two huge volumes of the Library of America's "Reporting World War II," a compilation of the journalism from those days that seemed to its editors fittest to endure, although it would have lain forgotten still without their curiosity and their initiative.

What struck me most in these men and women was not just how magnificently they rose to the occasion but how much more they were able to learn than their editors at the home desk or their audience at far civilian remove.

These reporters had done what Stein told Marlowe in *Lord Jim* that we all must do, which is to "in the destructive element immerse." The destructive element is where the shock of recognition happens to be far more accessible to those who are buffered than to those who buffet. As the back knows more than the lash, the target knows more than the gun.

Because these reporters were stipulated non-combatants, they were certifiably only targeted. And so they quickly learned that war's supremely challenging moments arrive not when the soldier is ordered to kill but when he is called upon to rescue.

The victim, here as everywhere, is a more compelling figure than the victimizer, and that fact of life becomes patent as these chronicles proceed into the summer of 1945, when the Strategic Air Command rode triumphantly above cities tendered helpless to defend themselves, and the balance of heroic opportunity shifted all the way from the bombers to the bombed.

And, in that key, when we reach John Hersey's *Hiroshima*, the terminal entry in these volumes, we are confounded to find that it is not just the story of suffering we had originally taken it to be as much as it is a story of coping. In the end, Hiroshima's victims uniting and striving to heal themselves own the last word that speaks in these pages from the Second World War.

These reporters came upon that lesson in the only place they could meet it, as men and women not of the rear echelon but of the line. Of all this noble company, Ernie Pyle, whom I never had much chance to read at the time, stands above the rest because he most fully incarnated what a reporter ought to be.

Pyle went again and again wherever the wont extremes waited, the unconscripted man bound by conscience to the comradeship of the conscripted, and enduring by free will what they were compelled to endure by necessity. By instinct, in the destructive element he immersed, and I have no evidence that he had ever read *Lord Jim* and needed Stein's instructions to do it. But I did.

I do not mean to suggest that our standards have declined from these days. Any of these reporters would have drawn pride and profit from going about with Neil Sheehan and David Halberstam in Vietnam and with Roy Gutman and John Burns in Bosnia and with Peter Arnett just about anywhere.

Then too, almost nothing in our coverage of the Soviet Union provided noticeable illumination before the late eighties and it didn't cast its highest light until David Remnick came to Moscow carrying the treasure of the literary sensibility that forbade him to stop with one or two of the great novels of Dostoyevsky but pushed him on to *Poor Folk*, which, however lesser a work, manages to tell you most of all you need know about what life was like on the collective farms.

For Remnick knew a secret, which took me so long to learn that I was well down the road before I went to Mississippi and found out that Faulkner wasn't weaving fantasy at all but was instead soberly working off the files of country weeklies. Ever since, I have shunned the researches of social science and depended upon the novelists and have since come across no Sovietologist as useful as Chekhov and no guide to the incorrigibilities of rulers and ruled in Central America as Conrad's *Nostromo*.

No reporter, however good, can avoid realizing that the novelist is his better; but both know that the victim is in the end most of the story. Since the victim is and probably will ever be less and less able to come to us, the reporter who is worth his salt recognizes that his one commanding duty is to go out himself and look for the victim.

And that is why I so much fear that the futurists may be right and that in time to come the accountants will have had their way and the reporter will slip into the category of surplus labor and affliction to the profit margin.

That would be sad. I won't say that it would be tragic, because I have been taught not to indulge in hyperbole, even when it is as true to the facts of the case as I feel it to be in this one.

A Little Boy with Ol' Blue Eyes

12 • 15 • 96

Frank Sinatra's retirement has been announced once again but this time not by him but on his behalf, a circumstance allowing us the inference that he won't be lingering with life much longer than he used to on the last notes of other lovely songs. He ever did the fullest duty to his art, and now he is leaving us with the duty to sum him up.

My betters have already done that. One day I was dealing with Ella Fitzgerald, and the subject of Sinatra came up and her intruder-mistrusting voice suddenly softened and she said, "Frank. Just this little guy telling this story. That's all you have to be."

In 1956, Nelson Riddle thought to employ the Hollywood String Quartet as backup for Sinatra's *Close to You* album. The HSQ found Sinatra as demanding as Schoenberg had been six years before, when it recorded "Verklärte Nacht" and so gratified its composer that he felt himself fully defined and registered his satisfaction by writing the liner notes. Sinatra asked not a whit less than Schoenberg, and Eleanor Aller, the HSQ's cellist, has remembered the delight of the challenge and fulfillment as "the sort of thing in which you just enjoy every minute, because the man is so musical."

And so those made newly aware of the summit of America-bred chamber music that was the Hollywood String Quartet would do well to catch those four on "The Lady Is a Tramp" and understand that the HSQ's glorious decade belongs not only to Schoenberg and Schubert but to Frank Sinatra, too.

For Frank Sinatra knew, as every artist must, that there is no such thing as trash that cannot be transcended. He also knew the second great lesson, which is that everything is there to be stolen if you have the taste to confine your larcenies to the worth-taking. We cannot appreciate the work if we overlook its elements of creative plagiarism.

The porkpie hat and the walk into the shadows of loneliness with the light at his back are all taken intact from the "One for My Baby" that Fred Astaire consummated in the unjustly forgotten movie *The Sky's the Limit*. I remember when Sinatra was trying to put together a sextet for the Kennedy Inaugural and finally had to tell Milton Berle, "Look, Milton, the only way you'll ever learn to sing is to listen to Billie Holiday and find out how to play out a note." The Lord had given him his voice; mother wit and a magpie's cunning account for the enduring distinction of the rest.

Our relations were always cordial, however fleeting, but it didn't take too long to recognize the puritanical little boy beneath the skin. Once we passed a few minutes after a Kennedy rally in Los Angeles. Sinatra was in the full fit of enchainment in the great clan's thrall, and said how great they all were: "Jack, Jackie, the ambassador, Bobby, and every one of them."

He had to confess, all the same, that he was coming to doubt that Peter Lawford, the brother-in-law, had the moral fiber befitting his grand connections.

"Do you mean to say," I, puzzled, asked, "that, when you and Sammy Davis throw a wild night, Peter Lawford comes along?"

"Yes," Sinatra replied. "That's just what I mean."

And he did, because at bottom he believed—and could rise every morning and believe again—that love is eternal and fidelity is a sacred trust. There and only there was his secret. What would Don Giovanni be except merely coarse bouffe if the Don could not so unvaryingly persuade himself that each fresh object of trifling fancy is his lifetime's love?

No, if you want to know why Frank Sinatra will intrude himself into the bloodstream of our memories if we survive to a hundred and five, forget the grown man he never became and look for the little boy he could not quite stop being, because that is the little boy who goes about searching for and singing about the love that will always last.

Unjust Advances Behind Bars

1 • 5 • 97

When bedtime comes for the guests at the prison California delicately identifies as its Central Women's Facility, the loudspeaker is reported not infrequently to announce, "All you bitches and whores get into your rooms."

One little-noticed index of our advance toward gender equality is a 400 percent increase in the number of women in prison since 1980. The majority of new arrivals are drug offenders, and their rise reflects the criminal society where the man deals and the woman carries the stuff and is thus the easier to catch.

Organized feminism has paid small attention to this mark of progress and displays infinitely livelier concern for prisoners chafing under glass ceilings than those sealed round with stone walls. This neglect is now handsomely redeemed by the report on sexual abuse of women in state prisons that Human Rights Watch's Women's Rights Project has called "All Too Familiar."

Most female prisoners serve their terms in an atmosphere where the ratio of men to women corrections officers is at least two to one. Women's Rights Watch cannot, in justice, object to men guarding women because it is too sensible not to concede that most men tend to be decent. Its proper grievance is, rather, that there are no rules to inhibit those who aren't and are allowed free play to treat their prisons as their deer park.

We would argue foolishly if we suggested that convicted miscreants have not forfeited most of their rights. But we would argue infamously if we denied them any redress for violations of the very body that is pretty much all still theirs.

The occasions of redress for the abused are rare, stingy and disdainful of the equities owed to the respectable. Sexual harassment has been so prevalent in the corrections department of the District of Columbia, capital of the free world, that last year eight of its female employees filed and won a suit against the department. They were awarded $1.4 million in damages.

A few months before, a civil jury had found a District of Columbia corrections lieutenant guilty of raping a woman inmate. The defendant claimed consent. The plaintiff's attorney pointed out the reality that there is no such thing as consent in prison, and the jury agreed. Her reward was a $5,000 judgement against the district. Such is the scale of penalties for delinquent prison officials: more or less $175,000 for every employee you have left subject to sexual harassment and $5,000 for every inmate you have allowed to be raped.

Small though this fallen but still proud woman's victory was, it shines as a signal triumph over the universal jailhouse rule that no prisoner's word can be taken against her guard's. Georgia goes so far in discounting any prisoner's unsupported testimony as to refuse to accept it even when the complainant passes and the complained-against fails a lie detector test.

Still, Georgia deserves some credit for trying, however easily discourageable it may be. In 1992, the Georgia Department of Corrections fired the deputy warden for security at its women's center for rape and prisoner intimidation. After the county prosecutor had dropped the attendant criminal charges, the accused was rehired elsewhere at captain's pay.

We would deceive ourselves, however, if we traced all these evils to a male guard force alone. The Women's Rights Project is replete with complaints against doctors, high school equivalency teachers and even one chaplain. Even women wardens are an insecure assurance. In the eighties, Illinois installed Jane Higgins as warden of its women's facility. She busied herself especially with misconduct. When she left, a more complaisant sister took her place, and reforms ceased. We men can always count on a woman to do what we want to have done.

Once Ain't for Always

6 • 12 • 97

An Explanation of My Title: Historical scholarship, that ragbag of myth, holds that once in 1927, while recording at the Columbia Studios, Bessie Smith had run through all her prepared material and then found herself with enough time left for another song and no way to use it except by making up the lyrics as she went along.

The result was "Lost Your Head Blues" and one of Bessie's supposed improvisations was:

> *Once ain't for always*
> *And two ain't but twice.*

The beauty of the lines was inexplicable and so was their meaning. Exegeses of Bessie's work have always tended to err in the direction of the coarse; and we pursued the mystery of the import of these words for the longest while among esoterica of sexual reference far beyond our own puny experience.

But we never solved their puzzle; and it teased me into late middle age until suddenly I understood. Bessie had meant to speak not about some unfamiliar variety of sexual congress but about a human condition that, if it is not universal, has inescapably been my own.

To say that once ain't for always is to remind us that to have done what we ought to have done is no assurance that we will do it the next time we ought and that to have left undone what we ought to have done is no condemnation to the leaving of all future oughts undone.

"Lost Your Head Blues" has since resided in me as the revelatory text for a life history that has been a continual process of confronting and suppressing one bad part of my character and then finding and struggling to suppress quite another bad part on and on and probably unto the last breath.

Now it has occurred to me that I may not be alone in this condition and that it might, as Clarendon put it, be not unuseful to the curiosity if not the conscience of mankind to attempt a memoir each of whose chapters would record some new discovery and transient overcoming of another deformed aspect of my nature. That is what I will try to do if the Lord has the kindness to allow me time to complete my recitals of successive combats with devils who once surprised with their newness and are now old and apparently old, gone, and replaced. Only His hand can finally spare me from unexpected encounters with some next one.

I came back from the war with nothing scarred about my person except a cartridge clip shot from my fatigue trouser pocket north of Bataan in February of 1945.

In the years before its disappearance I would occasionally happen upon it in a bureau drawer and be reminded less of how close life's wounds scrape than how unaware they take us when they do.

We had been whiling an afternoon away in a firefight where we had, as amateurs do, been wasting our stocks of ammunition, and a squad of Japanese stragglers had been, as professionals must, disciplinedly conserving theirs. Now and then we would subside from our clamors, and one of them would fire a single round to set us off again and advance the hour when we would have used up our stores and be forced to let them be.

Somewhere in the midst of these futilities, I felt a light slap, smelled smoke at my haunch, and looked down to see the .45 caliber cartridges ascending and scattering from my side pocket. If you make the most of the noise long enough, you settle into the delusion that there is no one in the room except yourselves.

And so I at once took it for granted that someone in our troop had shot too close from my rear and yelled out to straighten the line. A Philippine scout as raw as we and fatally more anxious to please stood up to obey my unfranchised command, was shot under the eye, and fell among his brains.

The work of the day went profitlessly on for another hour before his comrade scouts picked up the body and carried it for deposit upon the bamboo porch where his mother was standing. He had died the soldier's death in a war scarcely half a kilometer from the ground where he had learned to walk. I told the mother and brothers and sisters around her that he had been brave. All he had been, of course, was dumbly respectful of a thoughtless, hasty and unauthorized order. I also said how sorry we all were, which commonplace and guilt-unconscious nicety could hardly, since I had no Tagalog, have reached her there among the mute and immutable sorrows of the East.

Back at our outpost, I looked at my violated cartridge clip. Its lips had been parted so neatly as to give free play to its spring. The top cartridge must have exploded, which would explain the clap and the smoke. The shot had then come from the front and would near to a certainty have passed by unnoticed if it hadn't struck this piece of metal jutting out too far behind my own flesh to have served it for shielding.

We spoke of the dead scout that evening with too much more sentimentality than sentiment, and then so far forgot him as not even to wonder about the funeral where we might have formed a useless but not unfeeling guard of honor. He had died to make no difference between his freedom from harsh but seldom-seen conquerors and his deference to callous liberators it had been his misfortune to understand too little and to trust too much.

We would soon forget everything about him except the startling ruddiness of the heap of his brains. Young men are careless people and never so much a danger to themselves and others as when most of what they are seeking is relief from boredom.

For what else but boredom could have brought me to such engagements uncompelled by the will and irrelevant to the desires of my commanders and driven to them by that least bearable of boredoms, the one that turns life to lead for those who feel denied every function of use and value?

I had come to the South Pacific doubly deprived of purpose because my military speciality and my assigned duty had already withered into obsolescence. My training had been as a radio operator assumedly equipped to send and receive International Morse Code at a speed of twenty-five words a minute. My wrist was stiffer and my fist infirmer than this rating attested; and these disabilities might have troublesomely betrayed themselves if the continuous wave transmissions of dots and dashes had not been outmoded by voice radio awhile back.

Since the Signal Corps had so small a residual need for my superseded skills, it could not be blamed for shuffling me off to its even-worse-superseded ground-observer service. There had existed an age when the air spotter had been a valued instrument for early warning of a hostile flight's approach and had occasionally earned himself a modest portion of legend. But the development of radar had long since pushed him nearer and nearer to wherever the observation balloon had gone before him.

Even so, radar had its blind spots; and ground-observer teams went on being deployed to points of isolation on the unlikely chance that some Japanese plane might fly between mountains and hedgehog over peaks and so conceal itself from the radar's beam that only human eyes could detect it. It was so hard to take pride in having no excuse for being except as insurance against all-but-inconceivable circumstances that I took to self-identification as "Forward Observer attached to the Air Force," a desperate essay at being mistaken for those artillerymen who had something real to do and did it under conditions that could stand a man's hairs on end. Everyone else with a title to dignities larger than our own went on speaking of us as "groundhogs."

It did not take long, for the burden of being survivor and relic not just of one but of two of the auxiliary arts of warfare so weighed me down with my uselessness that I took to bobbing up whenever two or three were to be gathered together for adventures lurid as anticipation and pallid as experience.

For a while at Lae in New Guinea, I took to patrolling with an Australian Sixth Division squad fleshed out by veterans of the European Theater. Two or three among them had been harried from Greece through Crete and at last turned fiercely to bay in North Africa. Then, having followed and endured the gloomy Anzac destiny of profiting the Empire's interests more abundantly than their own, they had been recalled to face up to the Japanese advance upon their own home continent.

They had walked from Port Moresby over the Kakota Trail and down toward Buna, formed themselves as though on parade, and, singing "Waltzing Matilda," marched straight forward until the Japanese opened up from the embankments that would be as close to Australia as they would ever thereafter go. Whatever the case, such was the legend, told, as always with the Aussies, by others than themselves. The reality was sufficiently superb, for in that week, the Australian Sixth and the American 23rd had won the Battle of Buna and decided the New Guinea campaign two years before I threw my feather's weight into the balance.

My Aussies knew that their business was done, that they were indisposed to further goes, and had settled into nights of reminiscence and days of desultory patrols, whose unoffending objective was to remind the enemy's leftovers that they were beaten and would be senseless to act otherwise. There are more fruitful ways to pursue the illusions of adventure than with companions who have already nobly undergone the destruction of most of their own. And so we spent our days scouring for nothing; and I can barely recall sensing, let alone confronting, a foe armed and dangerous.

My comrades could have taught me all manner of craft; and I have no doubt that they would have handsomely done so if some laboratory exercise had been forced upon them. As it was I picked up only two lessons. One was never to set forth for marsh or crag without first shining your shoes. The other was what I came to think of as the "Lick."

I noticed early on that each of the squad's elders had the habit of touching some part of his body—usually the crotch or abdomen—before entering some spot of brush where insecurities might hide. Later on, when I had strayed into patrols less secure against hazard, I caught myself now and then sweeping my hand across my forehead just above the eyebrow and could fairly hear the interior voice whispering that, if I were not hit there, I would be hit nowhere. And then I understood the tic for what it was, the talismanic gesture that restores the delusions of invulnerability and is the faint suggestion of recoil that defines the countenance of the him or the her who has known the supreme crisis.

I have recognized its look on the face of a woman just after her first child has been born and as surely I have marked it upon the drunken soldier with his forged leave pass and have noted his distinction from the arresting MP half again as tall and with his traded-for or extorted paratrooper boots crowing on his feet. From then on I understood that what had conveyed me to these wanderings had not merely been boredom but an almost possessed desire to earn that look and some lodgment with those who had been there.

To have departed ashamed of myself from as many places as I had before and would again had bound me as with iron to the need to leave this one at least without cause for apology. We always must of course, and so too would I soon and three times over, once for cowardice, once for the coarsest breach of the decencies of warfare, and a third time that would have been worse than either if I had not been summoned back from its almost overmastering temptations just in time.

And so, from dreams of being more than I could ever be, I went on volunteering for anything that was not kitchen police and, for what now seems to have been an eternity, I was cheated in each and all.

The B-17 crews gave me leave to ride a few times on their bomb runs to Wewak, whose official status as last bastion of the Japanese air arm in Australian New Guinea was already dissolving into an abstraction. I would sit at the .50-caliber machine gun station in the belly turret with naught to challenge and little to enchant me except the vistas of the coral seas.

I further played my spectatorial part in five or so assault landings upon beaches so obscure that most of them slip by without mention in the shorter histories of the war, and even I cannot say for sure how many they were.

Upon discharge I was issued five campaign ribbons, three of them with the arrow that signified—and in my case oversuggested—repetitive encounters with hostile beachheads. One such arrow certified my service under conditions of combat in the Admiralty Islands, which I had never seen. But then the army is never so generous as with compliments that cost it nothing; and my papers credited me with ten

D-Day landings, four of them over and done with while I was yet stateside.

But then, if I had indeed played these four fictional roles, it is hard to imagine them as much different from the routine our commanders would never vary and our enemies could never interrupt. We would tune our radios to a Japanese frequency that as usual told us precisely where we were going and as always promised to redden the seas with our blood when we got there. We would bed down as well as we might against bulkheads neither tropic air nor moonlight could soften until we made our half-slumbering way down the rope to the landing craft.

Military convention had fixed our appointment for two hours after the infantry's first wave. The wait was a spectacle whose gauds never ceased to delight, with the great cruisers—we never rated a battleship—grumbling behind us and the little destroyers firing the streams of their rockets into vacant beaches. Then, as though to announce the break of day, the B-17s would let loose their bombs for majestic descent in orderly stacks into trackless forests while the infantry fanned out no farther than it needed to establish room for an airstrip, a communications system, supply tents, a hospital, space for the Salvation Army's doughnut wagons, and like necessaries for this way station to the next leapfrog in General MacArthur's vision.

We would debark to the anticlimax of flailing our shovels and tools against the coral and contriving foxhole enough to shelter us for a night's sleep before being told, as we quite often wouldn't be, what we were then supposed to do.

No image from these undifferentiated excursions has kept so vivid an impress in my memory as one from a half-lit morning off Sansopar when I was sitting in my stall in the landing craft and reading *Victory*. I had arrived at the passage where Axel Heyst, beset by peril on presumably civilized premises, remembers "with regret the gloom and the dead stillness of the forests at the back of the Geelvink Bay, perhaps the wildest, the unsafest, the most deadly spot on earth from which the sea can be seen."

I looked up and there before me spread the forests at the back of the Geelvink Bay, wild and gloomy and still as the tomb to be sure yet all else but unsafe for me in my armor-surrounded immunity. No other moment in New Guinea drew me so close to an epiphany; and yet, having been received as it were on loan from Conrad, it was not enough my own to realize fulfillments more complete than those quasi-epiphanies accessible to any tourist with his guidebook.

And so it was as tourists still that we debarked upon the Luzon beaches off the Lingayen Gulf in January of 1945. We arrived, however, heartened by prospects of employments less empty than had been our lot. The Air Force had at last taken account of the inanition of its ground-observer teams and thought to change their duty to voice radio guidance for the fighter bombers in their works of close support for the infantry. We would transmit the grid coordinates of enemy positions to pilots who could then match them with their own flight maps and avoid mistaken inflictions upon our own troops.

These chores were sufficiently simple to accord with the generally low estimate of our competence; but they offered our first promise of actual service as far as, if no farther forward than, a battalion headquarters. We had even been indulged with a dress rehearsal directing P-51 sorties around the road to Bagulo and escaping serious damage to our credit.

But our sentence to limbo was not yet commuted; and we docilely resumed the ground observer's otiose existence and went down the road toward Mazilla and stopped at Aglao to mount guard against the improbable apparition of a hostile plane that had eluded the radar's notice and might take the advancing infantry unaware.

We were welcomed as liberators by the first authentic civilians to speak to us in the past thirteen months, established our outpost in their barrio's most impressive hutch, and began keeping our object-unrewarded watch around the clock.

One early evening—our third in office—one of our new neighbors came on the run to report that he had sighted a full Japanese company half a kilometer away and grouping for an attack on Aglao.

There were four of us Yanks and at least fifteen Philippine scouts, the makings of a respectable garrison. We nonetheless panicked like so many tourists, stammered our excessive alarms in a message to the rear echelon, shot up our radio, snatched our codebook, and scuttled a full kilometer down the hill followed pell-mell by scouts overdependent on the leadership of Americans who could display no more inspiring symbol of leadership than the spectacle of their heels in flight.

We spent a haunted night in the brush until the sun was high enough to embolden us to sneak back to Aglao. We found her peaceable as ever and all our stores pillaged to the last K-ration can and all but the last thread. We had been well and thoroughly set up. The only enemy in the neighborhood had been the cunning hidden somewhere beneath the fair face of our welcomers.

We had earned ourselves a court-martial and would, I suppose, have gotten one if persons of substance had mistaken anything we did for stuff that mattered for good or ill. The rear echelon sent up a new radio and a fresh stock of rations and spared itself the bother of reproaches. We had been relieved of every inconvenience except the ignominy whose weight bore down upon each and all of us ever present and never spoken of.

Our looters had overlooked one of my shirts; and, since to ask supply for a reissue of clothing would have been to call further attention to my shame, I had to make do with that shirt and the one I had worn on that night of worst disgrace. And so the discovery of the little I would ever know about war was carried through with two shirts, one pair of fatigue trousers, and the last pair of socks that I would wash and let dry every night while I stood my watch barefoot.

If the war had ended that night, I doubt that I could thereafter have found stomach to mention my part in affairs that, after continually denying me all opportunity for tactile experience, had finally deprived me of all dignity. But life sometimes blesses us with reprieves; and, having encumbered myself with dishonor fleeing a fantasy of the Japanese, I would find a kind of redemption running away from the fact of them.

A squad from the 38th Division set up in Aglao the week after our debasement; and we joined its daily patrols in company with the scouts. Our searches brought us into five or so skirmishes, bloodied only twice on our side and, so far as I can judge, only once on theirs.

The Japanese had lost their corner of the war and were much too shrewd at cover and concealment for us to catch them unless boredom impelled them to stand and fight. I have often wondered why they cared. Perhaps it was the itch to instruct.

They were the only authentic, because the most fully completed, soldiers with whom I would in my dealings ever reach intimacy; and no apprentice could ever want for better teachers or reasonably expect to stay alive with ones less meagerly equipped with armament.

They closed school on us one afternoon in March just after we hit upon a straggler scrounging in a *comote* patch. Our leadman shot him and he stumbled and presumably fell in a grove. We were too cautious to follow since one of him argued more of them; and we moved up to a hill overlooking a rice paddy and stretched ourselves prone in the skirmisher line.

And then just down and to our left we saw a Japanese soldier carrying on his back the comrade we had left wounded, and all down the line we opened up on him. There were at least twenty meters between him and any cover at all; and he walked them like a farmer at his plow with all that metal hurling death around without ever straining beyond the solemn and deliberate majesty of his stride. My war was not overabundant with specimens of bravery in its purest essence; but this one will do for a good many.

He kept walking and we kept firing enough to leave him dead ten times over and we never hit him once. Some guardian angel had saved us from the ultimate infamy of killing a soldier carrying a wounded man off the field. I am no witness to the end of this one's trek, because we noticed two others setting up one of those rickety-ticky Japanese machine guns across the way and turned our weapons toward them. And then the ambush was sprung.

It was work of the highest art. They had used the interval of our malevolent distraction to emplace snipers in the trees behind and they were firing at us from the rear with reports so close and loud as to make me think that they were using my shoulder for a gun rest. The machine gun commenced to tap like a woodpecker; and we took our departure with sufficient discipline to pick a route for the rout as near as we could keep to the foliage at the rice paddy's border.

I was next to last in the line of retreat with the Browning Automatic rifleman behind me; and I ran while that silly machine gun putt-

putted behind me and the two carbines fairly burst my eardrums from overhead and the little shots were splitting apart when they hit the grass around me, until I at last fell gasping behind a tuft of cane stalks.

It was only fifty yards to absolute safety; and I was familiar enough with the woodpecker to know that its gunners could only fire five times before having to stop and push the drum back in order to start again. The full limit of demand upon me was to stay low, count five putts, and then get up and run ten or so yards toward total security. The gunners dealt their ration from what sounded like an increasingly comfortable distance; and then just as I was picking myself up for another dash, the BAR man called out that he had been hit.

The last minute or so had been consumed with desperate efforts to seem invisible to everyone behind me; and I dedicated the next ten seconds to seeming deaf as well. I lay there fixed in denial that I had heard this voice in its distress. I was in that moment as quit of the war as if the copy of my discharge papers had lain for a century in Washington's files. My vow to go home with no grounds for apology had already been twice violated; and I should surely had done it a third time if the BAR man had not cried out against that awful silence, "Oh, don't go away and leave me."

No words other than those particular seven could have brought him my help or me some shoring-up of my honor in its ruins. But these served for the miracle of taking me back to where seconds before I would not have gone for God or man; and, when I went to see what might be done for him, I covered the distance erect and uncaring what the enemy might see in the numbed conviction that my life was now forfeit anyway.

His wound was in the right thigh and none too bad a one; but he was too damaged to walk and too large for me to carry. I fiddled with fingers scarcely more practical than sticks to mount his BAR and contrive some impression that he was yet fit for combat, wished him a peaceful wait, and, without time to waste with deals of concealment, I ran across what no longer resounded as the field of one-sided fire and down the trail to find bearers stronger than myself.

I found my comrades in a commendable condition of calm, and explained why we would have to return. They prepared to follow me without a flicker of dubiety; and before we went, I handed my Thompson machine gun to a scout and took his carbine instead. The Thompson had been my talisman; to watch the arc of .45 caliber bullets exiting its muzzle was to feel safe and shielded from all man's malice. The carbine had no such claim on reason or superstition; but neither was of consequence by then and even weaponry wasn't, because I knew to a dead certainty that here was the hour of my last breath. The carbine's point was that it was lighter than the Thompson; a twig would have been better still.

We made our way through the heaviest of silences upward to where his mates gathered up the BAR man while I stood with my rifle pointed across that lately dreadful field in a counterfeit of the protective cover I had lost the will to provide. I had simply become a target. The enemy across the way let us be; the twenty minutes that had begun with our coarse denial of all gallantry toward one of them was ending with their free and easy tender of chivalry toward one of us.

A while afterward I came upon those pages where Antoine de St. Exupéry recalls his flight on reconnaissance to Arras to observe and report on the deployments of the French in a place from which the Germans had already driven them. He had come down for a closer look at the lines and, as he descended alone, naked and surrounded by the puffs from the antiaircraft guns, he became suddenly aware that war is the acceptance of death.

So I had lived once in that state of acceptance in that unforgettable paddy near Aglao and it would never happen again. I took to wondering how many occasions before the fatal last are allowed a soldier for feeling all his sensations distilled into those of the target that can no longer act for itself but only wait for death to dispose as it chooses. Once in hospital—for jungle rot—I put the question to Sergeant Herman Boetcher, a great soldier indeed; and he answered that he well knew the sense of the accepted death because he had undergone it five times. A few weeks after he came out of hospital, I read that he had been killed. So the limit for acceptances of death is perhaps six.

By sunset back in Aglao we were surprised by how much light we could make of the afternoon. There is a curious spiritual uplift in being done to so delicious a turn. The BAR man had been hurt just enough for a chance to go home and none of the rest of us was the worse for the day. We laughed more delightedly still when word came that the Japanese were walking guard formation in their renewed pride not a hundred yards away. And so they were, or anyway one of them imperturbably was, more than a hundred yards off but well within .30-caliber range.

I am embarrassed to confess that I did not render him the salute that was his due.

There could not have been more than six of them and there were never fewer than twenty of us; and our advantage in metallic weight was far crueler than in numbers. I myself carried more killing power on my shoulder than all of them could summon up with their .25-caliber single-shot carbines.

We had been taken by surprise but we had not entirely lost our heads; and it would be by no means unreasonable to inquire why, instead of withdrawing in order, we did not respond as patrols are expected to and simply turn our weapons on these overmatched enemies and transform their ambush into their terminal disaster. I have once or twice asked myself the same question. Respect for our betters perhaps; and in any case rather more than just as well.

They had made out of us the stuff of what must have been the last clear Japanese victory in the Pacific, and they deserved the satisfactions of a pride that had outlasted what may or not once have been their arrogance.

I recovered my Thompson and some of my aplomb; and we returned to our patrols the next day and for a week or so and, outside of an indecisive brush or so, never intimately engaged them. It was now near the end of March and we had been more than two months in Aglao. The normal span of our languid duties was D-Day plus nineteen. Our very existence had been forgotten; and, for two or three days, we went so far as to close down communications with net control and take off like the addicts we had become to join our old fellow travelers from the 38th on patrols around the Wewak Dam.

At last we were recalled to headquarters. I came down out of the hills as one who, while in no sense a tiger, had feasted and been near feasted upon by tigers and would never be the poor thing he had been before. I told myself with entire assurance that I had for all time to come dammed and copper-lined the turbulent bank-caving river of my life and that I would never again flinch or flee from anything and that, most especially, I would never go away and leave anyone. It had been true: once ain't for always.

But it is a truth with two faces. One of them looks back and is a consolation. The other looks forward and is a warning. We had been back in the rear area for no more than a week when the sound of the guns awoke me in the night and I came out of the tent to see the little white tracers that identified what had to be the last airworthy Japanese Betty in the whole of Luzon. If I had really been what I thought I had become, I would have gazed serenely at her futile gallantry and tried to conceive whence she had come and to where she could possibly return. Instead I surrendered to my old thought-conquered self and scuttled in aimless terror from tree to tree. Once indeed ain't for always.

I knew then that timidity and, yes, cowardice would be the permanent tenants of my interior and that I could never hope to trust my courage and would have to settle for preserving my dignity, a virtue whose keeping depends upon constant care to protect it from takings by surprise. It would be some years more before I discovered the equal worthlessness of my assurance that I would never again go away and leave anyone.

"Trespassing"

I remain at a loss to guess what my mother and my father might have had in common except for being each the child of a losing side. Even that would have been a tie too tenuous to bind, since neither had inherited the ruin of an ill-fortuned cause remotely like the other's. My mother's family had been beaten in the Civil War and my father's in some obscure skirmish of greed in the Gilded Age.

I was three years old when he died. We had been living in Radnor in a white house that belonged to but can hardly be said to have incarnated the Main Line of Philadelphia. I have retained only two images of him: one was of waking, no doubt discontentedly, and seeing his gigantic and fecklessly fearsome form beside my bed with a slipper half-uplifted in his hand. The other was a day or so before he died. My brother and I were playing in the hall and he shouted, "God damn it, Sally, can't you keep them quiet?"

Such is the whole tenebrous body of my memory of my father. If these scenes are hardly stuff for the hearths where we warm our hands in the chilly passages of life, I have never thought to assign them any part of the dreary child and dreadful adolescent I would be, which may explain why they had sat so steadily and vividly in my consciousness ever since instead of burrowing down beneath it for that expensive disinterment in middle age as genuine traumas are supposed to extort. We jest at scars who were too numb to feel the wound; and, if I have any notion of my father, it is of one of those familiar personages who can mount degrees of the clamor of impact without producing much in the way of lasting effects.

Even long after he was gone, I never to my shame developed the civilized curiosity to ask my mother what he had been like. If I had, it is doubtful that she would have been forthcoming, because at the earliest convenience after his interment, she took us back to Baltimore to live with her father and her sister. It was not a household where his ghost had much chance of finding its shrine. Mother kept his photograph in her bedroom for a few years; he had the dashing—even rather flamboyant—good looks not to be found in the faces of the men in my mother's family, and he seems to have taken a pride unworthy of a gentleman in a possession which, I aggrievedly noticed, he had clearly not bequeathed to me, because he had chosen to have it displayed in profile. A pose that was excusable for John Barrymore, who wore his face for a living, somehow seemed an excess of vanity in someone who wore it only to a stockbroker's office.

My mother's nostalgia for her brief term of enlistment as a Kempton was so all else but manifest, and my Aunt Virginia's horror at the idea that anyone could have been was all too much so that I between them had little trouble with the surmise that my father's family was provisional in status, obscure in history, and neither able nor disposed to struggle with the vulgarity attendant upon its origins. The provisional, the obscure and the vulgar happen of course to have become the qualities that defined my own existence and I have since recognized that they are essential to the enjoyment of life. But they were not encouraged in my mother's family and I was trained to disapprove of anything that was not approved of there, including myself.

I used to think of the Kemptons as having traveled with romantic and picturesque splendor from rags and back down to rags in a single generation. That image, however derisive it might affect to be, had the high and lurid color familiar to childish fantasies; the surges and plunges of the Kemptons could hardly have been as precipitate as I imagined. There was no disputing my grandmother's vulgarity; she retained much of the prettiness of the village belle, not to say even more of the marks of resentment and disappointment that are so often the rewards of special opportunities open to that calling. A woman born to the unpretentious assurance of social acceptance does not, after all, name her daughters Hortense Vivienne, Inez and Santa Lucia. But the Kemptons cannot have been all that parvenu. They had established themselves well enough before their fall to equip my aunts to marry so more than handsomely as to recoup at the altar whatever their father had lost in the counting house. For all my Aunt Virginia's conviction that my father had been above himself in marrying my mother, he had, as against his sisters, contracted lamentably. Our condescension toward the Kemptons seems odder still since my Aunt Tonnie was distinctly grander than anyone in her sister-in-law's family and wore hats the size of umbrellas and had her picture in the rotogravures.

All that, to be sure, was as nothing when set against the tidal fact that my mother's mother had been a Virginia Randolph. I do not know what it is about the Randolphs, but, whatever it may be otherwise, it is a beating of wings from a height so great that anyone with Randolph in his name habitually flourishes it in his signature as a mark of the hereditary and irreducible refinement exemplified in, say, William Randolph Hearst, to whom my poor grandmother Kempton would scarcely owe the tiniest apology. The line began with Col. William Randolph of Turkey Island, Virginia, who had eight sons; and the distribution of his blood over ten generations makes it likely that no Randolph is more closely related to any of the others than Muhammed Ali Baba, a piece of reality that has never inhibited every Randolph from claiming near kinship with every Randolph of a distinction more seemly than Hearst's. My Great-Aunt Evie used to refer to John Randolph of Roanoke as she might to a great uncle when he could not have been more than an eighth cousin.

The most notable of the otherwise inconspicuous leaves put forth by our own branch had been my great-grandfather, Alfred Magill Randolph, Episcopal Bishop of Northern Virginia and Civil War chaplain to general Robert E. Lee, an office that he himself must have thought the least strenuous of possible labors at salvation since no Virginian of his time could conceive of a priest as holy as that particularly penitent. But then the Randolphs were wonderfully liberated from the compulsions of strenuosity; their uttermost exertions were in the line of charm. I owe to their beguiling example the conviction that charm is the only absolute virtue, which has deprived me ever since from any steady flow of the impulse to moral outrage.

My great-grandfather's memory is still cherished in the Virginia Episcopacy; and I have been told that its theological seminary devoutly preserves a bank draft that bears the inscription, "I heartily endorse this check, Alfred Magill Randolph."

My father's ghost would probably have been happier for a rest in soil and so might my mother and I. My grandfather Ambler's home was an outpost of exile from a Virginia where gallantry had insufficiently availed; and neither of us could have found readier atmosphere for deepening her conviction and developing my suspicion that neither of us was of the stuff that measures up.

I don't recall ever hearing anyone at Eight East Preston Street say outright that to have suffered a misfortunate was to have committed a trespass; but no one needed to; that sentiment could no more have commanded the household if it had been written in letters of flame on the living room wall.

My mother had married in haste and among strangers and she had compounded the sin with the bad luck of a widowhood too precipitate and sons too far from doing for themselves. The airs around her were heavy with unspoken reproaches; and she set out almost immediately to look for a job, prodded in all likelihood far more insistently by perceived obligations of atonement than by realistic fears of penury.

She worked at Hutzler Brothers, the department store, for the next thirty-three years and starting as a saleslady in toys and then in boys clothing and ending as adviser to brides and buyer for wedding dresses. She had acquired the pride of a function and I the unforgivable shame of her being reduced to the need to have one. I did not know anybody else whose mother worked. But then I was unacquainted with any family except my own that lived among the florist shops and taverns extinguishing all claims to dignity that my part of Preston Street might once have had as a fit quarter for residents of the class my aunt used to refer to as "people you know." My cousins the Thomases lived on Calvert street two blocks away; but their house had white marble steps with shiny brass balustrades; and, though Henry Thomas was always polite, I could feel in our encounters that he thought of me as a child visitor from the slums and I once had the embarrassment of a moment when he thought me out of hearing and felt free to refer to me and my brother as "my tough cousins."

We lived then on an otherwise abandoned island of the genteel in a sea of the disreputable. Every wave assailed but none could quite wash over us. Even my family could not be impervious to the changes around it but we could resist them in all ways available, most of which are apt to seem in retrospect rather ridiculous. We lived insulated by our history and surrounded by its memorials, fragments whose dim powers to evoke were further obscured by our curious incapacity to inform. I grew up in a home suffused with memories unvaryingly unreliable.

To have named your child after the author of the Fugitive Slave Law scarcely suggests an over-acute ear for the spirit of one's age; and, years later, when I gently teased my mother for encumbering me with this impropriety, she turned out to have no idea who James Murray Mason might be. She had simply named me after my grandfather, who, she supposed, must have been named after his grandfather, the Senator from Virginia, the Confederate Ambassador to the Court of St. James, and object of disdain in the autobiography of Henry Adams. He was an ancestor the scholarly neglect of whose doings more than contented me; but, all the same, I was surprised that any figure still existed, however vaguely in history, could be totally unknown to his great-granddaughter.

We are curious creatures. I am so far from proud of my name as to feel it an embarrassment and as gratified by the results of James Murray Mason's failures as a diplomat as I was ashamed of his most substantial legislative success, which was to write a law that degraded the interstate commerce clause into an instrument for the pursuit and harassment of escaped slaves.

And, even so, I bridled when I first read Henry Adams' disdainful reflections on the maladdress of my great-great-grandfather's efforts to win the British to a cause that no amount of gallantry could quite excuse. Blood and family have a way of rising up to assert an inexplicable claim that has endured through years when we took for granted its casting off or anyway its supersession by newer blood and later families; and I look back on this earliest of all and recognize it as the stamp that engraved me with the ineradicable cast of that Confederate soul, whose allegiance to a lost cause that was by no means the good one commits it to every other lost cause, however tainted, and allies it with Prince Rupert against the New Model Army and then with Algernon Sydney against the Stuarts, with Marie Antoinette against the French Assembly, then with Danton against Robespierre, and then with Robespierre against Thermidor, and at last with the Marshals of France against the armies of a united Europe. I had enough conscience to draw the line against Hitler and the common sense to do the same to Leon Trotsky; but otherwise, a cause has but to be lost to gain what inadequate service it may find in being my own.

"My Funeral"

5 • 8 • 97

I should like my burial service to take place at the Church of St. Ignatius of Antioch and to follow as closely as its rector deems fit the Order of the Burial of the Dead prescribed by the 1559 Book of Common Prayer, which can be found in my bookcase. It is my preference that there be no reference to my name except in its proper place after "for it has pleased to deliver this [name] . . ." If there is to be music I should like it to be the Sanctus and the Agnus Dei from the Byrd Three-Part Mass and the Purcell Funerary Verses, which will, to be sure, have been spoken elsewhere but deserve two hearings if anything in the language does.

And it would be a pleasant and heartfelt gesture to the low church of my boyhood if the congregants sang "Ten Thousand Times Ten Thousand."

James Murray Kempton
November 20, 1989

Sources

"I'll Still Take Roosevelt" first appeared in *The Johns Hopkins News-Letter*, on 10/6/36. It is published here for the first time in book form.

"Last Boat for Jerusalem" is an excerpt of the pamphlet *Socialism Now! Democracy's Only Defense*, published by the Young People's Socialist League in 1941. It is published here for the first time in book form.

All for Mr. Davis: The Story of Sharecropper Odell Waller, coauthored with Pauli Murray, was first published in pamphlet form by the Workers Defense League in 1941. It is published here for the first time in book form.

"The Wobblies and Tom Clark" first appeared in *The New York Post*, on 8/2/49. It is published here for the first time in book form.

"Christmas in Shallmar, Maryland" first appeared under the title "IV—Christmas in Shallmar, Md." in *The New York Post*, on 12/22/49. It is published here for the first time in book form.

"Women Pickets Only 'Floozies' to Tennessee Troops," first appeared in *The New York Post*, on 6/7/50. It is published here for the first time in book form.

"Huntsman, What Quarry?" first appeared in *The New York Post*, on 4/29/52. It is published here for the first time in book form.

"A Night Thought" first appeared in *The New York Post*, on 6/11/53. It is published here for the first time in book form.

"Bad Day at the Track" first appeared in *The New York Post*, on 3/11/54. It is published here for the first time in book form.

"The Real Davy" first appeared in *The New York Post*, on 6/21/55. It is published here for the first time in book form.

"Intruder in the Dust" first appeared in *The Progressive*, on 11/1/55. It is published here for the first time in book form.

"The Way It's Got to Be" first appeared in *The New York Post*, on 2/9/56. It appeared in *America Comes of Middle Age: Columns 195–1962* (E. P. Dutton, 1963).

"All the Saints" first appeared in *The New York Post*, on 3/7/56. It is published here for the first time in book form.

"Buckley's National Bore" first appeared in the July 1956 edition of *The Progressive*. It is published here for the first time in book form.

"Daughter of the Furies" first appeared in *The New York Post*, on 1/29/57. It appeared in *America Comes of Middle Age: Columns 1950–1962* (E.P. Dutton, 1963).

"The Inheritance" first appeared in *The New York Post*, on 6/19/57. It appeared in *America Comes of Middle Age: Columns 1950–1962* (E. P. Dutton, 1963).

"Loyalty" first appeared in *The New York Post* on 8/14/57. It is published here for the first time in book form.

"The Wrong Man" first appeared in *The New York Post*, on 8/15/57. It appeared in *America Comes of Middle Age: Columns 1950–1962* (E. P. Dutton, 1963).

"The Big Cheese" first appeared in *The New York Post*, on 4/2/58. It appeared in *America Comes of Middle Age: Columns 1950–1962* (E. P. Dutton, 1963).

"Ten Days That Shook" first appeared in *The New York Post*, on 9/24/59. It appeared in *America Comes of Middle Age: Columns 1950–1962* (E. P. Dutton, 1963).

"Let Me Off Uptown" first appeared in *The New York Post*, on 9/21/60. It appeared in *America Comes of Middle Age: Columns 1950–1962* (E. P. Dutton, 1963).

"A Seat on the Bus" first appeared in *The New York Post*, on 3/25/61. It appeared in *America Comes of Middle Age: Columns 1950–1962* (E. P. Dutton, 1963).

"The Saddest Story" first appeared in *The New York Post*, on 6/5/62. It appeared in *America Comes of Middle Age: Columns 1950–1962* (E. P. Dutton, 1963).

"I would like to talk to you tonight quite personally . . . ," is the text of an address delivered at Manhattan Center, New York City, on 7/7/62. It appears here in book form for the first time.

"Visiting Hours" first appeared in *The New York Post*, on 8/6/62. It appeared in *America Comes of Middle Age: Columns 1950–1962* (E. P. Dutton, 1963).

"Back at the Polo Grounds" first appeared in the August 1962 edition of *Sport*. It is published here for the first time in book form.

"The Clarity of A. Philip Randolph" first appeared in the 7/6/63 edition of *The New Republic*. It appeared in *Rebellions, Perversities, and Main Events* (Times Books, 1994).

"The March on Washington" first appeared in the 9/4/63 edition of *The New Republic*. It appeared in *Rebellions, Perversities, and Main Events* (Times Books, 1994).

"Romans," coauthored with James Ridgeway, first appeared in the 12/7/63 edition of *The New Republic*. It appeared in *Rebellions, Perversities, and Main Events* (Times Books, 1994).

"The Champ and the Chump" first appeared in the 3/7/64 edition of *The New Republic*. It appeared in *Rebellions, Perversities, and Main Events* (Times Books, 1994).

"The Meritocracy of Labor" first appeared in the 2/2/65 edition of *The New Republic*. It appeared in *Rebellions, Perversities, and Main Events* (Times Books, 1994).

"Robert George Thompson: American" first appeared in *The New York World-Telegram*, on 1/26/66. It appeared in *Rebellions, Perversities, and Main Events* (Times Books, 1994).

"Four Days in Mississippi" first appeared in the 7/1/66 edition of *The Spectator*. It is published here for the first time in book form.

"K. Marx: Reporter" first appeared in the 6/15/67 edition of *The New York Review of Books*. It appeared in *Rebellions, Perversities, and Main Events* (Times Books, 1994).

"The Underestimation of Dwight D. Eisenhower" first appeared in the September 1967 edition of *Esquire*. It appeared in *Rebellions, Perversities, and Main Events* (Times Books, 1994).

"Responses to 'Liberal Anti-Communism Revisited'" is excerpted from a symposium that first appeared in the September 1967 edition of *Commentary*. It is published here for the first time in book form.

"Thoughts on Columbia" first appeared in *The New York Post*, on 4/30/68. It is published here for the first time in book form.

"Illusion to Reality" is excerpted from the pamphlet *Law & Disorder: The Chicago Convention and Its Aftermath* (Chicago: D. Myrus, 1968). It is published here for the first time in book form.

"A Victory for Proper Manners" first appeared in the 3/7/70 edition of *The Spectator*. It is published here for the first time in book form.

"The Panthers on Trial" first appeared in the 5/7/70 edition of *The New York Review of Books*. It is published here for the first time in book form.

"One underappreciated advantage to being a pauper . . ." was originally read aloud on the CBS radio program *Spectrum* on 9/9/71. It is reproduced here for the first time.

"My Last Mugging" first appeared in the December 1971 edition of *Playboy*. It appeared in *Rebellions, Perversities, and Main Events* (Times Books, 1994).

"Incompetency, American Style" first appeared in *Newsday*, on 2/26/72. It is published here for the first time in book form.

"Our war with North Vietnam . . ." was originally read aloud on the CBS radio program *Spectrum*, on 1/30/73. It is reproduced here for the first time.

"The streakers seem to have disappeared . . ." was originally read aloud on the CBS radio program *Spectrum*, on 3/21/74. It is reproduced here for the first time.

"Witnesses" first appeared in the 6/10/76 edition of *The New York Review of Books*. It appeared in *Rebellions, Perversities, and Main Events* (Times Books, 1994).

"Yes, the Ferry is Far from Perfect" first appeared in *The New York Post*, on 5/18/78. It is published here for the first time in book form.

"We Owe the Mob a Lot" first appeared in *The New York Post*, on 3/25/78. It is published here for the first time in book form.

"The Making of the Pope" first appeared in the 9/11/78 edition of *New York*. It appeared in *Rebellions, Perversities, and Main Events* (Times Books, 1994).

"A Name for a Crime" first appeared in *The New York Post*, on 10/15/78. It is published here for the first time in book form.

"Offsides for False Modesty" first appeared in *The New York Post*, on 11/2/78. It is published here for the first time in book form.

"The Scribblers' Choice" first appeared in *The New York Post*, on 9/18/80. It appeared in *Rebellions, Perversities, and Main Events* (Times Books, 1994).

"Saving a Whale" first appeared in the 6/11/81 edition of *The New York Review of Books*. It appeared in *Rebellions, Perversities, and Main Events* (Times Books, 1994).

"The Sad Secrets of an Assassin's Mind" first appeared in the 10/15/81 edition of *Rolling Stone*. It is published here for the first time in book form.

"Captain Jolly Hasn't Noticed We're Adrift" first appeared in *Newsday*, on 1/6/83. It is published here for the first time in book form.

"Mussolini in Concert" first appeared in the 4/14/83 edition of *The New York Review of Books*. It appeared in *Rebellions, Perversities, and Main Events* (Times Books, 1994).

"The Ambivalence of J. Robert Oppenheimer" first appeared in the 12/1/83 edition of *Esquire*. It appeared in *Rebellions, Perversities, and Main Events* (Times Books, 1994).

"Mrs. Velasquez and the Politicians" first appeared in the 2/2/84 edition of *The New York Review of Books*. It is published here for the first time in book form.

"'If I Leave You, Baby, Count the Days I'm Gone'" first appeared in *Newsday*, on 4/29/84. It is published here for the first time in book form.

"Example of Police Restraint Ends in Coma—and Death" first appeared in *The Los Angeles Times*, on 6/26/84. It is published here for the first time in book form.

"Pride and Prejudice" first appeared in *Newsday*, on 12/5/84. It appeared in *Rebellions, Perversities, and Main Events* (Times Books, 1994).

"Splendors and Miseries on Gramercy Park" first appeared in the January 1985 edition of *House and Garden*. It is published here for the first time in book form.

"Parade's End" first appeared in the 6/13/85 edition of *The New York Review of Books*. It is published here for the first time in book form.

"The Landlord State" first appeared in *The Baltimore Sun*, on 9/5/85. It is published here for the first time in book form.

"Report from Nicaragua" first appeared in *Newsday*, on 6/27/86. It appeared in *Rebellions, Perversities, and Main Events* (Times Books, 1994).

"If RICO Wins, We Lose" first appeared in *Newsday*, on 3/8/87. It is published here for the first time in book form.

"Verdict on a City" first appeared under the title "Four Dead and Justice Lay Dying" in *Newsday*, on 6/17/87. It appeared in *Rebellions, Perversities, and Main Events* (Times Books, 1994).

"Bessie Smith: Poet" first appeared under the title "Bessie's Inalienable Blues" in *Newsday*, on 7/5/87. It appeared in *Rebellions, Perversities, and Main Events* (Times Books, 1994).

"Strange Landscape at Passion's Height" first appeared in *Newsday*, on 8/15/87. It appeared in *Rebellions, Perversities, and Main Events* (Times Books, 1994).

"Turning Seventy, Just by Chance" first appeared in *Newsday*, on 12/17/87. It appeared in *Rebellions, Perversities, and Main Events* (Times Books, 1994).

"Hostage to History" first appeared under the title "Soviet Past Slows Move Into Future" in *Newsday*, on 6/19/88. It appeared in *Rebellions, Perversities, and Main Events* (Times Books, 1994).

"The Beggar of Gracie Mansion" first appeared in *Newsday*, on 8/11/88. It is published here for the first time in book form.

"Undertaking Roy Cohn" first appeared in the Autumn 1988 edition of *Grand Street*. It appeared in *Rebellions, Perversities, and Main Events* (Times Books, 1994).

"Bike Theft as a Point of Departure" first appeared in *Newsday*, on 10/22/88. It is published here for the first time in book form.

"On Clemency for Jean Harris" first appeared in *Newsday*, on 10/13/88. It is published here for the first time in book form.

"My File Is Haunted by Hoover" first appeared in *Newsday*, on 5/14/89. It is published here for the first time in book form.

"The Proof That Trump Is a Self-Made Man" first appeared in *Newsday*, on 6/4/89. It is published here for the first time in book form.

"Death, Life in Painting, Exhibition" first appeared in *Newsday*, on 11/17/89. It is published here for the first time in book form.

"In the Oddly Delightful Company of Guerrillas" first appeared in *Newsday*, on 12/3/89. It appeared in *Rebellions, Perversities, and Main Events* (Times Books, 1994).

"Unsentimental Education" first appeared in *Newsday*, on 9/3/91. It appeared in *Rebellions, Perversities, and Main Events* (Times Books, 1994).

"Oh, for Brawls of Yesteryear" first appeared in *Newsday*, on 4/12/92. It is published here for the first time in book form.

"Let Me Be Wrong About Clinton" first appeared in *Newsday*, on 5/27/93. It is published here for the first time in book form.

"A Raisin in the Sun" first appeared in the 3/24/94 edition of *The New York Review of Books*. It appeared in *Rebellions, Perversities, and Main Events* (Times Books, 1994).

"Brave Instincts, Affirming Dignity" first appeared in *Newsday*, on 12/1/94. It is published here for the first time in book form.

"The Reporter's One Commanding Duty" was delivered as an address at Colby College on 11/9/95. It is reproduced here for the first time.

"A Little Boy with Ol' Blue Eyes" first appeared in *Newsday*, on 12/15/96. It is published here for the first time in book form.

"Unjust Advances Behind Bars" first appeared in *Newsday*, on 1/5/97. It is published here for the first time in book form.

"Once Ain't for Always," first appeared in the 6/12/97 edition of *The New York Review of Books*. It is published here for the first time in book form.

"Trespassing" is a compilation of pages excerpted from a draft manuscript of Kempton's unfinished memoir, available in the Murray Kempton papers, 1940–1997, at Columbia University's Rare Book and Manuscript Library. The manuscript pages were evidently typed from Kempton's own handwritten pages in June 1997, shortly after his death, but the exact date of their composition by him is unclear. Another extant part of this memoir was published posthumously in *The New York Review of Books* (see the above citation, "Once Ain't for Always"). These pages, however, are published here in edited form for the first time, and the title is the choice of this editor.

"My Funeral" is the text of a note signed by Kempton on 11/20/89, reproduced in the program for his memorial service at St. Ignatius of Antioch Episcopal Church, New York City, 5/8/97. It is published here for the first time in book form.

Acknowledgments

This book would not have been possible without Helen Epstein, who was a great source of insight and encouragement throughout. All of us who cherish Murray Kempton's work are indebted to Barbara Epstein, her mother, and I am grateful for the invitation to join my meager efforts with hers. I thank the many writers, editors, and publishers who shared their memories of Murray Kempton with me and volunteered their assistance at various points, including Jeff Alexander, Richard Brookhiser, Christopher Buckley, Paul Buhle, Jean Casella, Vivian Gornick, D. D. Guttenplan, Lewis Lapham, Larry McShane, Victor Navasky, Rick Perlstein, David Remnick, Marion Elizabeth Rodgers, Lucy Sante, Gene Seymour, Charlotte Sheedy, Scott Sherman, Peter Slevin, Sam Tanenhaus, Dhoruba bin Wahad, Steve Wasserman, and Garry Wills. Sarah Fan and Jamie Fuller commissioned the article in *Lapham's Quarterly* that led to this book. My special thanks go to Kevin Boyle, Christopher Corbett, Rebecca Corbett, Joshua Clark Davis, Dora Korewa, George Derek Musgrove, Darryl Pinckney, and Emily Wilson.

My work on this book was funded in part by a Rubys Artist grant from the Robert W. Deutsch Foundation; I thank Ruby Lerner and Sonja Cendak for their support of Baltimore artists and writers. I was helped by librarians and archivists at several institutions, including Johns Hopkins University, the University of Maryland, Baltimore County, and the New York Public Library. I am especially grateful to Melissa Cabarcas, Thai Jones, Melina Moe, and the staff of the Rare Book and Manuscript Library at Columbia University.

Shortly before she died in 2023, Sally Kempton told me she was looking forward to seeing her father's work in print again after so long. I regret that this book was not finished in time for her to see it. I'm further grateful to Arthur Kempton, Christopher Kempton, and David Kempton.

Thanks to Dan Simon for seeing the worth in this project, and to everyone at Seven Stories Press. Most of all I have to thank Lisa Adams at the Garamond Agency for her generosity and good counsel.

Index of Titles